EX
LIBRIS

ADOLF
GRÜNBAUM

Errata

Chapter 6
Page 244, line 25: "have already discussed in chapter 3" should read "shall discuss in chapter 8."
Page 247, line 23: "viewpoints" should read "view points."

Chapter 10
Page 375, line 18: "only" should read "also."

VALIDATION IN THE
CLINICAL THEORY OF
PSYCHOANALYSIS

PSYCHOLOGICAL ISSUES

HERBERT J. SCHLESINGER, *Editor*

Editorial Board

VALIDATION IN THE CLINICAL THEORY OF PSYCHOANALYSIS

A STUDY IN THE PHILOSOPHY OF PSYCHOANALYSIS

ADOLF GRÜNBAUM

INTRODUCTION BY
PROFESSOR PHILIP S. HOLZMAN

Psychological Issues
Monograph 61

INTERNATIONAL UNIVERSITIES PRESS, INC.
Madison, Connecticut

Library of Congress Cataloging-in-Publication Data

Grünbaum, Adolf.
    Validation in the clinical theory of psychoanalysis : a study in the philosophy of psychoanalysis / Adolf Grünbaum ; with an introduction by Philip S. Holzman.
      p. cm. — (Psychological issues ; monograph 61)
    Sequel to: The Foundations of psychoanalysis.
    Includes bibliographical references and indexes.
    ISBN 0-8236-6722-7
    1. Psychoanalysis—Philosophy. 2. Clinical psychology—
—Philosophy. 3. Freud, Sigmund, 1856–1939. I. Grünbaum, Adolf.
Foundations of psychoanalysis. II. Title. III. Series.
    [DNLM: 1. Psychoanalysis. 2. Psychoanalytic Theory. W1 PS572
monograph 61 / WM 460 G887v]
BF173.G766 1993
150.19′5′01—dc20
DNLM/DLC
for Library of Congress   92-48956
                                                       CIP

Manufactured in the United States of America

To Robert Sonné Cohen
with affectionate gratitude
for
fifty years of devoted friendship

CONTENTS

PREFACE

Over half of this Monograph is a sequel to the author's 1984 book *The Foundations of Psychoanalysis: A Philosophical Critique* (hereafter *Foundations*).

The reception of that earlier work in the psychoanalytic community bespeaks the relevance of this sequel and is illustrated by responses from several psychoanalysts:

1. Robert Wallerstein's 1986 Freud Anniversary Lecture "Psychoanalysis as a Science: A Response to the New Challenges" was avowedly "intended primarily as a response to Grünbaum" (*J. Amer. Psychoanal. Assn.*, 36:6, 1988).

2. In *Psychoanalysis: A Theory in Crisis* (1988, pp. xiii–xiv), Marshall Edelson wrote:

> The most telling outside challenge to psychoanalysis has been the questions raised by Adolf Grünbaum about its empirical foundations and mode of inquiry. The most telling manifestations of the difficulties in which psychoanalysis now finds itself are both the lack, for the most part, of a cogent response to these questions (I except my own work, of course), and the various kinds of responses these questions have received instead.

3. The psychoanalyst-philosopher Carlo Strenger introduced his 1991 monograph in the *Psychological Issues* series, entitled *Between Hermeneutics and Science*, as follows (pp. 4–5):

> In a series of publications culminating in his [Grünbaum's] *The Foundations of Psychoanalysis* (1984), he has presented a critique of the evidential foundations of psychoanalysis, unprecedented in its clarity and incisiveness. . . .
>
> The bulk of this essay . . . is an attempt to present versions of claims of the hermeneuticist conception of psychoanalysis, which stand up to the sharp critique it has been subjected to by Grünbaum.

The present Monograph goes beyond *Foundations* in the following principal respects:

1. It contains my new basic critique of the psychoanalytic theory of transference in its role of an *etiologic* theory: As it turns out, etiologic transference interpretations rest on fallacious causal inferences from so-called "meaning connections" between mental states. Moreover, just these unsound inferences are the stock-in-trade of the "hermeneutic" reconstruction of psychoanalysis, which charges Freud with a "scientistic self-misunderstanding."

2. It joins the issue with Marshall Edelson's defenses of the investigative viability of the single-subject case study method.

3. As a spin-off from the import of the serious placebo challenge to psychoanalysis, this Monograph presents the author's new account of the placebo concept across *all* of medicine *and* psychotherapy.

4. Whereas in *Foundations* I objected that Freud's dream theory was evidentially ill-founded, the burden of the present book is to give two new basic reasons for presuming the theory to be false.

5. It gives an appraisal of Freud's triadic *psychology* of religious belief in theism.

6. Since Popper's most detailed charge of pseudo-science against psychoanalysis in 1983 could not be examined for inclusion in the 1984 *Foundations*, the present Monograph shows in what ways his diagnosis of the scientific liabilities of psychoanalysis is both mistaken and incoherent.

Professor Philip Holzman, with the editorial support of Professor Herbert Schlesinger, originally suggested the preparation of this Monograph. They recommended that I also include—in somewhat updated form—several papers of mine that had antedated *Foundations* by a few years, because these publications had not been conveniently available as originally published. Four such papers have been integrated with the other chapters.

I am very grateful to Professor Holzman for having taken the initiative to bring this Monograph into being, and also for contributing his valuable *Introduction*.

It is believed in some quarters that ever since Freud developed psychoanalysis as a therapy, the transaction between the analyst and the patient in the clinical setting has yielded telling evidential support for the cardinal psychoanalytic hypotheses. Indeed, there are those who believe that the viability of the Freudian enterprise rests on just such *clinical validation*. As they would have it, the entire analytic legacy—both explanatory and therapeutic—*stands or falls* with the support for its principal tenets *from the treatment setting* (Wallerstein, 1988, p. 27).

No wonder, therefore, that those practicing analysts who hold this view react with dismay when confronted by a fundamental challenge to their cherished assumption. Very understandably, those who see their doctrine in jeopardy may find it more difficult to be receptive to my demurrer than it is for me to issue it, as I do in the succeeding chapters. After all, whatever the fortunes of my polemic against Freud's clinical arguments and against post-Freudian variants on them (Grünbaum, 1984, chap. 7) in the marketplace of ideas, my own professional craft as a philosopher is not put at risk by the outcome.

Yet I submit that those who do have a stake in the viability of psychoanalysis as a theory or a therapy owe it to themselves to consider my doubts, although Peter Gay (1988, p. 745) deemed them obsessive: "The most formidable among the skeptics, who has made the credibility of Freudian science (or lack of it) into an obsessive concern for a decade, is the philosopher Adolf Grünbaum." In the first place, I do *not* rule out the possibility that, granting the weakness of Freud's major clinical arguments, his brilliant theoretical imagination may nonetheless have led to correct insights in some important respects. Hence, I allow that a substantial vindication of some of his key ideas may perhaps yet come from well-designed extraclinical investigations, be they epidemiologic or experimental. Conceivably, it might even come from *as yet unimagined* new clinical research designs (Grünbaum, 1986, p. 276). In the second place, if such a reliable new footing is ever to be achieved for Freud's theory, it is essential to have a clear appreciation of the range and depth of the difficulties besetting its extant defenses. Analysts ignore these defects at their peril. A similar lesson emerges, in confluence with my views, from Holzman's recent admonition (1985).

Eagle (1983) has contended in detail that the upshot of my assessment of Freud's classical arguments applies no less to the neorevisionist doctrines of self psychology, and of recent object relations theory.

The following chapters are offered in the spirit of a philosophical inquiry into some of the principal issues that arise in establishing the validity of the clinical theory of psychoanalysis.

ACKNOWLEDGMENTS

Chapter 1 originated in my 1982 Presidential Address to the American Philosophical Association (Eastern Division). This address was published under the title, "Freud's Theory: The Perspective of a Philosopher of Science" in *Proceedings and Addresses of the American Philosophical Association*, vol. 57, September 1983, pp. 5-31. The present chapter 1 is a modified and updated version of this publication, which appears here by permission of the American Philosophical Association.

Chapter 2 is drawn from the psychoanalytic portion of my essay "The Degeneration of Popper's Theory of Demarcation," which appeared under my copyright in *Freedom and Rationality: Essays in Honor of John Watkins*, ed. F. D'Agostino and I. Jarvie, Dordrecht: D. Reidel, 1989, pp. 141-161; it was also published in the Italian philosophical periodical *Epistemologia*, vol. 12, 1989, pp. 235-260. This chapter is derived originally from a section of the sixth of my eleven *Gifford Lectures,* delivered in Scotland in 1985.

Chapter 3 has been published, in somewhat different forms, under my own copyright, as "The Placebo Concept in Medicine and Psychiatry" in *Psychological Medicine*, vol. 16, 1986, pp. 19-38; in *Non-Specific Aspects of Treatment*, ed. N. Sartorius and M. Shepherd, published for the World Health Organization, Bern and Toronto: Hans Huber Verlag, 1989, pp. 7-38; also in *Thinking Clearly about Psychology: Essays in Honor of Paul E. Meehl*, ed. D. Cicchetti and W. Grove, Minneapolis: University of Minnesota Press, 1991, vol. 1: Matters of Public Interest, pp. 140-170. A German translation appeared in *Kritische Betrachtungen zur Psychoanalyse*, ed. A. Grünbaum, Heidelberg, Germany: Springer Verlag, 1991, pp. 326-357. This chapter first originated in rudimentary, shorter form in my "The Placebo Concept," which appeared in *Behaviour Research and Therapy*, vol.

19, 1981, pp. 157-167; it then appeared in intermediate form as "Explication and Implications of the Placebo Concept," in *Placebo: Theory, Research, and Mechanisms*, New York: The Guilford Press, 1985, pp. 9-36.

I thank Dr. Thomas Detre and Dr. Arthur K. Shapiro for useful expository comments on the first draft of this paper. Furthermore, I am grateful to Dr. Jennifer Worrall, as well as to Dr. John Worrall, who offered some perceptive suggestions for clarifying some of the formulations in my earliest publication on this subject (Grünbaum, 1981). Sections from this earlier paper are used by permission of Pergamon Press, Ltd.

Chapter 4 is an extensively revised and much enlarged version of the following two papers: "The Theory of Transference Qua Key Flaw in the Psychoanalytic Case Study Method," presented in the "Psychoanalytic Dialogue" Session, held on December 20, 1986 at the Annual Meeting of the American Psychoanalytic Association in New York City, and "The Role of the Case Study Method in the Foundations of Psychoanalysis," delivered at the Conference on the Humanities and the Sciences, held at Cornell University in April 1987. It is a modified version of an article published, under my own copyright, in *The Canadian Journal of Philosophy*, vol. 18, 1988, pp. 623-658; it also appeared in *Die Philosophen und Freud*, ed. H. Vetter and L. Nagl, vol. 3 of *Wiener Reihe: Themen der Philosophie*, Vienna: R. Oldenbourg, 1988, pp. 134-174.

I am much indebted to Professor Melford E. Spiro, who is both a distinguished anthropologist and a psychoanalyst, for a number of critical comments on the first of two earlier versions above. His commentary prompted considerable expository clarification of my arguments, and the correction of a nosologic error. I am also grateful to the psychoanalyst Rosemarie Sand for an insightful reading of the earlier version that stimulated me to deal with additional issues. This chapter was dedicated to Professor Paul K. Feyerabend on the occasion of his sixty-fifth birthday.

Chapter 5 is a revised, shortened version of my essay in the philosophical quarterly *Noûs*, vol. 14, September 1980, pp. 307-385. It appears here under a new title by permission of the editor of *Noûs*. It was originally dedicated to the memory of the philosopher Richard Rudner.

Chapter 6, which appears here for the first time, is devoted to a critical response to Marshall Edelson's efforts of (1984) and (1988). An earlier version was delivered as one of my eleven *Gifford Lectures* in Scotland in 1985.

Chapter 7 appeared in the "Irrationality" issue of the philosophical periodical *The Monist*, vol. 70, 1987, pp. 150-192. It is reprinted here by permission of the editor. It was also published in Italian as *Psicoanalisi E Teismo,* with an Introduction by Alessandro Pagnini, entitled "Grünbaum e la filosofia analitica della religione," Naples and Rome: Edizioni Scientifiche Italiane, 1991.

Chapter 8 is a revised version of an essay that first appeared, under a slightly different title, in *Testing Scientific Theories*, ed. J. Earman, Minnesota Studies in the Philosophy of Science, vol. X, Minneapolis: University of Minnesota Press, 1983, pp. 315-347. It appears here by permission of the University of Minnesota Press. Parts of it were also incorporated in my (1984).

Chapter 9 was first published, though in a different form, under my own copyright in the European journal *Erkenntnis*, vol. 19, 1983, pp. 109-152. This periodical features the philosophy of science. The earlier version of chapter 9 was entitled "Logical Foundations of Psychoanalytic Theory" and was part of a *Festschrift* issue in honor of Wolfgang Stegmüller.

Chapter 10 originated in a paper I delivered at the conference "Freud and the History of Psychoanalysis" (Third Hannah Conference), held at Trinity College, University of Toronto, in October 1990. That paper was published under my copyright in the volume of proceedings under the conference title by the Analytic Press, ed. by Toby Gelfand and John Kerr, 1992.

Just as in the case of all of my earlier books, Elizabeth McMunn did yeoman's work, ranging from bibliographic research to revising the earlier format of the chapters and typing the final manuscript. I am greatly indebted to her for that substantial assistance. In addition, I appreciate the help of Judith Nestico, who typed the final addenda.

Lottie M. Newman, who is well known for her superb editorial skills, gave me the benefit of them throughout the typescript by her entries and suggestions. I am much in her debt for the ensuing improvements in the final text.

INTRODUCTION

During the past decade, I have found it especially welcome and instructive to read Adolf Grünbaum's brilliant and incisive critical analysis of the nature of the scientific enterprise within psychoanalysis. Yet, not always do I agree with him, particularly since I regard psychoanalysis not as a unified theory, but rather as many theories loosely tied together. The theories are heterogeneous in content and in level of abstraction, and they appear scattered among Freud's papers in both older and newer versions, more as working, tentative formulations than as a final systematic theory. One such group consists of theories of thought processes; another group is concerned with conceptions of development; and still another group is a complex of clinical theories focused on psychopathology and treatment. While some attain a certain theoretical and stylistic elegance, others are rather poorly stated and exist primarily in a "pretheoretical" form. Some are models rather than theories, and have the form of analogies, comparisons, or constructions that help one visualize a complex mechanism or structure, rather than precise statements of functional relations between variables.

Still, Freud's writings have been treated by most of the psychoanalytic community as received doctrine, quarantined from sharp critical examination of the kind that Professor Grünbaum has conducted in these papers. Grünbaum's deft criticism of Popper's claim that psychoanalysis is inherently not falsifiable and is therefore a pseudoscience established him as an authoritative critic who could clear away the misunderstandings and flummery in Popper's assertions and could point to genuine issues that needed to be addressed.

Adolf Grünbaum speaks eloquently for his views in the ten papers collected in this volume. His views deserve respectful study, and, in his words, psychoanalysts may dismiss his challenge, but only at their peril. The papers not only call attention to inconsistencies, fallacies, and soft spots in the corpus of psychoanalytic theory, but they also point to ways that scientists can generate new vigor into what appears to be a fading beacon that once lit the way to deep psychological insights, especially into the darker side of human psychology.

Consider some of the signs of decline: First, there is decreasing mention of psychoanalytic contributions in the empirical literature. Psychoanalytic journals are now seldom cited in published empirical studies. No doubt this reflects the fact that most psychoanalytic journal articles are, generally speaking, essays rather than scientific examinations of phenomena. The case study has remained almost the only source of "data" for dealing with theoretical issues in psychoanalysis and has even been used erroneously in attempts to validate some major propositions (viz. chapter 4).

A related point concerns the shortage of psychoanalytically sophisticated scientists who can make research use of the privileged access psychoanalysts have to the irrational side of human behavior and to the coloration given to relationships by sexual and aggressive urges.

The sociological structure of psychoanalysis has been that of a free-standing academy. For whatever reason, psychoanalytic institutes have remained outside of the university systems. Therefore, they have isolated themselves from the kind of serious questioning by students and colleagues in allied and neighboring disciplines that can act as corrective guides. The training institutes have been guided by noteworthy authoritarian governance, in which probing questions, such as those raised by Professor Grünbaum in this collection, have been parried by impugning the motives of the questioner (see Holzman, 1976).

A science grows by successive corrections from cumulative knowledge, obtained by experiment and logical examination, but not by revelation. Approaching truth is always a matter of continual approximations. None of our beliefs can escape revision. For a science to grow, it is necessary to test the range and validity of the hypotheses offered to explain the various phenomena under investigation. This is the spirit of the ten papers that make up this book.

Adolf Grünbaum is no stranger to philosophers and to many psychoanalysts. He is a past president of the American Philosophical Association as well as of the Philosophy of Science Association. He is the Andrew Mellon Professor of Philosophy at the University of Pittsburgh, founder and chairman of that University's Center for the Philosophy of Science, and Research Professor of Psychiatry in its School of Medicine.

Adolf Grünbaum was born in Cologne, Germany, on May 15, 1923. In 1938 he and his family fled the Nazi persecutions and immigrated to the United States. He attended Wesleyan University (Connecticut) where he studied mathematics, physics, and philosophy. After serving in the Army of the United States in an intelligence unit interrogating German academics during World War II, he returned for graduate studies at Yale University. There he earned an M.S. in physics, and a Ph.D. in philosophy. His dissertation on Zeno's paradoxes was written under the direction of the distinguished philosopher of science, Carl G. Hempel. Grünbaum's subsequent work on the philosophical problems of space and time established him as clearly one of the foremost contemporary authorities on the philosophy of physics.

Grünbaum's interest in psychoanalysis was whetted by Popper's critique. He doubted that psychoanalysis could be so cavalierly classified as a pseudoscience. In the course of examining Popper's criterion for scientific status, Grünbaum realized that he needed to become thoroughly versed in the theoretical richness of psychoanalysis. Beginning in 1975, he began to read Freud's works systematically. Soon, in a series of superbly reasoned and vigorously argued papers, he established a new level of criticism that was both appreciative of the brilliance of Freud's writings and yet uncompromisingly clear about their defects.

In 1981, I heard Adolf Grünbaum lecture at the Boston Colloquium for the Philosophy of Science, when he pointed up many of the knotty methodological issues in psychoanalysis. I became convinced that the earlier vigor of psychoanalysis could be reestablished by taking up the arguments, criticisms, and challenges that Grünbaum presented. I discovered that although by then he had published much about psychoanalysis, Grünbaum's papers had largely appeared in philosophical journals that are not easily available to the psychoanalytic community. I thought it would be helpful to collect several of his seminal papers in *Psychological Issues* and thereby to make them available to psychoanalysts and others interested in the scientific status of psychoanalysis.

Together, Professor Grünbaum and I selected four of his papers; they appear in the present volume as chapters 1, 5, 8, and 9. In 1984, during the preparation of this volume, Grünbaum's book, *The Foundations of Psychoanalysis: A Philosophical Critique,* was published. There have been extraordinarily many responses to that book, and Professor Grünbaum has, in turn, reacted to the critiques. Both he and I believed that a collection of his papers should reflect the ongoing, constructive dialogue that was taking place as a consequence of both his 1984 book and a subsequent piece in *Behavioral and Brain Sciences* (1986), with comments from 39 invited respondents and Grünbaum's rejoinder. Therefore, Grünbaum engaged in a process of revising and updating for this volume the four chapters originally chosen for inclusion, and added six more chapters that address further crucial questions in psychoanalysis as well as offer a new systematization of the theory of placebogenic phenomena not only in psychiatry but in medicine in general. The result is a volume that contains much new material, responses to earlier criticisms, and some older papers otherwise not easily available.

In these papers Grünbaum contends that psychoanalysis should be held to the standards of empirical science, and accordingly he takes issue with those, such as Habermas and Ricoeur, who would make of psychoanalysis merely an interpretative, hermeneutic, or "critical" discipline. He further argues effectively that psychoanalytic propositions can be taken seriously as scientific statements since in principle they are amenable to empirical scrutiny by generally agreed on standards of scientific procedure. Yet he indicts psychoanalysts for their frequently flawed reasoning and for their failure to seek appropriate and uncontaminated observational opportunities to evaluate their assertions. In pursuing these issues, Grünbaum demonstrates his superior sophistication about psychoanalysis compared with those philosophers who participated in the celebrated debates of 1959 (Hook, 1959). He has read Freud's principal papers with great care and he has treated them with the seriousness commanded by other major theoretical systems. The sheer richness of Freud's psychoanalytic theoretical statements, the abundance of his ideas about human behavior, the multitude of areas into which those ideas proliferate, elevate the Freudian corpus above many less ambitious theories in influence and generality. The very fact of this elevated status requires a systematic examination of its logical and epistemic status, equal to that accorded to other great statements on human psychology. That is the purpose, essence, and gravamen of Grünbaum's examination.

Grünbaum's writing style is at times colorful and dramatic. In his efforts to probe the essence of an argument, he can pull out all the stops: italics as a point is emphasized; a sweeping rhetorical crescendo as a conclusion is demonstrated and an obfuscation exposed; derision as he catches a writer in a grave but avoidable error; labyrinthine paragraphs as he leads the reader to and from basic premises in order to plumb the depths of an issue. He is a tough critic. He uncovers gloss, and he will not suffer superficial arguments and sloppy thinking. He presses his arguments exuberantly to teach and to reason. The reader will at once be made aware of his integrity as a critic, his honesty as a communicator, and his demands that we join him in intensive examination.

These are timely papers. It is always risky to prophesy where and how advances will appear, but it seems to me that in the next several years advances in psychoanalysis will come from probing examinations of its basic premises. Whatever new directions are charted, whether they be in the therapy or in the science, they will require the kind of logical and informed scrutiny that Professor Grünbaum engages in. Psychoanalysis must therefore be clear about its premises, its evidence, its logic. It must also search for methods of validation worthy of its rich hypotheses. I hope that these papers will stimulate both the crafting of those methodological tools and the adopting of an undefensive, clear mode of inquiry. Both are necessary for accomplishing credible advances. In my opinion, joining Grünbaum in this serious but unsparing colloquy can reintroduce productive ferment into psychoanalytic thought, for he asks us to accompany him in applying the kinds of critical standards that would be appropriate to evaluate psychoanalysis as a serious generator of scientific knowledge.

Philip S. Holzman
Harvard University
Cambridge, Mass.

February 17, 1992

1

THE PSYCHOANALYTIC ENTERPRISE AND ITS "HERMENEUTIC" CONSTRUAL: A DISPUTATION

INTRODUCTION

It is well known that Freud was hardly the first thinker who postulated *unconscious* processes in order to explain much conscious psychic life and overt conduct. In Plato's dialogue the *Meno*, we encounter a slave boy who had never studied geometry. Yet by just showing him a diagram and asking him appropriate questions, his interlocutor was able to elicit geometric truths from him. This phenomenon is then used by Plato to interpret the acquisition of conscious knowledge as the recall of information, which the soul had unconsciously stored in the meantime.

In the early nineteenth century, the German philosopher Johann Herbart, who died fifteen years before Freud was born, taught that conscious mental life is affected by subliminal processes, which function like ideas, except for being beneath the threshold of focal awareness (Fancher, 1973, p. 12). Moreover, Arthur Schopenhauer had claimed, *before* Freud, that consciousness resists the intrusion of unpleasant thoughts and perceptions. Indeed, Schopenhauer was Freud's precursor in the field of psychopathology even to the extent of enunciating, in very general terms, that repressed ideation is pathogenic (Ellenberger, 1970, p. 209)! No wonder that Thomas Mann had a sense of déjà vu when he read Freud, after delving into

1

Schopenhauer. Furthermore, Eduard von Hartmann published his *Philosophy of the Unconscious* when Freud was thirteen years of age. There, von Hartmann gave wide explanatory scope to unconscious processes (Ellenberger, 1970, p. 210).

The founding father of psychoanalysis died in 1939. Several decades thereafter, new experimental findings have prompted cognitive psychologists to conclude that unconscious ideation plays a cognitive role in mental life that even Freud had not envisioned. In fact, despite some similarity between the *cognitive* unconscious of recent psychology and Freud's *dynamic* unconscious, there are also important differences between them that should not be glossed over. For example, there is a sense in which the psychoanalytic unconscious is *affect*-laden (Freud, 1915c, Section III), and its contents are deemed to be recoverable by lifting their repression. By contrast, the implicit problem-solving capabilities of the cognitive unconscious are neither repressed nor conscious. Thus, therapists who have used subliminal techniques to increase self-esteem, or to induce weight loss, are feeling reassured by the new recognition that a substantial portion of *cognitive* activity is, in fact, unconscious.

But one factor that may have made psychoanalytic theory so extraordinarily influential in some segments of our culture was Freud's particular articulation of the assumed *causal* role of unconscious processes. It is a measure of this influence, at least in the United States, that the Science section of the *New York Times* (January 24, 1984), no less than the *New Yorker, Time* and other such magazines, gave wide publicity to Jeffrey Masson's book (1984) about Freud, which purports to contain highly derogatory revelations about his lack of intellectual integrity. To boot, Janet Malcolm (1981) gave prominence to Peter Swales's allegation that one of Freud's paradigmatic examples of a memory lapse pertained to a shady episode involving Freud himself, who had supposedly impregnated his own sister-in-law, and had then taken her to Italy for an abortion. Indeed, the intellectual and cultural historian Peter Gay (1985, 1988)—to name only one—invokes psychoanalytic theory *uncritically*, as if it were holy writ. And he applies it to generate so-called psychohistory (Lifton, 1980).

Yet, in my view, Freud's massive elaboration of *clinical observations* into his own doctrine of hidden motives still cries out for further careful scrutiny. By the same token, I contend, such scrutiny is at least equally imperative in the case of the various *post*-Freudian, revisionist versions of psychoanalysis. Although the specific content of their theories of psychic conflict is more or less different, they also rely on Freud's clinical methods of validating causal inferences (Eagle, 1983; Grünbaum, 1984, chap. 7). I shall be challenging just these causal inferences. And it will be an immediate corollary of my challenge that it applies not only to Freud's own original hypotheses, but also to any and all post-Freudian versions of psychoanalysis that rely on his clinical methods of justifying causal claims. After all, the changes made by post-Freudians in the specific content of the founding father's theory of psychic conflict (repression) hardly make the *validation* of the revisionist versions more secure!

Therefore, as Morris Eagle documented in a recent publication (1983), those analysts who have objected to my critique as anachronistic have simply not come to grips with it. For example, such inadequate engagement is present, in my view, in the recent Freud Anniversary Lecture "Psychoanalysis as a Science: A Response to the New Challenges," given by Robert Wallerstein (1986), a former president of the International Psychoanalytical Association. As he tells us (1988, p. 6, n.1), "The Freud Anniversary Lecture was intended primarily as response to Grünbaum." Yet he does not come to grips at all with the gravamen of my challenge: *Even if clinical data could be taken at face value as being uncontaminated epistemically*, the inability of the psychoanalytic method of clinical investigation by free association to warrant causal inferences leaves the major pillars of the clinical theory of repression ill-supported.

The heart of Freud's distinctive theory of repression is not just that we harbor repressed memories, thoughts, desires, and feelings. Instead, it is that sexual repressions are the *crucial pathogens* of mental disorders, that repressed infantile wishes are the generators of our dreams, and that various sorts of repressed, unpleasant thoughts *engender* our slips of memory, the tongue, the ear, the eye, the pen, etc.

Freud referred to these various sorts of unsuccessful, bungled actions collectively in German as *Fehlleistungen*, or misbegotten performances. And James Strachey, the principal translator of Freud's psychological works into English, coined the new term *parapraxes* to denote them *generically* in English. But the Vienna-born American psychoanalyst Bruno Bettelheim (1982) deplored this translation. The German word *Fehlleistungen*, he tells us, has a familiar, mellifluously humanistic ring, even smacking of poetry. By contrast, according to Bettelheim, the technical term *parapraxes* allegedly has a coldly scientific tang. Thus, as he would have it, the Englishman Strachey has misportrayed the psychoanalytic enterprise to the English-speaking public by giving a misleading scientific twist to it. Freud, we are asked to believe, wanted psychoanalysis to be a branch of the humanities, but deplorably Strachey made it appear as if Freud worshiped the natural sciences and idolatrously intended psychoanalysis to be a natural science! Strachey created this allegedly false impression by insidiously mistranslating Freud's key German vocabulary. Let me just say very briefly that Bettelheim's indictment of Strachey is, I believe, an unfortunate exegetical fabrication which, alas, grasps at straws. For example, one need only read the German original of Freud's 1933 lecture "Über eine Weltanschauung," which appeared only six years before he died, to see that Bettelheim's complaint is a hermeneutic red herring. In that lecture, Freud declared that "psychoanalysis has a special right to speak for the scientific *Weltanschauung*" (p. 159), the word *scientific* being intended in the sense of the *natural* sciences.

The contemporary philosophic spokesmen for the so-called hermeneutic reconstruction of psychoanalysis have even gone further than Bettleheim by condemning Freud for an alleged "scientistic" misunderstanding of his own clinical theory. As we know, the word *scientism* is a derogatory term, used to refer to a misguidedly utopian, intellectually imperialistic worship of science. Thus the hermeneutic philosophers, such as Jürgen Habermas and Paul Ricoeur, claim that even Freud's *aspiration* to build a scientific depth psychology was misguided from the outset. In my book (1984) and below, I argue that these hermeneutic criticisms are based on misconceptions of both the content and the methods of the natural sciences. Furthermore, I contend, in chapter 4 that Karl Jaspers and the hermeneutic philosophers have mishandled so-called "meaning connections" between mental events vis-à-vis causal connections between such states. As against their claim that Freud assigned much too little explanatory significance to thematic kinships ("meaning connections"), I maintain that he fallaciously gave much too much explanatory weight to them. Therefore, in this chapter, I shall try to give a kind of overview of some parts of my appraisal of Freud's own principal arguments for the *cornerstone* of his entire edifice: the theory of repression, or psychic conflict. His theory of psychopathology was the logical and historical foundation of his entire theory of repression.

FREUD'S NOTION OF SCIENTIFIC STATUS

Throughout his long career, Freud insisted that the psychoanalytic enterprise has the status of a natural science. As he told us at the very end of his life, the explanatory gains from positing unconscious mental processes "enabled psychology to take its place as a natural science like any other" (1940a, p. 158). He went on to declare: "Psycho-analysis is a part of the mental science of psychology. . . . Psychology, too, is a natural science" (1940b, p. 282). Clearly, he was *not* using the term "science" here metaphorically. Earlier, Freud had firmly rebuffed the antinaturalism and methodological separatism that was championed by the *Geisteswissenschaften* movement as a framework for psychology and the social sciences. Its votaries deemed causal explanations to be endemic to the natural sciences in view of the lawlike causal connections featured by these disciplines. And they rejected such nomothetic causal explanations as generically alien to the humanistic sciences. As they saw it, the aim of the study of man ought to be the "hermeneutic" quest for idiographic understanding by such methods as empathy and intuitive self-evidence (Möller, 1976, 1978). In diametrical opposition to this view of the task of psychology, Freud (1933) proclaimed:

. . . the intellect and the mind are objects for scientific research
in exactly the same way as any non-human things. Psycho-analysis has a special right to speak for the scientific *Weltanschauung.* . . . If . . . the investigation of the intellectual and emotional
functions of men (and of animals) is included in science, then it
will be seen that . . . no new sources of knowledge or methods of
research have come into being [p. 159].

In 1895, the psychoanalytic method of clinical investigation
by means of free association was only a fledgling mode of inquiry. Likewise, Freud's clinical theory of psychopathology was
still nascent. At that very early juncture, he gave a neurophysiological twist to the notion of a scientific psychology. And he
couched his then vision of a neurological underpinning for
psychic processes in the reductionistic physical idiom of material particles. This biophysical notion animated his 1895 "Project for a Scientific Psychology." Yet Freud abandoned his reductionistic program within only two years of having
enunciated it. As he wrote in retrospect: "every attempt . . . to
discover a [brain] localization of mental processes, every en-
deavour to think of ideas as stored up in nerve-cells and of
excitations as travelling along nerve-fibres, has miscarried completely" (1915c, p. 174).

By 1900, the legacy of the abandoned neurological model
had become the postulation of a bipartite structure of the mind
whose principal component systems were the unconscious and
the so-called preconscious (1900, chap. 7). The contents of the
preconscious system, if not actually conscious, are deemed
readily accessible to consciousness. But only the clinical techniques of psychoanalysis are held able to unlock the gates to
the unconscious system. Freud now pointedly eschewed the
original neurological connotations of the technical vocabulary
he had introduced in the 1895 Project. Yet he retained this
terminology for use in a purely mentalistic sense. Thus, the
erstwhile excitation or "cathexis" of a *neuron* has now become
the cathected state of an *idea* or *memory*. Likewise, a train of
thought is now held to involve the *flow* of cathexes from one
idea to another, so that *psychic energy* is invested in the mental
representations of objects. And the two component systems of
the mind were assumed to differ in regard to permitting the

flow of psychic energy toward tension discharge. Later, Freud modified his bipartite structural model of the unconscious and the preconscious, when he replaced it by *three* agencies whose functions need not detain us (1923a, pp. 12-59; 1933, pp. 57-80).

These successive models of the structure and function of the psychic apparatus are often denominated as the "metapsychology" of the psychoanalytic edifice (Laplanche and Pontalis, 1973, p. 250). The separation of the clinical theory of repression from that metapsychology within the edifice is not always sharp. Yet it is vital to appreciate to what marginal epistemic status Freud relegated its metapsychological part, amid steadfastly claiming natural-science status for his construction overall. The metapsychological models, he tells us, are "a speculative superstructure of psychoanalysis, any portion of which can be abandoned or changed without loss or regret the moment its inadequacy has been proved" (1925b, pp. 32-33; see also 1914c, p. 77). And he added pointedly: "But there is still plenty to be described that lies closer to actual experience." The "plenty . . . that lies closer to actual experience" is, of course, none other than his *clinically* based theory of personality, psychopathology, and therapy. The centerpiece of that corpus of hypotheses is the theory of repression, which features his compromise model of neurotic symptoms, as well as of manifest dream content and of various sorts of slips. These phenomena are deemed "compromises" in the sense of being *substitutive gratifications* or outlets, for they are held to be conatively vicarious surrogates. Moreover, the clinical theory of repression is often couched in personalist language.

But in conspicuous contrast to his depiction of the metapsychology as "a speculative superstructure" which can be sloughed off, if need be, "without loss or regret," Freud explicitly deemed his clinical theory to be "the most essential part" of what he had wrought, for, as he told us, "the theory of repression is the cornerstone on which the whole structure of psychoanalysis rests. It is the most essential part of it" (1914b, p. 16).

Thus, when Freud unswervingly claimed natural science status for his theoretical constructions throughout his life, he did so first and foremost for his evolving clinical theory of personality and therapy, rather than for the metapsychology of psychic energy flow. After all, he had been chastened in his early reductionistic exuberance by the speedy demise of his neurobiological model in 1896. Thereafter, he never made the scientific status of the clinical theory parasitic on its would-be subsumption under a primordially scientific metapsychology! Instead, he then perennially claimed his theory of personality and therapy to be authenticated by *direct* and cogent evidential support originating on his office couch and in his self-analysis. In brief, during all but the first few years of his career, Freud's criterion of scientificity was methodological and not ontologically reductive.

Critique of Habermas's Charge of "Scientistic Self-misunderstanding"

The leading spokesmen for the so-called "hermeneutic" construal of Freud's clinical theory have given wide currency to an exegetical thesis that I have just shown to be a myth. This is ironic, since the hermeneuticians see themselves as guardians of the faithful exegesis of texts. According to the philosophers Jürgen Habermas and Paul Ricoeur, and the late psychoanalyst George Klein, Freud attributed natural-science status to the clinical theory by *misextrapolation* from its would-be reduction to the primordially scientific metapsychology. Indeed, Habermas (1971) chides Freud for having fallen prey to a far-reaching "scientistic self-misunderstanding" (pp. 246-252). According to this complaint, Freud's misunderstanding was "scientistic," because he idolatrously endowed the clinical theory with natural-science status under the ideological aegis of the metapsychology. Furthermore, Freud's view was purportedly a *self*-misunderstanding, because it issued in a philosophical misconception of the very nature of his own clinical theory. Finally, Freud's alleged misconstrual of the clinical theory was far-reaching, if only because it thwarted the recognition of psychoanalysis as a paradigmatically depth-hermeneutic mode of inquiry, as the only tangible example of a science incorporating methodical self-reflection, and as potentially prototypic for the other sciences of man (Habermas, 1971, chap. 10).

As recently as 1981, Ricoeur again endorsed Habermas's allegation of "scientistic self-misunderstanding" (p. 259). And, in an earlier work, Ricoeur hailed the *failure* of Freud's clinical theory to qualify as an empirical or natural science by the received standards as the basis for "a counterattack" against those who deplore this failure (1970, p. 358).

Habermas, Ricoeur, and Klein each give more or less detailed *arguments* for actually denying natural-science status to Freud's clinical theory in principle. In the present chapter, I need to confine myself largely to Habermas, whose views have become influential not only in philosophy but also in some of the social sciences. I concentrate mainly on his arguments in the conviction that they are representative of the mode of reasoning offered by the others.

It is to be clearly understood that far from questioning the etiologic and therapeutic hypotheses of Freud's clinical theory, these hermeneuticians claim to take them for granted without ado. What they purportedly tried to controvert are rather the philosophical tenets that, as they see it, Freud had misguidedly grafted onto those hypotheses. Hence in my appraisal of their views, I shall refrain from challenging the credentials of Freud's clinical hypotheses. But, as we shall see thereafter, there are ample grounds for such a challenge.

It is one of Habermas's cardinal theses that the *lawlike* causal nexus present in the causality of nature does *not* inhere in the therapeutic dynamics of the psychoanalytic process of "self-reflection." He presents this denial by reference to a patient's conquest of a neurosis whose salient manifestation is rigidly *repetitive* behavior. And Habermas's astonishing pivotal contention is that the etiologic causal connection which was operative in the pathogenesis of the neurosis is itself "dissolved" when the patient overcomes his affliction in therapy (1970, pp. 302, 304; 1971, pp. 256-257). More explicitly, as Habermas would have it, whenever a neurotic overcomes the repetition compulsion by the lifting of his pathogenic repressions, this psychoanalytic self-reflection has actually "dissolved" and "overcome" the very *causal connection* that had previously linked the pathogen to the neurotic behavior (1971, p. 271). Yet, in the domain of the laws of nature, there is no counterpart to this alleged overcoming of a causal connection "as such." Hence Habermas uses the Hegelian term "causality of fate" to refer to the sort of fragile causal linkage that, he tells us, is "dissolvable," because it can purportedly be "subdued" by the therapeutic "power of reflection."

But, regrettably, the reasoning he uses to establish this "causality of fate" is a mere tissue of errors. The most damaging of these mistakes becomes clear from the rationale used by Breuer and Freud when they founded psychoanalysis. In 1893, they enunciated the following epoch-making etiologic hypothesis: In the pathogenesis of a psychoneurosis, repression plays the generic causal role of a *sine qua non* (1893, pp. 6-7; 1893-95, pp. 29-30). The impetus for this assumption avowedly came from their belief that the therapeutic gains from their method of treatment were causally attributable to the cathartic retrieval of traumatic memories, which their patients had repressed. Once they had decided that such lifting of repressions is therapeutic, they wished to *explain* its remedial efficacy. And, as they soon realized, the desired explanation could be given deductively by the etiologic postulate that repression is causally necessary not only for the initial development of a neurotic disorder, but also for its maintenance. Clearly, if a repression of type R is indeed the causal *sine qua non* for the presence of a neurosis of kind N, then it follows that the removal of R will actually issue in the obliteration of N. Hence any patient who rids himself of R and thereupon becomes emancipated from N plainly *instantiates* that R is the causal *sine qua non* for the presence of N. Amazingly enough, Habermas claims that this very causal linkage itself is dissolved by the patient's therapeutic achievement. But surely the instantiation of a causal connection cannot possibly also qualify as the dissolution of this linkage! Hence Habermas's notion that a therapeutic achievement can "overcome" an etiologic linkage by dissolving it is deplorably incoherent.

What the patient has indeed overcome is his pathogenic repression as well as his neurosis, but hardly the causal connection between them. To terminate an *effect* by undercutting the cause required for its production is patently *not* tantamount to overcoming the causal connection that links them. On the contrary, it is to *illustrate* it. Hence in Freud's clinical theory, just as in physics or in somatic medicine, there can be no question at all of "dissolving" a causal linkage between an antecedent C and its effect E on the strength of terminating the recurrence of E by preventing the further realization of C. Thus, when a surgeon removes a gall bladder full of gall stones, this sudden *absence* of the cause of the gall colics effects their cessation. But patently, this therapeutic achievement leaves wholly intact the causal linkage between the *presence* of moving gall stones and the colics, which is the *etiologic* connection. Yet by parity with Habermas's specious reasoning, one could deduce the inanity that, in this somatic context, the patient himself "dissolves" the causal connection between the *presence* of the pathogen and its painful effect as follows: By taking medication that literally dissolves his gall stones, the patient terminates the continued recurrence of his colics. In virtue of yielding this ludicrous suspension of somatic causality as well, Habermas's muddled account boomerangs. For his notion of "overcoming" a causal linkage was avowedly *not* applicable to the "causality of nature" in *somatic* medicine or physics, but distinctively only to the therapeutic dynamics of the psychoanalytic process of "self-reflection"! Far from having elucidated the role of causality in psychoanalysis, Habermas's callow importation of the causality of fate has only obfuscated it (see Grünbaum, 1984, Introduction).

The causality of fate is not the only major causal doctrine enlisted by Habermas to contrast psychoanalysis with the natural sciences. He considers the application of psychoanalytic generalizations, which he calls "general interpretations" (1971, p. 259), to the life history of a particular analysand. Such application generates particular interpretations that combine into a personalized narrative. When offered to the individual patient by the analyst, particular interpretations are presumed to be stated in the *intentional* clinical language of desires, affects, fantasies, sensations, memories, and the like (p. 272). Habermas speaks of these motivational imputations and reconstructions as deriving from the "hermeneutic application" of general interpretations to the life of a particular analysand.

Now, he is concerned to contrast the logic of such hermeneutic utilization with the corresponding application of lawlike principles in the nomothetic empirical sciences to particular cases. And his paradigm for the latter sort of instantiation of the antecedent of a physical law is given by " 'this stone' is considered, for example, as 'mass' " (p. 265). Claiming that "this subsumption is unproblematic" (p. 265), he proposes to *contrast* it logically with an instantiation of a general interpretation in psychoanalytic practice. In the empirical sciences, he tells us "we can base explanations on context-free laws. In the case of hermeneutic application, however, theoretical propositions are translated into the narrative presentation of an individual history in such a way that a causal statement does not come into being without this context" (pp. 272-273). Hence he maintains that "general interpretations do not make possible context-free explanations" (p. 273). In brief, his thesis is that—in contrast to psychoanalysis—explanations in physics are generically based on context-free, ahistorical laws. And its enunciation concludes the chapter he entitled "The Scientistic Self-misunderstanding of Metapsychology," with the subtitle "On the Logic of General Interpretation" (chap. 11).

But to the serious detriment of this further dichotomy of his, there are telling counterexamples to it from venerable principles of physics. And these counterexamples likewise will be seen to redound to the utter discredit of the following equally grandiose assertions by the hermeneutician (or hermeneut) H. G. Gadamer (1975), who wrote: "It is the aim of science to so objectify experience that it no longer contains any historical element. The scientific experiment does this by its methodical procedure" (p. 311). But how, one asks, does the scientific experiment have this ahistorical import? Gadamer reasons that the experimental method of science predicates confirmation on *repeatability to such a degree* that he feels entitled to conclude: "Hence no place can be left for the historicality of experience in science" (p. 311). Now, in order to give my counterexamples to the purported dichotomy of context-dependence, I need to adduce concrete examples from the laws of physics.

As shown by the laws of classical electrodynamics, Habermas and Gadamer have drawn a *pseudo* contrast between the nomothetic and human sciences. A number of these laws embody a fundamental dependence on the history and/or context of the object of knowledge. Indeed, in some of the basic laws of electromagnetism, context-dependence is far greater than was ever contemplated in even the most exhaustive of psychoanalytic explanatory narratives, or in any recapitulation of human history. Readers who find the impending details from physics too technical need only retain their pertinent import for the issue at hand. The moral I claim emerges even from the simple examples below of the rubber band and of Coulomb's law.

Consider an electrically charged particle having an arbitrary velocity and acceleration. We are concerned with the laws governing the electric and magnetic fields produced by this point charge throughout space *at any one fixed time t.* In this theory, the influence of the charge on any other test charge in space is postulated to be propagated with the finite velocity of light, in contrast to the instantaneous propagation familiar from Newton's action-at-a-distance theory of gravitation. But the *non*instantaneous feature of the propagation of the electrodynamic influence contributes to an important consequence: At any space point P, the electric and magnetic fields at a given time t depend on the position, velocity, and acceleration the field-producing charge had at an *earlier* time. That earlier time depends, in part, on the distance traversed by the influence arriving at P at time t after having traveled from the charge to P with the velocity of light.

Clearly, the greater the distance traversed by the influence by the time t of its arrival at point P, the earlier its origination time. Thus, for space points at ever larger such distances in infinite space, the origination time will be ever more remotely past. In short, as the distance of a field point becomes infinitely large, the origination time of the influence determining the electric and magnetic field intensities at that point at the fixed time t goes to past infinity.

It thus turns out that at *any one instant t*, the electric and magnetic fields produced throughout infinite space by a charge moving with arbitrary acceleration depend lawfully on its own *particular entire infinite past kinematic history!* The pertinent lawlike equations specify the fields as functions of the aforestated kinematic attributes possessed by the charge at the appropriate earlier times (Page and Adams, 1940, p. 144). Pertinently enough, in a classic treatise, the relevant upshot of these electro-dynamic laws has been stated as follows: "expressions for the complete field of an element of charge [throughout space at any one time] involve . . . its entire [infinite] past history" (p. 161).

Though the individual histories of each of two or more charged particles can be very different indeed, the electrody-namic laws accommodate these differences amid being general. The generality derives from the form of the lawlike functional dependencies of the electric and magnetic field intensities on the earlier accelerations, velocities, and positions of the field-producing charge. But the latter's individual history consists of the infinite temporal series of the particular values of these kinematic attributes (variables).

As against Habermas, I submit that these electrodynamic laws exhibit context-dependence with a vengeance by making the field produced by a charge for any one time dependent on the particular entire past history of the charge. And, to the detriment of Gadamer, these delayed-action laws are based on replicable experiments but resoundingly belie his thesis that "no place can be left for the historicality of experience in science." Indeed, by being a special case of one of these laws, even Cou-lomb's simple inverse square law for the electric field is highly *history-dependent* by holding only if the field-producing charge has been at rest *for all past time* (Page and Adams, 1940, p. 161).

Some hermeneuticians may retort that these physical cases do not capture the relevant sense of "history," as if to say: "What is all-important here is *how* past states count in the deter-mination of present behavior, not just *that* they count." Patently, it is anything but a liability to my argument that I rely on the following banal fact: The Freudian narratives adduced by Habermas are psychological, whereas my examples of context-dependence are avowedly physical. Indeed, the qualitative dis-tinction between the respective *domains* of application of psy-choanalytic generalizations on the one hand, and physical laws on the other, is *obviously presupposed by Habermas's thesis* of asym-metry of context-dependence between the two domains, *no less*

than by my argument against it! But this assumed ontological difference is itself unavailing to Habermas's thesis that there is an
asymmetry of context-dependence, whenever general propositions are applied explanatorily to particular instances. He rules
out *simpliciter* just the sort of ingredience of history in physical
laws that I have multiply documented: As he would have it
(1971, pp. 272-273), in the natural sciences, the laws are *invariably* context-free *and* remain so, when applied to explain particular cases, whereas concrete psychoanalytic explanations are
generically context-dependent. Thus, the stated attempt to
parry my critique fails, if only because it modifies, rather than
rescues, Habermas's contention. Besides, the modification is
unavailing to the alleged asymmetry, since the adduced plati-
tude—that Freudian narratives are *psychological*—is patently insufficient to sustain the asymmetry. These considerations were
lost on Peter Rudnytsky (1990, p. 145) who wrote: "But that
Grünbaum could suppose that the 'history' of a particle is comparable to that of a human being attests to his utter incompre-
hension of the essential insight of hermeneutics since Dil-
thy. . . . perhaps Grünbaum could place the particle on the
couch and ask it to narrate its 'history' to him!"

There are other instructive cases of context-dependence of
laws of physics that reveal further the poverty of Habermas's
supposed paradigmatic example of " 'this stone' is considered . . . as 'mass' " (1971, p. 265). These cases exhibit so-called
"hysteresis" in the sense that a property of a physical system,
induced by a given present influence upon it, depends not only
on that present influence, but also on the *past history* of variation
of that influence (Considine, 1976, p. 1335). One such case is
the hysteresis behavior of highly magnetizable metals (e.g., iron,
cobalt, nickel), which are known as "ferromagnetic." Thus, the
present response of the ferromagnetic material to one and the
same external magnetic influence will depend on the prior magnetization *history* of the given sample. More generally, suppose
that such material is subjected to a cycle of magnetization and
demagnetization by a suitable alternation in the external magnetic influence; and let that cycle be depicted graphically by
plotting the induced internal magnetization against the external magnetizing field. Then the one complete initial cycle of

magnetization and demagnetization will be represented by a closed curve ("hysteresis loop"). Significantly, the dependence of the behavior of the ferromagnetic sample on its *history* then makes itself felt *overall*: The closed curve representing the initial cycle will *never* be retraced by subsequent cycles of demagnetization and remagnetization (Efron, 1967, p. 694). Other examples in physics in which the response of materials to current influences is sensitive to the history of their prior exposure to like influences are furnished by solids that exhibit *elastic* hysteresis. Even rubber bands display a like behavior.

The array of context-dependent physical laws I have adduced seem tailor-made as insuperable difficulties for the second of Habermas's alleged causal dichotomies. I trust that the context-dependence of the physical cases I have developed either matches or surpasses the degree of any such dependence encountered when general clinical hypotheses are applied to particular patient histories. Habermas's paradigm of the stone that has mass epitomizes the generic notion of a situation in physics on which he relied to buttress his purported dichotomy. He and Gadamer have managed to parlay the severe limitations of their own personal scientific horizons into a *pseudo* contrast between the humanistic disciplines and the natural sciences. Indeed, it is a sad commentary on our intellectual culture that by trading on their stone-age notions of physics, they have been able to gain adherents to their view. Here we have yet another example of the penchant to erect grandiose doctrines about the sciences of man on the sand of callow myths as to the content of the natural sciences.

Habermas likewise makes several *epistemic* allegations to vindicate his reproach of "scientistic self-misunderstanding" against Freud's own construal of the clinical theory. Here I can deal with only one of these contentions (see further, Grünbaum, 1984, Introduction).

The logic of validating the general hypotheses of Freud's clinical theory is one of the major themes of Habermas's hermeneutic epistemology. The pivotal claim of his account is that the patient is the ultimate epistemic arbiter of these general psychoanalytic postulates, which he calls "general interpretations" (1971, p. 261). Within the confines of analytic therapy, these universal hypotheses are used to generate *particular* interpretations pertaining to the individual lives of specific patients. For example, the analyst employs psychoanalytic generalizations retrodictively to construct an etiologic scenario for the pathogenesis of a patient's disorder.

In the context of the clinical setting, Habermas downgrades the doctor cognitively *vis-à-vis* his patient by endowing the analysand with an epistemic *monopoly* in the testing of the *particular* interpretations pertaining to his own life history. As he puts it, "analytic insights possess validity for the analyst only after they have been accepted as knowledge by the analysand himself" (1971, p. 261). Having claimed that the patient is thus cognitively preeminent, Habermas infers that "the success and failure [of a psychoanalytic construction] cannot be intersubjectively established" (p. 266). Thereupon he assumes that induction from just such particular interpretations is the *sole* means for *validating* Freud's universal hypotheses, and not merely for elaborating these generalizations heuristically (p. 259). Hence he concludes that patients enjoy privileged epistemic access as follows: "the validity of general interpretations depends directly on statements about the object domain being applied by the 'objects,' that is the persons concerned, to themselves" (p. 261). Habermas relies on this contention, in turn, to arrive at the methodological dichotomy that general interpretations are not governed by the same criteria of validation as the universal hypotheses of the empirical sciences (pp. 261-266).

It appears that the tenability of this dichotomy depends on the merits of Habermas's cognitive tribute to the patient. Note that if the analysand were actually the ultimate epistemic arbiter, as depicted by Habermas, then the patients treated by psychoanalysts would have truly formidable cognitive powers. Each patient would then be not only the best judge, but ultimately the *sole* judge of what was in fact the cause of his neurotic disorder, what engendered his sundry dreams, and what induced his lapses of memory, various slips of the tongue, and other bungled actions. Moreover, in Habermas's account, the cognitive monopoly of patients, taken collectively, likewise extends to *universal* psychoanalytic hypotheses. Hence the validation of Freud's etiology of obsessional neurosis, for example, would ultimately rest entirely on the collective verdicts of those treated for this affliction.

I contend that this epistemic thesis is a house of cards, no less than Habermas's two alleged causal dichotomies. One important reason will have to suffice here (see, further, Grünbaum, 1984, Introduction). As background for it, note that Habermas tacitly and peremptorily banished all *extra*clinical testing of general psychoanalytic hypotheses from consideration. He simply took it for granted that the treatment setting is the sole arena for any and all validation or disconfirmation of these universal propositions. Just for argument's sake, let me assume that if one were to confine all testing to the clinical investigations carried out by the doctor-patient dyad, then the analyst can confirm an interpretation only on the authority of his patient's prior certification of its validity.

Even then, it would hardly follow that the clinical setting is the principal arena for the well-designed testing of general psychoanalytic hypotheses, let alone the sole arena (see chapters 4-6 and 8-10 below). But if extraclinical tests of at least some of these hypotheses are feasible, as indeed they are, then patients in analysis surely do not have the cognitive monopoly that Habermas conferred on them. In fact, as I shall now show by an example I have developed elsewhere (Grünbaum, 1984, chap. 1), some important psychoanalytic postulates are testable by *epidemiologic* findings, *without* any recourse to data from the analytic treatment setting, let alone to the experiences of patients when their repressions are being undone in that clinical milieu. But since this example has been questioned by Gill[1] (unpublished), let me issue the *caveat* that it pertains to *Freud's* explicitly stated etiology of paranoia, and not to Gill's own version thereof.

Freud's etiology of paranoia postulates that *repressed* homosexual love is *causally necessary* for being afflicted by paranoid delusions (1915a, pp. 265-266). When the pathogenically required intensity of repression exists, it is partly engendered by the strong social taboo on homosexuality (Grünbaum, 1986, p. 268). Thus, the detailed pathogenesis of paranoia envisioned by Freud warrants the following prediction: A significant decline in the social sanctions against this atypical sexual orientation should issue in a noticeable decrease in the incidence of

---

[1]Merton M. Gill, meeting of Rapaport-Klein Study Group, June, 1983.

paranoia. Incidentally, this prediction alone refutes Karl Popper's claim that psychoanalytic theory is not testable, a contention I shall show to be multiply wanting in chapter 2 (see also Grünbaum, 1984, chap. 1).

It was revealed only very recently that in 1893, Tchaikovsky was very probably blackmailed into suicide under threat of exposure of a homosexual liaison (Brown, 1980, pp. 626-628). This tragic episode is a measure of the lethal power possessed by the ban on homosexuality in the Christian world less than a century ago. Tchaikovsky's suicide occurred at the pinnacle of his career, less than a week after the St. Petersburg premiere of his celebrated Pathétique symphony. Yet for the past nine decades, the standard biographies of him listed cholera as the cause of his death at the age of fifty-three (Dorian, 1981). During that time, there has been a marked decline in the taboo on homosexuality, despite the best efforts of Anita Bryant. Perhaps it is therefore not too early now to begin garnering appropriate statistics on the incidence of paranoia, with a view to ascertaining in due course whether these epidemiologic data bear out the psychoanalytically expected decline or disconfirm it. In either case, the testing of this Freudian etiology will be clearly intersubjective, in salient contravention of Habermas's thesis.

What then is the merit of the reproach by Habermas and Ricoeur that Freud fell prey to a "scientistic self-misunderstanding"? I submit it was not Freud, but these hermeneuticians themselves, who forced the clinical theory of psychoanalysis onto the Procrustean bed of a philosophical ideology demonstrably alien to it. For, as I have argued, they first trumped up a mythic exegesis of his own perennial notion of scientificity, and then used an antediluvian paradigm of the natural sciences to boot. So much for the unjustified demand of the hermeneuticians that we abjure the very standards of validation by which Freud himself wanted his theory to be judged. In chapter 4, I shall deal critically with the hermeneuticist complaint that Freud paid insufficient explanatory heed to "meaning connections" or thematic kinships between mental states. Indeed, I shall argue that he was all too ready to inflate them into *causal* connections.

APPRAISAL OF FREUD'S ARGUMENTS FOR THE PSYCHOANALYTIC
THEORY OF REPRESSION

Avowedly, his ideals *or* criteria of scientific validation are
roughly those of hypothetico-deductive or quasistatistical inductivism (Freud, 1914c, p. 77; 1915b, p. 117; 1925b, p. 32),
and he took adherence to them to be the hallmark of the scientific probity he claimed for his theory. Hence it behooves me
to appraise Freud's *arguments* for his monumental clinical theory of personality and therapy by his own standards. The verdict I shall reach on this basis is hardly predicated on the imposition of some extraneous methodological purism. Nor can it
be parried by the retort that psychoanalysis is a science *sui
generis*, a riposte that is unavailing in any case, if only because it
could likewise be invoked to vindicate mesmerism, Mary Baker
Eddy's Christian "science," biblical creationism, etc. Nor yet
does my application of Freud's avowed norm of scientific rationality to psychoanalysis imply that I deem this touchstone to be
the criterion of demarcation between science and nonscience.
In short, I shall grant Freud his own canon of scientific status
in addressing the following key question: Did his clinical arguments vindicate the knowledge claims he made for his evolving
theory by labeling it "scientific"?

My answer will be twofold: The reasoning on which Freud
rested the major hypotheses of his edifice was fundamentally
flawed, even if the probity of the clinical observations he adduced were not in question (Grünbaum, 1984, Part II). Moreover, far from deserving to be taken at face value, clinical data
from the psychoanalytic treatment setting are themselves epistemically quite suspect (Grünbaum, 1984, chap. 2; 1986, pp.
275-277).

The central causal and explanatory significance enjoyed by
unconscious ideation in the entire clinical theory rests, I submit,
on two cardinal inductive inferences drawn by Breuer and
Freud. As we are told in their joint "Preliminary Communication" (1893, pp. 6-7), they began with an observation made
after having administered their cathartic treatment to patients
suffering from various symptoms of hysteria. In the course of

such treatment, it had turned out that, for each distinct symptom S afflicting such a neurotic, the victim had *repressed* the memory of a trauma that had closely preceded the onset of S and was thematically cognate to this particular symptom. Besides repressing this traumatic memory, the patient had also strangulated the affect induced by the trauma. In the case of each symptom, our two therapists tried to lift the ongoing repression of the pertinent traumatic experience, and to effect a release of the pent-up affect. When their technique succeeded in implementing this twin objective, they reportedly observed the dramatic disappearance of the given symptom. Furthermore, the symptom removal *seemed* to be durable.

Impressed by this treatment outcome, Breuer and Freud drew their first momentous *causal* inference. Thus they enunciated the following fundamental therapeutic hypothesis: The dramatic improvements observed after treatment were produced by none other than the cathartic lifting of the pertinent repressions. But before the founders of psychoanalysis credited the undoing of repressions with remedial efficacy, they had been keenly alert to a rival hypothesis, which derived at least *prima facie* credibility from the known achievements of the admittedly suggestive therapies. On that alternative explanation of the positive outcome after cathartic treatment, that benefit was actually wrought by the patient's credulous expectation of symptom relief, not by the particular treatment ritual employed to fortify his or her optimistic anticipation. Breuer and Freud believed they could rule out such an account of treatment gains. As explained below in chapter 3, I shall refer to it as "the hypothesis of *placebo effect*." In an attempt to counter this challenge, they pointed out that the distinct symptoms had been removed *separately*, so that any one symptom disappeared only after leaving a *particular* repression. But Breuer and Freud (1893, p. 7) do not tell us why the likelihood of placebo effect should be deemed to be lower when several symptoms are wiped out *seriatim* than in the case of getting rid of only one symptom.

They saw very clearly that the threat posed by the rival hypothesis of placebo effect could be ominous. Unless they could meet it convincingly, it would totally abort their inference of a bold and, in fact, historic *etiological* postulate from their funda-mental therapeutic tribute to the undoing of repressions. In-deed, I shall argue that, to this day, the *whole* of the clinical psychoanalytic enterprise is haunted by the mortal threat from the very live possibility of placebo effect. As will emerge, the continuing failure of psychoanalytic research to discredit this altogether reasonable challenge gravely jeopardizes the very foundations of Freud's entire clinical theory. The clinical hypotheses comprise not only the asserted therapeutic efficacy of lifting repressions, but also the repression etiologies of the psychoneuroses, as well as the compromise models of manifest dream content and of sundry sorts of "Freudian slips."

At the time, Breuer and Freud believed their therapeutic results had ruled out the dangerous rival hypothesis of placebo effect. Having inferred the remedial efficacy of undoing re-pressions, they thought, furthermore, that this posited thera-peutic potency inductively spelled a paramount *etiologic* moral, that is, a coexisting ongoing repression is *causally necessary* for the *maintenance* of a neurosis N, and an original act of repres-sion was the causal *sine qua non* for the origination of N. This second ground-breaking causal inference was animated by their supposition that the repressed traumatic memory "acts [patho-genically] like a foreign body which long after its entry must continue to be regarded as an agent that is still at work" (1893, p. 6). The heuristic value of adopting this analogy becomes patent upon recalling that the inferred etiology yielded a *deduc-tive* explanation of the supposed remedial efficacy of lifting repressions, for, as I noted above, if an ongoing repression R is causally *necessary* for the pathogenesis *and* persistence of a neurosis N, then the removal of R must issue in the eradication of N.

Here and throughout, I have been at pains to emphasize that, according to Freud's etiologies and principle of "causal overdetermination," repression is only a *necessary* rather than both a necessary and sufficient condition for neurosogenesis. Thus, in Grünbaum (1984, pp. 109-110), I wrote that Freud held that "the development of a disorder N after an individual I suffers a pathogenic experience P depended on I's hereditary vulnerability. Hence, his universal etiologic hypotheses typically asserted that exposure to P was *causally necessary* for the development of N, *not* that it is causally sufficient." Nonetheless, in a lengthy editorial review of my book (1984), the analyst Wallace (1986, p. 382) saw fit to erect the following straw man: "a lack of precision in Grünbaum's understanding of the repression theory of neurosis and an insufficient appreciation of the concept of overdetermination vitiate much of his argument. Repression was never posited as the *necessary and sufficient* condition for neurosis, but only as a *necessary* precondition." Alas, this fabrication is representative of Wallace's own rigor of thought and reading. Besides, in Freud's technical parlance (1895b, p. 136), repressions qualify as "specific causes" (prior to Freud's abandonment of solutions to the problem of the "choice of neurosis"), and not, as Wallace claims, as "preconditions."

Note that the affect attached to a traumatic experience E can be *suppressed* (strangulated), but there may still be conscious awareness of this pent-up affect. Thus the affect attached to E can be suppressed without also being repressed (1915c, pp. 177-178). For example, Breuer's pioneering patient Anna O. felt disgust at the sight of seeing a dog drinking water from a glass, but she "said nothing as she wanted to be polite" toward the dog's owner (1893-95, p. 34).

But the cognitive repression of E can be *lifted without undoing E's* affective *suppression*. Indeed, as Breuer and Freud report, the implementation of just this latter scenario was almost always therapeutically unavailing: "Recollection without [release of the attached pent-up] affect almost invariably produces no [therapeutic] result" (1893, p. 6). Thus, it would be empirically false to deem the *mere* lifting of the cognitive repression of E *without* catharsis causally sufficient for the removal of the symptom S.

Hence we must endeavor to construe the Breuer-Freud etiology of psychoneurosis so that it does *not* entail this empirical falsehood. Yet it would have this untoward consequence, if it were taken to assert that *both* cognitive repression *and* affective suppression of E are causally *necessary* for neurosogenesis. On the other hand, just that undesirable false consequence is averted—as Carl Hempel and Morris Eagle have each re-marked to me—by articulating the founding etiology of psycho-analysis as follows: Either cognitive repression or affective sup-pression of E, i.e., *at least one* of the two, is causally necessary for neurosogenesis, rather than both. This version of the etiology would explain the purported therapeutic finding that the *ca-thartic* lifting of the repression—i.e., the undoing of the af-fective suppression as well as of the cognitive repression—is causally sufficient for symptom removal. Yet this same version would *not explain*, but only allow the observation, made by Breuer and Freud, that mere recall without release of pent-up affect is "almost invariably" unavailing therapeutically.

Though the discharge of pent-up affect is thus deemed *thera-peutically* essential, to accompany the cognitive retrieval of the repressed memory of E, it would be cumbersome to say so whenever one speaks of the presumed therapeutic role of lift-ing repressions. Therefore, brevity is served by the expository practice of simply crediting the therapeutic gain to the restora-tion of repressed memories, but with the understanding that affect-release is to be co-present.

It is essential to bear in mind that the posited *therapeutic* effi-cacy of retrieving repressed memories had provided the *sole* epistemic warrant for the cardinal etiologic postulate. This cog-nitive dependence was hardly lessened when Freud replaced Breuer's hypnotic technique by the innovative method of free association as the means for uncovering repressed mentation. In fact, though it is widely overlooked, *the attribution of therapeu-tic success to the removal of repressions not only was but, to this day, remains the sole epistemic underwriter of the purported ability of the patient's free associations to certify causes*. These associations were deemed to be a reliable *investigative* avenue leading to the detec-tion of the pathogens of neuroses. Indeed, one of Freud's (1900, p. 528) justifications for the use of free association as a *causally probative* method of *dream investigation* is that it is "identi-cal" with the one used to "resolve hysterical symptoms; and there the correctness of our method is warranted by the coinci-dent emergence and disappearance of the symptoms." In short, Freud adduces *therapeutic success* to vouch for the "correctness of our method" of free association as causally probative for etiologic research in *psychopathology*.

Freud could not have been more explicit in his assertion that therapeutic success is his epistemological basis for regarding free association as a reliable method for attributing a pathogenic role to repressions uncovered by means of it. And just that cardinal thesis of his has been overlooked by a number of my critics (e.g. Sachs, 1989), who have accused me of mistakenly assigning a fundamental role to therapeutic gain in Freud's basic rationale for deeming free association to be etiologically probative in the search for the pathogens of neuroses.

Thus, they have turned a blind eye to the fact that at the start of Breuer's collaboration with Freud, the latter heralded his belief in the therapeutic rationale for the *etiologic probativeness* of lifting repressions, when he declared: "For Breuer learnt from his first patient that the attempt at discovering the determining cause of a symptom was at the same time a therapeutic manoeuvre" (Freud, 1893, p. 35). Moreover, some of my critics have misunderstood, if not caricatured, my account of the relevance of therapeutic success in this context.

I never made the callow claim that when Freud used free association to arrive at the presumed pathogens of the affliction in any given case—e.g. in that of a paranoiac—he justified his belief in the etiologic probativeness of the method by pointing to therapeutic success in *every* such case. On the contrary, I said that once Freud had convinced himself of such probativeness by presumed therapeutic successes in *some* cases, he was confident that he could also consider the method etiologically reliable even in cases (such as victims of narcissistic neuroses like paranoia) in which he did not expect any therapeutic success. Thus, in my reply to Frank Cioffi's misrepresentations, I wrote: ". . . free association was gradually assumed to be an autonomous source of causal information, without reference to its initial therapeutic basis—or appeals to treatment gains in individual case histories—providing the etiologic pieces of the jigsaw puzzle" (Grünbaum, 1986, p. 273).

Incidentally, Freud's statement of his therapeutic argument for the probativeness of free association contains a slip of the pen that becomes apparent from his original German wording, but which has no bearing on the merits of my case. As we know, the patient's symptoms hardly first emerge simultaneously with their therapeutic dissipation. Yet Strachey translated Freud correctly as having spoken of "the coincident emergence and disappearance of the symptoms." It would seem that Freud meant to speak of the *resolution* (German: "Auflösung"), rather than of the emergence ("Auftauchen"), of the symptoms as coinciding with their therapeutic dissipation.

Analysts such as Strachey (1955) and Eissler (1969) have hailed free association as an instrument comparable to the microscope and the telescope. It is asserted to be a trustworthy means of etiologic inquiry in the sense of licensing the following *causal inference*: Let a causal chain of the analysand's free associations be initiated by his neurotic symptoms and issue in the emergence of previously repressed memories; then, we are told, this emergence qualifies as *good evidence* that the prior ongoing repression of these memories was actually the *pathogen* of the given neurosis.

Whereas all Freudians champion this causal inference, a number of influential ones have *explicitly renounced its legitimation* by the presumed *therapeutic dynamics* of undoing repressions. To *them* I say: *Without* this vindication, or some as yet unknown other warrant, not even the tortures of the thumbscrew or of the rack should persuade a rational being that free associations can *certify* pathogens or other causes! *Without* the stated *therapeutic* foundation, this epistemic tribute to free associations rests on nothing to date but a glaring causal fallacy; even that foundation turns out to be quite flimsy. Therefore, it is unavailing to extol the method of clinical investigation by free association as a trustworthy resource of etiologic inquiry, while issuing a modest disclaimer as to the therapeutic efficacy of psychoanalytic treatment. One is dumbfounded to find that noted psychoanalysts such as George S. Klein have done just that (1976, pp. 36-38). Also amazingly, the well-known analyst Judd Marmor (1968) conjectured that it was the accidental need to earn his livelihood as a psychiatric practitioner that drove Freud "to utilize his investigative tool [of free association] simultaneously as a therapeutic instrument" (p. 6). In brief, those who have made it fashionable nowadays to dissociate the credentials of

Freud's theory of personality—the so-called "science"—from the merits of psychoanalytic therapy are stepping on thin ice indeed. How very thin will shortly become clear from my scrutiny of the arguments put forward by the mature Freud, in place of those that he had championed while he was still Breuer's junior collaborator. This conclusion has been challenged by Sachs (1989). But the challenge has been rebutted by Erwin (1992).

Soon after Freud had begun to practice without Breuer, it became devastatingly plain that they had been all too hasty in rejecting the rival hypothesis of placebo effect. The remissions achieved by additional patients whom Freud himself treated cathartically turned out *not* to be durable. Indeed, the ensuing pattern of relapses, additional treatment, ephemeral remissions, and further relapses gainsaid the attribution of therapeutic credit to the lifting of those repressions that Freud had uncovered. Ironically, he began to be haunted by the triumph of the hypothesis of placebo effect over the fundamental therapeutic tenet that Breuer and he had originally enunciated, for he recognized that the vicissitudes of his personal relations to the patient were highly correlated with the pattern of symptom relapses and intermittent remissions. In his own view, this correlation "proved that the personal emotional relation between doctor and patient was after all stronger than the whole cathartic process" (1925b, p. 27). But once the repression etiology was thus bereft of therapeutic support, the very cornerstone of psychoanalysis was completely undermined (Ellenberger, 1972, p. 279). Hence at that point, the new clinical psychoanalytic structure tumbled down and lay in shambles.

Nonetheless, Freud was undaunted. Although the excavation of *adult* repressions had been a therapeutic failure, he conjectured that the uncovering of much earlier ones dating from childhood and sexual in content might well eradicate the neurosis. He hypothesized further that the patient's free associations would lead to the certification of the early pathogen required for the existence of the affliction (1896, pp. 194-199). As he reports, the very early repressions that then emerged were in fact thematically sexual. But when his patients improved and he gave therapeutic credit to the lifting of these childhood repressions, he was apparently no longer able to adduce the *separate* symptom removals invoked earlier to hold the rival hypothesis of placebo effect at bay. At this stage (1896), his attribution of remedial efficacy to the disclosure of hidden affect-laden mentation took the form of declaring such insight to be at least causally *necessary* for a cure. Furthermore, Freud's rehabilitation of the generic repression etiology in a new sexual version was now directly built into this newly avowed therapeutic role of insight as follows: Insight could extirpate a neurosis *only if* it afforded the victim conscious mastery of the particular repression causally required by the pathogenesis of his disorder.

In fact, as I have documented elsewhere (Grünbaum, 1984, chap. 2), from 1896 onward through at least 1917, Freud thought he could claim clinical support for the following extraordinarily strong conjunction of clinical propositions (1909a, p. 104; 1914a, pp. 155-156; 1916-17, p. 452): A neurosis can be dependably eradicated *only* by the conscious mastery of the repressions that are causally required for its pathogenesis, *and* only the therapeutic techniques of psychoanalysis can generate this requisite insight into the specific pathogen. I shall designate this conjunction of two causally necessary conditions as "Freud's Master Proposition." Its significance will receive detailed attention in chapter 5, but in the present overview chapter, I am concerned to point out that once he had equipped himself with the intellectual arsenal contained in it, he was entitled to make a whole series of claims each of which is of the first importance for the validation of his enterprise. I shall now develop the ensuing cardinal theses.

1. If a patient has been cured, then the etiologic interpretations his doctor gave him, at least in the later stages of the analysis, must have been correct or close to the mark. By the same token, insofar as the substantial remission of symptoms can bespeak a genuine cure, this treatment outcome confirms that the analyst has correctly identified the specific pathogen via the patient's free associations. Hence, collectively the successes achieved by psychoanalytic treatment vouch for the truth of

the Freudian theory of personality, including its specific etiologies of the psychoneuroses, and even its general hypotheses about psychosexual development.

As a further corollary, the psychoanalytic probing of the unconscious is vindicated as a method of etiologic investigation by its therapeutic achievements. This method has the remarkable capacity to validate major causal claims by essentially retrospective inquiries, *without* the burdens of prospective longitudinal studies employing experimental controls. Yet these causal inferences are not vitiated by *post hoc ergo propter hoc*. Magnificent, if true!

2. The clinical data furnished by successfully treated neurotics do not result from self-fulfilling predictions. Thus, these data are exonerated from the charge that they forfeit their probative value. According to this reproach, even a patient who engages in frequent emotional outbursts against his analyst will comply with him doctrinally, like a pupil, despite the doctor's best efforts to forego overt or covert communication of his theoretical expectations. Such epistemic contamination of the patient's sundry responses will occur willy-nilly, it is charged, because the psychoanalyst will unconsciously yet persuasively insinuate his anticipations in a myriad of subtle ways. And since the analysand has sought out an avowedly Freudian therapist for help, he will want to please the authority figure on whom he now so greatly depends. The ensuing intellectual deference makes for *self-fulfillment* of the analyst's theoretical expectations, and thereby for the *spuriousness* of the vauntedly abundant clinical confirmations.

Freud (1954, pp. 334-337) had been stung when even his long-time confrère Wilhelm Fliess dropped this skeptical bombshell, which rankled. Yet to his great credit, Freud eloquently came to grips with its grave challenge, emphasizing that it "is uncommonly interesting and must be answered" (1916-17, p. 447). He then met it head-on by enlisting his Master Proposition in his lecture on "Analytic Therapy" (p. 452) to authenticate clinical data as probatively legitimate. Thus, if the patient's assent to his analyst's interpretations is epistemically reliable after all, credence may be reasonably given to the patient's introspective *self*-observations, once his repressions no longer hold his motives in distorting and obfuscating thrall.

3. *Only* psychoanalytic treatment can effect genuine cures of neuroses (1916-17, p. 458). But *if* Freud's therapy does enjoy such preeminence, then it can warrantedly take credit for the recoveries of patients *without* statistical comparisons with the results from untreated control groups, or from controls treated by rival modalities (pp. 461-462). Moreover, when analytic therapy does score remedial triumphs, these gains are *not* placebo effects. For if the first conjunct of the Master Proposition is to be believed, the working through of the patient's unconscious conflicts is the decisive therapeutic factor, although the analyst's role as a parent surrogate serves as an ice-breaker. Freud did recognize that the analysand's so-called "transference" attachment to his doctor plays such a catalytic role in the earlier stages of treatment (1926b, p. 190). Yet he evidently singled out the patient's correct etiological insight as the one quintessential ingredient "which distinguishes [the therapeutic dynamics of] analytic treatment from any kind of treatment by suggestion" (1914a, pp. 155-156; 1916-17, pp. 450-452).

As long as Freud felt entitled to champion his Master Proposition, he could have confidence in the three sets of remarkable theses I have just formulated. With one stroke, he had redeemed his promise (1916-17, pp. 446-447) to nullify the twofold indictment that suggestion is at once the decisive agent in his therapy and the cognitive bane of the psychoanalytic method of investigation. In this way, etiologic hypotheses—which do not themselves pertain at all to either the dynamics or the outcome of analytic therapy—nonetheless were *epistemically parasitic* on therapeutic results, if only to legitimate the probity of the clinical data on which they were predicated. Yet new evidence then severed the dazzling link Freud had forged in the Master Proposition between the conquest of a neurosis and the patient's discernment of its pathogens.

Indeed, by 1926, Freud himself repudiated the therapeutic indispensability of his type of treatment, and he demoted the psychoanalytic conquest of the analysand's resistances to the status of a mere expeditor of recoveries that were in the offing anyway. As he put it modestly: "as a rule our therapy must be content with bringing about more quickly, more reliably and with less expenditure of energy than would otherwise be the case the good result which in favourable circumstances would have occurred of itself" (1926a, p. 154). But just such spontaneous remission *belies* the Master Proposition. Once the latter became defunct, even spectacular therapeutic successes became probatively unavailing for the validation of the generic repression etiology by means of that Proposition. To boot, Freud (1937a) reported ruefully that a satisfactory psychoanalysis is not even prophylactic against the recurrence of the affliction for which the analysand was treated, let alone does it immunize him against the outbreak of a different neurosis. Far from holding out hope for cures, Freud essentially confined the prospects to palliation. But the import of this therapeutic pessimism is shattering. Even if the Master Proposition were true, it would need the existential premise of documented cures in order to vouch for the etiologies inferred by means of free association.

As if this were not enough, in recent decades, comparative studies of treatment outcome from rival therapies have failed to reveal any sort of superiority of psychoanalysis within the class of therapeutic modalities that exceed the spontaneous remission rate, gleaned from the (quasi) untreated controls.[2] There is no such evidence, if only because the requisite comparative studies for *long-term* psychoanalysis have yet to be carried out. This result further impugns the Master Proposition, which entails that only analytic therapy can effect genuine cures of psychoneuroses.

But if analytic treatment is not superior to its rivals in the pertinent diagnostic categories, it becomes quite reasonable—though *not* compelling—to interpret its therapeutic achievements as placebo effects. If so, then the therapeutic successes of psychoanalysis are *not* wrought after all by the patient's acquisition of self-knowledge, much to Socrates' sorrow. In this vein, the psychiatrist Jerome Frank (1973) has contended that the analyst, no less than his competitor, heals neurotics by supportively counteracting their demoralization, not by excavating their repressions. Indeed, Frank's hypothesis even allows rival

---

[2]For a very brief digest of the summary literature on treatment outcome, see Grünbaum (1977, pp. 235-250, and chap. 5 here). Detailed, argued accounts are given by Prioleau et al. (1983), Smith et al. (1980), Rachman and Wilson (1980), and Strupp et al. (1977).

therapies to have differential effects by virtue of their differential abilities to mobilize agencies common to all of them. The shared techniques for such mobilization usually include well-practiced rituals, a special vocabulary, a knowledgeable manner, and the therapist's charisma. To be sure, it is still arguable that psychoanalytic treatment gains are *not* placebogenic. But, as some noted analysts have conceded, the following damaging fact remains: "All-pervading" psychic improvements or even cures can be effected by such rival modalities as behavior therapy, and also by extraclinical life events (Malan, 1976, pp. 147, 172-173, 269). Hence Freud's Master Proposition became untenable.

It emerges that this collapse completely undercuts the pivotal therapeutic argument given by the mature Freud to validate his repression etiology of the psychoneuroses *and* to authenticate the probative value of the clinical data generated by the psychoanalytic method. Thus, the ominous reproach that epistemic contamination by suggestion makes for bogus confirmations bedevils clinical validation after all. Moreover, no empirically viable surrogate for the discredited Master Proposition capable of yielding Freud's desired conclusions even seems to be remotely in sight. In my 1984 book and in chapters 5 and 8 below, I referred to the argument based on the Master Proposition as Freud's "Tally Argument" for reasons given there. Sachs (1989) claimed that this attribution to Freud is exegetically unwarranted. But Erwin (1992) has discredited Sachs's objections. And I shall show elsewhere that Sachs's proposed alternative reading *trivializes* Freud's entire case in his "Analytic Therapy Lecture" (1916-17).

But it may well be asked impatiently: Why could Freud not dispense with therapeutic arguments altogether and rely instead on other sorts of clinical evidence to furnish support for his specific etiologies? In reply, I shall contend in chapters 4-6 and 8-9 that the genuine confirmation of his etiologies by intraclinical observations is epistemically rather hopeless, at least foreseeably. For now, I shall give but a few reasons that, in my view, collectively warrant this dismal conclusion, since later chapters will develop them in detail.

1. Freud conjectured that the development of a neurosis N by an individual I depended not only on I's exposure to pathogenic experiences P, but also on I's hereditary vulnerability. His universal etiological hypotheses typically asserted that exposure to P is causally necessary for the pathogenesis of N, not that it is causally sufficient. Any such hypothesis entails the universal *retrodiction* that all those afflicted by N had suffered P.

In the context of this entailment, Freud's Rat-Man case has been invoked to maintain that the psychoanalytic etiology of obsessional neurosis would have been confirmed by clinical evidence corroborating the occurrence of the pertinent retrodicted experience P during the Rat-Man's early childhood (Glymour, 1980, p. 272).

Now suppose, for argument's sake, that in his analysis the Rat-Man had reported having retrieved the distant memory of the traumatic sexual event retrodicted by Freud. And assume further for now that credence can be given to so early a memory under the suggestive conditions of a psychoanalysis. Then it is vital to appreciate that the mere retrospective authentication of the bare occurrence of the early trauma hardly bespeaks the *causal relevance* of this event to the pathogenesis of the Rat-Man's obsessions. Surely the mere traumaticity of an event does not itself attest to its etiologic relevance. The human condition would be much worse than it already is if every psychic blow became the specific pathogen of a neurosis. Yet prominent psychoanalysts have reasoned that the causal relevance of an experience P to a neurosis N is supported by the mere fact that those who are beset by N and suffered P instantiate the retrodiction entailed by Freud's etiology (Waelder, 1962, pp. 625-626). Such an inference is no better than *post hoc ergo propter hoc*, as will be shown in detail in chapters 4 and 8, where Freud's reasonings in the Rat-Man case will be examined extensively.

But what if we could also assume that the clinical setting has the epistemic resources to certify *retrospectively* that all available victims of neuroses *other than N* had been *spared* the experience P? Even under this sanguine assumption of retrospective certifiability, the envisaged retrospective clinical testing design is *confined* to the class of neurotics. This confinement restricts the probative import of the putative findings. At best, they might bespeak the etiologic relevance of the experience P to N *within* the class of neurotics, but would *not* lend credence to the Freudian claim of pathogenic relevance in the wider class of *persons*.

2. Some analysts have told us that the patient himself is able to determine by *introspection* whether the repressed P was in fact the pathogen of his disorder, once he no longer represses the memory of this episode (Waelder, 1962, pp. 628-629). But this thesis of privileged epistemic access to the causes of psychopathology does not bear scrutiny.

Substantial evidence recently marshaled by cognitive psychologists has shown (see chap. 5) that even in the case of *consciously* motivated behavior, a subject does not enjoy special cognitive access to the discernment of the motivational causes of his various actions. Though the subject often does have direct access to the individual conscious contents of his mental states, he has only *inferential* access—just like outside observers—to such causal linkages as actually connect some of his own mental states. The possession of direct access to the content of momentary states of attention or felt affect is a far cry from being uniquely privy to the actual existence of a hypothesized causal nexus between, say, certain infantile experiences and specified adult personality dispositions. No less than in the case of causal hypotheses pertaining to physical states, the subject's avowal of causal connections between his own mental states is based either on the fallible inferences drawn by himself, or on those carried out by members of his subculture to whom he gives credence. Hence these avowed causal linkages may be fancied or actual. In short, when a subject attributes a causal relation to some of his own mental states, he does so—just like outside observers—by invoking theory-based causal schemata endorsed by the prevailing belief system.

More often than not, a patient who sought treatment from a Freudian doctor already brings some psychoanalytic beliefs into the therapy, or is at least receptive to etiologic interpretations of his conduct based on the analyst's theoretical stance. No wonder analytic patients then find the rationale offered to them credible. But this credulity is hardly tantamount to privileged cognitive access to the validity of the ambitious causal claims central to the etiologic reconstruction of the given dysfunction.

As we saw earlier, the same gullibility may also be responsible for the analysand's therapeutic gains. These may be due to his *belief* in his doctor's etiologic reconstruction rather than to the undoing of his repressions. But just as the patient has no direct introspective access to the pathogenesis of his affliction, so also his introspections do not afford him privileged epistemic access to the cause of his therapeutic progress. He is surely not in a better position to make such a causal attribution than his analyst. Indeed, two Freudian investigators of the dynamics of psychotherapies have issued the following agnostic disclaimer: "Psychoanalysts, like other psychotherapists, literally *do not know* how they achieve their [remedial] results" (Luborsky and Spence, 1978, p. 360).

3. Freud himself emphasized that the patient's poor mnemic performance often simply fails to authenticate the childhood event retrodicted via his etiology (1920a, p. 18; 1937b, pp. 265-266). As I shall document (chap. 5), his writings also multiply attest to the *unreliability* of purported adult memories of early childhood episodes that had presumably been retrieved by the analysis after being repressed. More recently, research on memory has furnished telling empirical evidence that the patient's supposed ability to achieve *non*inferential veridical recall of very early repressed experiences is largely a myth.

Experimental studies acknowledged by analysts themselves (Marmor, 1970) have borne out the therapist's contaminating regimentation of purported memories recovered by free association. It can be granted, of course, that requirements of consistency or at least overall coherence do afford the analyst *some* check on what the patient alleges to be bona fide memories. And it is to be understood that the epistemic discounting of early childhood memories purportedly retrieved by the adult patient is not a wholesale derogation of adult memories in daily life. But the malleability of adult memories from childhood by suggestion is epitomized by a report from Piaget (Loftus, 1980, pp. 119-121), who thought he vividly remembered an attempt to kidnap him from his baby carriage along the Champs Elysées. He recalled the gathered crowd, the scratches on the face of the heroic nurse who saved him, the policeman's white baton, the assailant running away. However vivid, Piaget's recollections were false. Years later his nurse confessed she had made up the entire story, which he then internalized as a presumed experience, under the influence of an authority figure.

That psychoanalytic treatment ought not to be regarded as a *bona fide memory-jogging* device emerges more generally as a corollary of at least three sets of recent research findings elaborated by Loftus (1980): (1) the remarkable extent to which human memory is malleable; (2) the interpolative reconstruction and bending of memories by theoretical beliefs or expectations; and (3) the penchant, under the influence of leading questions, to fill amnesiac gaps by confabulated material. Earlier we saw that theoretical beliefs rather than direct introspection determine the subject's verdicts on causal relations between his own mental states. Similarly, the interpolative reconstruction and bending of memories by theoretical beliefs combine with the malleability of memory by suggestion to generate pseudomemories of events that never occurred, especially when they are temporally remote. In short, the retrospective testing design of the psychoanalytic setting cannot even reliably authenticate the bare occurrence of the retrodicted childhood experience *P*, let alone its pathogenic role.

It emerges that the proposed clinical vindication of the repression etiology *without* reliance on the dynamics of Freud's therapy is no less a fiasco than his attempted therapeutic validation. Two main reasons for this additional failure are: (1) The testing design of the analytic setting appears incompetent to warrant that the retrodicted childhood experience *P* was, if actual, also pathogenic; (2) the retrospective methods of this clinical inquiry cannot even reliably authenticate the bare occurrence of *P*. To my knowledge, besides the sorts of arguments I have canvassed, there are no other *clinical* defenses of Freud's sexual repression etiology of the neuroses.

Hence I draw the following major conclusions: His sexual version of this generic etiology is now devoid of cogent clinical support, just as Breuer's nonsexual cathartic etiologies, which Freud had disavowed as clinically ill-founded. Furthermore, *this collapse of the psychoanalytic etiology, I maintain, basically impugns the investigative cogency of free associations in the conduct of etiologic inquiry. For Freud had enunciated his fundamental rule of free association as a maxim of clinical research, because he thought that associations governed by it had reliably certified the unconscious pathogens of the neuroses.* Yet just this epistemic tribute is now seen to be gratuitous. Finally, Freud is left helpless to rebut the charge that clinical data forfeit their probative value by epistemic contamination through suggestion, a complaint for which there is good evidence. But, for the sake of argument, assume nonetheless that there is no such forfeiture of probative value, and that the patient's clinical responses can be taken at face value after all. It is of fundamental importance to appreciate that *even if the clinical data were thus uncontaminated, they would still utterly fail to sustain the causal hypotheses of the psychoanalytic clinical theory of psychopathology*, as I have argued.

I must emphasize that these bleak results are equally devastating to the currently fashionable revisionist versions of psychoanalysis that go under the names of Kohutian "self psychology" and of "object relations theory." Insofar as these post-Freudian theories are indeed recognizably psychoanalytic, they do of course embrace some version of the repression etiology. Furthermore, they rely epistemically on free association in the clinical investigation of purported pathogens and other unconscious determinants of behavior, while lifting repressions as one means to effect therapy (Eagle, 1984a). But, I submit, precisely to the extent that these outgrowths of Freud's ideas are thus recognizably psychoanalytic in content as well as in method of inquiry and therapy, my epistemic critique of Freud's original hypotheses applies with equal force to the etiologic, developmental, and therapeutic tenets of these successors (Eagle, 1983; Grünbaum, 1983 and 1984, chap. 7). In the context of the therapeutic theories espoused by the post-Freudian neorevisionists, I have advisedly depicted the undoing of repressions as just "one means" of effecting therapy. The need for this qualification has been stressed by Eagle (1984a, 1984b). As he points out, the Kohutian self psychologists place less therapeutic emphasis on insight into prior repressions than on the therapist's "empathic mirroring," coupled with the patient's feelings of identification with and idealization of the doctor. But precisely insofar as there is such divergence from the orthodox psychotherapeutic tenet, the warrant for labeling the revised doctrine "psychoanalytic" becomes seriously questionable.

In any case, Eagle (1984a, 1984b) has argued tellingly that the etiologic and therapeutic claims of self psychology and of object relations theory rests epistemically on bases even more dubious than those of Freud's corresponding hypotheses. Hence it would be unavailing to adduce the post-Freudian neo-revisionist credos in an attempt to blunt the force of the doubts I have raised against orthodox psychoanalysis.

As a direct corollary, we are now able to appraise the psycho-analytic theory of dreams as well as Freud's account of sundry sorts of slips or "parapraxes," although the theory of dreams will receive detailed scrutiny in chapter 10. I gave my critique of the theory of slips in 1984 (chap. 4). Both of these renowned hypotheses attribute a decisive *causal* role to repressed ideation. These two causal attributions were and have remained auda-cious, if not foolhardy, extrapolations from the etiologic func-tion that Freud has ascribed to repression in his explanation of psychopathology. As later chapters will explain, whereas he claimed to have therapeutic evidence for postulating this patho-genic role, he never produced any independent clinical support for these two momentous extrapolations. As we learn in the opening pages on the method of dream interpretation, the first extrapolation consisted of simply enlarging the epistemic role of free association from being only a method of etiologic in-quiry aimed at therapy, to serving likewise as an avenue for finding the purported unconscious causes of dreams (1900, pp. 100-101).

Having found that his patients reported their dreams while freely associating to their neurotic symptoms, he drew the infer-ence that "a dream can be inserted into the psychical chain that has to be traced backwards in the memory from a pathological idea. It was then only a short step to treating the dream itself as a symptom and to applying to dreams the method of inter-pretation that had been worked out for symptoms" (p. 101). Yet, far from being only heuristic in Freud's view, this cavalier *extrapolative* adoption of the symptom model for manifest dream content was avowedly also probative. As he argued: "We might also point out in our defence that our procedure in interpreting dreams [by means of free association] is identical with the procedure by which we resolve hysterical symptoms; and there the correctness of our method is warranted by the coincident emergence and disappearance of the symptoms" (p. 528). *Mutatis mutandis*, the same remarks apply to the further extrapolation that slips are likewise minineurotic symptoms. Therefore the claim that the method of free association can reliably certify the unconscious motives of dream formation and of parapraxes is cognitively parasitic on the prior thesis that this method can certify repressions to be the pathogens of neuroses.[3]

But in virtue of the extrapolative justification given for the repression models of dreams and of parapraxes, their epistemic fortunes are dependent on those of Freud's theory of *psychopathology* (1925b, p. 45; 1900, p. 149). As a consequence of just this epistemic dependence, the ravages from the demise of Freudian psychopathology and of free association as a tool of etiologic certification extend, with a vengeance, to the psychoanalytic theory of dreams and of sundry sorts of "slips."

Originally, Freud had claimed that free association, like Breuer's cathartic method, can certify the required cause of a neurosis in virtue of the method's ability to cure the illness. As Freud put it, "Breuer learnt from his first patient that the attempt at discovering the determining cause of a symptom was at the same time a therapeutic manoeuvre" (Breuer and Freud, 1893, p. 35). But, as we saw, the arguments for deeming free association capable of certifying pathogens were not viable. And in the wake of their collapse, Freud's extrapolation does not furnish even the *shadow* of a good reason for supposing that associations governed by his "fundamental rule" can reliably certify the unconscious causes of dreams and of parapraxes.

Indeed, as far as I know, Freud's disciples, either orthodox or revisionist, have yet to produce any sound reason for crediting free association with the ability to pick out the causes of

---

[3]In Grünbaum, 1984, chap. 5, I have argued that neither Freud's (1900) own account of his Irma specimen dream, nor Erikson's (1954) attempt to give an orthodox psychoanalytic interpretation of it, can serve to accredit free association as a reliable means for certifying dream motives.

dream formation. Hence I claim that the emergence of repressed infantile wishes via free associations triggered by the
recall of anxiety dreams and nightmares cannot warrant the
hypothesis that these dreams are engendered by such wishes.
Indeed, whatever evidence there may be from commonsense
psychology that certain particular dreams were generated by
unfulfilled wishes, it has now turned out that free association
does not have the probative power to *underwrite* this verdict.

THE FUTILITY OF HERMENEUTICS WITHOUT CAUSATION

Faced with the bleak import of such a skeptical indictment,
psychoanalysts will be intent on salvaging their legacy in some
form. Some of them will then be understandably receptive to a
rationale that promises them absolution from their failure to
validate the cardinal hypotheses of their clinical theory. Be of
stout heart, they are told, and take a more radical *hermeneutic*
turn than the one considered above and in chapter 4. Freud,
they learn, brought the incubus of validation on himself by his
scientistic pretensions. *Abjure his program of causal explanation*,
some hermeneuticians beckon them, and you will no longer be
saddled with the harassing demand to justify Freud's causal
hypotheses. One such hermeneutic advocate illustrated this repudiation of causation as follows: "the meaning of a dream
does not reside in some prior latent dream [content], but in the
manifest dream and the analysand's associations of it" (Steele,
1979, p. 400). The blandishments of this renunciatory stance
include the comforting assurance that the practicing analyst is
immune to taunts from critics who dispute the cost effectiveness
of his therapy. Even for the Freudian psychohistorians, the
hermeneutician has the glad tidings that henceforth they can
hold their heads high as protagonists of a newly legitimated
kind of humanistic discipline. In short, the claim is that the
challenge to provide validation of the causal propositions has
been obviated, and that the continuing demand for it has therefore become an anachronism.

As against the generic disavowal of causal attributions advocated by some hermeneuticians, I maintain that it is a nihilistic,

if not frivolous, trivialization of Freud's entire clinical theory. Far from serving as a new citadel for psychoanalytic apologetics, the embrace of such hermeneuticians is, I submit, the kiss of death for the legacy that was to be saved. On the other hand, insofar as other hermeneuticians, Ricoeur (1981), for example, do countenance the retention of causal hypotheses in psychoanalytic explanations, they are no less obligated to substantiate these hypotheses by cogent evidence than the orthodox Freudians whom they pilloried as scientistically addicted.

Let me illustrate my case against the stated acausal hermeneutic construal of psychoanalytic significance by reference to an allegedly Freudian lapse of memory that has figured as a paradigmatic instance in the literature (Grünbaum, 1984, chap. 4). To say that a slip of the tongue, pen, ear, eye, or of memory is genuinely "Freudian" is to say that it was engendered by a *repressed* motive. Thus Freud assimilated a seemingly insignificant slip of the tongue to the status of a minineurotic symptom by regarding this lapse as a *compromise* between a repressed motive that crops out in the form of a disturbance, on the one hand, and the conscious intention to make a certain utterance, on the other.

The pertinent paradigmatic instance of a lapse of memory involves the forgetting of the Latin pronoun *aliquis* (someone), which a young man Y omitted when reciting a line from Virgil's *Aeneid* (Freud, 1901, chap. 2). Freud supplied the missing word and enjoined Y to use the restored word as the point of departure for free associations. After a tortuous chain of such associations, punctuated by some interjections from Freud, it emerged that Y had been harboring a presumably repressed fear. An Italian girlfriend, he suspected apprehensively, had become pregnant by him. Freud then told him that this repressed anxiety had undeniably produced his *aliquis* lapse. But Y doubted any such causal nexus, although he was fully aware that his worry was genuine.

Now let me contrast Freud's account of this lapse with the hermeneutic claim that Y's slip lends itself to acausal and yet psychoanalytic interpretation.

The orthodox rationale for calling on Y to let the restored word initiate his free associations was clear. Having deemed the lapse to be a minineurotic symptom, Freud attributed its occurrence *causally* to the operation of some repression. When *Y* asked him to *explain* how the forgetting of the pronoun had been brought about, Freud promised to identify the causally relevant repression by winnowing the free associations triggered in *Y* by the restored word *aliquis*. He then used the surfacing of *Y*'s previously repressed pregnancy worry from these particular associations as grounds for concluding that this very fear—while as yet being repressed before the memory lapse—had caused *Y* to forget that word. Freud held this inference to be licensed by the principle that a repression *R* present before the commission of a parapraxis by a person *X* qualifies as its cause, if *R* emerges into *X*'s consciousness in the wake of free associations triggered by his awareness of the content of his error.

I do not profess to know at all what did cause *Y*'s slip, but, as an immediate corollary of my earlier arguments, I claim that if *Y*'s repressed worry did cause him to forget *aliquis*, Freud has completely failed to supply cogent evidence for this causal nexus. This failure to justify his causal inference deserves censure, even if one could grant him quite generally that the analyst does not inject epistemically contaminating influences into the sequence of the associations, as he contended (1923c, p. 238). Seriously flawed though it is, Freud's account nonetheless does offer an explanation of slips *qua slips* by purporting to have identified unconscious motives *for their occurrence*.

I submit that the alleged interpretive meaning furnished by the acausal hermeneutic rationale is altogether insensitive to the fact that the word *aliquis* figured in a *lapse* of memory. Whatever that hermeneutic meaning, I claim that it is *not* the meaning *of a slip qua slip* at all! To be sure, the afore-cited hermeneutician, no less than the orthodox analyst, sifts the free associations elicited from *Y* by the restoration of the forgotten word to his awareness. Yet the hermeneutic view now at issue demurely disclaims the postulation of causes (Steele, 1979, p. 400), and thus forsakes the causal import of treating a slip as a minineurotic symptom. According to this construal, the interpretive meaning to be revealed by the winnowing of *Y*'s associations avowedly has no *causal* relevance to the fact that *aliquis* did figure in a lapse. How then can the interpretive meaning revealed by the associative content of *aliquis* be held to be the significance of the *forgetting* of *aliquis*, rather than simply the associative import of that word per se, regardless of whether it had been forgotten or not? Indeed, on the acausal hermeneutic rationale, why should *Y* be asked to associate to the word *aliquis* rather than to one of the words in the line from Virgil that he had *not* forgotten? Since the emerging meaning is not the meaning of a slip *qua* slip, how can this acausal rationale provide a reason for supposing that the associations to a *forgotten* word are richer in interpretive meaning—whatever that is—than the associations to nonforgotten words, or to other associatively evocative items in the subject's life? How then can the hermeneutician see himself as having given any reconstruction at all of Freud's theory of slips *qua* slips? Here and in chapter 4 we see again how a hermeneutic construal becomes a mischievous device of obfuscation (Grünbaum, 1988, 1989).

What of the reply that, though the associations do not bespeak a cause of a slip, they reveal a great deal about the current psychological makeup of the person who has them? I retort by asking: On what basis does the advocate of *acausal* hermeneutics infer the psychological makeup of a person from the latter's free associations? Does the inference rely tacitly on presumed causal linkages between personality structure and associational output? If so, the acausalist is not entitled to invoke them, if only because the validation of causal connections would require nonhermeneutic methods he is unwilling to license. But let us suppose the generalizations used to draw the requisite inferences as to the associating person's makeup are not causal. Even then, it is at best unclear how they can be validated short of adopting the very methods the hermeneutician rejects as "scientistic."

Similar considerations warrant the conclusion that the acausal hermeneutic rationale so truncates the repression etiology of the psychoneuroses as to trivialize that etiology *qua* theory of psychopathology. A like verdict serves to convict the stated acausal version of the received theory of dreams, as Moore has argued in his telling critique of hermeneutic "rationalization without causation" (1983, pp. 32-34).

Menaker (1982) has argued that Freud's one-time disciple Otto Rank repudiated his erstwhile search for *causes* of personality development, thereby abandoning his own thesis of the role of the birth trauma. Instead, Rank claimed an acausal creative role for an individuating will, a notion that is *not* explanatory even if it seems elevating to some.

CONCLUSIONS

In this first chapter, I set out to present just some of the highlights of my appraisal of Freud's principal *arguments* for his monumental clinical theory of personality and therapy. This scrutiny was based on his own avowed inductive standards.

So far, I have made no mention of the results obtained in actual attempts to test some parts of psychoanalytic theory experimentally. Such laboratory tests of psychoanalysis are discussed in a book by the *pro*-Freudian English psychologist Paul Kline (1981). In this work, Kline tries to refute the extremely skeptical conclusions offered by Hans Eysenck and Glenn Wilson (1973). Interestingly enough, Freud himself told us that "In [psycho]analysis, however, we have to do without the assistance afforded to [other] research by experiment" (1933, p. 174).

In my view, the debate between Eysenck and Kline yields essentially the same verdict as the one I have drawn from the *clinical* evidence offered by Freudians. So far, the evidence available from the laboratory has provided no significant support for any of the major hypotheses of psychoanalytic theory or therapy. Let me give two brief but important illustrative examples, which will also convey what I mean by the term *major hypothesis* in this context.

Freud hypothesized that strongly *repressed* homosexual desires are the causal *sine qua non* for the pathogenesis of paranoid delusions. The experimenter Harold Zamansky (1958) attempted to test this etiologic hypothesis (Grünbaum, 1986, pp. 269-270). But this investigator himself makes only the following quite modest claim for his findings: "Though the present experiment has demonstrated a greater degree of [repressed] homosexuality in men with paranoid delusions than in nonparanoid individuals, these results *tell us nothing* about the role which homosexuality plays in the development of these delusions" (quoted from Zamansky's study, as reprinted in Eysenck and Wilson [1973, p. 308]; italics added). In the same vein, I claim more generally: It is not enough to provide evidence for the existence of a *mechanism* of repression, which was already postulated before Freud by Herbart, among others. The point is that there is no good experimental evidence for Freud's much stronger claim that specific sorts of sexual repressions are *causally necessary* for the production of designated kinds of mental disorders. In fact, Kline (1981) admits as much in the following disclaimer: "Many of the Freudian claims concerning the neuroses have simply never been put to the objective test. . . . Thus, the hypotheses which have been put to the test are usually those where convenient measures are at hand rather than those most crucial to the theory" (p. 437).

The psychoanalytic theory of dream production by repressed infantile wishes furnishes a second illustration of my thesis that there is a poverty of experimental support for Freud's *cardinal* postulates. His theory of dream interpretation is appraised by the psychoanalytically oriented psychologists Fisher and Greenberg (1977). On the construal they deem most reasonable, its central thesis is that dreams express (vent) not only wishes, but sundry drives or impulses that originate in the unconscious (pp. 46-47). But, besides opting for some revisions, they make two sobering points: (1) Even if one can show that a dream does, indeed, express a certain impulse, there are, at present, still no scientifically reliable means of warranting that the impulse originated in the unconscious sector of the psyche (p. 47); and (2) the available "findings are *congruent* with Freud's venting model. But . . . they do not specifically document the model" (p. 53); moreover, "the data . . . are encouraging but not definitively validating with respect to Freud's venting model" (p. 63).

Yet, despite issuing these vital admonitions, Fisher and Greenberg permitted themselves to *begin* their summary by declaring that Freud's model "seems to be supported by the scientific evidence that can be mustered" (p. 63). By thus sliding from compatibility ("congruence") with the theory into *support* for it, these friends of psychoanalysis have lent substance to Popper's complaint against the methodological behavior of some of Freud's sympathizers, although Popper's critique of psychoanalytic theory as such is largely unsound, as I shall argue in chapter 2 (Grünbaum, 1984, chap. 1; 1986, pp. 266-270; 1989).

Several conclusions issue from my appraisal of the arguments that Freud and his disciples have rested on their observations:

1. Insofar as the evidence for the major causal hypotheses of the psychoanalytic corpus is now held to derive from the productions of patients in analysis, this warrant is remarkably weak. All the same, there is some plausibility, I believe, in the psychoanalytic claim that there exist such defense mechanisms as repression, denial, rationalization (in Ernest Jones's sense), reaction formation, and projection. But, as I have emphasized, psychoanalytic theory goes far beyond asserting that repression operates in these defense mechanisms. Besides claiming the bare operation of a mechanism of repression, the theory assigns a crucial causal role to it in pathogenesis, dream formation, and in the generation of slips. And, I claim, just that causal role is questionable.

2. Despite the poverty of the clinical credentials, it may still turn out that Freud's brilliant theoretical imagination was actually quite serendipitous for psychopathology or the understanding of some subclass of slips.

As I noted elsewhere (Grünbaum, 1984, pp. 202-204), very recently a psychologist claimed to have found genuine *experimental* support for the psychoanalytic theory of speech errors (Motley, 1980). He did indeed furnish telling laboratory evidence for the causal relevance of cognitive-affective mental sets, and even of personality dispositions to oral misreadings consisting of phoneme switchings. In this way, the experimenter showed that *semantic* influences produced by the speaker's mental sets, and external to the intended utterance, effected a pre-articulatory semantic editing of the words to be pronounced.

Valuable though they were, the results from these ingenious experiments were probatively irrelevant to the Freudian theory of slips of the tongue; the mental sets the investigator manipulated as his independent variable were *not repressed* ideation. By being conscious (or preconscious) states instead, they failed to realize the initial conditions required by Freud's theory. In fact, as I have pointed out (Grünbaum, 1984, p. 203), the observed misreadings can all be explained by a rival psychological theory that allows *only* conscious motivational influences as generators of slips. It remains to be seen what a properly designed test would show. I refer the reader to my 1986 paper (pp. 269-270) for my appraisal of *other* experimental findings, which are likewise less than favorable.

3. In view of my account of the epistemic defects inherent in the psychoanalytic method, it would seem that the validation of Freud's cardinal hypotheses has to come, if at all, mainly from well-designed *extra*clinical studies, either epidemiologic or even experimental. But that appraisal is largely a task for the future.

2

THE DEGENERATION OF POPPER'S CRITIQUE OF PSYCHOANALYSIS

INTRODUCTION

Karl Popper, on the one hand, and the descriptive or hermeneutic phenomenologists, on the other, have offered radically different, influential diagnoses of the failure of psychoanalytic theory to pass scientific muster. As Popper (1974) would have it, "Freud's theory . . . simply does not have potential falsifiers" (p. 1004) and is therefore nonscientific. But, in his view, the time-honored inductivist conception of scientific rationality was unable to detect this fundamental flaw. Thereby it purportedly failed to give a correct diagnosis of the scientific bankruptcy of the psychoanalytic enterprise (Popper, 1962, pp. 33-38, 255-258; 1974, pp. 984-985; Grünbaum, 1984, pp. 103-107). Therefore, Popper (1962, p. 256) concluded: "Thus there clearly was a need for a different criterion of demarcation" between science and pseudoscience, other than the inductivist one. In this way, psychoanalysis served as the gravamen and benchmark of his case for the superiority of his own falsifiability criterion of demarcation.

In my book (1984, p. 280), I argued for the following contrary thesis:

It is ironic that Popper should have pointed to psychoanalytic theory as a prime illustration of his thesis that inductively countenanced confirmations can easily be found for nearly every theory, if we look for them . . . *it is precisely Freud's theory that furnishes*

49

poignant evidence that Popper has caricatured the inductivist tradition by his thesis of easy inductive confirmability of nearly every theory!

But, as he tells us in his 1983 volume, chapter 2 contains his first "published *detailed* analysis of Freud's method of dealing with falsifying instances and critical suggestions" (p. 164, n. 1; italics added). When I was completing my 1984 book on psychoanalysis, Popper's (1983) volume was not yet available to me. In my later (1986, pp. 266-269) reply to him, I made only a cursory critical remark about his 1983 account of Freud's scientific miscarriage. Here, I shall therefore deal with his most recent and fullest treatment of this issue in adequate detail.

According to Karl Jaspers, Paul Ricoeur, and Jürgen Habermas, Freud misunderstood his own theory "scientistically" by giving far too little weight to "meaning connections" between mental states, as distinct from causal connections. In their view, hermeneutic victory can be snatched from the jaws of Freud's scientific defeat, once we appreciate that the hermeneutic discernment of so-called meaning connections is at the heart of the psychoanalytic enterprise (Jaspers, 1974; Habermas, 1971, chap. 11; Ricoeur, 1970, 1981). Elsewhere, I have argued that this criticism basically misidentifies both the source and the import of Freud's scientific shortcomings: Far from giving too little explanatory weight to "meaning connections" (thematic affinities), Freud endowed them with much too much explanatory significance, drawing fallacious causal inferences from them (see chapter 4 below).

Therefore, I can confine the present paper to Popper's (1983) volume. Frank Cioffi (1985, 1988) has published two ill-tempered replies to my earlier criticisms of Popper's charge of pseudoscience against psychoanalysis. It is a mark of Cioffi's mode of disputation that in 1988, he makes no mention at all of my 1986 paper, in which I painstakingly dealt with his objections to my book, as he knows. In 1986 (pp. 271-273), I also documented his exegetical fabrications and straw men. Erwin (1992) has given a careful defense of my views against Cioffi. I can now refer the reader to my chapter 4 below to see my most detailed treatment of Freud's Rat-Man case, which undercuts Cioffi's objections to my handling of that case history.

POPPER'S 1983 MISDIAGNOSIS OF FREUD'S SCIENTIFIC FIASCO

Let me begin with a retrospect on Popper's treatment of the topic prior to the appearance of his 1983 Postscript.

Throughout his career, Popper has repeatedly made two claims: (1) Logically, psychoanalytic theory is irrefutable by any human behavior; and (2) in the face of seemingly adverse evidence, Freud and his followers always dodged refutation by resorting to immunizing maneuvers. According to (1), *none* of the deductive consequences of Freud's hypotheses are refutable by potentially contrary empirical evidence. But clearly, this charge of unfalsifiability against psychoanalytic theory *itself* does not follow from the *sociological* objection that Freudians are not responsive to criticism of their hypotheses. After all, a theory may well be invalidated by known evidence, even as its true believers refuse to acknowledge this refutation. Besides, if Popper were right that "Freud's theory . . . simply does not have potential falsifiers" (1974, p. 1004), why would it have been necessary at all for Freudians to *dodge* refutations by means of immunizing gambits? Popper's (1) and (2) seem incoherent.

Ironically, it emerges clearly from some of Popper's other doctrines that the recalcitrance of Freudians in the face of falsifying evidence, however scandalous, is not at all tantamount to the irrefutability of their theory. As he tells us, theories, on the one hand, and the intellectual conduct of their protagonists, on the other, "belong to *two entirely different 'worlds'* " (1974, p. 144). Yet because Popper sometimes discusses them in the same breath, my response to his views on psychoanalysis takes both into account. My principal objection to him pertains to his logical thesis of empirical irrefutability, although I argued (1984) that he also used gross oversimplification to make his case for his sociological objection to Freud's evasive methodological behavior.

Indeed, contrary to Popper, Freud unflinchingly issued some important theoretical retractions in response to acknowledging the emergence of refuting evidence. A telling case in point is furnished by his 1926 landmark revision of his prior views on the causal relation between repression and anxiety. Freud wrote:

> It was anxiety which produced repression and not, as I formerly believed, repression which produced anxiety.
>
> It is no use denying the fact, though it is not pleasant to recall it, that I have on many occasions asserted that in repression the instinctual representative is distorted, displaced, and so on, while the libido belonging to the instinctual impulse is transformed into anxiety. But now an examination of phobias, which should be best able to provide confirmatory evidence, fails to bear out my assertion; it seems, rather, to contradict it directly. . . . It is always the ego's attitude of anxiety which is the primary thing and which sets repression going. Anxiety never arises from repressed libido. . . . I believed I had put my finger on a metapsychological process of direct transformation of libido into anxiety. I can no longer maintain this view [1926a, pp. 108-109].

In a volume on Popper's philosophy, Popper (1974, Book II) had claimed—once again—that psychoanalysis is an empirically untestable psychological metaphysics, which does "not exclude any physically possible human behaviour" (p. 985). From this allegation of empirical unfalsifiability, he immediately drew the fallacious inference (p. 985) that psychoanalysis indeed can, in principle, *explain* any actual behavior. Thus, on the heels of saying that Freud's and Adler's theories do not exclude any possible human behavior, Popper tells us that "whatever anybody may do is, in principle, explicable in Freudian or Adlerian terms."

But if a theory, in conjunction with particular initial conditions, *does not exclude* any behavior at all, how can it deductively *explain* any *particular* behavior? To explain deductively is to exclude: as Spinoza emphasized, to assert (entail) p is to deny every proposition incompatible with it. Note that in psychoanalytic theory, just as in Newton's physics, for example, lawlike statements cannot explain particular behavior without initial conditions: without *suitable* initial velocity specifications, Newton's laws of motion and gravitation do not yield an elliptical orbit for the earth under the gravitational action of the sun. Hence, if no potential behavior could falsify psychoanalysis under given initial conditions I, then this theory, *cum* I, could not

explain any actual behavior deductively. *A fortiori*, if the theory
T were unfalsifiable, it could not explain *all* such behavior, as
Popper believes. Furthermore, if the conjunction *T* and *I* fails
to explain some particular behavior *b* deductively, then *I* and *b*
cannot confirm (support) *T* hypothetico-deductively. Thus, if
psychoanalysis were unfalsifiable, how could any actual behavior—let alone *all* physically possible behavior—be explained by
it so as to confirm it inductively, as Popper claims (1962, p. 35)?
On the contrary, the alleged unfalsifiability would *preclude* such
hypothetico-deductive confirmability.

According to psychoanalytic theory, in both genders, repressed homosexual desires are the causal *sine qua non* of paranoia, whatever the variations in the delusional modes of this
psychosis. The modes include delusions of persecution, jealousy, grandeur, and heterosexual erotomania (Freud, 1915a,
1922); earlier Freud gave a more tentative statement (1911, pp.
59-65). Thus, every sort of paranoiac is an arena for the psychic
conflict between homosexual impulses, and the need to banish
them from consciousness as objectionable to avoid emotional
distress, such as disgust, shame, or guilt (1905b, p. 127 and pp.
157-159). In brief, his or her delusions (of persecution, etc.)
are the *unconscious defense* against the conscious emergence of
the forbidden homosexual cravings. And this defense is mediated by two defense mechanisms: (1) Reaction formation, which
converts the homosexual love into hatred toward the love object; i.e., once a dangerous impulse has been largely repressed,
it surfaces in the guise of a more acceptable contrary feeling;
(2) projection of the ensuing hatred from the lover by imputation to the beloved.

In 1915, Freud published a paper entitled "A Case of Paranoia Running Counter to the Psychoanalytic Theory of the
Disease." The pertinent case is that of a woman suffering from
persecutory delusions. As suggested by the very title of this
paper, Freud saw her case history as at least potentially supplying a *refuting instance* or disconfirmation of the particular sexual
etiology he had posited for this patient's type of psychosis. In
this vein, he notes (p. 265) that the patient's conduct might well
supply evidence that she is *not* beset by a conflictual struggle

against unconscious homosexual impulses. To take a contemporary putative example, imagine a self-declared lesbian, who is
also paranoid, and living in San Francisco as the avowed lover
of another woman. Suppose also that she is publicly active in
the gay rights movement there. Freud emphasizes that if there
are indeed empirical indications of such freedom from repressed homosexuality on the part of a paranoiac, then the
person in question would *count against* the psychoanalytic etiology of paranoia. The posited case would be a contrary instance,
because this etiology declares intense repressed homosexuality
to be a *sine qua non* for paranoia.

As Freud points out, furthermore (1915a, p. 265), the hypothesized etiologic role of repressed homosexuality leads "to
the necessary conclusion that the persecutor must be of the
same sex as the person persecuted." But, if so, it becomes important to determine empirically to what extent the supposed
persecutors are actually of the *same* gender as the persecutees.
Since the delusions of persecution are themselves conscious,
this empirical determination of gender does not require the
techniques of psychoanalytic investigation as such, and is therefore extraclinical in that sense. It is, of course, logically possible
that any and every paranoiac feels persecuted *only* by members
of the *opposite* sex. For this reason alone, Freud's etiology is
falsifiable by a finite number of such instances in the face of
Popper's own denial of such falsifiability!

What then are the known findings among paranoiacs as to
identity or difference of gender? And does Freud conclude that
his etiology of paranoia would simply be refuted by fancied
persecutors of the *opposite* sex?

His answer to the first question is unequivocal: "In psychiatric
literature there is certainly no lack of cases in which the patient
imagines himself persecuted by a person of the opposite sex"
(1915a, p. 265). Indeed, the paranoid young woman of his case
history sought out a lawyer for protection against the imagined
persecutions by a young man with whom she had been having
an affair. As Freud admits, in the light of his homosexual etiology of paranoia, it "seems strange that a woman should protect
herself against loving a man by means of a paranoic delusion"
(p. 268). How then, if at all, does Freud propose to reconcile

such cases with the requirement of gender identity that he himself had deduced from his homosexual etiology of paranoia?
His reply takes the form of two claims that are, in principle,
empirically testable. First, he reports "as a rule we find [in para-
noia] that the victim of persecution remains fixated . . . to the
same sex" (p. 271). Furthermore, he maintains, wherever a
supposed persecutor is of the *opposite sex*, then investigation will
reveal *this* antagonist to be only a secondary one, whom the
paranoiac imagines to be in collusion with an *original primary*
persecutor of the *same* sex.

But are there statistics bearing out the first claim that the
great majority of paranoiacs believe themselves to be persecuted by members of the *same* sex? Even if there are such statistics, neither Freud nor his followers have provided evidence
to support his crucial further thesis that for any presumed
persecutor of the opposite sex, there demonstrably exists a person of the same sex who was the *original* object of the paranoiac's persecutory delusions. Indeed, to the extent that, in the
case of oppositely sexed persecutors, psychoanalysts *fail* to find
the primary, gender-identical persecutor required by their theory, their etiology of paranoia is *disconfirmed*.

There are further reasons for concluding that the psychoanalytic etiology of paranoia may actually be disconfirmed. As
Fisher and Greenberg (1977) have pointed out, "the appearance of overt homosexual . . . acting out in the paranoid would
represent a contradiction . . . of Freud's theory of paranoia" (p.
259). How so? That theory makes the following conditional
prediction: If a person does not strongly repress homosexual
impulses, then this person will *not* be paranoid. But any individual who is openly and publicly a highly active practicing homosexual surely qualifies as a person who does *not* strongly repress
his or her homosexuality. If that same individual also exhibits
strong delusions of persecution toward, say, various members
of the opposite sex, then this flamboyant homosexual gives a
strong observable indication of being paranoid. Yet, according
to the prediction derived from Freud's etiology, just such an
openly active homosexual should *not* be paranoid.

It should not be unduly difficult for extraclinical researchers
to sample the population of avowedly practicing homosexuals

of either sex to determine whether there are any paranoiacs among them. In fact, presumably it is not a very risky bet to suppose that there are. And, if so, their existence casts strong doubt on the psychoanalytic claim that all paranoiacs are *repressed* homosexuals. Yet Zamansky (1958) believes to have produced experimental support for it, which I find dubious (Grünbaum, 1986, pp. 269-270).

In sum, the psychoanalytic etiology of paranoia is empirically falsifiable or disconfirmable, and Freud explicitly said so in his 1915 paper. As he noted (pp. 265-266), empirical indicators can bespeak the absence of strongly repressed homosexuality as well as the presence of paranoid delusions. Thus, empirical indicators can fallibly discredit the stated etiology.

Hence, this example has an important *general* moral: Whenever empirical indicators can warrant the *absence* of a certain theoretical pathogen P as well as a *differential diagnosis* of the *presence* of a certain theoretical disorder D, then an etiologic hypothesis of the strong form "P is causally necessary for D" is *fallibly* refutable. The etiology will be falsified or disconfirmed by any victim of D who has *not* been subjected to the avowedly required P. For the hypothesis *predicts* that anyone not so subjected will be spared the miseries of D, a prediction having significant prophylactic import for child rearing. Equivalently, the etiologic hypothesis *retrodicts* that any instance of D was also a case of P. Hence if there are empirical indicators as well for the *presence* of P, then this retrodiction can be empirically instantiated by a person who instantiates both N and P. Thus, Glymour's (1974) account of Freud's case history of the Rat-Man points out that Freud's specific etiology of the Rat-Man's obsession with his father's death was fallibly falsified by means of disconfirming the retrodiction that Freud had based on it. (But see chapter 4, section B, for the several auxiliary hypotheses on which this falsification was predicated.)

Popper undertook to write on the falsifiability of psychoanalysis. He was apparently unaware of Freud's 1915 paper on paranoia, whose mere title would have alerted him to the testability of the Freudian theory of psychopathology, or would at least have made him aware of the fact that Freud had entertained its falsifiability. Indeed, it is a measure of the inadequacy of Popper's psychoanalytic scholarship that, by his own account, he was first made cognizant of such testability by William Bartley. As we learn from an insert in Popper (1983, p. 169), in 1980, Bartley pointed out to him that the existence of a homosexually active paranoiac is *ruled out* by Freudian theory, because it demands that the homosexuality of paranoiacs be strongly repressed, rather than active. But Fisher and Greenberg (1977, p. 259) had already emphasized this prohibition, as we saw.

It so happens that Bartley gave this example to Popper during the discussion of my own paper at the July 1980 London Symposium on Popper's philosophy. As I had argued in that paper, Freud's theory implies that the decline in the social taboo on homosexuality in communities like San Francisco should, in due course, issue in a decreased incidence of paranoia in both sexes. This quasi-statistical prediction is quite compatible with Freud's allowance for a "multiplicity of mechanisms of repression proper" (1911, p. 68), which include autochthonous developmental factors that are independent of exogenous social taboos. Hence I contended that Freud's etiology of paranoia would be discomfirmed epidemiologically by the failure of the quasi-statistical prediction to materialize.

Let us now see how Popper reacted to Bartley's example. In context, the relevant passage in Popper (1983, p. 169) reads as follows:

> I cannot think of any conceivable instance of human behaviour which might not be interpreted in terms of either [Freud's or Adler's] theory, and which might not be claimed, by either theory, as a 'verification'.
> * Added 1980 [by Popper]. The last sentence of the preceding paragraph is, I now believe, too strong. As Bartley has pointed out to me, there are certain kinds of possible behaviour which are incompatible with Freudian theory—that is, which are excluded by Freudian theory. Thus Freud's explanation of paranoia in terms of repressed homosexuality would seem to exclude the possibility of active homosexuality in a paranoid individual. But this is not part of the basic theory I was criticizing. Besides, Freud could say of any apparently paranoid active homosexual that he is not *really* paranoid, or not *fully* active.

This retort strikes me as unfortunate for the following reasons:

1. To justify Popper's original thesis of nonfalsifiability, it was necessary to *show*—not just to assert peremptorily—that there simply are no potentially falsifying empirical instances in the case of psychoanalytic theory, as he claimed anew in his 1974 reply to Lakatos (p. 1004). In that reply, Popper asserts that Newtonian physics does have potential empirical falsifiers, which could be neutralized only by using immunizing strategies, such as modifying some auxiliary hypotheses of the Newtonian corpus. Thus, he admits that Newtonian physics can be immunized against falsification. By the same token, his assertion of its falsifiability presupposes "disregarding the possibility of immunizing stratagems." But in 1974 he then claimed a contrast between Newtonian theory and psychoanalysis as follows: "And this is the heart of the matter, for my criticism of Freud's theory was that it simply does not have potential falsifiers" (p. 1004). Furthermore, "I cannot describe any state of affairs concerning Mr. Smith—say about his behaviour—which would need immunization [i.e., which would require neutralization by immunization of the theory] in order not to clash with Freudian theory" (p. 1005). But despite Popper's own admitted inability to describe such a case, the documented ability of others to do so shows how wrong he was to have inflated his mere suspicion of the empirical irrefutability of psychoanalysis into a thesis of unfalsifiability. Plainly, his own reported inability to think of contrary instances was, at best, grounds for a mere suspicion of nonfalsifiability. Worse, Popper flatly contradicts his thesis of nonfalsifiability: (a) In the Postscript (1983, p. 173), he tells us in italics that "*anxiety dreams constitute a refutation of the general* [Freudian] *formula of wish-fulfillment*"; (b) Popper assumes falsifiability when he complains that Freudians use immunizing gambits to neutralize contrary evidence.

2. It is important to note how Popper tries to practice damage control by qualifying and hedging his more recent admission that the case of a homosexually active paranoiac does contradict his thesis. Thus, he immediately resorts to *two* immunizing maneuvers, which are disingenuous, I submit, besides being demonstrably unsuccessful, as we shall now see.

He admonishes us that Freud's repression etiology of paranoia "is not part of the basic theory I was criticizing." Yet we are left completely in the dark as to just what does count for him as the "basic" part of psychoanalytic theory, *and why*. In effect, Popper asks us to overlook that, throughout his career, he had leveled the charge of nonfalsifiability *tout court*, rather than only against a so-called "basic" part of the theory, whose identity he strangely fails to specify. Indeed, as we saw (Popper, 1974, p. 1004), he wrote: "my criticism of Freud's theory was that it simply does not have potential falsifiers."

Vague as it is, even his claim that Freudian etiologic theory is *not* "basic" to psychoanalysis is simply untenable. As any student of the subject knows, both historically and logically, precisely the theory of psychopathology, which features the repression etiology of the neuroses, is the *most foundational* part of Freud's edifice. Thus, as we know, its architect had ample reason to declare: "The theory of repression is the cornerstone of which the whole structure of psycho-analysis rests. It is the most essential part of it" (1914b, p. 16).

Not content with being disingenuous, the kettle calls the teapot black, when Popper (1983, p. 163) writes against Freud:

> I wish to criticize Freud's way of rejecting criticism. Indeed I am convinced that Freud could have vastly improved his theory, had his attitude towards criticism been different. . . .
> This self-defensive attitude is of a piece with the attitude of looking for verifications; of finding them everywhere in abundance; of refusing to admit that certain cases do not fit the theory.

In response, I find it hard not to exclaim: "Physician heal thyself."

Moreover, Popper wants to take out an insurance policy in case his immunizing resort to the alleged non"basicality" of the theory of paranoia is not seen by others as a vindication. So he comes up with the following (1983, p. 169): "Besides, Freud could say of any apparently paranoid active homosexual that he is not *really* paranoid, or not *fully* active." In this way, Popper wants to claim that this kind of case does not discredit his lifelong thesis of irrefutability about psychoanalysis after all.

To this I say two things: (1) In regard to Freud's scientific honesty, the question is not whether he *could* save his etiology of paranoia in this way, but only whether he *would* try to do so. His 1915 paper shows explicitly that, in fact, he did not, although his epistemic reasoning there is problematic in other respects, as I have pointed out; (2) Popper's depiction of what Freud *could* say to neutralize the counterexample does not help to sustain Popper's thesis of irrefutability, as I shall now show.

Assume we grant that Freud could evade falsification by the case of the paranoid active homosexual in the farfetched manner proposed by Popper. Then surely a like gambit is available to a physicist, *mutatis mutandis*, to neutralize unpalatable contrary evidence, so as to parry the refutation of his theoretical hypothesis, as I shall soon illustrate. Yet Popper claims falsifiability for physics, even though he explicitly *predicates* it on "disregarding the possibility of immunizing stratagems" (1974, p. 1004). What is sauce for the goose is, I submit, also sauce for the gander. Thus if, as Popper claims, the physical scientist does *not* forfeit the falsifiability of his hypotheses in the face of immunizing maneuvers that are surely available to that scientist, why then should Freud have to acknowledge irrefutability merely because he too could adopt such stratagems?

As Popper would have it, Freud "could" evade refutation by pleading that even the most promiscuous homosexual is not "fully active" after all. But Freud's etiology of paranoia had explicitly declared that *strongly repressed*, intense homosexuality is the *sine qua non* of paranoia (1915a, p. 265; 1922, p. 228). Even an average homosexually active paranoiac violates this declared necessary condition. A *fortiori*, an erotomanically active paranoid homosexual clearly violates it.

Could Freud still say, as Popper (1983, p. 169) suggests, that the active homosexual is "not *really* paranoid," no matter how delusional his behavior? To deal with this question, let me first recall a relevant moral from a paper by Carnap (1936, 1937). He acknowledged over fifty years ago that in physics, no less than in somatic medicine or psychology, empirical data are *not sufficient conditions* for the presence of hypothesized states, which they are taken to manifest. Instead of being sufficient conditions for the theoretical states, empirical indicators *under-determine* such states, and betoken their presence only more or less probabilistically. Thus it is a commonplace, even among laymen, that an X-ray or even the more refined tomogram or cat-scan does not guarantee any one somatic diagnosis. Hence if the repudiation of a psychiatric diagnosis of paranoia is an immunizing option open to Freud, then a like gambit of rediagnosis is available to a radiologist, when expectations based on the original diagnosis fail to materialize.

By the same token, tracks in Wilson cloud chambers *may* actually bespeak the existence of as yet unknown particles, rather than the passage of those postulated entities that physicists now (fallibly!) take them to attest. Hempel has reminded us that even a circular array of iron filings does not guarantee the presence of a magnet deductively. And, as Wesley Salmon (1959) noted, the same holds in psychoanalysis. True, even patent delusions of intense persecution are only probabilistic evidence of paranoia. But Popper's appeal to the fallibility of a differential diagnosis, and to the possibility of rediagnosis is misleading as a basis for singling out psychoanalysis as remaining irrefutable, even in the face of the example of a homosexually active paranoiac.

In sum, to the detriment of Popper's vaunted contrast between the testability of physical theory and psychoanalysis, the rescuing option that, according to him, is open to Freud, could likewise be exercised, *mutatis mutandis*, in physics so as to preclude refutation of *its* hypotheses. For example, if the measured charge of an electron turned out *not* to accord with theoretical expectations or requirements, a physicist *could* say—in Popper's sense of "could"—that the particle in question is "not *really* an electron." Besides, as I have illustrated (1984, pp. 121-123), when Freud did retract a differential diagnosis to preserve a specific causal hypothesis, he was sensitive to the need for independent evidence in favor of the alternative diagnosis.

In chapter 1, I called attention to a quasi-statistical prediction derivable from Freud's theory of paranoia. This prediction qualifies as "risky" by Popper's standards, since it is "novel" with respect to rival theories of paranoia that do *not* yield it. By the

same token, the failure of the prediction would also disconfirm
Freud's etiology of paranoia.

Far from supporting his nonfalsifiability thesis, Popper's
(1983) account of the case of the homosexual paranoiac evidently relies on just the kinds of immunizing maneuvers he is
quick to reject when others engage in them. In any case, as
we saw, his account seems incoherent: Only a few pages after
discussing the paranoia example, he deals with Freud's dream
theory and astonishingly declares it to be a "simple fact . . . that
*anxiety dreams constitute a refutation of the general formula of wish-
fulfillment*" (1983, p. 173). Thus, by Popper's own appraisal,
the dream theory must be falsifiable, since it had already *been*
falsified by anxiety dreams, when Freud first proposed it! And
this clear acknowledgment of falsifiability is hardly tempered
in the *logical* sense by Popper's detailed complaint against
Freud's own evidential disposal of *prima facie wish-contravening*
dreams, such as anxiety dreams and nightmares. After all, in
Popper's conception, theories are so-called third-world objects
that have a logical life of their own, as it were, apart from the
attitudinal scientific integrity of their propounders.

As we know, Freud relied on the distinction between the
manifest and latent content of a dream to claim that a latent
wish engenders even those dreams whose manifest content is
anything but wish-fulfilling. And Popper's (1983) critical comment on this distinction is the following:

> Freud repeatedly re-affirms his programme of revealing the la-
> tent content of every anxiety dream as a wish-fulfillment. . . . *Yet
> Freud never carries out his programme; and in the end he gives it up
> altogether*—without, however, explicitly saying so [p. 165].
> The reason why Freud does not carry out his original pro-
> gramme of showing (by way of detailed analyses such as he is
> wont to give) that all anxiety dreams are wish-fulfillments is,
> clearly, that in the end he no longer believed in it. . . . I should
> be the last to criticize such a change of mind. But the change is
> not a conscious correction, or the admission of a mistake [p. 167].

As we learn from Popper's Postscript (1983, pp. 164, 172),
the psychoanalytic theory of dreams in particular was historically a major inspiration of his falsifiability criterion of demarcation. Moreover, though Popper hails Freud's interpretation of

dreams as "a great achievement," he nonetheless considers it to be his own centerpiece for leveling the following reproach: *"But it is a fundamental mistake to believe that, because it is constantly being "verified", it must be a science, based on experience"* (p. 172).

Yet, as we know from the old inductivist tradition of Francis Bacon and John Stuart Mill, Popper's admonition here just carries coals to Newcastle by echoing one of the salutary injunctions familiar from precisely that legacy of eliminative inductivism. Freud's wish-fulfillment theory of dream production is clearly a causal hypothesis. I have argued on earlier occasions (1979a; 1984, p. 280) that the demands made by that inductivist patrimony for validating such a strong hypothesis are clearly not met by the so-called "verifications" adduced by Freudians: As I recalled above from my 1984 book, *it is precisely Freud's theory that furnishes poignant evidence that Popper has caricatured the inductivist tradition by his thesis of easy inductive confirmability of nearly every theory.* Hence inductivistically untutored claims of confirmations made by psychoanalytic zealots cannot serve Popper's advocacy of his falsifiability criterion of demarcation as a replacement for the received Bacon-Mill inductivist criterion, which was in vogue when he came upon the philosophic scene.

Thus, *malgré lui*, the upshot of Popper's account of the psychoanalytic theory of dreams seems to be as follows: Since this part of Freud's corpus is known to be false, it is falsifiable. Hence, I submit, precisely because—*qua* "third-world" object—the dream theory itself is falsifiable—it is *scientific* by Popper's criterion of demarcation. This conclusion is, of course, compatible with Popper's distinct claim that Freud was aware of the falsity of the dream theory, but was unwilling to admit it explicitly.

In the face of his proclamation of unfalsifiability, Popper has a highly incongruous attitude toward psychoanalytic explanations. If, as he says, psychoanalysis is indeed unfalsifiable, then it cannot make any risky empirical predictions, because such predictions run the risk of turning out to be false. Hence, if Popper is to be believed, psychoanalysis cannot be corroborated observationally by successful risky predictions, as demanded by his standards of corroboration. Yet, in his view, explanations based on a completely uncorroboratable theory are presumably pseudoexplanations. Indeed, if psychoanalysis does yield the surfeit of explanations deplored by him, then its explanations cannot be genuine, precisely because they explain too much, as it were.

Unabashed by such apparent corollaries of his account, Popper not only enlists psychoanalytic theory to provide several explanations, but even explicitly declares his belief in its essential substantive correctness. Let me document these very odd twists.

1. In 1950 (pp. 16-17), Popper invokes Freud's unconscious defense mechanism of "reaction formation" to "explain," as he claims, how Heraclitus embraced two *prima facie* contradictory ideas. But if such Freudian hypotheses as the existence of conflict, actuated by unconscious fear and resistance, are untestable, as Popper thinks, how can they have enough *empirical import* to explain Heraclitus's utterances by Popper's standards of *bona fide* scientific explanations?

2. In 1962 (p. 49), Popper wishes to explain the adoption by some people of a "dogmatic attitude," as distinct from a "critical attitude." In the quest for such an explanation, he registers "a [purported] point of agreement with psychoanalysis" when suggesting the following causal hypothesis: "most neuroses may be due to a partially arrested development of the critical attitude . . . [due] to resistance to demands for the modification and adjustment of certain . . . responses. This instance in its turn may perhaps be explained, in some cases, as due to an injury or shock, resulting in fear." Yet, according to psychoanalytic theory, dogmatic rigidity may be seen as a manifestation of neurotic conflict, but hardly as a contributory *cause* of the neurosis itself. To this extent, Popper's purported "agreement with psychoanalysis" here seems spurious.

3. In 1962 (p. 275, n. 52), Popper tries to make diagnostic and explanatory use of Freud's theory of the oedipal conflict, which postulates ambivalent feelings toward the father that include hostile, aggressive and even murderous impulses. Thus Popper declares: "One need not believe in the 'scientific' character of psycho-analysis (which, I think, is in a metaphysical phase) in order to diagnose the anti-metaphysical fervour of positivism as a form of Father-killing." But, on his account of

psychoanalysis, how can the putative desire for father-killing yield anything but an *ad hoc* pseudoexplanation of the positivist antipathy to metaphysics? What competing explanations, if any, did Popper canvass? He makes no mention of any.

4. Let us be mindful of Popper's complaints against the spurious verifications of Freud's dream theory. Then one is simply dumbfounded to learn that he has no hesitation to declare his belief in its essential correctness. As he amazingly puts it (1983, p. 164):

> . . . in spite of severe shortcomings . . . it [Freud's dream theory] contains, beyond any reasonable doubt, a great discovery. I at least feel convinced that there is a world of the unconscious, and that Freud's analyses of dreams given in his book are fundamentally correct, though no doubt incomplete.

But, if the dream theory—though purportedly falsified by anxiety dreams—is unfalsifiable, then there can be no corroborating evidence for it by Popper's standards. Therefore, we are left to wonder how he can know "beyond any reasonable doubt" *without corroborating evidence*, that Freud's dream theory "contains . . . a great discovery." If the distinction between the manifest and latent content of a dream is discredited by anxiety dreams, and Freud's wish-fulfillment hypothesis is false, just what *is* the purported great discovery? Indeed, since Popper believes that (the bulk of) Freud's dream analyses are essentially correct, if incomplete, how can the pivotal distinction between the manifest and latent dream content fail to be sound?

In chapter 10, I shall develop two new major reasons for presuming that Freud's dream theory is false.

THE DEGENERATION OF POPPER'S CRITERION OF DEMARCATION

In the Postscript (1983, pp. 163-164), Popper's avowed purpose of treating the dream theory is to show the following: "that the problem of demarcation is not merely one of classifying theories into scientific and non-scientific ones, but that its solution is urgently needed for a critical appraisal of scientific theories, or allegedly scientific theories." Yet ten pages later—at the

66 VALIDATION: CLINICAL THEORY OF PSYCHOANALYSIS

end of the section on Freud's theory (p. 174)—Popper tells us amazingly enough that "from the beginning", his "problem of demarcation . . . certainly was not a problem of classifying or distinguishing some subject matters called 'science' and 'metaphysics.' " But this concluding disclaimer *flatly contradicts* the first conjunct of his initially stated motive for dealing with the psychoanalytic dream theory. By the same token, this concluding disclaimer here is patently incompatible with two of his earlier landmark reports, as we shall now see.

Thus in his 1953 Personal Report on the development of his entire philosophy of science, which is reprinted in 1962, he informs us that, beginning in 1919, when he was seventeen years of age, his problem was "to distinguish between science and pseudo-science . . . [or] 'metaphysics' " (1962, p. 33). In his Replies to Critics (1974, p. 984), he explains that his criterion of demarcation

> . . . is more than sharp enough to make a distinction between many physical theories on the one hand, and metaphysical theories, such as psychoanalysis, or Marxism (in its present form), on the other. This is, of course, one of my main theses; and nobody who has not understood it can be said to have understood my theory.

Evidently, in 1983, he insouciantly repudiates just this major, central tenet of his whole philosophy without ado. By the same token, he now denies his repeated other historical accounts of the aim that inspired his criterion of demarcation, starting in 1919. And, as we shall now see, this 1983 retraction occurs on the heels of a qualified, hedged disavowal that plainly serves as an immunizing stratagem for his prior vindication of his notion of demarcation by reference to psychoanalysis and Marxism. Thus, that stratagem in the Postscript (1983, p. 174) runs as follows:

> . . . it hardly matters whether or not I am right concerning the irrefutability of any of these three theories [i.e., psychoanalysis, Adlerian psychology, and Marxism]: here they serve merely as examples, as illustrations. For my purpose is to show that my "problem of demarcation" was from the beginning the practical

problem of assessing theories, and of judging their claims. It
[the problem of demarcation] certainly was not a problem of
classifying or distinguishing some subject matters called "science"
and "metaphysics." It was, rather, an urgent practical problem:
under what conditions is a *critical appeal to experience* possible—one that could bear some fruit?

But, if—as Popper tells us here—the stated three theories are
not essential to the vindication of his falsifiability criterion of
demarcation, and are mere illustrations, then I must ask: What
other theories for which scientificity has been wrongly claimed
can be adduced to furnish such a vindication *vis-à-vis* the much
older criterion of evidential support, which he wants to replace
as unduly permissive? And as for stating conditions under
which a "critical appeal to experience" is possible, Francis Bacon
had demanded—three centuries before Popper—that the validation of a given theory *T* requires data that are *contrary* to *T's*
rivals or competitors, while being positive instances of *T*.

In an article on psychoanalysis in a German newspaper, the
journalist Dieter Zimmer (1982, pp. 18-19) quotes Popper on
the status of psychoanalysis. According to that article, Popper
characterized it in 1982 as a subject for "weak heads" (*Schwach-
köpfe*). If this report is authentic, how does it square with Popper's stated tribute to Freud's dream theory and with his own
explanatory invocation of psychoanalysis in the cases I cited?

Several conclusions seem to me to emerge from my scrutiny
of Popper's portrayal of psychoanalytic theory *vis-à-vis* his falsifiability criterion of demarcation:

1. Popper's indictment of the Freudian corpus—or of its unspecified "basic" portion—as inherently unfalsifiable has fundamentally misdiagnosed its failure as a scientific theory. More
often than not, the intellectual defects of psychoanalysis are
too subtle to be detected by his criterion of demarcation. For
example, there is no systematic published critique by him of
Freud's method of free association, *qua* purported method of
causal validation. Yet just that method is *the* method of clinical
investigation in psychoanalysis. Alas, Popper's myth of nonfalsifiability has entrenched itself in current philosophic folklore.
Examples of its inveterate enunciation abound. Thus, in a very
recent issue of *The New Republic*, we are told that "Freudian

explanations" are "beyond the reach of empirical falsification" (Wright, 1988, p. 30).

2. As a perspective on the nature of Freud's theory, Popper's portrayal is not viable. Yet perhaps it has had some value sociologically by putting psychoanalysts on notice to become more accountable scientifically. But it is unclear whether it actually had that effect on their attitudes.

3. Popper's (1983) notion of demarcation has become a kind of degenerative philosophical research program in Imre Lakatos's sense of that term.

This said, let me gladly make an acknowledgment: My own scrutiny of psychoanalysis was prompted by my initial doubt as to the soundness of Popper's portrayal of it.

3

THE PLACEBO CONCEPT IN
PSYCHIATRY AND MEDICINE

INTRODUCTION

In the first chapter, we had occasion to assume, at least for argument's sake, that certain categories of patients who are treated by analysts fare better, on the whole, than suitable untreated control groups. But it then became important to pose a key question as to the *process dynamics* of psychoanalytic treatment: Are the surplus *outcome* gains presumably achieved by analyzed patients actually wrought by the insight engendered as a result of using Freud's etiologies in the analysis of their transference and resistance? Or is the posited better therapeutic outcome a *placebo effect* instead, as purported by critics of psychoanalytic process doctrine?

As we saw in chapter 1 (sec. 3), the answer to this question is crucial to the tenability of Freud's "Master Proposition," and hence to the viability of his cardinal defense in 1916-17 of the whole analytic enterprise, a defense which I have dubbed "the Tally Argument."

It is a commonplace that the placebo concept invoked against the orthodox process-dynamics of analytic therapy is a *generalization* of the traditional pharmacological notion. Yet just this more inclusive concept cries out for clarification: One need only look at the received jargon of the medical and psychiatric literature on placebo therapies to notice that it is conceptually bewildering to the point of being a veritable Tower of Babel,

69

rife with confusions. True, various authors have offered rival explications of the placebo notion. I contend, however, that these other writers have fallen quite short of providing an adequate clarification. Yet the missing explication is not only imperative for psychiatric and medical therapeutics generally, but also propaedeutic for the rigorous appraisal of Freud's Tally Argument. And since chapter 5 will offer such an appraisal, it now behooves me to offer the desired elucidation of the family of notions consisting of placebo therapy, placebo effect, and placebo control. In so doing, I shall give some illustrations from psychoanalysis while ranging broadly over somatic medicine and psychiatry.

Just what is the problem of identifying an intervention or treatment t of one sort or another as a placebo for a target disorder D? One set of circumstances, among others, in which the need for such an identification may arise is the following: After the administration of t to some victims of D, some of them recover from their affliction to a significant extent. Now suppose that there is cogent evidence that this improvement can indeed be causally attributed at all to some factors or other among the spectrum of constituents comprising the dispensation of t to a patient. Then it can become important to know whether the therapeutic gain that ensued from t in the alleviation of D was due to *those particular factors* in its dispensation that the advocates of t have theoretically designated as deserving the credit for the positive treatment outcome. And one aim of this chapter is to articulate in detail the bearing of the answer to this question on whether t qualifies generically as a placebo or not.

The proverbial sugar pill is hardly the sole placebo capable of producing therapeutic benefits for ailments other than hypoglycemia and other glucose deficits. Indeed, the long-term history of medical treatment has been characterized as largely the history of the placebo effect (Shapiro and Morris, 1978). After all, it is not only the patients who can be unaware that the treatments they are receiving are just placebos for their disorders; the physicians as well may mistakenly believe that they are administering nonplacebos for their patients' ailments, when they are actually dispensing placebos, while further enhancing the patients' credulity by communicating their own therapeutic faith. For example, as we shall see, surgery for angina pectoris performed in the United States during the 1950s turned out to be a mere placebo. Unbeknown to the physicians who practiced before the present century, most of the medications they dispensed were at best pharmacologically ineffective, if not outright physiologically harmful or even dangerous. Thus, during all that time, doctors were largely engaged in the unwitting dispensation of placebos on a massive scale. Even after the development of contemporary scientific medicine some 80 years ago, "the placebo effect flourished as the norm of medical treatment" (Shapiro and Morris, 1978, p. 371).

The psychiatrist Jerome Frank (1973) has issued the sobering conjecture that those of the roughly 200 psychotherapies whose gains exceed those from spontaneous remission do *not* owe such remedial efficacy to the *distinctive* treatment factors credited by their respective therapeutic advocates, but succeed for other reasons. Nonetheless, Frank admonishes us not to disparage such placebogenic gains in therapy, at least as long as we have nothing more effective. And even in internal medicine and surgery, a spate of recent articles has inveighed against downgrading placebogenic benefits, the grounds being that we should be grateful even for small mercies. Yet the plea not to forsake the benefits wrought by placebos has been challenged on ethical grounds: The injunction to secure the patient's informed consent is a demand whose fulfillment may well render the placebo ineffective, though perhaps not always (Park and Covi, 1965).

The physician Arthur K. Shapiro is deservedly one of the most influential writers in this field of inquiry. He has been concerned with the history of the placebo effect (1960) and with the semantics of the word "placebo" (1968), no less than with current empirical research on placebogenic phenomena in medical and psychological treatments (Shapiro and Morris, 1978). Thus, in his portion of the last-cited paper, he refined (1978, p. 371) his earlier 1971 definition of "placebo" in an endeavor to codify the current uses of the term throughout medicine and psychiatry. The technical vocabulary employed in Shapiro's earlier and most recent definitions is standard terminology in the discussion of placebo therapies and of experimental placebo controls, be it in pharmacology, surgery, or psychiatry. Yet just this standard technical vocabulary, I submit, generates confusion by being misleading or obfuscating, and indeed cries out for conceptual clarification. Thus, it is my overall objective to revamp Shapiro's definitions substantially so as to provide a clear and rigorous account of the placebo notion appropriate to current medicine and psychiatry.

CRITIQUE, EXPLICATION, AND REFORMULATION OF SHAPIRO'S DEFINITION

CRITIQUE

While some placebos are known to be such by the dispensing physician—though presumably not by the patient—other placebo therapies are mistakenly believed to be nonplacebos by the physician as well. Mindful of this dual state of affairs, Shapiro's definition of a placebo therapy makes it clear that, at any given stage of scientific knowledge, a treatment modality actually belonging to the genus placebo can be of the latter kind rather than of the traditionally recognized first sort. To capture both of these two species of placebo therapy, he casts his definition into the following general form, in which the expression "=def." stands for the phrase "is definitionally equivalent to":

Therapy t is a placebo therapy
=def. t is of a kind A OR t is of kind B.

Any definition of this "either-or" form is called a "disjunctive" definition, and *each* of the two independent clauses connected by the word "or" is called a "disjunct." For example, suppose we define a "parent" by saying:

Person X is a parent
=def. X is a father OR X is a mother.

This is clearly a *disjunctive* definition. And it is convenient to refer to each of the separate clauses "X is a father" and "X is a mother" as a "disjunct." Thus, the sentence "X is a father" can obviously be regarded as the first of the two disjuncts, while the sentence "X is a mother" is the second disjunct. Hence, for brevity, I thus refer respectively to the corresponding two parts of Shapiro's actual disjunctive definition (Shapiro and Morris, 1978):

> A *placebo* is defined as any therapy or component of therapy that is deliberately used for its nonspecific, psychological, or psychophysiological effect, or that is used for its presumed specific effect, but is without specific activity for the condition being treated [p. 371].

Shapiro goes on to point out at once that the term "placebo" is used not only to characterize a treatment modality or therapy, but also a certain kind of experimental control:

> A *placebo*, when used as a control in experimental studies, is defined as a substance or procedure that is without specific activity for the condition being evaluated [sic]. . . .

> A *placebo effect* is defined as the psychological or psychophysiological effect produced by placebos [p. 371].

All of the conceptual puzzlement warranted by these three statements arises in the initial disjunctive definition of a "placebo therapy." For it should be noted that this definition employs the tantalizing words "nonspecific effect," "specific effect," and "specific activity" in unstated *technical* senses. Once these terms are elucidated, the further definitions of a "placebo control" and of a "placebo effect" become conceptually unproblematic. Hence let us now concentrate on the disjunctive definition of a "placebo therapy," and see what help, if any, Shapiro gives us with the technical terms in which he has expressed it. Contrary to the belief of some others, I make bold to contend that his explicit comments on their intended construal still leave them in an unsatisfactory logical state for the purposes at hand.

In their joint 1978 paper, Shapiro and Morris elaborate quite vaguely on the key concept of "specific activity" as follows:

> Specific activity is the therapeutic influence attributable solely to
> the contents or processes of the therapies rendered. The crite-
> rion for specific activity (and therefore the placebo effect) should
> be based on scientifically controlled studies [p. 372].

They provide this characterization as part of a longer but
very rough delineation of the complementary notions denoted
by the terms "specific" and "nonspecific," locutions that are as
pervasive as they are misleading or confusing in the literature
on placebos. Thus, they make the following comment on the
definition of "placebo" given above, which I amplify within
brackets:

> Implicit in this definition is the assumption that active treatments
> [i.e., nonplacebos] may contain placebo components. Even with
> specific therapies [i.e., nonplacebos] results are apt to be due to
> the combination of both placebo and nonplacebo effects. Treat-
> ments that are devoid of active, specific components are known
> as pure placebos, whereas therapies that contain nonplacebo
> components are called impure placebos. . . . Treatments that
> have specific components but exert their effects primarily
> through nonspecific mechanisms are considered placebo ther-
> apies. . . .
>
> The key concept in defining placebo is that of "specific activity."
> In nonpsychological therapies, specific activity is often equated
> with nonpsychological mechanisms of action. When the specific
> activity of a treatment is psychological [i.e., in psychotherapies
> that derive therapeutic efficacy from those particular factors in
> the treatment that the pertinent theory singles out specifically as
> being remedial] this method of separating specific from nonspe-
> cific activity is no longer applicable. Therefore, a more general
> definition of specific activity is necessary. Specific activity is the
> therapeutic influence attributable solely to the contents or pro-
> cesses of the therapies rendered [i.e., the therapeutic influence,
> if any, that derives solely from those component factors of the
> therapy that are specifically singled out by its advocates as deserv-
> ing credit for its presumed efficacy]. The criterion for specific
> activity (and therefore the placebo effect) should be based on
> scientifically controlled studies. . . . In behavior therapy, some
> investigators have utilized "active placebo" control groups
> whereby some aspects of the therapy affect behavior but those
> aspects differ from the theoretically relevant ingredients of con-
> cern to the investigator [pp. 371-372].

This passage urgently calls for clarification beyond what I have supplied within brackets. In particular, the terms "specific activity" and "nonspecific effect," though standard, are anything but clear. Yet, as the authors emphasize further on, it is by virtue of a treatment's *lack* of so-called "specific activity" for a given target disorder that this treatment *objectively* qualifies as a placebo, regardless of whether the dispensing physician believes the treatment to have actual placebo status or not. They import this emphasis on the irrelevance of belief to generic placebo *status* into their definition. There, in its first paragraph, a disjunction makes explicit provision for the presence of such belief on the part of the dispenser, as well as for its absence. In the first disjunct, it is a placebo that the physician *believes* himself or herself to be giving the patient, and the doctor is right in so believing. In the second disjunct, the physician believes himself or herself to be administering a *non*placebo, but he or she is definitely mistaken in so believing.

In either case, a placebo is actually being dispensed, be it wittingly or unwittingly. For brevity, I distinguish between the two situations to which these disjuncts pertain by saying that the treatment is an "intentional placebo" in the former case, while being an "inadvertent placebo" in the latter. Note that if a treatment t is actually not a placebo generically while its dispenser or even the whole professional community of practitioners believes t to be one, then t is precluded from qualifying as a "placebo" by the definition. To earn the label "intentional placebo," a treatment not only must be *believed* to be a placebo by its dispenser, but must also actually *be* one generically. Thus, therapists have administered a nonplacebo in the erroneous belief that it is a placebo. For example, at one time, some psychoanalysts used phenothiazines to treat schizophrenics in the belief that these drugs were mere (anger-reducing, tranquillizing) placebos; they presumed them to be ineffective for the psychic dissociation and the pathognomonic symptoms of schizophrenia. But controlled studies showed that these medications possessed a kind of therapeutic efficacy for the disorder that was not placebogenic (Davis and Cole, 1975a, 1975b).

Incidentally, besides not being placebos for schizophrenia, the phenothiazines turned out to be capable of inducing the

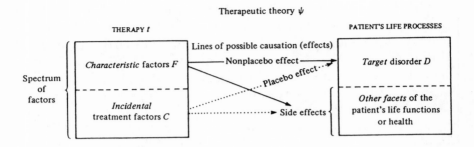

Figure 1. Illustration of therapeutic theory Ψ, used in clarifying the definition of "placebo."

negative side effects of parkinsonism, at least transiently (Blakiston's *Gould Medical Dictionary*, 1972, p. 1130). But the motor impairment manifested in parkinsonism is attributed to a deficiency of brain dopamine. Thus the unfavorable parkinsonian side effect of the phenothiazine drugs turned out to have *heuristic* value because it suggested that these drugs block the dopamine receptors in the brain. And since the drugs were also effective nonplacebos for schizophrenia, the parkinsonian side effect raised the possibility that an excess of dopamine might be implicated in the etiology of schizophrenia. In this way, a *biochemical* malfunction of the brain was envisioned quite specifically as causally relevant to this psychosis (Kolata, 1979).

Let me now specify the terminology and notation that I employ in my rectifying explication of "placebo," using the diagram shown in figure 1. Overall, there is some stated or tacit therapeutic theory, which I call "Ψ." Now Ψ designs or recommends a particular treatment or therapy *t* for a particular illness or target disorder *D*. In the left-hand box of figure 1, I generically depict a treatment modality or therapy *t*. Note that it contains a spectrum of ingredients or treatment factors. For example, the theory Ψ may insist that if it is to recommend surgery for the treatment of gallstones, then the surgical process must obviously include the removal of the gallstones, rather than a mere sham abdominal incision. I want a name for those treatment factors that a given theory Ψ thus *picks out* as the defining characteristics of a given type of therapy *t*. And I call these factors the "characteristic factors *F*" of *t*. But Ψ recognizes that besides the characteristic factors F, the given therapy normally also contains other factors which it regards as just incidental. For example, a theory that deems the removal of gallstones to be therapeutic for certain kinds of pains and indigestion will assume that this abdominal surgery includes the administration of anesthesia to the patient. To take a quite different example, when Freud recommended psychoanalytic treatment, he insisted on the payment of a hefty fee, believing it to be perhaps a catalyst for the patient's receptivity to the therapeutic task. Furthermore, a therapeutic theory may well allow that a given therapy includes not only known incidental factors, but also others that it has failed to recognize. And the letter C in the diagram, which labels "incidental treatment factors," is intended to apply to both known and unknown factors of this type.

Turning to the right-hand box in figure 1, we note that the patient's life functions and activities are generically subdivided into two parts: the target disorder D at which the therapy t is aimed, and then the rest of his or her functions. But there may well be some vagueness in the circumscription of D. Both its pathognomonic symptoms and the presumed etiological process responsible for them will surely be included in the syndrome D. Yet some nosologists might include, while others exclude, certain accessory manifestations of D that are quite secondary, because they are also present in a number of other, nosologically distinct syndromes. Somewhat cognate conceptual problems of taxonomic circumscription arose in chemistry upon the discovery of isomerism, and even in the case of chemical isotopy.

Finally, in the middle of figure 1, arrows represent some of the interesting possible causal influences or effects that may result from each of the two sets of treatment factors. Thus, one or more of the characteristic factors F may be remedial for the target disorder D, or the F factors may have no effect on D, or the F factors conceivably could make D even worse. By the same token, these factors F may have these three kinds of influence on other facets of the patient's health. And any of these latter effects—whether good or bad—will be called "side effects." Now *if (and only if) one or more of the characteristic factors do have a positive therapeutic effect on the target disease D, then the therapy as a whole qualifies generically as a nonplacebo for D.* This is the situation that is depicted in the diagram by the words "nonplacebo effect" in the horizontal solid arrow from *F* to *D*.

It is vital to realize that, in figure 1, the causal arrows are intended to depict *possible* (imaginable) effects, such that the given treatment factors may have various sorts of positive *or* adverse effects on the target disorder, or on other facets of the patient's health. Thus, the diagram can be used to depict a nonplacebo therapy as well as a placebo therapy. In the former case, there is an actual beneficial causal influence by the characteristic factors on *D*, whereas in the latter case such an influence does not—as a matter of actual fact—exist, though it is imaginable (logically possible).

Similarly, the incidental treatment factors *C* may or may not have positive or negative effects on *D*. Furthermore, these factors *C* may have desirable or undesirable effects *outside* of *D*, which we again call side effects. If the incidental factors do have an effect on *D*, we can refer to that effect as a "placebo effect," even if the therapy qualifies overall as a generic nonplacebo by containing therapeutically effective characteristic factors. For example, suppose that the characteristic factors in a certain chemotherapy are effective against a given kind of cancer, at least for a while, so that this chemotherapy is a nonplacebo for this affliction. Then this therapeutic effectiveness may well be *enhanced*, if the dispensing physician communicates his or her confidence in this therapy to the patient. And if there is such enhancement, the treatment factors *C* do indeed produce a positive placebo effect on *D*, a situation depicted in the diagram by the broken diagonal arrow. Thus we can say that *whether a given positive effect on D is or is not a placebo effect depends on whether it is produced by the incidental treatment factors or the characteristic ones.* (For *other* placebo effects see p. 96.)

Let me now use the preceding informal preliminary account to give a more systematic and precise characterization of the genus placebo as well as of two of its species, thereby also revamping Shapiro's definitions.

A treatment process normally has a spectrum of constituent factors as well as a spectrum of effects when administered for the alleviation of a given target disorder D. Effects on the patient's health not pertaining to D are denominated "side effects." Though the term "side effects" often refers to *undesirable* effects outside D, there is neither good reason nor general agreement to restrict it in this way. As I soon illustrate, the therapeutic theory Ψ that advocates the use of a particular treatment modality t to remedy D demands the inclusion of certain characteristic constituents F in any treatment process that Ψ authenticates as an application of t. Any such process, besides qualifying as an instance of t according to Ψ, will typically have constituents C other than the characteristic ones F singled out by Ψ. And when asserting that the factors F are remedial for D, Ψ *may* also take cognizance of one or more of the noncharacteristic constituents C, which I denominate as "incidental." Thus, Ψ may perhaps attribute certain side effects to either F or C. Indeed, it may even maintain that one or another of the incidental factors affects D—say, by enhancing the remedial effects that it claims for F. In short, if a doctor is an adherent of Ψ, it may well furnish him or her with a therapeutic rationale for administering t to a patient afflicted by D, *or* for refraining from doing so.

For instance, consider pharmacological treatment, such as the dispensation of digitoxin for congestive heart dysfunction or of nitroglycerin for angina pectoris. Then it is perfectly clear that the water with which such tablets are swallowed, and the patient's awareness of the reputation of the prescribing cardiologist, for example, are incidental treatment factors, while the designated chemical ingredients are characteristic ones. But Freud also specified these two different sorts of treatment factors in the nonpharmacological case of psychoanalytic treatment, while recognizing that some of the incidental factors may serve initially as catalysts or icebreakers for the operation of the characteristic ones. Thus, he identified the characteristic constituents as the educative and affect-discharging lifting of the patient's presumed repressions, effected by means of overcoming ("working through") the analysand's resistance to their conscious recognition in the context of "resolving" his or her "transference" behavior toward the doctor. And Freud depicted the patient's faith in the analyst, and the derivation of emotional support from that authority figure, as mere catalysts or icebreakers in the initial stage of treatment—factors that are incidental, because they are avowedly quite incapable of extirpating the pathogenic causes, as distinct from producing merely cosmetic and temporary relief.

Hence Freud stressed tirelessly that the patient's correct, affect-discharging insight into the etiology of his or her affliction is the one quintessential ingredient that distinguishes the remedial dynamics of his treatment modality from any kind of treatment by suggestion. Treatments by suggestion, he charged, leave the pathogenic repressions intact, and yield only an ephemeral cosmetic prohibition of the symptoms (see Grünbaum, 1984). In the same vein, Freud came to maintain early in his career that the characteristic factors of Erb's electrotherapy for nervous disorders were therapeutically unavailing, and that any gains from treatment with that electric apparatus were achieved by its incidental factors.

EXPLICATIONS AND REFORMULATIONS

The schematic diagram in figure 1 can serve as a kind of glossary for the notations Ψ, t, F, and C that I have introduced. Using this notation, I shall offer several explications, which supersede those I have offered much earlier (Grünbaum, 1981). In the first of these explications, which pertains to the "intentional" species of placebo, the fourth condition (d) is somewhat tentative:

1. A treatment process t characterized by a given therapeutic theory Ψ as having constituents F, but also possessing other, perhaps unspecified incidental constituents C, will be said to be an "intentional placebo" with respect to a target disorder D, suffered by a victim V and treated by a dispensing practitioner P, just when the following conditions are jointly satisfied: (a) none of the characteristic treatment factors F are remedial for D; (b) P believes that the factors F indeed all *fail* to be remedial for D; (c) but P also believes that—at least for a certain type of victim V of D—t is nonetheless therapeutic for D by virtue of containing some perhaps even unknown incidental factors C

different from F; and (d) yet—more often than not—P abets or at least acquiesces in V's belief that t has remedial efficacy for D by virtue of some constituents that belong to the set of characteristic factors F in t, provided that V is aware of these factors.

Note that the first of these four conditions explicates what it is for a treatment type t to have the objective generic property of being a placebo with respect to a given target disorder D. The objective property in question is just that the characteristic constituents F of t are actually not remedial for D. On the other hand, the remaining three of the four conditions describe the property of belonging to the species of intentional placebo, over and above being a placebo generically. And, clearly, these three further conditions pertain to the beliefs and intentions of the practitioners who dispense t and of the patients who receive it. In particular, they render whether the therapist is *intentionally* administering a generic placebo to the patient, rather than unaware of the placebo status of the treatment. But notice that the fourth condition would require modification, if there were enough cases, as has been suggested, in which a patient may benefit therapeutically even after being *told* that he or she is receiving a generic placebo. On the other hand, the fourth condition apparently still suffices to cover those cases in which surgeons perform appendectomies or tonsillectomies solely at the behest of their patients, who, in turn, may be encouraged by their families. The need to accommodate such interventions has been stressed by Piechowiak (1982, 1983).

The caveat regarding the fourth condition (d) is occasioned by a report (Park and Covi, 1965) on an exploratory and "paradoxical" study of 15 adult neurotic outpatients, who presented with anxiety symptoms. The treating therapists did provide support and reassurance, yet "the responsibility for improvement was thrown back to the patient by means of the paradoxical statement that he needed treatment but that he could improve with a [placebo] capsule containing no drug" (p. 344). Of the 14 patients who remained willing to receive the capsules for a week, 6 *disbelieved* the purported pharmacological inertness of the capsules, and 3 of them even experienced "side-reactions," which they attributed to the pills (p. 342). But the 3 patients who did firmly believe in the doctor's candid disclosure of inertness improved after 1 week, no less than the "skeptics," who thought they were receiving an effective nonplacebo after all. Hence Park and Covi concluded that "unawareness of the inert nature of the placebo is not an indispensable condition for improvement on placebo" (p. 342). Yet, as these authors acknowledged at once, in so small a sample of patients, improvement may have occurred "in spite of" the disclosure as a matter of course, under *any* sort of treatment or even as a matter of spontaneous remission. And since it is quite unclear whether the moral drawn by Park and Covi is at all generalizable beyond their sample, I have let the fourth condition stand.

Piechowiak (1983) also calls attention to uses of diagnostic procedures (e.g., endoscopy, stomach X-rays) when deemed unnecessary by the physician, but demanded by the anxious patient suffering from, say, cancerphobia, who may even believe them to be therapeutic. In the latter sort of instance, the gastroenterologist may justify an invasive procedure to himself or herself and the patient, because when the expected negative finding materializes, it may alleviate the patient's anxiety as well as the vexatious somatic effects of that anxiety. In some cases (e.g., Wassermann test for syphilis), the patient may be under no illusions as to the dynamics by which this relief was wrought, any more than the doctor. But Piechowiak is concerned to point out that in other cases (e.g., angiography), the patient may well conceptualize the diagnostic intervention as *itself* therapeutic. And hence this author suggests the assimilation of these latter cases to intentional placebos. In this way, he suggests, account can be taken of the cognizance taken by doctors of the therapeutic beliefs of their patients—beliefs that are psychological realities, even if they are scientifically untutored.

As we have seen, a particular treatment modality *t* derives its identity from the full set of its characteristic treatment factors, as singled out by the therapeutic theory that advocates the use of *t* in stated circumstances. Hence therapies will be distinct, provided that they differ in at least one characteristic factor. By the same token, therapies whose distinct identities are specified in each case by two or more characteristic factors can have at least one such factor in common without detriment to their distinctness, just as they can thus share one or more incidental factors. Indeed, as I illustrate later, a shared factor that counts as characteristic of one therapy may qualify as merely incidental to another. And clearly these statements concerning factors common to distinct therapies hold for somatic medicine and psychotherapy alike.

Thus, in *either* of these two classes of healing interventions, a therapy that qualifies as a nonplacebo for a certain target D derives precisely this therapeutic status from the remedial efficacy of some or all of its characteristic factors. Yet it may share these efficacious ingredients with other, distinct therapies that differ from it in at least one characteristic factor. In fact, one or all of the common factors may count as only incidental to some of the other therapies. And it is to be borne in mind that a therapy having at least one remedial characteristic ingredient is generically a nonplacebo, even if the remaining characteristic factors are otiose. Hence a therapy t can be a nonplacebo with respect to a particular D, even if all of its efficacious characteristic treatment ingredients are common to both t and distinct other therapies!

Unfortunately, Critelli and Neumann (1984) run foul of this important state of affairs by concluding incorrectly that "the common-factors criterion . . . appears to be the most viable current definition of the placebo for the study of psychotherapy" (p. 35). They see themselves as improving on Shapiro's explication of the placebo concept, at least for psychotherapy. Yet they actually impoverish it by advocating the so-called "common-factors definition" (for psychotherapy), which they do not even *state*, and by altogether failing to render the two species of placebo adumbrated in the 1978 definition given by Shapiro and Morris. Besides, Critelli and Neumann contend that Shapiro's explication of the notion of a generic placebo suffers from his abortive attempt to encompass somatic medicine and psychotherapy simultaneously. But once I have completed my thorough recasting of Shapiro's pioneering definition below, it will be clear that—contrary to Critelli and Neumann—his endeavor to cover medicine and psychotherapy with one definitional stroke is *not* one of the defects of his explication.

Turning now to placebo *controls*, we must bear in mind that to assess the remedial merits of a given therapy t^* for some D, it is imperative to disentangle from each other two sorts of possible positive effects as follows: (1) those desired effects on D, if any, actually wrought by the characteristic factors of t^*; and (2) improvements produced by the expectations aroused in both the doctor and the patient by their belief in the therapeutic efficacy of t^*. To achieve just such a disentanglement, the baseline measure (2) of expectancy effect can be furnished by using a generic placebo t in a control group of persons suffering from D. For ethical reasons, informed consent has presumably been secured from a group of such patients to be "blindly" allocated to either the control group or the experimental group.

Ideally, this investigation should be a triply blind one. To say that the study is triply blind is to say the following: (a) the patients do not know to which group they have been assigned; (b) the dispensers do not know whether they are administering t^* or t; and (c) the outcome assessors do not know which patients were the controls. But there are treatment modalities—such as surgery and psychotherapy—in which the *second* of these three sorts of blindness obviously cannot be achieved.

By subtracting the therapeutic gains with respect to D in the control group from those in the experimental group, investigators can obtain the sought-after measure (1) of the incremental remedial potency of the characteristic factors in t^*. And, for brevity, one can then say that with respect to D, the generic placebo t functions as a "placebo control" in the experimental evaluation of the therapeutic value of t^* as such. More briefly, the placebo served in a controlled clinical trial of t^*.

As will be recalled, the relevant definition of that term given by Shapiro and Morris (1978, p. 371) reads as follows: "A placebo, when used as a control in experimental studies, is defined as a substance or procedure that is without specific activity for the condition being evaluated." But just this characterization of a "placebo control," as used in experimental studies in medicine or psychotherapy, is in dire need of emendation. As they would have it, "the condition" D is "being evaluated" in an experimental study employing a placebo control. But surely what is being

evaluated instead is the conjectured therapeuticity of a designated treatment t^* (substance, procedure) for D. And I suggest
that their definition of a placebo control be recast as follows. A
treatment type t functions as a "placebo control" in a given
context of experimental inquiry, which is designed to evaluate
the characteristic therapeutic efficacy of another modality t^* for
a target disorder D, just when the following requirements are
jointly satisfied: (1) t is a *generic placebo* for D, as defined under
the first condition (a) in the definition above of "intentional
placebo"; (2) the experimental investigator conducting the
stated controlled trial of t^* believes that t is not only a generic
placebo for D, but also is generally quite harmless to those
victims of D who have been chosen for the control group. And,
as I have noted, the investigator's reason for using t as a placebo
control when evaluating the characteristic therapeutic value of
t^* for D is as follows: especially if t^* is expensive or fraught with
negative side effects, clinicians wish to know to what extent, if
any, the beneficial effects on D due to its characteristic treatment factors *exceed* those produced by its incidental ones.

When schematized in this way, some of the complexities inherent in the notion of a placebo control are not apparent. To
their credit, Critelli and Neumann (1984) have perceptively
called attention to some of the essential refinements in psychotherapy research:

> [I]t is imperative that test procedures be compared to realistic
> placebo controls. Too often in the past, false claims of incremen-
> tal effectiveness have resulted from the experimental use of pla-
> cebos that even the most naïve would not mistake for genuine
> therapy. There appears to be a tendency for experimental place-
> bos to be in some sense weaker, less credible, or applied in a less
> enthusiastic manner than treatments that have been offered as
> actual therapies. At a minimum, placebo controls should be
> equivalent to test procedures on all major recognized common
> factors. These might include induced expectancy of improve-
> ment; credibility of rationale; credibility of procedures; demand
> for improvement; and therapist attention, enthusiasm, effort,
> perceived belief in treatment procedures, and commitment to
> client improvement [p. 38].

Having issued this salutary caveat, these authors claim that
"current [psycho]therapies have yet to meet the challenge of

demonstrating incremental effects" (p. 38). Yet one of the reasons they go on to give for posing this challenge relies on their belief that treatment factors common to two or more therapies *must* be—in my parlance—incidental rather than characteristic ingredients. As I have pointed out, however, formulations invoking this belief tend to darken counsel. Here too, placebo controls cannot be *doubly* blind.

Suedfeld (1984) likewise addresses methodological (and also ethical) problems arising in the employment of placebo controls to evaluate psychotherapy. As he sees it, "the necessity for equating the expectancy of the active [nonplacebo] and placebo treatment groups implies the acceptance of the null hypothesis, a position that is better avoided" (p. 161). To implement this avoidance, he advocates the use of a "subtractive expectancy placebo," which he describes as follows:

> It consists of administering an active, specific therapeutic procedure but introducing it with the orientation that it is inert with respect to the problem being treated. In other words, the client is led to expect less of an effect than the treatment is known to produce. The Subtractive Expectancy Procedure avoids the need to invent or find an inert technique, attempts to create initial differences in expectancy which can be substantiated by the rejection of the null hypothesis, and also makes it feasible to assess the specific effect of an active treatment in a design with one treated and one untreated (control) group [p. 161].

Here I am not concerned with the pros and cons of the subtractive expectancy placebo procedure advocated by Suedfeld *qua* alternative to the null hypothesis on which my definition above of a "placebo control" is implicitly predicated. Whatever that balance of investigative cogency, there can be little doubt that some of the ideas in Suedfeld's paper are illuminating or at least suggestive. Besides, I appreciate his several citations of my initial paper, "The Placebo Concept" (Grünbaum, 1981). There I made concrete proposals for the replacement of the standard technical vocabulary used in the placebo literature, precisely because of the Tower of Babel confusion that is engendered by it.

Alas, in criticism of Suedfeld, I must point out that his exposition is genuinely marred by just the penalties of ambiguity, obscurity, and confusion exacted by the received placebo vocabulary, because he unfortunately chooses to retain that infelicitous terminology for the formulation of his ideas. As we shall see in due course, the terms "active," "specific," and "nonspecific" are especially insidious locutions in this context. Yet these ill-fated terms, and their cognates or derivatives, abound in Suedfeld's presentation. In any case, so much for the notion of a placebo control.

Recently there have been interesting conjectures as to the identity of the incidental constituents C that confer somatic remedial potency on medications qualifying as intentional placebos for some Ds with respect to certain therapeutic theories. It has been postulated (J. Brody, 1979) that, when present, such therapeutic efficacy derives from the placebo's psychogenic activation of the secretion of substances as follows: (1) pain-killing endorphins, which are endogenous opiatelike substances; (2) interferon, which counters viral infections; and (3) steroids, which reduce inflammations. Indeed, the physiological mechanisms involved are believed to be operative as well in the so-called miracle cures by faith healers, holy waters, and so-called quacks. As an example, there is evidence from a study of dental postoperative pain (Levine et al., 1978) that endorphin release does mediate placebo-induced analgesia. And this suggests analgesic research focusing on variables that affect endorphin activity (Levine et al., 1979).

So far I have explicated only one of the two species of placebo *therapy* adumbrated in the disjunctive definition given by Shapiro and Morris (1978). Hence let me now explicate their second disjunct, which pertains to the second species of placebo.

2. A treatment process t characterized by a given therapeutic theory Ψ as having constituents F will be said to be an "inadvertent placebo" with respect to a target disorder D, suffered by a victim V and treated by a dispensing practitioner P, just when each of the following three conditions is satisfied: (a) none of the characteristic treatment factors F are remedial for D; (b) but—at least for a certain type of victim V of D—P credits these very factors F with being therapeutic for D, and indeed he or she deems at least some of them to be causally *essential* to the remedial efficacy of t; also (c) more often than not, V believes

that t derives remedial efficacy for D from constituents belonging to t's characteristic factors, provided that V is aware of these factors.

It is to be clearly understood that, as before, the first condition (a) codifies the *generic* property of being a placebo. The second condition (b) of this second explication renders the following: P denies that t's efficacy, if any, might derive mainly from its incidental constituents. Here the third condition (c) is subject to the same caveat (Park and Covi, 1965) that I have issued for the fourth condition (d) in my first explication above.

CLARIFYING COMMENTS

Let me now add four sets of clarifying comments on my explications, because of questions put to me by Edward Erwin (personal comunication, 1981), a philosopher of psychology.

1. Clearly, it was the intentional species of placebo that was denoted by the term "placebo" in its original pharmacological use. And its use in Shapiro's definition to denote as well what I have called the inadvertent species constitutes a *generalization* of the genus placebo, prompted by the sobering lesson of the history of medicine that most treatments were inadvertent rather than intentional placebos, and often harmful to boot! But the tacit intuitions of many people as to what a placebo is are strongly geared to its original status in pharmacology. No wonder that these intuitions call for identifying the intentional species of placebo with the entire genus. Consequently, some people will be ruffled by the fact that, in my explication of the *generalized* use of the term, the generic property of being a placebo is, of course, considerably less restrictive than the property of being an intentional placebo. For, as is clear from the codification of the generic placebo property in the first condition (a) of both of my explications, any treatment t qualifies generically as a placebo for a given target disorder D merely on the strength of the failure of *all* of its characteristic factors F to be remedial for D.

But once the source of the counterintuitiveness is recognized, it should be dispelled and should occasion no objection to my explication of the generic property. Furthermore, in the generalized generic sense of "placebo," a treatment t does belong to the genus placebo even if its characteristic factors exacerbate D, since exacerbation is a particularly strong way of failing to be remedial for D. Surely, it is the failure of the *characteristic* treatment factors to be *remedial* for D that is at the heart of the notion of a placebo therapy, *not* their failure to have an *effect* on D, either bad or good. And the failure of a practitioner who dispenses a harmful inadvertent placebo t to be cognizant of its ill effect hardly detracts from t's objective status as a generic placebo. Nor does the malaise of those who would invoke the favorable *etymological* significance of the term "placebo" in order to forbid a generalized generic concept that fails to exclude the envisaged untoward case. Either species of placebos can *undesignedly* exacerbate D! History teaches that many well-intended treatments were *worse than useless*.

Finally, note that if one were to define a generic placebo therapy t *alternatively* as one whose characteristic factors are *without effect* on D, it would have the consequence that a *non*placebo t would either exacerbate D or be remedial for it, or would have a merely neutral effect on it. But in my definitional scheme, one or more of the characteristic factors of a *non*placebo must be positively therapeutic.

2. There are treatments only *some* of whose characteristic factors F are therapeutic for a given D, while the therapeutic theory Ψ that advocates their dispensation claims that *all* of the factors F are thus remedial. For example, it has recently been claimed (Kazdin and Wilson, 1978) that in the systematic desensitization brand of behavior therapy, which is an effective treatment for certain phobias, only one of its three F factors is thus therapeutic, while the other two appear unavailing. What, it might be asked, is the classificatory verdict of my explication as to whether a therapy whose characteristic factors comprise both efficacious and otiose members qualifies generically as a nonplacebo?

To answer this question, note that within the class of treatments for any given D, any member t will belong to the genus placebo exactly when *none* of its characteristic factors are remedial for D. Therefore any therapy whose characteristic factors include *at least one* that is therapeutic for D will pass muster as a nonplacebo. Evidently it is not necessary for being a nonplacebo that all of the F factors be remedial. It follows that, in the absence of further information, the designation of a given therapy—such as desensitization in the example above—as a nonplacebo does not tell us whether only some of its characteristic factors are remedial or whether all of them are. But this fact hardly militates against either my explication or the usefulness of the concept of nonplacebo as rendered by it.

Upon recalling Shapiro and Morris's cited characterizations of "pure" and "impure" placebos (1978, p. 372), we see that my construal of the generic placebo notion explicates what they call a "pure placebo." Their "impure placebos" are, as they put it vaguely, "treatments that have specific components but exert their effects primarily through nonspecific mechanisms" (p. 372). This sort of treatment does count as a nonplacebo, according to my formulation. But my parlance can readily characterize their so-called impure placebos by saying the following. Although the characteristic ingredients of these therapies do make some therapeutic contribution, this remedial effect is exceeded by the therapeutic benefit deriving from the *incidental* treatment factors. This quantitative vagueness is, of course, not my problem but theirs.

3. It must not be overlooked that my explication of "placebo" is relativized not only to a given target disorder D, but also to those characteristic factors that are singled out from a particular treatment process by a specified therapeutic theory Ψ. It is therefore not my explication but a given theory Ψ that determines which treatment factors are to be classified as the characteristic factors in any one case. And by the same token, as I illustrate presently, the given therapeutic theory Ψ (in medicine or psychiatry) rather than my explication determines whether any factors in the physician-patient relationship are to count as only "incidental." Clearly, for example, a particular psychiatric theory might well designate some such factors as being characteristic. And just this sort of fact prompted Shapiro and Morris to disavow the common restriction of "specific activity" to "nonpsychological mechanisms of action," and to offer their "more general definition of specific activity" cited above.

An example given to me in a discussion at Maudsley Hospital in London called my attention to allowing for the possible *time-dependence* of the effects of *incidental* treatment factors. In pharmacological research on rats, it was noticed that the effects of injected substances were enhanced after a while, via Pavlovian conditioning, by the continued presence of blue light. That light can be deemed an incidental treatment factor throughout, I claim, although its effects will vary as time goes on. Hence I reject the suggestion that once the blue light has begun to potentiate the effects of the injected substances, the light must be reclassified to become a characteristic treatment factor, after starting out as a merely incidental one.

The divergence between Jerome Frank's (1973) theory of healing as persuasion on the one hand, and such psychotherapeutic theories as Freud's or Hans Eysenck's on the other, will now serve to illustrate three important points as follows. (a) As is evident from my explication, it is the given therapeutic theory Ψ rather than my explication of "placebo" that decides *which* treatment factors are to be respectively classified as "characteristic" and as "incidental." (b) Precisely because my analysis of the placebo concept does make explicit provision for the dependence of the memberships of these classes on the particular theory Ψ at hand, it allows for the fact that rival therapeutic theories can *disagree* in regard to their classification of particular treatment factors as "characteristic," no less than in their attribution of significant therapeutic efficacy to such factors. (c) Hence, the relativization of the classification of treatment factors to a given theory Ψ that is built into my explication prevents seeming inconsistencies and confusions, generated when investigators want to assess the generic placebo status of a therapy t across rival therapeutic theories, and without regard to whether these theories use different characteristic factors to identify t.

In the language and notions of my explications, Frank's (1973, pp. xv-xx) view of the therapeutic status of the leading rival psychotherapies can now be outlined. For *each* of these treatment modalities t and its underlying theory Ψ, he hypothesizes that t is as follows:

1. A generic placebo with respect to the characteristic treatment factors singled out by *its own* particular Ψ.
2. An inadvertent placebo with respect to the beliefs of those dispensers of t who espouse Ψ.
3. Therapeutically effective to the extent that the patient's hope is aroused by the doctor's healing symbols, which mobilize the patient's sense of mastery of his or her demoralization.

As is clear from the third item, Frank credits a treatment ingredient *common* to the rival psychotherapies with such therapeutic efficacy as they do possess. But his categorization of each of these therapies as a generic placebo rather than as a nonplacebo is now seen to derive just from the fact that he is tacitly classifying as "incidental," rather than as "characteristic," all those treatment factors that he deems to be therapeutic. In adopting this latter classification, he is speaking the classificatory language employed by the theories underlying the various therapies, although he denies their claim that the treatment ingredients they label "characteristic" are actually effective.

Yet in a language suited to Frank's own therapeutic tenets, it would, of course, be entirely natural to label as "characteristic" just those treatment factors that his own theory T deems remedial, even though these same ingredients count as merely incidental within each of the psychotherapeutic theories rejected by him. And if Frank were to couch his own T in that new classificatory language, then he would no longer label the leading psychotherapies as generic placebos, although he would be holding the same therapeutic beliefs as before. It should now be clear that by explicitly relativizing to a given Ψ the classification of particular treatment factors as "characteristic" or "incidental," no less than by relativizing their respective therapeutic efficacy to a particular D, my explication obviates the following sort of question, which is being asked across unspecified, tacitly presupposed therapeutic theories: If the effectiveness of a placebo modality depends on its symbolization of the physician's healing power, should this ingredient not be considered a *characteristic* treatment factor?

4. In a paper devoted mainly to the ethical complexities of using placebo control groups in psychotherapy research,

O'Leary and Borkovec (1978) write: "Because of problems in devising a theoretically and practically inert placebo, we recommend that the term *placebo* be abandoned in psychotherapy research" (p. 823). They propose to "circumvent the ethical concerns inherent in placebo methodology" (p. 825) by devising alternative methods of research control. In this way, they hope to assure as well that "the confusion associated with the term *placebo* would be avoided" (p. 823).

But I hope it will become clear from my comparison of my explication above with the usual parlance in the literature that these confusions indeed can be avoided without abandoning the placebo concept in any sort of therapeutic research. Nor do I see why the theoretical identification of a particular incidental treatment factor that is effective for *D* rather than "inert" ever has to be detrimental to therapeutic research.

Logical Defects of Received Vocabulary

On the basis of my explications, I can now make two sets of comments on the logical defects of the key locutions commonly employed as technical terms throughout the medical and psychiatric literature on placebos.

1. We are told that any effect that a placebo has on the target disorder *D* is "nonspecific." But a placebo can have an effect on *D* that is no less sharply defined and precisely known than the effect of a nonplacebo. To take a simple example, consider two patients *A* and *B* suffering from ordinary tension headaches of comparable severity. Suppose that *A* unwittingly swallows the proverbial sugar pill and gets no relief from it, because it is indeed pharmacologically "inert" or useless for such a headache *qua* mere sugar pill. *A* stoically endures his or her discomfort. Assume further that *B* consults his or her physician, who is very cautious. Mindful of the potential side effects of tranquillizers and analgesics, the doctor decides to employ a little benign deceit and gives *B* a few lactose pills, without disabusing *B* of his or her evident belief that he or she is receiving a physician's sample of analgesics. Posit that shortly after *B* takes

the first of these sugar pills, the headache disappears altogether. Assume further that B's headache would not have disappeared just then from mere internal causes. Both of these
conditions might well apply in a given case. Thus B assumedly
received the same headache relief from the mere sugar pill as
he or she would have received if a pharmacologically *non*inert
drug had been slipped into his food without his knowledge.

Clearly, in some such situations, the therapeutic effect of the
sugar pill placebo on the headache can have attributes fully as
sharply defined or "specific" as the effect that would have been
produced by a so-called "active" drug like aspirin (Frank, 1973).
Moreover, this placebogenic effect can be just as precisely described or known as the nonplacebogenic effect of aspirin. In
either case, the effect is complete headache relief, even though
the sugar pill as such is, of course, pharmacologically inert for
headaches whereas aspirin as such is pharmacologically efficacious. It is therefore at best very misleading to describe as "nonspecific" the *effect* that the placebo produces on the target disorder, while describing the at least qualitatively like effect of the
nonplacebo as "specific." Yet just such a use of the terms "nonspecific" and "specific" as modifiers of the term "effect" is made
in Shapiro's above-cited definition of "placebo," in a leading
treatise on pharmacological therapeutics (Goodman and Gilman, 1975), in a German work on psychoanalysis (Möller,
1978), in a German survey article on placebos (Piechowiak,
1983), and in a fairly recent article on treatments to reduce
high blood pressure (A. P. Shapiro et al., 1977). Equally infelici-
tously, Schwartz (1978, p. 83) speaks of a "nonspecific placebo
response." Why describe a treatment effect as "nonspecific" in
order to convey that the incidental treatment factors, rather
than the characteristic elements, were the ones that produced
it? Relatedly, D. F. Klein (1980) points out that when a placebo
counteracts demoralization in a depressed person, it is wrong-
headed to describe this therapeutic outcome as a "nonspecific"
effect. After all, the demoralization and the effect on it are
quite specific in the ordinary sense.

Worse, as it stands, the locution "specific effect" is quite ambiguous as between the following two very different senses: (a)
The therapeutic effect on D is wrought by the characteristic

("specific") factors F of the therapy t; or (b) the remedial effectiveness of t is specific to a quite small number of disorders, to the exclusion of a far more multitudinous set of nosologically different afflictions and of their respective pathognomonic symptoms. Most writers on placebos, though not all, intend the first construal when speaking of "specific effect." But others use the term "specific" in the second of these senses. Thus, as we shall see in greater detail further on, according to whether the effects of a given therapy are or are not believed to be "specific" in the *second* sense above, H. Brody (1977, pp. 40-43) classifies that *therapy* as a "specific therapy" or as a "general therapy." And he wishes to allow for the fact that the placebogenic remedial efficacy of the proverbial sugar pill is presumed to range over a larger number of target ailments than the nonplacebogenic efficacy of widely used medications (e.g., penicillin). In an endeavor to make such an allowance, he uses the belief in the ability of a therapy to engender "specific effects" in the second sense above as the touchstone of its being a nonplacebo. In addition, Shepherd (1961) has pointed out yet another ambiguity in the loose use of "specific" and "nonspecific" to designate treatment factors in psychopharmacology. And Wilkins (1985, p. 120) speaks of "nonspecific events" not only to refer to treatment factors *common* to rival therapies, but also to denote life events outside the treatment process altogether. How much better it would be, therefore, if students of placebo phenomena banished the seriously ambiguous use of "specific" as a technical term altogether.

As if this degree of technical confusion were not enough, the misleading use of "specific" in the sense of "nonplacebo" is sometimes encountered alongside the use of "specific" in the usual literal sense of "precise" or "well defined." Thus, when Miller (1980) writes that "placebo effects can be quite specific" (p. 476), the illustrations he goes on to give show that here "specific" has the force of "quantitatively precise." But in the very next paragraph, he uses the term "specific" as a synonym for "nonplacebo" when reporting that "it is only in the past 80 years that physicians have been able to use an appreciable number of treatments with specific therapeutic effects" (p. 476).

Indeed, the placebo research worker Beecher (1972), who is renowned for investigating the role of placebos in the reduction of pain, entitled one of his essays "The Placebo Effect as a Non-specific Force Surrounding Disease and the Treatment of Disease." But even metaphorically and elliptically, it seems inappropriate to speak of the placebo *effect* as being a nonspecific *force*, as Beecher does repeatedly.

On the basis of the explications I have given, it is appropriate to speak of an *effect* as a "placebo effect" under two sorts of conditions: (a) Even when the treatment t is a *non*placebo, effects on D—be they good, bad, or neutral—that are produced by t's incidental factors count as placebo effects, precisely because these factors wrought them; and (b) when t is a generic placebo whose characteristic factors have harmful or neutral effects on D, these effects as well count as placebo effects (see pp. 88-89). Hence, if t is a placebo, then *all* of its effects qualify as placebo effects.

2. Shapiro and Morris (1978) tell us in their definition that a placebo "is without specific activity for the condition being treated." And, as we recall, they contrast "active treatments" with placebos by saying that "active treatments may contain placebo components" (p. 371). Yet they also tell us that "in behavior therapy, some investigators have utilized 'active placebo' control groups" in which "some aspects of the therapy affect behavior but those aspects differ from the theoretically relevant ingredients of concern to the investigator" (p. 372). Furthermore, in the common parlance employed by two other investigators, even placebos that are acknowledged to be "potently therapeutic" or "effective" (for angina pectoris) are incongruously dubbed "inactive" just because they are placebos (Benson and McCallie, 1979). And Beecher (1972) emphasizes that some placebos "are capable of *powerful action*" (p. 178), while contrasting them with treatments that he and others call "active" to convey that they are indeed nonplacebos.

By contrast to Beecher's use of "active," Bok (1974) tells us that any medical procedure, "whether it is active or inactive, can serve as a placebo whenever it has no specific effect on the condition for which it is prescribed" (p. 17). Thus, in Bok's parlance, placebos may be said to be "active" (p. 17) and "place-bos can be effective" (p. 18), but they must be devoid of so-called "specific effect." Yet just what is it for a placebo to be "active"? Clearly, a placebo therapy as a whole *might* be produc-tive of (remedial or deleterious) effects on the target disorder while being devoid of significant (negative or positive) side ef-fects, or it may have only side effects. On the other hand, it might have both kinds of effects. And it matters therapeutically, of course, which of these effects—if either—is produced by any particular placebo. Hence clarity will be notably served by explicitly indicating the *respect* in which a given placebo inter-vention is being said to be "active." Yet such explicitness is lacking when Bok tells us, for example, that there is a clear-cut "potential for damage by an active drug given as a placebo" (p. 20). Thus it is only a conjecture just what she intends the term "active" to convey in the latter context. Is it that there are phar-macologically induced side effects in addition to placebogenic effects on the target disorder D? By the same token, her usage of "inactive" is unclear when she reports that "even inactive placebos can have toxic effects" (p. 20), even though she goes on to give what she takes to be an illustration. Bok's concern with placebos focuses, however, on ethically questionable dis-pensations of intentional placebos. But if a treatment is truly remedial, why should it matter to the patient that the treatment is *technically* a placebo relative to the therapist's theory?

Evidently there are divergences among writers on placebos in regard to the usage of the term "active." But they tell us in one voice, as Bok does, that a placebo procedure "has no specific effect on the condition for which it is prescribed" (p. 17). To this conceptually dissonant discourse, I say: In the case of a placebo it is, of course, recognized that incidental treatment factors *may* be potently remedial for D, although the character-istic ones by definition are not. And if some of the incidental constituents are thus therapeutic, then the actual specificity of their activity—in the ordinary sense of "specificity"—clearly does *not* depend on whether the pertinent therapeutic theory Ψ is able either to specify their particular identity or to afford understanding of their detailed mode of action. Hence if some of the incidental constituents of t are remedial but presently elude the grasp of Ψ, the current inability of Ψ to pick them out from the treatment process hardly lessens the objective specificity of their identity, mode of action, or efficacy. A theory's current inability to spell out certain causal factors and to articulate their mode of action because of ignorance is surely not tantamount to their being themselves objectively "nonspecific" as to their identity, over and above being unknown! At worst, the details of the operation of the incidental factors are left unspecified.

Hence, despite the assumed present inability of the pertinent theory Ψ to spell out which particular incidental constituents render the given placebo remedial for D, it is at best needlessly obscure to say that these constituents are "without specific activity" for D and are "nonspecific." A *fortiori*, it is infelicitous to declare of any and every placebo treatment modality as a whole that, *qua* being a placebo, it must be devoid of "specific activity." It would seem that, when speaking generically of a placebo, the risk of confusion as well as outright unsound claims can be obviated by steadfast avoidance of the term "nonspecific activity." Instead, as I have argued earlier, the objective genus property of being a placebo should be codified as follows. With respect to the target disorder D, the treatment modality t belongs to the genus placebo just when its characteristic constituents *fail* to be remedial for D. Furthermore, clarity is served by using the term "incidental" rather than "nonspecific" when speaking of those treatment constituents that differ from the characteristic ones. In short, the generic distinction between placebos and nonplacebos has nothing whatever to do with the contrast between nonspecificity and specificity, but only with whether the characteristic treatment factors do play a therapeutic role for D or not. So much for my proposed rectifications of the misleading conceptualizations conveyed by the standard locutions whose confusion I have laid bare.

CLARIFYING RAMIFICATIONS OF MY EXPLICATIONS

As is clear from my formulation, the genus property of being a placebo is altogether independent of the belief of the dispensing practitioner as to whether the treatment in question is a placebo. But, equally clearly, the species property of being an inadvertent placebo is explicitly relativized to this belief, no less than the species property of being an intentional one. Thus, a placebo treatment t that qualifies as inadvertent with respect to one school of therapeutic thought may be explicitly avowed to have intentional placebo status in the judgment of another school. By the same token, advocates of t who do not even entertain the possibility of its being a placebo will be preoccupied with its characteristic constituents, to the likely disregard of incidental factors in t that may turn out to be remedially potent for D. Consequently, if patients who received treatment t register gains, such advocates will erroneously discount any remedial efficacy actually possessed by these incidental factors. Moreover, these theoreticians will give undeserved credit to the characteristic factors for any successful results that issue from t. As recounted in Beecher's classic (1961) paper "Surgery as Placebo," which is summarized by Benson and McCallie (1979), the history of surgical treatment for angina pectoris in the United States during the mid 1950s furnished a clear case in point.

Proponents of ligating the internal mammary artery claimed that this procedure facilitated increased coronary blood flow through collateral vessels near the point of ligation, thereby easing the ischemia of the heart muscle to which angina pectoris is due. And these enthusiasts then credited that ligation with the benefits exhibited by their surgical patients. But well-controlled, though ethically questionable, studies by skeptical surgeons in the late 1950s showed the following. When a mere sham bilateral skin incision was made on a comparison group of angina patients, then ligation of the internal mammary artery in randomly selected other angina patients yielded only equal or even less relief from angina than the sham surgery. Furthermore, the quality of the results achieved by the intentional placebo surgery was dramatic and sustained. Apart from subjective improvement, the deceived recipients of the sham surgery had increased exercise tolerance, registered less nitroglycerin usage, and improved electrocardiographically. Moreover, a similar lesson emerges from the use of a related surgical procedure due to Vineberg, in which the internal mammary artery was implanted into a tunnel burrowed into the myocardium. The results from this Vineberg operation (Benson and McCallie, 1979) suggest that placebogenic relief occurred even in a sizable majority of angina patients who had angiographically verified coronary artery disease. This history has a sobering moral. It bears further monitoring to what extent the positive results from coronary artery bypass surgery are placebogenic (Detre et al., 1984).

Now consider those who allow that such beneficial efficacy as a therapy t has could well be placebogenic. This group may thereby be led to draw the true conclusion that the characteristic factors do not merit any therapeutic credit. On the other hand, the therapeutic efficacy of a nonplacebo is enhanced if its incidental factors *also* have a remedial effect of their own. Thus, it has been found (Gallimore and Turner, 1977) that the attitudes of physicians toward chemotherapy commonly contribute significantly to the effectiveness of nonplacebo drugs. Again, Wheatley (1967) reported that in the treatment of anxiety by one particular nonplacebo drug, enthusiastic physicians obtained better results than unenthusiastic ones, although enthusiasm did not enhance the positive effect of tricyclic antidepressants on depression. Indeed, there may be synergism between the characteristic and incidental treatment factors, such that they potentiate each other therapeutically with respect to the *same* target disorder.

On the other hand, one and the same treatment may be a placebo with respect to the target disorder and yet may function as a nonplacebo for a secondary ailment. For example, when a viral cold is complicated by the presence of a secondary bacterial infection, a suitable antibiotic may serve as an intentional placebo for the viral cold while also acting as a nonplacebo for the bacterial infection. This case spells an important moral. It serves to discredit the prevalent stubborn refusal to relativize the placebo status of a medication or intervention to a stated target disorder, a relativization I have explicitly built into my definitions. For example, in the misguided effort to escape such relativization, Piechowiak (1983, p. 40) is driven to classify antibiotics as "false placebos." As he sees it, they are placebos because they are not pharmacologically effective for the typical sort of upper respiratory viral infection; but what makes them "false" placebos, in his view, is that they *are* pharmacologically potent (genuine medications, or in the original German, "echte Pharmaka") for other diseases (e.g., bacterial pneumonia).

But, according to this reasoning, "false" placebos are quite common. A telling illustration is provided by the following story reported by Jennifer Worrall, a British physician (personal communication, 1983). One of her patients, a middle-aged woman, complained of a superficial varicose leg ulcer. Worrall relates:

> [The patient] was very demanding and difficult to please and claimed to suffer continuous agony from her ulcer (although there were none of the objective signs of pain, such as sleep disturbance, increased heart rate and blood pressure, pallor and sweating). All of the many mild-to-moderate analgesics were "useless" [according to the patient] and I did not feel opiates were justified, so I asked the advice of my immediate superior. The superior [here referred to as "W."] saw the patient, discussed her pain and, with a grave face, said he wanted her to try a "completely different sort of treatment." She agreed. He disappeared into the office, to reappear a few minutes later, walking slowly down the ward and holding in front of him a pair of tweezers which grasped a large, white tablet, the size of [a] half-dollar. As he came nearer, it became clear (to me, at least) that the tablet was none other than effervescent vitamin C. He dropped the tablet into a glass of water which, of course, bubbled and fizzed, and told the patient to sip the water carefully when the fizzing had subsided. It worked—the new medicine completely abolished her pain! W. has used this method several times, apparently, and it always worked. He felt that the single most important aspect was holding the tablet with *tweezers*, thereby giving the impression that it was somehow too powerful to be touched with bare hands!

Some may find this episode amusing. Yet it has a devastating moral for the not uncommon claim that without regard to the *specified* target disorder, a pharmacological agent can qualify as a generic and even as an intentional placebo. Assume that, for the varicose leg ulcer that afflicted the given patient, vitamin C is a generic placebo even in high doses; this assumption allows that, in such large doses, it may have negative side effects. Furthermore, relying on W.'s findings, grant that for at least some patients suffering from a superficial leg ulcer, the administration of vitamin C as an intentional placebo in W.'s ceremonious manner ("with tweezers"!) is therapeutic for such an ulcer. Then surely such a placebo status for leg ulcer hardly detracts from the fact that, at least in sufficient doses, vitamin C is a potent nonplacebo for scurvy. And if Linus Pauling is to be believed, sufficiently high doses of this vitamin can even afford prophylaxis for certain cancers. In short, only conceptual mischief results from the supposition that the property of being a (generic) placebo is one that a treatment—be it pharmacological or psychiatric—can have *per se*, rather than only with respect to a stated target disorder.

Ironically, none other than the much-maligned proverbial sugar pill furnishes a *reductio ad absurdum* of the notion that a medication can be generically a placebo *simpliciter*, without relativization to a target disorder. For even a lay person knows that the glucose in the sugar pill is anything but a generic placebo if given to a victim of diabetes who is in a state of insulin shock, or to someone suffering from hypoglycemia. But if an antibiotic were a "false placebo" on the strength of the properties adduced by Piechowiak (1983), then—by parity with his reasoning—so also is the notorious sugar pill, the alleged paradigm of a "true" nonrelativized placebo. Even the diehards among the believers in intrinsic, nonrelativized placebos will presumably regard this consequence of their view as too high a price to pay. Nor would they ever think someone's Uncle Charlie to be a "false" uncle merely because Charlie is not also somebody else's uncle!

Suppose that, for specified types of diseases, a certain class of afflicted victims does derive placebogenic remedial gain from the use of a particular set of therapeutic interventions. Then it may become important, for one reason or another, to ascertain—*within* the classes of incidental treatment factors picked out by the pertinent set of therapeutic theories—which particular kinds of factors are thus remedial. This quest for identification can proceed across various sorts of treatment modalities (e.g., chemotherapy, radiation therapy, surgery), or may be focused more narrowly on factors within such modalities (e.g.,

surgery). Research during the past three decades has envisioned (1) that such placebogenic treatment gain may require
a so-called "placebo reactor" type of victim of disease, characterized by a specifiable (but as yet unspecified) personality trait or
cluster of such traits; or (2) that the therapeutic success of placebos may depend on certain kinds of characteristics or attitudes
possessed by the treating physician. It should be noted that my
explications of both the intentional and inadvertent species of
placebo have made provision for these two possibilities. Both
explications are relativized to disease victims of a specifiable
sort, as well as to therapists (practitioners) of certain kinds. As
it turns out, for some two dozen or so of proposed patient-trait
correlates of placebo responsiveness, the first hypothesis named
above—that of placebo reactivity—has been largely unsuccessful empirically, except for the following: Generalized chronic
anxiety has been frequently and reliably found to correlate with
placebo responsivity, notably in the treatment of pain (Gallimore and Turner, 1977). Yet in a 25-year series of studies of
placebo responsiveness in psychotherapy, Frank (1974) found
reason to discount the role of enduring personality factors in
the patient (see also Liberman, 1964). As for the second hypothesis, which pertains to the therapeutic relevance of the physician's communicated attitudes, I have already commented on
the demonstrated role of physician's variables among incidental
treatment factors in enhancing the therapeutic efficacy of nonplacebo drugs.

Having explicated the placebo concept by reference to Shapiro and Morris's proposed definition, I ought to comment on
the divergences between theirs and the one offered by H.
Brody (1977), which I have mentioned on page 95.

Shapiro and Morris's definition appeared in 1978 in the *second* edition of the Garfield and Bergin *Handbook of Psychotherapy
and Behavior Change*. But in the first edition of this *Handbook*,
which appeared in 1971, Shapiro alone had published an only
slightly different definition. This 1971 definition is not discussed by Brody (1977). But Brody claims rough consistency
between Shapiro's (1968) definition of "placebo effect" and his
own account of that notion. Hence I am concerned to point
out that there are several important divergences between the

construals of "placebo" given by Shapiro and Morris on the one
hand, and Brody on the other. And these differences are such,
I claim, that Shapiro and Morris render the generic placebo
concept implicit in the medical and psychiatric literature far
more adequately than Brody, notwithstanding the important
respects in which I have found Shapiro and Morris's definition
wanting.

The reader is now asked to recall my earlier remarks as to
the consideration that seems to have prompted Brody's introduction of his notion of a "specific therapy": the putative fact
that the placebogenic remedial efficacy of the proverbial sugar
pill is presumed to range over a larger number of target ailments than the nonplacebogenic efficacy of widely used medications (e.g., of penicillin). Then the essence of his account becomes quite clear from his proposed definitions of the following
terms: "therapy"; "specific therapy," which Brody avowedly
contrasts with "general therapy" (1977, p. 41); and finally, "placebo." Let me first cite these definitions and Brody's comment
on them. (For the sake of consistency, I am substituting the
abbreviations used up to this point in this article for Brody's
here.)

> 1) [t] is a therapy for condition [D] if and only if it is believed
>   that administration of [t] to a person with [D] increases the
>   empirical probability that [D] will be cured, relieved, or amel-
>   iorated, as compared to the probability that this will occur
>   without [t] [p. 38].
> 2) [t] is a specific therapy for condition [D] if and only if:
>   (1) [t] is a therapy for [D].
>   (2) There is a class A of conditions such that [D] is a subclass
>   of A, and for all members of A, [t] is a therapy.
>   (3) There is a class B of conditions such that for all members
>   of B, [t] is not a therapy; and class B is much larger than class
>   A.
>
> For example, consider how the definition applies to penicillin
> used for pneumococcal pneumonia. Penicillin is a therapy for
> this disease, since it increases the empirical probability of recov-
> ery. Pneumococcal pneumonia is one of a class of diseases (infec-
> tious diseases caused by penicillin-sensitive organisms) for all of
> which penicillin is a therapy; but there is a much larger class of
> diseases (noninfectious diseases and infectious diseases caused
> by penicillin-resistant organisms) for which penicillin is not a
> therapy [pp. 40-41].

It will be noted that Brody presumably intends the third requirement in the second definition to implement his stated objective of contrasting "specific therapy" with "general therapy"—an aim that, as we have seen, does *not* govern Shapiro and Morris's construal of "specific." For Brody's third requirement here makes the following demand. The membership of the class B of disorders for which *t* is believed to be *ineffective* has to be numerically greater than the membership of the class A of target disorders for which *t* is deemed to be remedial. But clearly, Shapiro and Morris's cited account of what it is for *t* to possess "specific activity" for *D* does *not* entail logically Brody's third restriction on the relative number of disorders for which *t* is (believed to be) therapeutic! For example, just think of how Shapiro and Morris would analyze the claim that aspirin is not a placebo for arthritis or tension headaches and that it affords nonplacebogenic prophylaxis for blood clotting and embolisms. Nor would Brody's third restriction seem to be often implicit in the medical and psychiatric usage of "specific therapy."

Yet Brody does deserve credit for pointing out, in effect, that the placebogenic efficacy of intentional placebos is believed to range over a larger number of target ailments, as a matter of empirical fact, than the nonplacebogenic efficacy of such medications as penicillin. This is *much less significant*, though, than he thinks: After all, the old sugar pill and penicillin alike have *placebogenic* efficacy, such that the sugar pill does not excel in regard to the number of target disorders!

The third of Brody's definitions reads:

> 3) A placebo is:
> (1) a form of medical therapy, or an intervention designed to simulate medical therapy, that at the time of use is *believed* not to be a specific therapy for the condition for which it is offered and that is used for its psychological effect or to eliminate observer bias in an experimental setting.
> (2) (by extension from 1) a form of medical therapy now believed to be inefficacious, though believed efficacious at the time of use.
>
> Clause 2 is added to make sense of a sentence such as, "Most of the medications used by physicians one hundred years ago were actually placebos" [p. 43; italics added].

A further major divergence between Brody's and Shapiro and Morris's definitions of "placebo" derives from the multiple dependence of Brody's generic placebo concept on therapeutic *beliefs*, in contrast to Shapiro and Morris's explicit repudiation of any such dependence of the generic notion of placebo. As shown by Brody's definition of "therapy" above, what renders a treatment a "therapy" in his construal is that "it is believed" to be remedial (by its advocates or recipients). Consequently, this dependence on therapeutic belief enters into Brody's definition of "specific therapy" via each of the three requirements that he lays down in his definition of that term above. On the other hand, no such belief-dependence is present in Shapiro and Morris's counterpart notion of "specific activity." As if this were not enough, Brody's definition of "placebo" invokes yet another layer of belief by requiring that "at the time of use," a placebo treatment be "believed not to be a specific therapy" for the target disorder, presumably by the doctor but not by the patient.

It is patent, therefore, that Shapiro and Morris's construal of the *generic* placebo notion, which we have seen to be objective rather than dependent on therapeutic beliefs, makes incomparably better sense than Brody's of such claims as "most of the medications used by physicians a century ago were actually placebos," a claim that Brody avowedly hopes to accommodate via the second requirement of his definition of "placebo." For on Shapiro and Morris's construal, physicians can in fact be *objectively* mistaken in deeming a treatment modality to be a nonplacebo. But on Brody's definition, it is merely a matter of a change in their therapeutic beliefs. For this reason alone, I have made Shapiro and Morris's definition rather than Brody's the focus of my explication.

Note that each of the two species of placebo therapy I have considered is defined by a *conjunction* of two sorts of statement: (1) an assertion of *objective fact* as to the therapeutic failure of *t*'s characteristic constituents with respect to *D*; and (2) claims concerning the *beliefs* held by the therapist and/or the patient in regard to *t*. Clearly, the belief-content of (2) does not lessen the objectivity of (1). Yet, in a reply to me, Brody (1985, p. 45) runs afoul of this point. For he thinks incorrectly that the belief-content of (2) negates the greater objectivity I have claimed for my definitions *vis-à-vis* his own *entirely belief-ridden* renditions of the pertinent concepts.

I hope it is now apparent that the customary notions and terminology of placebo research foster conceptual confusion, and that the adoption of the conceptualizations and vocabulary I have proposed would obviate the perpetuation of such confusion.

4

THE ROLE OF THE CASE STUDY METHOD IN THE FOUNDATIONS OF PSYCHOANALYSIS: FUNDAMENTAL EVIDENTIAL DEFECTS OF THE THEORY OF TRANSFERENCE QUA ETIOLOGIC HYPOTHESIS

INTRODUCTION

In my 1984 book on *The Foundations of Psychoanalysis*, I addressed two main questions: (1) Are the analyst's observations in the clinical setting reliable as "data"; and (2) if so, can they actually support the major hypotheses of the theory of repression or psychic conflict, which is the cornerstone of the psychoanalytic edifice, as we know? In the book, I argued for giving a negative answer to both of these questions. Clearly, if the evidence from the couch is unreliable from the outset, then this defect alone suffices to jeopardize the very foundations of the clinical theory. But, as I strongly emphasized, even if clinical data were *not* contaminated by the analyst's influence, the inability of the psychoanalytic method of clinical investigation by free association to warrant the required sort of *causal* inferences leaves the major pillars of the theory of psychic conflict ill-supported (1984, p. 172). Thus, I see a twofold threat to the psychoanalytic case-study method as a means of scientific inquiry.

Here we need to recall a caveat regarding post-Freudian apologetics for psychoanalysis from the Introduction to chapter

1. It is an immediate corollary of my challenge that it applies not only to Freud's own original hypotheses, but also to any and all post-Freudian versions of psychoanalysis that rely on his clinical methods of validating causal inferences, though the specific content of their theories of psychic conflict is different. After all, the alteration in the content of the hypotheses hardly makes their validation more secure. Therefore, as Morris Eagle documented in a recent publication (1983), those analysts who have objected to my critique as anachronistic have simply not come to grips with it. For example, such inadequate engagement is present, in my view, in the recent Freud Anniversary Lecture "Psychoanalysis as a Science: A Response to the New Challenges," given by Robert Wallerstein (1986), the current president of the International Psycho-Analytical Association. As he tells us (1988, p. 6, n. 1), "The Freud Anniversary Lecture was intended primarily as a response to Grünbaum." Yet he does not come to grips at all with the gravamen of my challenge: *Even if clinical data could be taken at face value as being uncontaminated epistemically*, the inability of the psychoanalytic method of clinical investigation by free association to warrant causal inferences leaves the major pillars of the clinical theory of repression ill-supported. Thus, I deem Marshall Edelson's comment (1988, p. 318) very telling:

> Referring to post-Freud developments in psychoanalysis *as a way of neutralizing Grünbaum* is apposite only if these developments make a difference with respect to the problems he has raised. Grünbaum could surely ask whether those who respond in this way to his critique make much of a case that these developments make that kind of difference.

I have asserted the inability of the method of clinical investigation to sustain the causal inferences that are required to validate the "major" psychoanalytic hypotheses. Thus, I must specify to what hypotheses I apply the labels "major" or "cardinal." Psychoanalytic theory goes well beyond asserting the bare existence of repression in the sense that we banish thoughts from consciousness or deny them entry: We are told that repression plays the crucial *causal* roles of producing neuroses, engendering dreams, and generating a very important subclass of slips

(Grünbaum, 1984, p. 188). Thus, when I speak hereafter of the "major" hypotheses of psychoanalytic theory in the foundational sense, I mean this cardinal trio of causal postulates.

My Scotch verdict ("not proven") on the major psychoanalytic hypotheses was disputed in an important recent paper by Lester Luborsky and his co-workers (1985), fetchingly entitled "A Verification of Freud's Grandest Clinical Hypothesis: The Transference." And Marshall Edelson has similarly demurred both in his vigorous paper "Causal Explanation in Science and in Psychoanalysis" (1986) and in his well-known earlier book *Hypothesis and Evidence in Psychoanalysis* (1984). I shall therefore want to explain just why I dispute the validity of the pivotal psychoanalytic hypothesis that the analysis of the adult patient's *transference* neurosis warrants Freud's *etiologic* reading of infantile sexuality. Such an elucidation has been lacking in my earlier writings.

A considerable number of other analysts have also joined the issue with me. They include several of the 39 contributors to the June 1986 issue of *Behavioral and Brain Sciences* (Grünbaum, 1986), which featured critical commentaries on my (1984) book, as well as my response to them.

In my (1986) "Author's Response" to my critics, I made some concessions to them concerning the following two items: (1) the evidential probity of the clinical data; and (2) the bare possibility that ingenious future psychoanalytic investigators just might come up after all with as yet unimagined clinical research designs, capable of validating the *causal* inferences required to sustain the core of their theory. Let me summarize these concessions.

As to the reliability of the data, I had claimed in my (1984) book that the investigative devices confined to the analytic setting "cannot reliably *sift* or decontaminate the clinical data so as to *identify* those that qualify as authentic" (p. 245). In response to Robert Holt's valuable commentary on this point, I modified my stance as follows:

> If future study of tape-recorded analytic sessions should turn out to be capable of disentangling contaminated data from valid data, as Holt surmises, then I shall appreciatively stand corrected, and will retract especially the statement from *Foundations*

I just cited. I have an important caveat, however. Suppose that Holt's hopes materialize, so that the valid and invalid data are separated. Even then, it may turn out that the vast majority of data needed to support the central psychoanalytic hypotheses are not valid! What then? I do understand that recorded analyses can be, and are being, used in a "relatively rigorous testing" of some kinds of psychoanalytic hypotheses, but I call attention to Holt's own stress on the very modest range of these particular hypotheses. . . .

Holt says: "It needs to be pointed out that most of the research so far conducted on recorded and transcribed psychoanalyses tests *particular* clinical hypotheses [in Benjamin Rubinstein's sense], which concern *individual patients*" [second emphasis added]. That, *I* observe, is still a long way from testing *explanatory* [*general*] psychoanalytic hypotheses as to the causal role of unconscious motives or fantasies in neuroses, dreams, or slips [1986, p. 276].

To this, I should add a further characteristic of *particular* clinical hypotheses, pointed out by Rosemarie Sand. Though some of these hypotheses invoke causal (etiologic) claims peculiar to psychoanalytic theory as such, others rely on causal assumptions made by *common sense* ("folk") psychology. An example of the latter is furnished by a male analyst's inference that a particular teenage female patient's low self-esteem—as manifested by her expectation of contempt from him—was caused by her lifelong awareness of her father's vilifications of her. But instances of the distinctively psychoanalytic subclass of particular clinical hypotheses are provided by Freud's attributions of the Rat-Man's obsessions to *repressions* of childhood hatred for his father. Just what is Sand's point in calling attention to the difference between the specified two subclasses of causal claims? It is that, in at least many cases, the evidential warrant for the commonsense attributions is likely to be much better than for the distinctly psychoanalytic ones. Readers of the psychoanalytic case histories should be mindful of this epistemological difference, so as not to extrapolate credibility from the one set to the other.

My second concession (1986, p. 279) was that I am no more inclined to put a cap on the ingenuity of intraclinical investigators than on that of extraclinical ones.

In Edelson's view (1988, chaps. 12 and 14), the qualifications I made in my Response (1986) definitely do not go far enough. And, in his 1986 paper, he uses his reading of the strategy of causal explanation deployed in Freud's Wolf-Man paper to develop his positive advocacy of the case-study method. He and I are in full agreement on the *heuristic* merits of the psychoanalytic clinical setting as an arena for *generating* hypotheses. Furthermore, we are also united in regarding the so-called "hermeneutic" versions of psychoanalysis as the kiss of death for it, at least *qua* theory of human nature (Edelson, 1988, pp. 246-251; Grünbaum, 1990a). Similarly, for the version put forward by the "descriptive phenomenologist" Karl Jaspers (1973), who was both a philosopher and a psychiatrist. But, as of now, Edelson and I differ on what research *within* the treatment setting can *foreseeably* deliver toward lending credence to the grand hypotheses of the clinical theory.

For the reasons I gave in my (1986) reply to Robert Holt, my focus now will not be on the questionable probity of the clinical data themselves, but rather on the difficulties of validating the important causal inferences of the theory by means of such data, even assuming that they may be taken at face value. In chapter 8 here and in my book (1984, chap. 8), I used Freud's (1909b) Rat-Man case history to illustrate these difficulties as well. But there are other important defects in it, which I have not previously adduced. These further key items from it, as well as salient reasoning in Freud's (1918) account of his Wolf-Man, will serve here, in turn, as additional instructive exemplars of specific fundamental flaws I see in the case-study method. By supplying just enough information on the relevant particulars from each of the two renowned case studies, I hope to enable even readers previously unfamiliar with them to follow the substance of my arguments.

But my arguments below will serve simultaneously to provide important additional grounds for the poverty of the hermeneutic philosophy of psychoanalysis (Grünbaum, 1990a).

According to the so-called "hermeneutic" reconstruction of classical psychoanalytic theory, the received scientific conception of the Freudian enterprise gave much too little explanatory weight to "meaning" connections between unconscious motives and overt symptoms. Thus, in a paper on schizophrenia, the German philosopher and professional psychiatrist Karl Jaspers (1974, p. 91) wrote: "In Freud's work we are dealing in fact with [a] *psychology of meaning*, not *causal explanation* as Freud himself thinks." The father of psychoanalysis, we are told, fell into a "confusion of meaning connections with causal connections." After Jaspers, Paul Ricoeur and Jürgen Habermas have elaborated the patronizing claim that Freud basically misunderstood what he himself had wrought. But it will be a corollary of this chapter that it is they, not Freud, who misconstrued the nature of the psychoanalytic enterprise.

In his book *Freud and Philosophy* (1970, p. 359), Ricoeur informs us that, contrary to Freud, psychoanalytic theory is a hermeneutic endeavor, as opposed to a natural science. Let us note that the noun "hermeneutics" was originally introduced in the seventeenth century as a name for Biblical exegesis, and was then much broadened to characterize *textual* interpretations quite generally. Alas, this term is also used in other senses, along with the adjective "hermeneutic," with resulting loss of clarity. Thus, these terms have been extended to refer to the interpretation of *psychological* phenomena *as such,* which feature mental states whose contents are designated as having "meaning."

Yet obviously, we interpret not only human behavior, thoughts, and feelings, but also such *physical* phenomena as x-ray films, tracks in Wilson cloud chambers and geological strata. In daily life, it is an *interpretation* or hypothesis to say that the table salt I taste at lunch is sodium chloride, just as it is an interpretive hypothesis to infer that a certain eye movement is a flirtatious, sexual gesture. Insofar as merely some kind or other of interpretation is involved, it is simply trivial to note that there is a *similarity* between the interpretation of a written text, on the one hand, and the psychoanalyst's interpretation of the patient's speech and gestures in the doctor's office as having socalled *unconscious "meaning."*

It is true, but unavailing to the hermeneutic reconstruction of psychoanalysis, that the challenge of puzzle solving is presented in *each* of the following two kinds of interpretive activities:

(i) Fathoming the hypothesized unconscious causal factors behind a symptom, dream, or slip by means of psychoanalytic interpretation

(ii) Ferreting out the *semantic* meaning of a *text*.

After all, the common challenge of problem-solving in each of these two cognitive activities hardly allows the assimilation of the quest for socalled *psychoanalytic* meaning to the search for the *semantic* meaning of a text. In particular, the psychoanalytic "meaning" of a symptom or a neurosis is essentially constituted by its *unconscious cause,* whereas the semantic meaning of a word is constituted by its sense and referent. As the analyst Edelson aptly put it: "For psychoanalysis, the *meaning* of a mental phenomenon is a set of unconscious psychological or intentional states. . . . these states would have been present in consciousness, instead of the mental phenomenon requiring interpretation, had they not encountered . . . obstacles to their access to consciousness" (1988, p. 247). In short, precisely because the repression of pertinent psychological states was only partly successful, they crop out in the compromise-formations of symptoms, manifest dream contents and slips. Just these manifestations of the unconscious then become the objects of psychoanalytic *motivational* interpretation. Hermeneuts have tried to invoke the fact that the title of Freud's *magnum opus* is "The Interpretation of Dreams," or, in German, "Die Traumdeutung." The German word for "meaning" is *Bedeutung.* But even in German common sense discourse, that noun, as well as its verb "bedeuten," are each used in both the Freudian motivational sense and in the semantic sense, as shown by the following illustrations:

(i) There is a German song "Ich weiss nicht was soll es *bedeuten,* dass ich so traurig bin"—translated: "I don't know what it *means* that I am so sad." Clearly, the song does not express puzzlement as to the semantic meaning of the term "so sad." Instead, it expresses curiosity as to the motivating psychological cause of the sadness.

(ii) The semantic sense is relevant when someone asks: "What does the word 'automobile' mean?" and receives the answer: "Literally, it means 'self-mover.' " Indeed, the German *Duden* Dictionary discusses a whole array of different uses of the verb "bedeuten," and of its cognate noun "Bedeutung," and in 1956, C.K. Ogden and I.A. Richards even published an entire book entitled *The Meaning of "Meaning."*

But unfortunately, the socalled "hermeneutic" philosophers, such as Ricoeur and Habermas, have fallaciously misused the following combination of facts: (i) The interpretation of a text is, at least in the first instance, the construction of a *semantic* hypothesis as to what it asserts, (ii) When the psychoanalyst bases imputations of unconscious motives to the patient on the patient's speech—rather than on behavioral indicators like weeping or certain gestures—the semantic content of that speech is only an *avenue* to the analyst's etiologic inferences as to the causally explanatory motives, and (iii) There is a school of literary criticism that deemphasizes the reader's aesthetic reaction to the prima facie semantic content of a poem or novel, in favor of biographical and motivational inferences concerning the personality and literary *intent* of the author.

Thus, it is no surprise that Ricoeur misleadingly and fallaciously misdepicted Freud's theory of repression as providing a socalled "semantics of desire," and he did so via misassimilating the following two sets of relations to one another: (i) the way in which the effect of an unconscious cause can manifest it and provide evidence for it, and (ii) the way in which a linguistic symbol represents its referent semantically or designates the attributes of the referent. It is precisely this misassimilation, together with basic misunderstandings of the natural sciences, that has enabled Ricoeur and Habermas to manufacture a methodological pseudo-contrast between the epistemology of causal hypotheses in the natural sciences and the psychoanalyst's search for the socalled unconscious meaning of the patient's symptoms and conduct.

Similarly, in a criticism of my views, the psychologist and hermeneutic Freudian Matthew Erdelyi offered the following platitudinous irrelevancy: "When one establishes the meaning of an unknown word from its context, one does not establish that the context has caused the unknown word" (1986, p. 234). However, this banality enables Erdelyi to overlook that the psychoanalyst generally knows the dictionary meanings of the patient's words, but has the difficult task of using them as merely one avenue to hypothesizing the unconscious causes of the patient's personality dispositions and life history. In short, Erdelyi and his hermeneutic colleagues simply conflate semantic with causally explanatory "meaning."

Their common aim is to make philosophic capital out of their semantic misemphasis by buying absolution for psychoanalytic motivational hypotheses from the criteria of validation that are routinely applied to causal hypotheses in the natural sciences. Yet Freud's interpretations of the unconscious "meanings" of symptoms, dreams, and slips are obviously offered as explanatory causal hypotheses.

Precisely this primacy of causal explanation in the psychoanalytic "interpretation" of the "meaning" of dreams as being causally motivated by unconscious wishes is mistakenly denied by those who seize on Freud's dream theory, and even on his self-analysis, as support for the hermeneutic reconstruction of psychoanalysis. Thus, the intellectual historian Michael Roth (1987) tells us incorrectly:

> *The Interpretation of Dreams* . . . marks a turning point in his [Freud's] thought; it is the start of psycho-analysis as a method and theory of interpretation *rather than as an explanatory theory.* The latter [i.e. providing an *explanatory* account] was an approach that characterized much of his work *prior to* his self-analysis . . . [my italics, Roth, p. 34].

Having miscontrasted psychoanalytic interpretation with psychoanalytic explanation, Roth first offers only obfuscation in his proposed articulation of the contrast, but then later flatly contradicts his allegation of a contrast. Thus, first we learn:

> But what does Freud mean by 'interpretation'? . . . Freud seems to say that everything is a sign or, to put it another way, that everything has meaning, and that meanings can be understood only as the result of a process of interpretation [p. 35].

But, later in the same chapter, Roth writes:

> Dream interpretation, then, revolves around . . . types of free association that aim at discovering the 'wish' within the dream.

The [associative] process that leads backward to the wish—interpretation—is the [temporal] reverse of the process through
which the dream itself was formed [p. 42].

But, the interpretation of the dream via the associative fathoming of its unconscious wish-motive is *of-a-piece* with the *causal
explanation* of the very formation of that dream, which rests on
the hypothesized "process through which the dream itself was
formed" in response to its wish-motive! Ironically, here Roth
seems to acknowledge unwittingly that the interpretation of the
manifest content as betokening a repressed wish-motive for its
formation is tantamount to the causal explanation of just that
content by means of the hidden wish-motive. Indeed, Roth
recognizes explicitly that the interpretation of the dream relies
crucially on Freud's hypothesis that during the dreamer's psychoanalysis, she or he associatively recapitulates *in temporally
inverse order* the causal process of dream production by an unconscious wish. Evidently, the purported associative disclosure
of that causal process is at once the vehicle for the causal explanation and the "interpretation" of the manifest dream content.

Thus, by Roth's own later account, he has offered a mere
pseudo-contrast between psychoanalytic interpretation and
Freudian causal explanation. And his claim that Freud's notion
of dream interpretation "marks a turning point" with respect
to his earlier understanding of psychopathology is erroneous,
if only because Freud conceptualized neurotic symptoms and
manifest dream contents as alike compromise formations (see
chapter 10). Indeed, the logical redundancy of the interpretive
"making sense" of human actions with their causal explanation
is acknowledged, in effect, by the hermeneut James Hopkins,
when he recognizes the causal role of human motives:

Our most basic and familiar way of understanding the activities
of persons—either our own, or those of others—is by interpreting them as actions resulting from motives [footnote omitted]
including beliefs and desires. . . . It is at once interpretive and
explanatory. It is interpretive because . . . assigning motives enables us to make sense of what people say and do. It is explanatory because we take the motives we thus assign to be causes
within persons which prompt their actions, and which, therefore,
serve to explain them [footnote omitted, 1991, p. 88].

When Hopkins says that motives "make sense" of actions as part of the causal explanation of conduct, he is conferring the role of "making sense" on the pertinent *species* of explanatory cause. But one can do likewise in physics: Just as there are motivational causes for our actions, so there are nuclear causes for the nuclear transmutation of hydrogen into helium in the interior of the sun, which results in solar radiation. Similarly, there are electromagnetic causes for the visible refraction of light. Hence we can speak of making nuclear and electromagnetic "sense" of these respective phenomena, no less some speak of making *motivational* sense of symptoms or actions.

Yet, if the ability of psychology to "make sense" of its phenomena renders that discipline "interpretative" or "hermeneutic," then evidently physics too qualifies as "hermeneutic." Then why not abandon the misleading talk about "hermeneutics" as just so much verbal ballast, and reserve that noun for its useful original designation of *biblical exegesis?*

Finally, the psychoanalyst Anthony Storr glaringly and explicitly conflates the psychoanalytic fathoming of the "sense" of a symptom with the semantic activity of understanding language. Thus, leading professional semanticists would undoubtedly be astonished to read the following claim by Storr, which he made in criticism of me: "Freud was a man of genius whose expertise lay in semantics. That is [*sic*], he was able to take the apparently inexplicable problems with which his patients confronted him and make both sense of their symptoms and coherent narratives of their lives" (1986, p. 260). But obviously, when the logician Frege spoke *semantically* of the sense and reference of a word, he was hardly talking about the way in which someone like Freud "made sense" *etiologically* of, say, the symptoms of paranoia as betoking repressed homosexuality.

Hailing the failure of Freud's theory to pass muster *qua* natural science, Ricoeur (1970, p. 358) called for a "counterattack" against those who *deplore* this failure. Finally, in this vein, Habermas (1971) advanced arguments of his own to conclude that Freud had fallen victim to a far-reaching "scientistic self-misunderstanding." The adjective "scientistic" is derogatory, since the noun "scientism" designates a misguidedly utopian, intellectually imperialistic worship of science. Habermas (1984, p. 249,

n. 25) tried to make short shrift of my critique of these theses (chap. 1; Grünbaum, 1984, Introduction), contending that I had made "the simple decision not to consider the hermeneutic character" of psychoanalytic theory. As he sees it, my disregard of the role of so-called hermeneutic meaning in psychoanalysis enabled me to adopt the device of "assimilating Freudian theory to the standard model of unified science, only to reject it for failing to measure up to its standards."

Clearly, there is a basic divergence here as to both the source and the import of Freud's theoretical shortcomings. As Jaspers, Ricoeur, and Habermas would have it, hermeneutic victory can be snatched from the jaws of scientific defeat, once we appreciate that the discernment of so-called meaning connections, as distinct from causal connections, is at the heart of the psychoanalytic enterprise.

The issues raised in this debate go far beyond psychoanalysis. As I shall argue, their proper resolution not only spells a major general moral for the human sciences, including *history*, but also has instructive counterparts in biology and even in physics. After I elucidate the concept of "meaning connection," one of the key lessons I shall draw will be the following: Meaning connections between the mental states of a given person *by themselves never attest* their causal linkage, even if these thematic connections are very strong. Typically, I shall argue, a good deal else is needed to vouch for a causal connection. This precept will emerge, I trust, from my analysis of just how Freud failed in his account of the relations between meaning kinships, on the one hand, and causal linkages, on the other. One important corollary of his miscarriage will be my claim that Freud gave *much too much explanatory weight* to meaning affinities, rather than much *too little* weight, as charged by Jaspers and the hermeneutic critics.

By the same token, we shall see that their diagnosis of his failure hardly rehabilitates psychoanalysis on new, viable hermeneutic foundations. Being a misdiagnosis, it merely baptizes some of Freud's fallacious reasoning by labeling it "hermeneutic science." Besides, Freud often displayed striking intellectual brilliance, even as he drew fallacious causal inferences from

mere meaning bonds. Yet, I submit, his critics from the hermeneutic camp have treated us to a miasma of confusions for the
sake of achieving forced ideological distortions of psychoanalytic theory *and* therapy. Their attempt to force psychoanalysis
onto their Procrustean bed derives, it seems, from their desire
to make the human sciences epistemologically independent
from the sort of cognitive accountability that is featured by the
natural sciences.

But what are the so-called "meaning connections" in this context? And just what are their relations to *causal* connections?
Let me strongly emphasize at the outset that I deplore and
regret the use of the term "meaning" in this context, because
it is ambiguous and lends itself to misleading use. I myself used
it here only because the philosophers I cite have seen fit to
employ it. Therefore, I shall generally speak of "thematic connections" or affinities rather than of "meaning connections."

THE RAT-MAN

Freud candidly reports a series of indoctrinating theoretical
explanations and *rebuttals* he presented to the patient, culminat-
ing in the declaration that repressed *infantile* experiences were
the crucial pathogens of the Rat-Man's obsessions:

> The unconscious, I explained, *was* the infantile; it was that part
> of the self which had become separated off from it in infancy,
> which had not shared the later stages of its development, and
> which had in consequence become *repressed*. It was the derivatives
> of this repressed unconscious that were [etiologically] responsible
> for the involuntary thoughts which constituted his illness [pp.
> 177-178].

Earlier, Freud had set the stage for attributing such decisive
etiologic significance to infancy: "Obsessional neuroses make it
much more obvious than hysterias that the [pathogenic] factors
which go to form a psychoneurosis are to be found in the patient's *infantile* sexual life and not in his present one" (p. 165).
Hence, if Freud's case histories are to bear out these claims, his
clinical evidence must be etiologically cogent with respect to

the hypothesized pertinent infantile episodes, and not just with respect to events in adolescence or adult life. After all, according to his theory, these later experiences qualify only as *precipitating* or other, lesser contributory causes.

What was the content of the obsessions, which the patient had suffered ever since childhood but with special intensity for some years just before seeking Freud's help? "The chief features of his disorder were *fears* that something might happen to two people of whom he was very fond—his father and a lady whom he admired" (p. 158). But, significantly, Freud offers quite distinct explanations for those of the patient's obsessions that featured *rats*, on the one hand, and those that featured his father's *death*, on the other. Indeed, he designates the rat cluster as "The Great Obsessive Fear" (pp. 165-173). Hence, first I shall deal in some detail with only the rat theme, but in due course will then turn to the death motif.

THE RAT THEME

Freud singles out the patient's reports of several episodes, beginning with the one that occasioned his initiative to seek treatment:

1. On a rest stop during military maneuvers, the Rat-Man sat next to an army captain, who *"was obviously fond of cruelty,"* who "had repeatedly defended the introduction of corporal punishment," and who described an oriental punishment in which *rats* are allowed to bore their way into the criminal's *anus* (p. 166). Upon hearing this tale of horror, the "idea" flashed through the patient's mind that someone administered just that rat punishment both to the woman who attracted him and to his father, who had been dead for years by then. But simultaneously, with this fantasy, he thought of a "sanction" he felt driven to adopt in order to prevent its fulfillment (p. 167).

2. During the same military rest stop, he lost his eyeglasses and wired the optician in Vienna to send him another pair c.o.d. by mail. That evening, the same captain handed him a package containing the new glasses, with the admonition that he must repay a certain lieutenant, who had paid the delivery

charges for him. But this demand triggered the thought that such reimbursement would bring the rat punishment upon both his father and lady friend, as well as the sanction that he must therefore refrain from it (p. 168). This sanction, in turn, was negated by the imperative thought that he must reimburse the lieutenant after all.

Yet the patient had already known by then that a young woman clerk at the post office had laid out the c.o.d. charges for him, with the remark that he could be trusted to repay her (p. 172). Freud conjectures that in contemplating amorous adventures upon the completion of his military service, the patient was torn between that female postal clerk and the pretty, inviting daughter of the owner of an inn, located near the post office (p. 211). But why does Freud deem this seemingly commonplace choice significant? He postulates (p. 211) that, for the patient, it was reminiscent of a sexual object choice faced long ago by his father: Prior to marrying the Rat-Man's mother, who was very well-to-do, his father "had made advances to a pretty but penniless girl of humble birth" (p. 198). Later (pp. 216-217), we learn that the Rat-Man's hesitation to marry his long-term inamorata was chiefly a matter of her inability to have children, a reluctance devoid of any economic motive.

3. "Once when the patient was visiting his father's grave he had seen a big beast, which he had taken to be a rat, gliding over the grave. He assumed that it had actually come out of his father's grave, and had just been having a meal off his corpse" (p. 215). In a footnote appended to the first of these two sentences, Freud points out that the beast on the grave was undoubtedly one of the weasels rampant in the Vienna cemetery.

But how did Freud *explain* those of the patient's obsessional thoughts that featured the dreadful rat theme? His etiologic inferences consist of several layers. Let us consider them in turn.

As he notes, "the first problem to be solved was why the two speeches of the Czech captain—his rat story [p. 166], and his request to the patient that he should pay back the money to Lieutenant A. [p. 168]—should have had such an agitating effect on him and should have provoked such violently pathological reactions" (p. 210; square-bracketed inserts in original).

Freud begins with the speculation that "As always happened with the patient in connection with military matters, he had been in a state of unconscious identification with his father, who had seen many years' service [p. 200] and had been full of stories of his soldiering days. Now it happened by chance . . . that one of his father's little adventures had an important element in common with the captain's request" (p. 210). The father had welshed on a gambling debt. In colloquial German, a gambler is designated by the term *Spielratte*, which literally means "play-rat." In the patient's mind, this designation purportedly established an associative connection between repaying money and rats. Freud opines, by way of further conjecture, that the recollection of the father's dereliction "was painful to him, for, in spite of appearances, his unconscious was filled with hostile strictures upon his father's character" (pp. 210-211).

Pleading here, as elsewhere, that he "can only give a very incomplete account of the whole business," Freud then maintains that, in the patient's mind, rats came to represent *money*. As grounds for this, Freud (p. 213) adduces three items: (1) When the patient was presented with the German word *Ratten* ("rats"), he had associatively produced the (phonetically similar) German word *Raten* ("monetary installments"); (2) in his obsessional deliria, the Rat-Man had coined a "regular rat currency" for himself, converting Austrian florins into numbers of rats "by way of the verbal bridge '*Raten—Ratten*' "; and (3) according to Freud's 1908 theory of *anal erotism* (pp. 168-174; see further 1913b, pp. 311-326), money is equated with both dirt and feces. And, in the present instance, Freud ventures the surmise that "What the rat punishment stirred up more than anything else was his *anal erotism*, which . . . had been kept in activity for many years by a constant irritation due to worms. In this way rats came to have the meaning of '*money*' " (p. 213). Moreover, as Freud would have it, the verbal bridge *Spielratte* enabled the captain's demand for repayment "to strengthen the money significance of rats" (p. 214).

In his initial account of the patient's report on the captain's rat tale, Freud offers his interpretation of the "very strange, composite expression" on the patient's face during the report (pp. 166-167). In reading that expression, Freud tells us, "I could only interpret it as one of *horror at pleasure of his own of which he himself was unaware.*" But why was such an interpretation unavoidable? As Freud relates without ado, when the patient spoke of the "idea" in his mind that his girlfriend and his father would become victims of the rat punishment, he had "evidently . . . censored" his report so as to eliminate "the stronger and more significant term 'wish', or rather 'fear' " (p. 167). Similarly, when the patient spoke of his "train of thought" that his father might die, Freud interprets this phrase as a "euphemism" for "wish" (p. 178, n. 1).

At this stage, it is vital, however, to be mindful of a major point: Until Freud can give a further or better reason for postulating the operation of hostile unconscious wishes, he has not even begun to build a case for his crucial subsequent inference that the patient's particular sorts of obsessions are a neurotic *defense* against these wishes. Later on, Freud does indeed offer a further rationale for the existence of the unconscious wishes he had inferred. This rationale includes both presumed events in the patient's early childhood, and the theoretical psychoanalytic principle of precise contrariety. According to that principle, "the unconscious must be the precise contrary of the conscious," such that "every fear corresponded to a former wish which was now repressed" (p. 180). But it will greatly facilitate our scrutiny of Freud's argument to defer the discussion of these further items.

Hence, for now, the important *etiologic* question is why anyone should suppose that the patient's severe *rat obsessions*—with their focus on his girlfriend, father, and money—should have been *engendered* even by the combination of the following factors: the captain's punitive personality, horrendous rat tale, and repayment demand; the patient's quite commonplace problem as to which of two girls to target for amorous pursuit, though purportedly reminiscent of one faced decades earlier by his father; the retrospective shame supposedly felt by the patient in the face of his father's role as a welshing *Spielratte*.

I pose the etiologic question in this way, if only because Freud himself had stated it as the problem of explaining why the captain's rat tale and repayment demand "should have provoked such violently pathological [obsessive] reactions" (p. 210). Remarkably enough, Freud himself tells us that a causal attribution of the patient's obsessions to the combination of these several factors alone overtaxed his own inferential credulity:

> Yet, in spite of all this wealth of material, no light was thrown upon the meaning [unconscious cause] of his obsessional idea until one day the Rat-Wife in Ibsen's *Little Evolf* came up in the analysis, and it became impossible to escape the inference that in many of the shapes assumed by his obsessional deliria, rats had another meaning still—namely, that of *children* [p. 215].

Thus, Freud allows that even the "wealth of material" he has adduced so far is etiologically unilluminating. One must share this bleak assessment of explanatory merit, if only because much of the information he has given us is itself a tissue of psychoanalytic *speculations*, ill-suited for contributing evidentially to the support of an explanatory etiologic hypothesis. For example, I regard as altogether farfetched, if not frivolous, the suggestion that the "rat" theme struck by the *word Spielratte* should make any contribution *at all* to forging a *causal link* from the patient's presumed feelings about his father's welshing to his severe rat obsession. It seems to me that almost any proposed causal account, however implausible, could be spuriously but greatly padded by assembling all sorts of allusive examples of this sort. And it would only beg the etiologic question at issue to retort, as other analysts have done, that the unconscious operates dynamically in just such allusive, illogical ways.

But if, as Freud allows, the wealth of prior material throws "no light" upon the cause (or unconscious "meaning") of the rat obsessions, how did the putative link between rats and *children* enable him to fathom the still missing, crucial pathogenic factors? As he sees it, the patient's childhood experience contained the essential etiologic scenario: At the age of 3 or 4, he had misbehaved *like a rat*, had been soundly beaten for it by his father, and had therefore borne him an abiding unconscious hatred ever since. As the patient had repeatedly heard from his mother, upon being punished for his naughty conduct, he had flown into a terrible rage, hurling abuse upon his father even while receiving his blows. When questioned anew, the mother "confirmed the story, adding . . . that he had been given the punishment because he had *bitten* some one," perhaps his nurse (p. 206). Freud elaborates on the dual theme of biting and punishment:

> The notion of a rat is inseparably bound up with the fact that it has sharp teeth with which it gnaws and bites. But rats cannot be sharp-toothed, greedy and dirty with impunity: they are cruelly persecuted and mercilessly put to death by man, as the patient had often observed with horror. He had often pitied the poor creatures. But he himself had been just such a nasty, dirty little wretch, who was apt to bite people when he was in a rage, and had been fearfully punished for doing so. He could truly be said to find a living likeness of himself in the rat. It was almost as though Fate, when the captain told him his story, had been putting him through an association test: she had called out a complex stimulus-word [see p. 210 n.], and he had reacted to it with his obsessional idea [pp. 215-216].

Freud then explicitly draws an *etiologic* inference partly from the *thematic kinship* between the culpability of roguish *biting*, on the one hand, and the intolerability of a *rat's* gnawing behavior, on the other. As he reasoned, the patient's latent memory of the cruel paternal castigation for biting had engendered repressed hostility toward the father. This antagonism, in turn, had engendered the *unconscious wish*—and thereby the *conscious fear*—that the father undergo the monstrous oriental punishment of anal rat penetration.

In brief, Freud sees the rat obsessions as the patient's *neurotic defense* against his own unacceptable punitive wishes toward his father. But assuming the occurrence of the punitive childhood scenario, the important issue of causation posed by this inference is *not* whether the severe paternal castigation for biting engendered hatred toward the father; instead the etiologic issue is whether that particular presumed hatred was the pathogen of the obsessive fear of the father's victimization by the oriental punishment. Therefore, when we address that issue in due course, we shall have to ask the following question: If we grant the existence of a causal link between the punitive childhood experience and hatred toward the father, does it support at all the etiologic hypothesis that this hatred, in turn, was the pathogen of the rat obsessions?

Freud sums up by encapsulating his belief in the etiologic contribution made by the stated thematic affinity: "According, then, to his earliest and most momentous experiences, rats were children" (p. 216). For good measure, Freud then adds that the patient "was extraordinarily fond of children," and that "the interest he was bound to feel in children" is "fully explained" by the infertility of his inamorata, whom he was therefore reluctant to marry (pp. 216-217). But here this piece of information is irrelevant, because it does nothing toward *linking* children to rats. And, as padding for Freud's case, it taxes the critical reader's patience even more than the prior play on the word *Spielratte*.

Yet, let us be mindful of Freud's decisive inferential leap to the hypothesized etiology of the rat obsessions, which occurs in his concluding aforecited declaration "and he [the patient] had reacted to it [the word "rat"] with his obsessional idea." Helpfully, Freud elaborates on his rationale for having made his theoretical leap. To unfold his more detailed etiologic scenario, he admittedly relies on his theories of infantile sexuality and of (dream) symbolism, reiterating that the rat obsession became pathogenically explicable only via the notion that rats represented children, besides money.

Besides conveying cruel lasciviousness, the punitive captain's rat tale activated both the patient's anal erotism (p. 213) and his unconscious memory of his traumatic childhood punishment for biting at the hands of his indignant father (p. 217). By being evocative of the cruel father, the captain also became a target of the Rat-Man's resurgent animosity. Somewhat more cautiously, Freud then infers that the patient's fleetingly conscious idea of the rat punishment besetting someone he liked "is probably to be translated into a wish such as 'You ought to have the same thing done to you!' aimed at the teller of the story, but through him at his father" (p. 217). Yet, in order to take his decisive etiologic leap, Freud invokes his principle of precise contrariety: The patient's obsessive *fears* of someone's infliction of the rat punishment upon his father and on his inamorata, we are told, are his *neurotic defense* against his own

unacceptable punitive wishes toward them, wishes whose existence Freud had previously inferred somewhat tentatively.

It emerges that his etiologic account turns fundamentally on
a cardinal thesis: The stated several *thematic affinities* between
the childhood castigation for *biting* and the tale of the *rat* punishment attested to the *causal linkage* between the punishment
and the obsessive fears, featuring rats in either a punitive or
chewing role. Hence I must examine the warrant for that key
thesis. In order to do so, let me first consider more generally
the special *further* conditions under which thematic affinity does
indeed warrant causal inferences.

As I shall illustrate presently, thematic kinships are not only
of various sorts but are also encountered in *varying degrees*,
ranging from very high to very tenuous. Yet it will be crucial
to appreciate the following impending moral: Even when the
thematic kinship is indeed of very high degree, it does not *itself*
license the inference of a causal linkage between the thematically kindred events. Thus, we shall consider a series of examples in their bearing on the inferrability of the causal relatedness among events or states featuring various sorts of
affinities or isomorphisms. A number of these examples are
deliberately drawn from areas *remote* from psychoanalysis.
Thereby, it will become clear that the issue of such inferrability
arises in a wide range of fields: What are the grounds for claiming that thematically kindred events are causally connected,
rather than akin just *by chance*?

1. Upon reading a young student's 10-page paper, the course
instructor notices that not only the details of its argument but
even its wording is uncannily reminiscent of an old encyclopedia article. Indeed, it turns out that the two texts agree verbatim. And despite the student's protestation of the originality of
his wording, the instructor confidently charges plagiarism.

Of course, this indictment relies on the *causal inference* that
the student had cribbed his paper. But what is the justification
for this inference? It is pertinent to spell out the implicit background knowledge on which it relies.

Consider all hand or typewritten texts exceeding, say, 2,500
words. In this class, focus on two subsets: (A) those which their

authors generated entirely by endeavoring to produce a verbatim transcription of another text; and (B) texts not produced entirely—or almost entirely—by *copying* from another one. As we know, people make errors of transcription. Hence, in subclass A, the frequency (probability) of verbatim agreement between two or more texts is not 100 percent, though it is rather high. By contrast, the incidence of verbatim agreement in subclass B is zero. Indeed, *every* case of verbatim agreement is produced by copying. Speaking elliptically, we can say that verbatim agreement is surely not a case of *"mere chance"* coincidence (correlation). Naturally, that's why the instructor was entitled to charge plagiarism.

But the moral I am concerned to draw from this otherwise trivial example is as follows: The instructor's entitlement to draw the causal inference that the student had cribbed the paper does *not* derive from the *mere* thematic affinity inherent in the verbatim agreement of the texts; instead, that inference relies crucially on the *additional* fact that essentially every case of verbatim agreement results from copying.

2. A tourist looking at an otherwise desolate beach notes that the sand reveals a string of configurations exhibiting the same shapes as the left and right shoes worn by humans. In short, the tourist observes a *geometric isomorphism*—or "thematic affinity"—between the sand configurations and the shoes. And he will then infer that a person wearing shoes had walked on the beach.

Yet the lesson of this example is essentially the same as that of the first one: The striking geometric kinship between the two shapes does not itself suffice to license the tourist's inference that the foot*like* configurations were, in fact, caused (produced) by the impact of human feet on the beach. To draw that inference, the tourist avails himself of a crucial piece of *additional* information: Footlike beach formations in the sand never or hardly ever result from the "mere chance" collocation of sand particles under the action of the air, such as some gust of wind. This further finding is thus that, within the class of beaches, the incursion of a pedestrian into the beach *makes the difference* between the absence and presence of the foot-like beach formations.

Just as the course instructor invoked the overwhelming probability that verbatim agreement of texts was *not* a matter of mere chance, so also the tourist relies on a like probability in drawing the *causal* inference that the sandy simulacrum of a human foot is, in fact, actually the trace or mark left by a human foot, and thus a *bona fide* foot*print* (Grünbaum, 1984, p. 63).

3. Two significantly different dreams will now serve to show that reliance on *mere* thematic "content connections" to draw causal inferences is a snare and a delusion. This moral will, of course, also apply to Freud's dream theory as a special case. In the first of the two dream examples, we shall have license to draw the causal inference that the manifest dream content was shaped by a salient component of the dreamer's waking experience on the day before. And this warrant will be seen to derive from reasoning of just the sort I articulated *à propos* of the case of *verbatim* agreement and of the footprint.

But my point in giving this dream example will be to contrast it with another kind: one in which it is demonstrably fallacious to invoke a content connection (thematic kinship) between the waking experience of the previous day and the manifest dream content as a basis for inferring a causal linkage between them. And the latter dream illustration will be only one of several that will exhibit the serious pitfalls of causal inferences in psychoanalysis that rely on mere thematic affinity. Without causal hypotheses, psychoanalytic dream theory is explanatorily sterile, since it claims to account for dream formation and instigation. Yet thematic "meaning connections" *as such* are the stock-in-trade of those champions of hermeneutics who are eager to nail psychoanalysis to their mast.

Let us turn to the first of my dream examples. The dreamer is a woman named Agnes. The night after her first visit to Frank Lloyd Wright's famous house "Falling Water" (in Ohiopyle, PA), she dreams about a house *just like it*, down to many of the fine details of its interior appointments. It is important that Agnes had never heard of Falling Water until the day of her visit, let alone seen a picture or description of it. Crucially, the very first time that Agnes's manifest dream content ever contained a simulacrum of Falling Water was the night after her daytime visit to that Frank Lloyd Wright house. It would seem that Agnes's visit *made a difference* to her having that dream. But this conclusion is *not* vouch-safed by the mere thematic affinity, though strong, between the mansion and her dream.

A psychologist concerned with explaining dream content can legitimately infer that her visit to Falling Water was causally relevant to the presence of a simulacrum of that mansion in her dream. And the warrant derives essentially from J. S. Mill's joint method, being analogous to that in the case of the footprint. But now consider a related dream example with the opposite inferential moral.

4. Assume that last night my manifest dream content included the image of some kind of house or other. In my urban life, I routinely see and frequent houses of some sort almost daily. Thus, my impressions on the day before this dream featured visual and tactile impressions of at least one dwelling. Indeed, over the years, on the day before a dream, my waking experience practically always includes seeing some domicile or other, *regardless of whether the ensuing manifest dream content then features the image of an abode or not!* In *this* case, unlike that of Agnes, seeing a house during the day does *not* make any difference to dreaming about a house the night after.

Evidently, when a house of some kind is an element of my manifest dream, the mere generic presence of a house theme in the prior day's waking experience does not meet the key requirement for being causally relevant to the presence of a house image in the dream: Seeing a house on the day before a dream does not divide the class of the day's waking experiences on the prior day into two subclasses such that the probabilities (frequencies) of the appearance of a house in the next dream *differ* as between the two subclasses. Indeed, precisely because I see houses practically daily, year in and out, my seeing a house on the day before a dream does not even divide the class of my waking experiences on the prior day into two subclasses. *A fortiori*, there is no division such that the two subclasses exhibit different probabilities of the stated sort. On the other hand, in Agnes's case, just these requirements for causal relevance are met.

Thus, there is a sharp contrast with the situation in the Falling Water dream: When some house image occurs in my dream last night, it is a mistake to attribute that image causally to my having seen one or more houses yesterday. In sum, despite their thematic affinity, it is eminently reasonable to conclude that the presence of the generic house theme both in yesterday's daytime experience and in last night's dream was a happenstance, rather than a case of causal linkage.

At this point, the reader may be shaking her (his) head in disbelief by having gotten the impression that my denial of causal relevance in the second dream example overlooks a rather obvious point: People might never have dreamt about houses *at all*, unless they had seen one before.

To avoid a misunderstanding of this denial of causal relevance, we need to distinguish between a *mere* necessary condition for the occurrence of an event, and a factor causally relevant to its occurrence. For example, breathing is a necessary condition for being paranoid, since it is required even for being alive; but breathing is hardly causally relevant to developing paranoia: Since nonparanoiacs breathe no less than paranoiacs do, breathing does not affect the incidence of paranoia. In short, breathing does make a difference to being alive, but not to developing paranoia.

Thus, in the case of dreaming, I do allow for the following necessary condition: People might never have dreamed about any house, unless they had seen one at some time or other in their lives. Yet, just as in the example of breathing and paranoia, this *mere* necessary condition for a house dream does not qualify as a causally relevant condition. To take another analogy: It is a necessary condition for dying to have been born earlier; yet a person's prior birth is not *also* causally relevant to his or her death, since all mortals alike were born, and the probability of death at some particular time is not affected by it (cf. Salmon, 1984, p. 128). By the same token, in the context of dreams as well, a state of type X may be a *necessary condition* for the occurrence of some other sort of state Y, although X is not causally relevant to Y. On the other hand, there is evidence that when women are going through a divorce, their dreams are thematically affected by it in a causally relevant way.

True enough, in the case of the generic house dream now at issue, the thematic affinity between the day's waking experience and the next dream is clearly much weaker than in the Falling Water example. But recall my earlier *caveat* that even in those examples featuring very strong thematic affinity, the mere presence of a very high degree of such kinship was quite insufficient to validate the causal linkage. Hence it would be quite wrong to believe that causal inferrability goes hand-in-hand with a high *degree* of *mere* thematic kinship.

An interesting psychoanalytic example of thematic affinity *without causal relevance* is furnished by Freud's ill-founded etiologic use of Otto Rank's notion of birth-trauma. Presumably, the baby's individuation and *separation* from the mother at birth was traumatic and anxiety-laden. But all humans alike undergo that traumatic anxiety, regardless of whether they are born normally or by Caesarean section à la Macduff in Shakespeare's *Macbeth*. Yet Freud invoked the thematic recapitulation of the presumed birth-anxiety in the later anxieties of adult life to claim that the early *universal* human experience accounts causally for the later one (1910b, p. 173). Here again the mere thematic connection between the earliest and later experience does not meet the requirements for the causal relevance of the former to the latter, since the required difference in probabilities is not involved.

5. As we know from American history, Thomas Jefferson and John Adams, who had been friends, died within a few hours of each other on the 50th anniversary of the Declaration of Independence, written by Jefferson with the aid of a draft to which Adams had contributed. Within the reference class of, say, long-term friends, the temporal proximity of events having the thematic affinities of death, careers in politics, and co-authorship is quite improbable. Nonetheless, I dare say that no professional historian would infer the existence of a causal linkage between the two deaths.

Nor would it do to infer that there was an *indirect* causal connection between these deaths, such that each of them is a partial effect of one and the same shared cause. Thus, even if there were both a God and a Satan, there is no basis for seeing the hand of either in the multiple correlations between the two deaths. On the other hand, a *common cause* is indeed implicated in the familiar fact that the probability of a storm occurring soon after a sudden barometric drop is appreciably greater than the probability of a storm in general: A pressure drop over a wider area is the *common cause* of both the sharp barometric drop and the storm, which are thereby linked indirectly. Thus, their common cause accounts for the positive statistical relevance of falling barometer readings to storms, as expressed by the stated comparison of the probabilities.

Instead of calling for such a common cause explanation, Jefferson's death and John Adams's demise call for *separate* causal explanations. The conjunction of these explanations may then also account for the otherwise improbable coincidence of the two deaths. In a recent article, Sober (1987) gave two other interesting types of examples to show that "Correlations, *per se*, do not cry out for common cause explanation."

6. As he points out in a case drawn from evolutionary theory (p. 466), there is a method of inference (so-called "cladistic parsimony") that operates on the following principle: When species match with respect to ancestral characteristics—which is one kind of thematic affinity—this similarity is not evidence of common descent; yet a match in regard to derived characteristics—which is another sort of thematic affinity—does qualify as evidence of a shared genealogy. Thus, "the mere existence of a [thematic] correlation between the traits of two species is not enough to justify a claim of common descent" (p. 466). In a still more recent and more extensive study, Sober (1988) has dealt with the problem of inferring common ancestry among species as a mere instance of the more general problem of just when one should postulate common causes. Sober's moral is to issue some important caveats in regard to the inferrability of a common cause. He develops this lesson by reference to a number of defects he claims to have detected in the "principle of the common cause" espoused by Reichenbach (1956, chap. IV, §19) and Salmon (1984, chap. 6).

7. Sober's other example (1987, p. 465) is furnished by the positive correlation between the cost of bread in England and the Venetian sea level: Both of the quantities have increased monotonically with time. However, this quantitative affinity

hardly betokens that it resulted from a common cause. Here again, *mere* affinity does not even warrant the presumption of such an indirect causal connection, let alone the inference of a direct linkage.

8. In the history of medical treatment, *mere* thematic affinity has sometimes been taken to betoken or presage therapeutic efficacy, much as a sign may attest to something. Thus, in the sixteenth century, Paracelsus gave the following advice: To cure the liver, treat with a herb that is shaped like a liver (Hacking, 1975, p. 42).[1] Nowadays, this inference of causal relevance strikes us as primitive, rather than as quaint. But I claim that its logical defects are no worse that those of causal inferences from *mere* thematic connections, which abound in many clinical case histories.

9. My final example comes from the weighty lesson spelled for etiologic inference by the explanatory fiasco in the case of Breuer's historic patient Anna O. (Bertha Pappenheim).

In 1896, Freud used the mere thematic affinity between a patient's particular experience and one of her individual symptoms to illustrate the suitability of the given repressed experience as an explanatory etiologic determinant of the pertinent symptom (1896, pp. 193-194; Grünbaum, 1984, pp. 149-150). In particular, he gives the following example:

> Let us suppose that the symptom under consideration is hysterical vomiting; in that case we shall feel that we have been able to understand its causation (except for a certain [hereditary] residue) if the analysis traces the symptom back to an experience which *justifiably produced a high amount of disgust*—for instance, the sight of a decomposing dead body [1896, pp. 193-194].

In short, on the basis of *mere* thematic affinity, Freud construes the symptom etiologically as outwardly *expressing* the aversion felt during the repressed disgusting experience. Was this construal warranted?

A very instructive answer is furnished by the case of the aversive affinity between Anna O.'s inability to drink water, and

---

[1] I am indebted to Wesley Salmon for this reference.

the traumatic disgust she had felt silently on seeing a companion's dog lapping water from a glass (Breuer and Freud, 1893, pp. 6-7; Freud, 1893, pp. 29-30). For his part, Breuer himself, we know, had the wisdom *not* to adduce the aversive kinship *itself* as his evidence for inferring that the repression and affective strangulation of the traumatic disgust had been the specific pathogen of Anna O.'s hysterical inability to drink (Grünbaum, 1984, pp. 177-180). Instead, he pointed to allegedly positive therapeutic results from his cathartic treatment as his evidence, rather than to the thematic kinship of aversion. But, as we know from Ellenberger's research (1970, pp. 483-484; 1972), Breuer's treatment of this patient was a therapeutic fiasco instead of a "talking cure" (Hirschmüller, 1989). Ellenberger put it in a nutshell: "Indeed, the famed 'prototype of a cathartic cure' was neither a cure nor a catharsis" (1972, p. 279). And, as I have argued elsewhere in detail (1984, pp. 180-184), Breuer's therapeutic failure showed that he had not removed the pathogens of Anna O.'s aversion to drinking water or of her other symptoms. Moreover, we know from Jung that Freud was quite aware of this debacle. Yet, as we recall, Freud told us that if we can uncover a disgusting experience, its mere aversive affinity to hysterical vomiting tells us "that we have been able to understand [the] . . . causation" of the vomiting.

Even the Anna O. episode alone should have given Freud much pause when he felt tempted to invoke such "meaning connections" as a justification for etiologic inferences. Alas, as we can now see very clearly, Freud did not heed that particular sobering moral from the demise of the cathartic theoretical edifice. Thus, we recall, in his Rat-Man case, he appealed to the thematic kinship between the punitive biting episode and the adult rat obsessions, even as he succumbed to the explanatory blandishment of an inferred etiologic linkage between them. But, as is now clear from the analysis of the preceding eight examples, the thematic connection adduced by Freud does not vouch for the etiologic role of the paternal punishment in the pathogenesis of the rat obsessions. And Freud simply begs the etiologic question here by trading on thematic affinity. Nor did Freud give any cogent reason for inferring the pathogenicity of the castigation by the father, if—in addition to the prior punitive biting episode—we also include the father's role as a "play-rat" (*Spielratte*), as well as the other thematically cognate events, such as the patient's concept of a rat currency. For, as we learned from the cases of *verbatim* agreement, the footprint and the Falling Water dream, none of these additional rat-theme-laden events go beyond thematic affinities to furnish cogent evidence for the *causal relevance* of these prior episodes to the rat obsessions, *even collectively*. Far from validating Freud's etiologic inferences, even a wealth of thematic affinities is quite insufficient to support the claim that the thematically cognate antecedents *made a difference* to the *occurrence* of the rat obsessions.

Inferences from thematic kinships play a pervasive role not only in picking out certain sorts of repressed ideation as the pathogens of neuroses, but also in other uses of free associations: (1) Selecting repressed infantile wishes from the glut of unconscious "dream thoughts" as the cardinal motives of dreams; and (2) picking out "motives of unpleasure" as the specific causes of slips from the plethora of thoughts uncovered when a patient freely associates to the content of a slip.

I have argued that it is always fallacious to infer a causal linkage between thematically kindred events from their *mere* thematic kinship. Yet, as illustrated by my example of Agnes's dream about Frank Lloyd Wright's Falling Water mansion (example 3), the existence of a strong content connection (high degree of thematic kinship) between two mental events, or two series of such events, hardly militates against there *also* being a causal linkage between them. Indeed, as shown by the example of verbatim syntactic and semantic agreement between two student papers (example 1), the direct or indirect causal linkage between them can be perspicuously lawlike. Thus, Freud should *not* be faulted for asserting, in principle, that some mental events can be linked *both* thematically *and* causally, though he mistakenly claimed entitlement to *infer* the latter linkage from the former alone. And when he explicitly asserted such entitlement, he was fully clear on the *distinction* between thematic connections and causal connections.

Yet, as noted above, Karl Jaspers (1974, p. 91) chides Freud: "In Freud's work we are dealing in fact with *psychology of meaning*, not *causal explanation* as Freud himself thinks." But since causal relevance is entirely compatible with thematic or "meaning" relevance, Jaspers's objection to Freud here rests on a pseudo-antithesis of either-or (cf. Grünbaum, 1984, pp. 69-83). Thus, there is no merit in Jaspers's indictment of Freud as having incurred a "confusion of meaningful connexions with causal connexions" (1974, p. 91), nor in his claim that "Freud's psychoanalysis" as being vitiated by "a misunderstanding of itself" (1974, p. 80), a patronizing charge echoed later on by Jürgen Habermas's equally ill-founded complaint of "scientistic self misunderstanding" (cf. Grünbaum, 1984, pp. 2-43; Jaspers, 1973, part 3, pp. 374-385).

As against these philosophers, it emerges from Freud's inferential failings that he gave *much too much* explanatory weight to thematic affinities, rather than too little, as they have charged. Indeed, mere meaning connections tell us nothing about the supposed unconscious *motives* or causes for symptom formation, dream genesis and the provenance of Freudian slips. Yet such a motivational account is precisely what psychoanalytic theory claims to offer.

I draw a twofold moral for the human sciences from my stated criticisms of Freud, and of his hermeneutic critics: (1) Let us indeed be alert to thematic connections, but beware of their beguiling causal pitfalls. *A fortiori* (2), narratives replete with mere hermeneutic elucidations of thematic affinities are explanatorily sterile or bankrupt; at best, they have literary and reportorial value; at worst, they are mere cock-and-bull stories. Patronizing hermeneutic sermons by Jaspers et al. against alleged scientistic misunderstandings of the role of meanings do nothing for the fruition of the psychoanalytic enterprise, or for any other *explanatory* theories of human psychology or of history. What they do, however, is foster *ideological hostility* to scientific thought. As I am concerned to show in this chapter, after a veritable cornucopia of brilliantly articulated meaning connections in Freud's case history of the Rat-Man, a validated etiology of the patient's obsessions remains deeply obscure to this very day—similarly for the Wolf-Man.

If the hermeneutic philosophers of psychoanalysis *do* countenance Freud's causal claims, how can they possibly hope to validate them other than by the methods familiar from the

natural sciences, which they decry? Ricoeur (1981, p. 263) belat-
edly, albeit *inadequately*, recognized the *causal* character of psychoanalytic motivational explanations, after having speciously
denied it in his book *Freud and Philosophy* (1970, pp. 359-360).
But the grudging, tendentious character of this recognition
soon becomes evident. As Ricoeur tells us, psychoanalytic theory "requires that the hermeneutics of self-understanding [in
terms of a narrative highlighting meaning connections] take
the detour of causal explanation" (1981, p. 264). Here the
grudging, loaded term "detour" is quite misleading as to the
content of psychoanalytic theory. Imagine a philosopher of human physiology saying that when our blood circulates between
our head and our feet, it takes "the detour" through our heart
pump! Moreover, which of Freud's case histories, I ask, illustrate Ricoeur's purported "detour"*qua* detour?

Thus the hermeneutic philosophers have tried to force psychoanalysis onto the Procrustean bed of their preconceived
philosophic notions about the human sciences. To implement
this program, they begged the epistemological questions by simply downgrading those features of the Freudian corpus that
did not fit their prior philosophic doctrines. And, as a normative recipe for the human sciences, their program seems to me
to darken counsel.

Carlo Strenger's (1991) *Between Hermeneutics and Science* devotes considerable attention to my writings (1984, 1986). In
regard to my (1984) book, he states that it offers "a critique of
the evidential foundations of psychoanalysis, unprecedented in
its clarity and incisiveness." But due to the length of the time
interval that elapsed between his completion of his 1991 book
and its publication, he was unable to take account of my 1988
and 1990 papers, from both of which I drew the present chapter 4. Yet these earlier papers contain a critique of hermeneutics going substantially beyond my 1984 arguments against it.

Therefore, I do not know whether this new critique would
incline Strenger to weaken the following description he gave of
his book: "The bulk of this essay (chapters 3 to 6) is an attempt
to present versions of claims of the hermeneuticist conception
of psychoanalysis, which stand up to the sharp critique it has
been subjected to by Grünbaum" (Strenger, 1991, p. 5).

In any case, Strenger's book does not offer a quasi-herme-neuticist gloss on the psychoanalytic theory of human nature at large, but confines itself largely to what he sees as a distinctly *post*-Freudian therapeutic strategy. Yet even within this limitation, it is unclear to what extent the kind of commonsense psychology he invokes is psychoanalytic in substance rather than primarily in name.

I must defer any further, more specific discussion of his welcome book to another occasion, since it was published just as the present monograph went to press.

THE PATERNAL DEATH MOTIF

As we recall, the patient's obsessions were not confined to the dreadful rat theme. They had also featured fears that his father might die. Indeed, the Rat-Man told Freud that thoughts of his father's death had often occupied him from a very early age, with depressing results. And such obsessional fears plagued him even when his father had already been dead for some years (1909b, p. 162). Remarkably enough, however, Freud does not offer the patient's repressed resentment of the paternal punishment for biting to explain his obsessional fears of the father's death, although these fears focused on the father no less than those featuring the father's falling prey to the rat punishment. And as Freud told us, the crucial pathogen of the rat obsession was furnished by repressed hostility toward the father, engendered by the unconscious memory of the cruel paternal castigation for biting. Why then was Freud not satisfied to adduce just that hostility as well to explain the patient's obsessive fears of the father's demise? If that antagonism actually generated the unconscious wish and conscious fear that the father undergo the monstrous oriental punishment of anal rat penetration, why not also the wish/fear that he be dead? In particular, why did Freud postulate instead a repressed paternal castigation for the *sexual* offense of *masturbation* to explain the obsessive fears of paternal death (pp. 205-206), while being satisfied to attribute the rat obsessions to the punishment for biting, a misdeed which he described as a "commonplace piece of naughtiness of a non-sexual nature" (p. 207 n.; cf. also p. 206)? Was it perhaps because rats are biting creatures and are thus thematically cognate to the castigation for *biting* in a way in which the father's death is not? No, that was not Freud's reason.

At first glance, it might seem that—by Freud's own standards of etiologic inference—there is some plausibility in his rationale for a separate sexual explanation of the obsessive fears of the father's demise. Freud called attention to evidence of a father-son conflict that intrudes into the son's erotic life. Thus we learn (p. 201): "Several years after his father's death [when the patient was 26 years old; pp. 256-257], the first time he experienced the pleasurable sensations of copulation, an idea sprang into his mind: 'This is glorious! One might murder one's father for this!'" The Rat-Man's thought that patricide might be a ticket to copulatory joy suggests that he saw his father as an obstacle to sexual fulfillment. The patient's own first report of imagining his father's death à propos of his love for a girl pertained to an episode at age 12 (p. 178), and he related recurrences of that thought from the times when he was 20 and 22 years old (p. 181). Freud then *extrapolated* the existence of this hostile idea backward into the patient's very early childhood (p. 183): "This wish (to get rid of his father as being an interference) must have originated . . . in his very early childhood . . . before he had reached the age of six . . . and things must have remained in the same state ever since."

It will turn out to be relevant to distinguish episodes in which the patient juxtaposed or linked his own erotic fulfillment with thoughts of his father's *death* from episodes in which no paternal death motif is involved, although they feature both sex and his father. Only a subclass of the former involve obsessive fears of the father's demise. As to the former, we can add the following example to those just mentioned: Six months before the father's death, when the patient was financially unable to marry the woman he loved, the idea had occurred to him that the father's demise might remove this financial obstacle; thereupon, however, he had wished not to get any inheritance as compensation for the loss of his parent (p. 179). But it is not altogether clear that such a reflection by a financially pressed son is a sign of hatred toward a parent, although its crass materialism apparently left the patient with guilt feelings. In the published text, Freud reports in italics that "shortly after his father's death," at age 21 the patient was overcome by "an impulsion towards masturbatory activities" (p. 203). But in the Original Record, Freud had put the same masturbatory episode in a rather different light: "He [the patient] began it [masturbation] when he was about 21—after his father's death, as I got him to confirm—because he had heard of it and felt a certain curiosity" (p. 261). It would seem that whereas the Original Record does not insinuate a causal linkage between the father's death and the patient's avowedly transitory self-gratification, Freud edited the text so as to contain just such a suggestion: He inserted the word "shortly" before the phrase "after his father's death" and left out the original qualifying word "about" before the age "21." Furthermore, Freud's private process notes tell us that the patient had not volunteered any temporal juxtaposition of his father's death with the onset of his passing autoerotic activities, but that Freud had coaxed it out of him. Nor do these notes provide any basis for Freud's published tendentious phrase "an impulsion towards masturbatory activities came over him [the patient]." All in all, therefore, there is little reason, if any, to interpret the pertinent temporal sequence as evidence for inferring that the patient took his father's death to be license for seeking erotic fulfillment, previously thwarted by paternal interference.

In the published case history, we are told that, once the Rat-Man's father was no longer alive, the patient nonetheless had the fantasy that he might reappear (p. 204). And, in the wake of such a fantasy, he would open the door late at night—as if to give his father access to his apartment—and would then take out his penis to look at it in the mirror (p. 204). The Original Record adds that, at the time, he was concerned that his penis may be too small, but was reassured by an ensuing partial erection (p. 302). Then, frightened by his own recognition of the pathological nature of his idea of permitting access to his dead father, he "freed himself from it by means of the thought 'if I do this [sexual mirror inspection], it will do my father harm' " (p. 303).

Now, in his process notes, Freud *interprets* this set of events as indicating that when the patient expected a visit from his father, "he carried out what he himself regarded as a substitute for masturbation, and thus defied his father" (p. 303). But is this interpretation clearly warranted? Why, for example, was it not a homosexual play for his father? And, furthermore, is the Rat-Man's own delusional idea that his sexual ritual would harm his dead father cogent evidence that his defiant hatred was actually the pathogen of his obsessive fears of his father's death? Freud himself gives us enough information to raise several objections.

Interestingly enough, as we learn from the process notes, the father was by no means the only person whom the patient imagined to be harmed by his own erotic activity: "When he [the Rat-Man] first masturbated he had the idea that it would result in an injury to someone he was fond of (his [female] cousin)" (p. 280). Moreover, "The patient had a charming little niece of whom he was very fond. One day this idea came into his head: '*If you indulge in intercourse, something will happen to Ella*' (i.e. she will die)" (p. 226). Besides, even in the case of his father, he thought that his own *non*sexual conduct too could bring harm: "His idea was . . . that if his father were alive he would be harmed by his laziness" (p. 300). And in the case of one Dr. P., the patient thought that his own mere wish that P. be dead could kill him (p. 299). Thus, he believed quite generally that his love and his hate were omnipotent (p. 234), declaring "my affects are omnipotent" (p. 279).

Indeed, he was convinced that this omnipotence was not even confined to just his affects:

> If he thought of someone, he would be sure to meet that very person immediately afterwards, as though by magic. If he suddenly asked after the health of an acquaintance whom he had not seen for a long time, he would hear that he had just died, so that it would look as though a telepathic message had arrived from him. If, without any really serious intention, he swore at some stranger, he might be sure that the man would die soon afterwards, so that he would feel responsible for his death [1913c, p. 86].

Clearly, sexual activity is hardly the only kind that triggers the patient's ominous premonitions. Nor do these forebodings of doom seem to focus with conspicuously greater frequency on his father than on others, not even in regard to the portent of death, although he may have felt them to be more intrusive when they featured his father. Then why suppose that, in the case of the father, the Rat-Man's superstitious premonition of harm had to be a manifestation of his *sexual defiance*? Yet Freud even adduces as evidence for such defiance two episodes of masturbation not involving the father at all but avowedly provoked by the beautiful blowing of a horn and by a beautiful passage in Goethe's *Dichtung und Wahrheit*. And he deems them relevant just because they *also* featured incidentally the breaking of a prohibition or command (1909b, pp. 203-204). This seems tendentious. Besides, it fallaciously trades on mere thematic affinity to claim that sexual defiance was a causal factor in the masturbation.

In fact, as early as at the end of the first session with the Rat-Man, Freud's etiologic reasoning is fallacious. He reports, as an initial retrodictive conclusion from a small sample, that all of his obsessional patients "invariably possess the characteristic of premature sexual activity" (p. 165). From this he drew the *causal* inference that "the factors which go to form" an obsessional neurosis "are to be found in the patient's *infantile* sexual life and not in his present one." However, as we know from John Stuart Mill's "method of agreement," even if we may assume the invariable presence of an earlier factor, it does not warrant the presumption that this antecedent is *also causally relevant*; instead, this prior presence calls for gathering further evidence bearing on the answers to the following questions: (a) Is the incidence of sexual precocity (or other designated infantile sexual factor) actually higher among obsessives than among non-obsessives; but more importantly, (b) is the incidence of obsessional neurosis among sexually precocious people *different* from its incidence among the erotically nonprecocious? In short, is there evidence that *designated* infantile sexual factors make a relevant difference? Until and unless such evidence is at hand, the invariably present sexual precocity retrodicted by Freud is at best etiologically heuristic, but clearly leaves the pathogenesis of obsessional neurosis moot. As we saw, *mutatis mutandis à propos* of the rat obsessions, the etiologic issue here is *not* whether a hypothesized paternal punishment for a *sexual* offense engendered hatred toward the father; instead the issue is whether *that* particular hatred was the pathogen of the obsessive fear of the father's death! And clearly, evidence for the former is not adequate support for the latter. Of course, here as elsewhere, lack of evidence for the pathogenicity of a hatred does not actually rule out its etiologic role.

It emerges that Freud's rationale for a *separate* sexual explanation of the obsessive fears of the father's death—as distinct from the rat obsessions—is flimsy. He rests his case for such a separate sexual account on his claim that the death obsessions occurred *à propos* of father-son conflict occasioned by the son's sex-object choices. But he reports only a relatively small number of episodes in which the patient himself mentioned such a temporal linkage. And, as we saw, death obsessions focusing on the father *or* on others hardly occurred *only à propos* of conflict with the father occasioned by sex-object choice. Moreover, all sorts of premonitions of doom occurred frequently in other contexts, clearly unrelated to such sex-oriented conflict. Thus, the relatively few episodes involving sex-related conflict with the father hardly warrant Freud's separate explanatory postulation of a paternal castigation for a *sexual* offense, as distinct from the childhood punishment *for biting*.

Freud may have been conscious of this evidential lacuna: He pads the Rat-Man's own reports of the few paternal sex-*conflict* episodes. Thus, first he tells us that the occurrence of the patient's childhood wish to see girls naked "was regularly accompanied" by "fearing that something dreadful would happen. This something dreadful was already clothed in a *characteristic indeterminateness* which was thenceforth to be an invariable feature of every manifestation of the neurosis" (p. 163; my italics). Earlier (p. 162), Freud had related: "In reply to a question he [the patient] gave an example of these fears: 'For instance, *that my father might die.*'" And on the heels of the declared "characteristic indeterminateness" of the diffuse apprehension of "something dreadful," Freud thinks that the Rat-Man's *mere example* entitled him to link the patient's voyeuristic wish to see a woman naked "confidently" to a death obsession *focused on his father*:

> But in a child it is not hard to discover what it is that is veiled behind an indeterminateness of this kind. If the patient can once be induced to give a particular instance in place of the vague generalities which characterize an obsessional neurosis, it may be confidently assumed that the instance is the original and actual thing which has tried to hide itself behind the generalization. Our present patient's obsessive fear, therefore, when restored to its original meaning, would run as follows: 'If I have this wish to see a woman naked, my father will be bound to die' [p. 163].

This induction from a *single instance* becomes the less credible, when taken in conjunction with Freud's own account of how he explicitly regimented the patient's responses in the first place. Thus, reportedly at age 12, the Rat-Man had been platonically in love with a little girl who was too small to elicit a desire in him to see her naked. But when she failed to reciprocate his affection adequately, "the idea had come to him that she would be kind to him if some misfortune were to befall him; and as an instance of such a misfortune his father's death had forced itself upon his mind" (p. 178). However, when the patient persisted in denying that his "train of thought" as to his father's demise betokened a death *wish*, Freud avowedly "broke off the argument with the remark that I felt sure this [episode at age 12] had not been the first occurrence of his idea of his father's dying [à propos of his love for a girl]; it had evidently originated at an earlier date, and some day we should have to trace back its history" (p. 179). No wonder that, in due course, Freud declared himself satisfied with the Rat-Man's ensuing responses: "I told him I thought he had now produced the answer we were waiting for. . . . The source from which his hostility to his father derived its indestructibility was evidently something in the nature of *sensual desires*, and in that connection he must have felt his father as in some way or other an *interference*" (p. 182).

There is yet another, quite different reservation against Freud's separate reliance on a paternal chastisement for "some sexual misdemeanor connected with masturbation" to explain the death obsessions, and on his invocation of a beating *for biting*—also administered by the father—to explain the rat obsessions: The case history published by Freud reports that the patient himself had no recollection whatever of either punishment (p. 205), but that, according to his mother, there had been only *one* paternal beating. Moreover, as she reported, at the age of 3, the patient had definitely been thrashed *for biting*, and "there was no suggestion of his misdeed having been of a sexual nature" (p. 206). But if indeed there was only one beating, how can Freud adduce severe physical punishments for two quite distinct sorts of offenses as the causes of the two kinds of obsessions? Is there not a *trade-off* between his two separate punitive explanations of the two sorts of obsessions? Does his etiologic account of the rat obsession not *forfeit* his explanation of the one featuring his father's demise and vice versa? Freud makes no mention of this *prima facie* forfeiture. And it is unavailing against it that he envisages the possibility (p. 207 n.) of the mother's having censored the sexual nature of her child's offense.

Yet, after all, could the one episode of paternal beating possibly furnish as well a sexual explanation of the death obsession, even though it was ostensibly given only for biting? Freud conjectures that although the father's intent was to administer the beating for biting, his son *conceptualized* the punitive intent as twofold, so that the one punishment episode can do double explanatory duty: "more than one version of the [punishment] scene (each differing greatly from the other) may be detected in the patient's unconscious phantasies" (p. 206 n.). In particular, "in constructing phantasies about his childhood the individual *sexualizes his memories*; that is, he brings commonplace experiences into relation with his sexual activity" (p. 207 n.). Indeed, without giving any details at all as to the patient's dreams or associations to them, Freud asks us to believe that "A deeper interpretation of the patient's dreams in relation to this [punitive] episode revealed . . . [that] his sexual desires for his mother and sister . . . were linked up [imaginatively] with the young hero's chastisement at his father's hand" (p. 207 n.). I know some psychoanalysts who are persuaded by Freud's imputation to the patient of a two-versions conceptualization of the single paternal beating. Yet, in the absence of any specifics whatever, others will be forgiven for doubting that the analysis of the adult Rat-Man's dreams can sustain Freud's retrodictive imputation of the patient's sexualization of his beating in early childhood. In fact, Freud concedes that supposed infantile punishments for sexual offenses "are apt to appear in a shadowy way in dreams" (p. 206 n.). Indeed, it would seem reasonable to extend this skepticism to such very long-term retrodictive inferences.

Oddly enough, there is an important discrepancy between Freud's published case history of the Rat-Man and the posthumously published "Original Record of the Case" in Strachey's translation (pp. 251-318). In the latter, we learn from the patient's report to Freud that, quite apart from the paternal beating at age 3, there was (at least) another one: "When he was a little boy (age uncertain, perhaps 5 or 6) he was lying between his father and mother and wetted the bed, upon which his father beat him and turned him out" (p. 284). Now suppose, just for argument's sake, that this patient recollection is authentic, and that furthermore the child did conceptualize the paternal beating for urination as *sexually* thwarting to the point of bearing his father an abiding grudge. In that case, Freud does not need to resort to the (farfetched) reliance on the patient's dreams to neutralize the stated damaging *trade-off* between his two separate etiologic explanations of the rat obsessions and death obsessions. But far from contributing to such obviation of the forfeiture of one of these two explanations, Strachey's own comment serves to undermine indirectly the authenticity of the patient's report of the second paternal beating:

> If there are occasional discrepancies between the record and the published case history, it must be borne in mind that the case continued for many months after the record ceased and that there was therefore every opportunity for the patient to correct his earlier accounts and for Freud himself to obtain a clearer view of the details [pp. 255-256].

In the same credulous vein, Peter Gay (1988, p. 262), adduces "the need for discretion" as one of the factors that "prevented Freud from making this case report complete."

On the other hand, could it be that there actually was a second beating, but that Freud "doctored" his case record for publication in the service of an oedipal etiology, mediated by child *fantasies*, as opposed to the rival maltreatment theory, which relies on real traumatic experiences? It has been argued quite generally that he engaged in such ideological editing (Sulloway, 1991). And this suggestion derives in the present case from Freud's own elaboration, in the Original Case Record, on the patient's report of the urination episode:

> His demeanour during all this was that of a man in desperation and one who was trying to save himself from blows of terrific violence; he buried his head in his hands, rushed away, covered his face with his arm, etc. He told me that his father had a passionate temper, and then did not know what he was doing [1909b, p. 284].

Indeed, as Mahoney (1986) has documented in his *Freud and the Rat Man*, other marked discrepancies between Freud's published account and his treatment process notes cast considerable doubt on his well-known claim that he had cured both of the patient's obsessions and restored his mental health (1909b, pp. 155, 207 n., 220, 249 n.). Thus, even if there is no trade-off between the etiologic explanations of the two obsessions, any psychoanalytic insight the Rat-Man achieved into the supposed pathogens of his obsessions cannot be credited with having been adequately curative. On the other hand, if there was such a cure after all, the very live possibility, if not likelihood, of trade-off jeopardizes Freud's contention that this recovery was wrought by the patient's *bona fide* psychoanalytic insights, since at least one of the two etiologic explanations may well have yielded *pseudo* insight. Yet Freud extols psychoanalytic treatment of obsessional neurotics as *uniquely* therapeutic: "We should not be justified in expecting such severe obsessional ideas as were present in this case to be cleared up in any simpler manner or by any other means" (1909b, p. 220).

Glymour (1974), Edelson (1984, chap. 11), I (Grünbaum, 1984, chap. 8), and Wallerstein (1986) have each claimed that Freud's sexual etiology of the Rat-Man's death obsessions was *disconfirmed* by the testimony of the patient's mother. At least in the case of Glymour and myself, this assertion of disconfirmation was predicated on the following assumptions: As she reported, during his childhood, the patient received only *one* beating from his father, and that severe punishment was not for a sexual offense but for biting, whereas Freud's theory had retrodicted a punitive paternal interference with the patient's childhood sexuality, presumably masturbation. Speaking for myself, implicit in this invocation of the mother's testimony were some additional assumptions: (a) As suggested by the aforecited comment by Strachey, we should discount as unreliable the patient's tale of further paternal punishment for urination in bed, which Freud records only in his Original Process notes, but does not mention at all in his published case history; (b) alternatively, if authentic, it is unclear that a punishment for urination would have been conceptualized by a male child as thwarting his sexual gratification, although Freud's theory of infantile sexuality would make such an imputation; (c) for the reasons I have given above, one should put no stock at all in Freud's totally undocumented appeal to the patient's dreams as evidence that the Rat-Man had also *sexualized* the paternal beating for biting by construing it as interference with his sexual desires for his mother and sister; and (d) Freud's etiologic scenario rests crucially on the supposition that the patient's unconscious hatred for the father as an erotic obstacle derived its indestructibility and pathogenic efficacy from punitive events during early childhood (1909b, pp. 177, 182-183). Hence evidence for sex-related father-son conflict *during adolescence and adulthood* does not impugn the disconfirmatory import derived from the foregoing considerations.

At this point, psychoanalysts may object that I have said nothing about Freud's reliance on so-called *transference* interpretations in the Rat-Man case in order to validate his sexual etiology. Therefore, let me consider how he invoked just such interpretations in that case, how he tried to justify them, and how Edelson and Luborsky have sought to vindicate him.

CAN TRANSFERENCE INTERPRETATIONS VALIDATE CHILDHOOD ETIOLOGIES?

As we shall see, Freud and other analysts have invoked interpretations of patient fantasies and dreams that focus on his *psychoanalyst* as a basis for drawing at least two sorts of etiologic inferences: (a) to validate hypotheses as to the *precipitating* cause of the patient's disorder; and (b) to warrant their claims as to the crucial pathogenic role of designated events in early childhood. Though the reasoning in drawing these two sorts of inferences is basically the same, it will be helpful expositorily to deal first with Freud's account of a purported precipitating cause in the Rat-Man case, as set forth in his separate section on "The Precipitating Cause of the Illness" (pp. 195-200).

According to psychoanalytic theory, the patient *transfers* onto the psychoanalyst feelings and thoughts that originally pertained to important figures in her or his earlier life. Thus, the patient is believed to behave toward her or his analyst *as though* the doctor were her or his father, mother, sister, or another significant person from the past. In this important sense, the fantasies woven around the psychoanalyst by the analysand, and quite generally the latter's conduct toward his doctor, are hypothesized to be *thematically recapitulatory* of childhood episodes. And by thus being recapitulatory, the patient's behavior during treatment can be said to exhibit a *thematic kinship* to such very early episodes. Therefore, when the analyst interprets these supposed reenactments, the ensuing interpretations are called "transference interpretations."

Astonishingly enough, Freud and his followers have inveterately drawn the following causal inference: Precisely in virtue of being thematically recapitulated in the patient-doctor interaction, the hypothesized earlier scenario in the patient's life can cogently be held to have *originally* been a pathogenic factor in the patient's affliction. In short, here the causal inference takes a somewhat different logical form from the one we encountered in our previous examples. There, Freud inferred the existence of a *direct* causal nexus between thematically kindred mental events from the mere fact of their thematic kinship. But in the context of his transference interpretations, the thematic reenactment is held to show that the early scenario had *originally* been pathogenic. And once this *etiologic* conclusion has been drawn, the patient's thematic reenactment in the treatment setting is also asserted to be *pathogenically* recapitulatory, rather than only thematically.

Freud presents the argument based on his transference interpretation *à propos* of trying to convince the Rat-Man that Freud had uncovered the *precipitating cause* of his patient's pathological incapacity for work. The circumstances surrounding the supposed precipitating cause were as follows: Sometime after his father's death, the Rat-Man learned from his mother that, upon the completion of his education, he will have the opportunity of marrying a daughter of a wealthy cousin of hers. And, as Freud explains, "This family plan stirred up in him a conflict as to whether he should remain faithful to the lady he loved in spite of her poverty, or whether he should follow in his father's footsteps and marry the lovely, rich, and well-connected girl who had been assigned to him" (p. 198). This bind, in turn, was a reenactment of a predicament into which his father had placed him, shortly before his death, by reprimanding him for imprudently keeping company with the impecunious lady (p. 201).

Though the patient acknowledged that he had been conscious of this conflict, he doubted that it had precipitated his crippling inability to work. Freud depicts this skepticism as sheer neurotic resistance. Why? It would seem because he had already begged the *etiologic* question on the basis of the following assumption: "The conflict at the root of his [i.e., the patient's] illness was in essentials a struggle between the persisting influence of his father's wishes and his own amatory predilections" (p. 200). But how did Freud rebut the patient's expressed etiologic skepticism? With the help of a fantasy focused on Freud, as he tells us, the Rat-Man "was forcibly brought to believe in the truth of my [etiologic] suspicion" by "the overwhelming effect of the perfect analogy between the transference phantasy and the actual state of affairs in the past." The "perfect analogy" is further attested, we are told, by the patient's dream about Freud's daughter's eyes. This perfect analogy, we learn, emerged after "an obscure and difficult period in the treatment," i.e., "after we [Freud and the patient] had gone through a series of the severest resistances and bitterest vituperations on his part" (pp. 199-200).

Now let us grant Freud's claim of "perfect analogy" to the following extent, at least for argument's sake: (a) The patient had seen an attractive young girl on the stairs of Freud's house, had taken her to be his daughter, and had assumed her to be rich; (b) the Rat-Man had interpreted Freud's patience with him in treatment as due to his doctor's desire to have him marry his daughter, a state of affairs that cast Freud in the role of blocking the patient's marriage to his impecunious lady friend, just as his father had done; and (c) when the Rat-Man dreamed of seeing Freud's daughter with two patches of dung for eyes, the dream *may* have been an expression of the conflict between marrying for filthy gain and marrying eyes beautiful. But the interpretation of the patches of dung in the dream is questionable: Freud gives no indication that the patient, rather than only he himself, associated these patches with the marriage conflict. Instead, he declares peremptorily: "No one who understands the language of dreams will find much difficulty in translating this one" (p. 200). Thus, as I see it, (a) the patient's psychoanalysis revived his memory of the conflict between marrying for love and marrying for money, as his parents had urged; (b) being preoccupied with this memory, as least partly because Freud was relentlessly harping on it in the analysis, the Rat-Man wove a fantasy around him that was *recapitulatory* of this marriage conflict; and (c) the same preoccupation may perhaps also have surfaced in the dream. Clearly, what makes a transference fantasy recapitulatory is that there is thematic kinship between the prior life events and the content of that fantasy. And the purported "perfect analogy" between them in this case is supposed to prepare the ground for drawing a special sort of causal inference from just that thematic recapitulation.

But, I claim, Freud's appeal to the above "perfect analogy" is a snare and a delusion. The crucial, urgent question is: On what grounds does he go on to claim that this recapitulatory "perfection" is at all evidence for the alleged *etiologic role* of the actual marriage-choice conflict as the precipitating cause of the

Rat-Man's inability to work? This claim seems to be a portentous blunder, because *it begs the etiologic question by just assuming that recapitulatory fantasies focused on the analyst are also* **pathogenically** *recapitulatory*! More explicitly, Freud is simply assuming that the original scenario had played the causal role of a pathogen in the patient's life, merely because certain features of the scenario were being thematically reenacted in the patient's fantasies about the analyst. How, I ask, can the reactivation, during the analysis, of a patient's conflict show at all that the earlier reactivation—by the mother's proposed family plan—had been the *precipitating pathogen* of the illness?

By the same token, I shall ask below: No matter how strongly recapitulatory, how can fantasies focused on the doctor be cogent evidence that a hypothesized or vividly remembered infantile prototype (simulacrum) of the conflict had been the crucial *original pathogen* of the patient's death obsessions? It is just fallacious, I submit, to claim with Freud, as many analysts do, that the conflictually recapitulatory character of the patient's transference fantasy is cogent evidence for identifying the mother's earlier conflict reactivation as the precipitating cause of the Rat-Man's illness. Neither the fact of being recapitulatory of a conflict, nor the fact that the setting for the recapitulation is a (bizarre) fantasy focused on the analyst, nor yet the combination of these facts shows that the reenacted scenario was pathogenically relevant in the first place as a precipitating cause! Yet this etiologic fallacy then inspired two of Freud's further fundamental tenets: First, the *investigative* thesis that the psychoanalytic dissection of the patient's transference behavior toward the analyst can reliably identify the original pathogens of her or his long-term neurosis; and second, the cardinal *therapeutic* doctrine that the resolution of the analysand's so-called "transference neurosis" is the key to overcoming her or his perennial problems. Indeed, the fallacious *etiologic* construal of the patient's thematic reenactments of earlier reactions seems to be aided or abetted by the very practice of *labeling* the patient's current conduct toward the analyst as occurring "in the transference."

Turning to the psychoanalyst's inference of the original crucial pathogen, I note the reasoning offered by Freud in his "On the History of the Psycho-analytic Movement":

The fact of the emergence of the transference in its crudely sexual form, whether affectionate or hostile, in every treatment of a neurosis, although this is neither desired nor induced by either doctor or patient, has always seemed to me the most irrefragable proof [original German: *unerschütterlichste Beweis*] that the source of the driving forces of neurosis lies in sexual life. This argument has never received anything approaching the degree of attention that it merits, for if it had, investigations in this field would leave no other conclusion open. As far as I am concerned, this argument has remained the decisive one, over and above the more specific findings of analytic work [1914b, p. 12].

This purportedly "irrefragable proof," I submit, deserves more attention *not* because its appreciation "would leave no other conclusion open," as Freud would have it; instead, I believe, the Rat-Man case, and other such concrete case histories, show how baffling it is that Freud deemed the etiologic transference argument cogent *at all*, let alone unshakably so. This is not to deny at all that the conduct of disturbed patients in analysis can be bizarre, ludicrous, inappropriate, and erotic. After all, the patient's extraordinary dependence on the doctor for help creates a very special situation.

In the face of the range and depth of the evidential flaws that vitiate Freud's argument in the Rat-Man case, Peter Gay's recent paean to it appears uncritically insouciant: "It brilliantly served to buttress Freud's theories, notably those postulating the childhood roots of neurosis. . . . Freud was not masochist enough to publish only failures" (1988, p. 267). No wonder that my doubts strike Gay as themselves an obsessional symptom: "The most formidable among the skeptics, who has made the credibility of Freudian science (or lack of it) into an obsessive concern for a decade, is the philosopher Adolf Grünbaum" (p. 745).

Marshall Edelson has offered a rebuttal to my denial of the cogency of the etiologic transference argument. In his 1984 book, he wrote:

. . . in fact, in psychoanalysis the pathogen is not merely a remote event, or a series of such events, the effect of which lives on. The pathogen reappears in all its virulence, with increasing frankness and explicitness, in the transference—in a new edition, a new version, a reemergence, a repetition of the past pathogenic events or factors.

[And Edelson elaborates:] The pathogen together with its pathological effects are, therefore, under the investigator's eye, so to speak, in the psychoanalytic situation, and demonstrating the causal relation between them in that situation, by nonexperimental or quasi-experimental methods, surely provides support, even if indirect, for the hypothesis that in the past the same kind of pathogenic factors were necessary to bring about the same kind of effects [p. 151].

But how does the psychoanalyst demonstrate, within the confines of his clinical setting, that the original pathogen is replicated at all in the transference, let alone such that the supposed *current* replica of the remote, early event is *presently* the virulent *cause* of the patient's neurosis? Having fallaciously identified a conflict as a pathogen because it reappears in the transference, many Freudians conclude that pathogens must reappear in the transference. And, in this way, they beg the key question I have just asked. How, for example, did Freud show that the Rat-Man's marriage conflict depicted in that patient's transference fantasy was the *current* cause of his *ongoing death obsessions*? Neither Edelson's book, nor his 1986 paper, offer a better answer. Thus, in the latter paper, he declares: "The psychoanalyst claims that current mental representations of particular past events or fantasies are constitutive [i.e., *current* operative] causes of current behavior, and then goes on to claim that therefore past actual events or fantasies are etiological causes of the analysand's symptoms." And Edelson concludes: "Transference phenomena are . . . nonquestion-begging evidence for . . . inferences about causally efficacious psychological entities existing or occurring in the here and now" (p. 110). But how do transference phenomena focusing on the analyst show a presumed current replica of a past event to be pathogenic in the here-and-now?

In chapter 6, I shall present a detailed critique of Edelson's other arguments for the feasibility of validating important causal hypotheses in psychoanalysis by means of clinical data.

A further concrete example can illustrate why I remain quite unconvinced. The well-known psychoanalyst Charles Brenner

(1976, pp. 43-44) discusses a patient whose inordinate adult fear of competing with other males is causally attributed to current repressed adult castration anxiety. How, I ask, is this attribution validated within the clinical setting? The analyst will reply that free associations to the patient's symptoms had led to the emergence of repressed castration anxiety. But I altogether reject this reply as unavailing: As I have painstakingly argued in my book (1984, chaps. 3 and 4), just such associative emergence is very poor evidence indeed for the inferred pathogenic role of the castration anxiety, even if we assume that the analyst did not subtly steer the patient's associations thematically toward castration anxiety.

But what of the (1985) paper by Luborsky and his coworkers, which claims verification of Freud's grand transference hypothesis? I must refer to my Response in the BBS symposium (Grünbaum, 1986, pp. 278-279). Suffice it to say here that the purported verification relies on a use of the term "causal" so permissive as to countenance that ordinary breathing is a "cause" of neurosis.

In the face of this state of affairs, it is remarkable to what extent the psychoanalytic theory of transference has penetrated the psychological doctrines of current folklore. For example, in a recent issue of the magazine *USAir*, an article on "Dealing with Difficult Bosses" (Rice, 1986) quotes Jerry Johnson of the Menninger Foundation as saying that troubles with the boss tend to stem from transference phenomena (pp. 32-34). Indeed, even psychiatrists who are hostile to psychoanalysis often refer to the doctor-patient relationship as "the transference." So much for the import of the Rat-Man case. Additional issues posed by it will be discussed in chapter 8 with respect to intraclinical testability.

THE WOLF-MAN

Edelson discusses the merits of *rival* causal explanations à *propos* of the Wolf-Man case (1986, pp. 119-120). Suppose, he says, that one theorist tells a coherent, *interconnected* causal story. Edelson points out that then

It is, of course, always possible to think up different explanations for each part of a causal story. However, to prefer a congeries of rival explanations for different data, all of which are explained by a causal story, violates the principle of parsimony. It also violates the principle of the common cause; that all these different explanations should be correct seems much more improbable than that one causal story is correct [p. 120].

I contend that, in practice, just such a statement of explanatory virtues and vices in the abstract can be quite misleading both for scientific validation at large, and with respect to psychoanalytic causal case histories in particular. Thus, note example 5 above.

Let me illustrate how the abstract principle of explanatory economy can vindicate *spurious* causal explanations. The example I am about to give is deliberately banal but, in my view, the moral it contains is by no means banal. Consider the large collection Alpha of human ailments that are known to remit spontaneously within, say, a month after onset. Now suppose, just for argument's sake, that everyone were a coffee drinker, and that we were told the following causal story by someone unaware of spontaneous remissions: Coffee drinking for one month cures all ailments in the class Alpha; thus, coffee consumption explains—in the lives of any of us—how we successfully got rid of the various ailments through interrelated chains of causation. Each time, we are asked to believe, coffee drinking for a month, together with other causes that had kept the given ailment from becoming fatal, produced the remission of the pertinent ailment. Moreover, as the coffee therapist points out, coffee drinking is stupendously predictive for the occurrence of such cures. Yet, as we all know, the fatal flaw in this grandiose causal story is that its patrons did not collect evidence as to whether coffee drinking *makes a difference* to the remissions in class Alpha. Had they done so, they would have found that the purported coffee cures would have occurred anyway, even if nobody drank coffee. And no appeal to explanatory parsimony, or to what Edelson calls "the principle of the common cause," can vindicate this causal story, even against a *congeries* of rival explanations of the various spontaneous remissions of different ailments, such as colds, temporary insomnia, hay fever, etc.

I claim that a similarly *spurious* explanatory economy employing Edelson's misuse of the common cause bedevils Freud's Wolf-Man study. Therefore I cannot share Edelson's explanatory tribute to that celebrated case history. Freud seems to meet Edelson's (1986, p. 104) desideratum of explaining not only diverse phenomena—such as the patient's wolf phobia and his childhood urination in the Grusha scene—but also the interrelations between them. Yet Freud demonstrably failed to heed Edelson's injunction that a causal explanation must supply "some appropriate argument, based on theoretically relevant evidence, for the scientific credibility of that explanation" (Edelson, 1986, pp. 124-125). Consider briefly the logical structure of Freud's causal story in the Wolf-Man case so that I can pinpoint the issue of scientific credibility.

Suppose we grant Freud the actual past occurrence of the so-called primal scene that he retrodicted ever so precariously from the adult patient's report of a dream he had had between the ages of 3 and 5 (1918, pp. 33-34). This scene of doglike sexual intercourse between his parents purportedly occurred when the patient was an infant of 18 months. Assume furthermore the universal occurrence of bisexuality in the so-called "complete" Oedipus complex, such that a male child can choose *either* parent as his sex object. Now postulate with Freud that, as a 4-year-old boy, the Wolf-Man had taken *his father* as a sex-object after his nurse Nanya had rejected him sexually. And note that this postulate of a homosexual object choice *just then* plays a vital role in Freud's explanation of the occurrence and timing of the subsequent wolf phobia (pp. 27 and 35). As he makes clear (pp. 36, 42, 46), without this *particular* assumption, the hypothesized primal scene could not have induced *castration* anxiety in the patient. And without that anxiety, the similarity between the upright posture of the father in the primal scene and the upright posture of the wolf in the fairy tale (p. 39) would hardly have attached terror to the wolves in the picture book with which the patient's sister had tormented him (pp. 16, 29, 39).

After Freud invoked the homosexual ("negative") form of the Oedipus complex to explain the wolf phobia, he relied on its *heterosexual* ("positive") form to explain why, as a 2½-year-old child, the patient had urinated when he saw the maid Grusha from the rear on her knees, scrubbing the floor. Here Freud again makes explanatory use of the Wolf-Man's unconscious memory of the primal scene as a common cause. But this time, the evocation of the posture his mother had in the scene is assumed to have triggered the little boy's *heterosexual* choice of his *mother* as a sex object (pp. 90-93), whereupon Grusha took his mother's place.

Alas, Freud provides no *independent* evidence at all for the particular sex-object choices that the little boy is presumed to have made at ages 2½ and 4 respectively. These choices are *not* deducible from the complete Oedipus complex hypothesis, although they *exemplify* it. And, as for the question whether the primal scene had actually occurred, Freud himself was sufficiently uneasy about it to speculate (pp. 57-58) that the scene may well have been the child's own mental fusion of a nonsexual event involving his parents with a recollected copulation by dogs. This supposed coalescence, he claims, greatly reduces the demands on our credulity. But in order to offer a plausible motive for the occurrence of the conjectured fusion, Freud concocts a new infantile wish, like a bolt out of the blue: "The inquisitive child's . . . wish, based on his experiences with the dogs, to witness his parents too in their love-making" (p. 58). Again, no independent evidence is offered for that new wish. Yet Freud was right that the belief in the actuality of the primal scene does tax our credulity. As the aged Wolf-Man himself told Karin Obholzer (1982, p. 36), "the whole thing is improbable because in Russia, children sleep in the nanny's bedroom, not in their parents'."

In the face of these evidential defects, does Edelson really want to claim merit for Freud's explanation of the little boy's incontinence in the Grusha scene, in virtue of explanatory parsimony and interrelatedness? Is this explanation better than the rival one that little 2½-year-old boys have been known to relieve themselves on floors, merely when their bladders make it very urgent? Does the rival assumption of commonplace urinary urgency, coupled with the sight of the water in Grusha's scrubbing pail, not enjoy better evidential support than Freud's explanation, which postulates the following: Under the influence of his unconscious memory of the primal scene, the little boy *just then* took his mother *rather than his father* as a sex-object? Does the network character of Freud's account compensate at all for its severe taxation of our credulity? I think not.

CONCLUSION

A number of distinguished analysts besides Freud have deemed the case histories of the Wolf-Man and the Rat-Man to be paradigms of good explanatory causal reasoning. Indeed, as Marcus reports (1984, p. 87), Freud's "celebrated account of the Rat Man . . . continues because of its unique qualities to be used today as a text for training psychoanalysts." But I see both patient histories as counterproductive advertisements for the case study method, precisely because I share Edelson's view that "Freud's intent in his case studies was to provide empirical evidence for causal claims" (1986, p. 90).

In sum, here I have tried to offer some of my *further* reasons for believing that if psychoanalysis is to have a future as a scientific enterprise, it very probably does not lie with the clinical case history method, but with other testing designs. The details of these other designs must be left to the creative ingenuity of future researchers. Yet, to this day the case study method has been the source of the evidence adduced by the vast majority of analysts to claim support for their theory of psychopathology, dream theory, theory of slips, and theory of psychosexual development. Thus, in concert with his psychoanalytic colleague J. A. Arlow, Wallerstein (1988, p. 27) declares: "Our confidence in our work will have to rely . . . on solid observational data, meticulously gathered in the analytic situation and objectively evaluated, for *it is upon this set of procedures that the claim of psychoanalysis to a place among the empirical sciences is based.*" But, as I have argued, just the evidence based on these clinical case history procedures continues to leave the major pillars of psychoanalysis poorly supported.

Relatedly, Philip Holzman (1985) has warned that the scientific potential of psychoanalytic theory will be destroyed by an arrestive fixation on the clinical setting as the probative arena of inquiry.

POSTSCRIPT (1992)

In the present chapter, I have repeatedly mentioned the following *necessary condition* for the *causal relevance* of an attribute or factor X to the occurrence of a property Y in a reference class C in which there are instances of X: X divides the class C into two subclasses, X's and non-X's, such that the respective probabilities of Y in these two subclasses are *different* (Salmon, 1984, pp. 32-33). And I added that modernized or refined statistical versions of the famous four methods of controlled inquiry articulated by John Stuart Mill (1887) serve to test the causal relevance of an X to a Y: Such controlled inquiry shows whether the presence of X *makes a difference* to the occurrence of Y.

Moreover, I claim that when X is an explanatory motive for an action Y, and thus "makes sense" of Y, then X is causally relevant to Y. And, as I argued in my (1984), evidence for the motivational species of causal relevance "in psychoanalysis, no less than in 'academic psychology' or medicine, has to rely on modes of inquiry that are refined from time-honored canons of causal inference pioneered by Francis Bacon and John Stuart Mill" (p. 47).

In criticism of me, James Hopkins has contended that "Because psychoanalysis is a psychology of motive, the Millian methodology that Grünbaum advocates seems radically inappropriate to it" (1991, p. 128). But on what grounds does Hopkins assert that "The Millian modes of inquiry that he [Grünbaum] endorses . . . seem inapplicable to motive" (p. 128)?

In an attempt to justify this thesis, Hopkins offers a characterization of Millian modes of inquiry that is demonstrably vitiated by red herrings. As he would have it:

> These are, roughly, correlational and eliminative methods: They are applied to items or properties that are observed to go together, to determine whether this co-occurrence is causal or accidental. So they are applied to A's and B's that are already given,

to investigate whether the A's actually cause the B's, as opposed, say, to accompanying them by chance.

Now as noted in the text it seems that we should not construe ourselves as simply *observing* that motives co-occur with the actions or wish-fulfillments that we take them to cause. Rather, surely, we are better represented as *hypothesizing* the various motives, in order to explain what we observe in terms of them. We thus treat motives as a species of unobserved causes, introduced to explain observed effects. This has two consequences. First, the putative causes and effects are not of the same observational status, as Millian methods presuppose. And second, the pair of items in question are already understood as cause and effect, and on non-Millian grounds [1991, p. 128].

But Mill's (1887) statement of his four methods talks about "instances" and about "phenomena" without imposing Hopkins's *contrived* requirement of direct observability. For example, Mill's method of concomitant variations is clearly applicable to the manipulation of the variables in the *theoretical* functional dependencies codifying scientific regularities (laws). Yet there are some phenomena in which the events to which the methods are applicable are indeed relatively observable.

Thus I can validate by means of these methods a supposed causal link between my conscious awareness of a derogatory remark and my introspectively experienced anger by noting, over a period of time and repeatedly, that the presence vs. the absence of insults *makes a difference* statistically to my becoming angry. Similarly, by finding that people who do not drink coffee recover from the common cold no less than coffee drinkers do, Mill's methods can be used eliminatively against the causal hypothesis that observed coffee drinking for, say, two weeks cures the observable symptoms of a cold.

Hopkins opines that Mill's methods "are applied to items or properties that are [directly] *observed* to go together" (my emphasis). But the issue is whether they are applied (applicable) *only* to "A's and B's that are already given" *observationally*. Alas, Hopkins slides fallaciously to the gratuitous requirement of direct co-observability. In so doing, he is unaware that, in controlled inquiries, it is commonplace to apply Mill's methods to A's and B's one or both of which are first *hypothesized* to exist on the basis of suitable empirical indicators. But they are "already given" *only after* thus having been hypothesized as theoretical entities.

How, other than by such theory-laden use of Mill's methods do scientists validate that (1) theoretically specified chemicals are carcinogenic, where the pathologist diagnoses the tumor by way of theoretical inference; (2) certain genes are oncogenic, (3) arsenic is lethal; (4) X-rays generated in Roentgen's cathode-ray experiments *caused* the formation of a picture of the bones of his moving hands on the (fluorescent) screen, (5) H.D.L. cholesterol plaques are causally relevant to coronary artery disease and death? By the same token, Hopkins can hardly deny that psychotherapy research on both treatment-outcome and treatment-process uses statistically refined versions of Mill's methods in a theory-laden way.

Indeed, when Breuer and Freud claimed therapeuticity for lifting repressions, they should have used Mill's methods to rule out the rival hypothesis of placebo effect by also noting the results from treatment in which no repressions were lifted. As we saw in chapter 1, the argument they actually gave instead against the placebo hypothesis was not cogent.

Hopkins's case against the applicability of Mill's methods to the validation of motivational explanations evidently founders on his red herring that "Millian methods presuppose" putative causes and effects to have "the same [direct] observational status." Thus, it is unavailing to Hopkins's posture against my Millian stance that in the context of imputing motives to others, rather than asserting their presence in oneself, "We thus treat motives as a species of unobserved causes, introduced to explain observed effects [behavior, action]." Though he preaches to the converted, he erects a straw-man, when he advises me that "we should not construe ourselves as simply *observing* that motives co-occur with the actions or wish-fulfillments that we take them to cause. Rather, surely, we are better represented as *hypothesizing* the various motives, in order to explain what we observe in terms of them."

It emerges that Hopkins has failed to sustain his thesis of the inapplicability of Mill's methods to the validation of explanations of human conduct by means of postulated motives. And it is no asset at all to his thesis, though obvious, that by the time we hypothesize that X motivationally (causally) explains Y, "the pair of items in question are already understood as cause and effect."

Hopkins deems it illuminating that the very description of a desire can be *goal-oriented* (p. 124, n. 9). For example, we can say that Smith desires to drink water, to eat food, or to have sex, instead of saying that she (he) is thirsty, hungry, or horny. But Hopkins thinks that from this otherwise innocuous commonplace, he can infer: "In understanding the description of a desire, therefore, we already know a central feature of its causal role, that is, what it is supposed to do" (p. 92). And from this, in turn, he concludes: ". . . the pair of items in question [motive and action] are already understood as cause and effect, and on non-Millian grounds" (p. 128). But Edward Erwin (1992) has argued decisively, in my view, that Hopkins committed a serious *non-sequitur,* when he inferred from the feasibility of target-oriented *descriptions* of desires that the validity of motivational (causal) explanations of actions by means of them is vouchsafed conceptually or *a priori,* rather than empirically by Mill's methods.

5

THE POVERTY OF CLINICAL OBSERVATIONS AS PROBATIVE EVIDENCE FOR PSYCHOANALYTIC THEORY AND THERAPY

INTRODUCTION

The influence of psychoanalytic theory in our intellectual culture has not only been enormous but may still be expanding, despite the marked decline of its *quondam* virtual hegemony in American psychiatry and psychotherapy. Avowedly, Freudian psychobiography and psychohistory have become a burgeoning field and have been given wide currency. Freud himself and Ambassador William Bullitt collaborated in a psychoanalytic study of Woodrow Wilson, published in 1967, while the historian Frank Manuel (1968) has given us a like portrait of Isaac Newton. In a similar vein, Abrahamsen (1977) has depicted Richard Nixon as victimized by a castrating mother. This characterization is laden with the etiologic hypothesis that the mother's purported domineering behavior expresses unresolved female penis envy which is held to have originated in the so-called phallic stage of infantile development. Lasch (1978) diagnoses American society as a "culture of narcissism," seething with a destructive oedipal rage, but masquerading under the pleasure principle. And in Mexico, even pastoral training in at least one diocese of the Roman Catholic Church has come under the sway of the Viennese genius: As reported by the Associated Press (Magri, 1979), the Pope met with one of the

167

bishops who had openly clashed with the Vatican over the use of psychoanalysis in training priests and monks in his diocese.

Undaunted by this pervasive ideological impact, I ask: What credence should we give to explanations in personality psychology, psychotherapy, psychohistory, and literary criticism or esthetics that are predicated on the soundness of much of Freud's intellectual corpus? For example, does *psychoanalytic* explanation of Hitler's behavior actually have far better warrant than, say, the diagnosis given by an exorcist who invokes literal Satanic possession? As for literary criticism, the *quondam* pro-Freudian literary critic Crews (1986) has argued caustically against the value of psychoanalytic explanations with reference to this chapter and to my book (1984).

Evangelists such as Billy Graham and Oral Roberts seem to have dramatically effected a durable restructuring of the personalities and emotions of some previously despairing born-again Christians. This outcome of evangelical "group therapy" has been explained psychoanalytically as resulting from a so-called "transference cure" (Fish, 1973) whose underlying mechanism is held to be libidinal. Granted that the impressive changes wrought by evangelists are produced by suggestion, one still wonders why one should put any epistemological stock in Ernest Jones's (1948, pp. 273, 291-292) hypothesis that these effects are attributable to a refocusing of the libidinal energy of repressed alloerotic impulses.

Like Freud himself, most advocates of his theory regard the analyst's many observations of the patient's interactions with him in the treatment sessions as the source of findings that are simply *peerless*, not only heuristically but also probatively. We are told that during a typical analysis, which lasts for some years, the analyst accumulates a vast number of variegated data from each patient that are evidentially relevant to Freud's theory of personality no less than to the dynamics and outcome of his therapy. Some leading analytic theoreticians have been concerned to *exclude* the metapsychology of Freud's psychic energy model, and *a fortiori* its erstwhile neurobiological trappings from the avowed purview of clinical validation. Therefore, it is to be understood that the term "psychoanalytic theory of personality" is here construed *within* the framework of the clinical theory to exclude the metapsychology of psychic energy flow.

The so-called "psychoanalytic interview" sessions are claimed to yield genuinely probative data because of the alleged real-life nature of the rich relationship between the analyst and the analysand. Hence the clinical setting is purported to be the arena of *experiments in situ*, in marked contrast to the contrived environment of the psychological laboratory with its superficial, transitory interaction between the experimental psychologist and his subject. In this vein, Kohut (1978) speaks of the clinical setting as "the laboratory of psychoanalytic treatment" (p. 523). Indeed the psychoanalytic method is said to be uniquely suited to first eliciting some of the important phenomena to which Freud's *depth* psychology pertains.

This superior *investigative value* of the analyst's clinical techniques is thus held to make the psychoanalytic interview at once the prime testing ground and the heuristic inspiration for Freud's theory of personality as well as for his therapy (Edelson, 1984, 1988). No wonder that five years before his death, Freud responded with almost patronizing disenchantment to Rosenzweig when the latter joyously reported *non*clinical *experimental* results that Rosenzweig took to be supportive of Freud's notion of repression (Rosenzweig, 1934, 1986). In a terse response of a few lines Freud (1934) replied, "I have examined your experimental studies for the verification of the psychoanalytic assertions with interest. I cannot put much value on these confirmations because the wealth of reliable observations on which these assertions rest make them independent of experimental verification. Still, it can do no harm."

The same stance is adopted by Jones (1959) in his "Editorial Preface" for Freud's *Collected Papers* (1959, vol. 1, p. 3), where he declared, the "clinical investigations" reported in these *Papers* "constitute the real basis of Psycho-Analysis" (p. 3). The same view is echoed by such diverse analytic authors as Hartmann (1959, p. 3), Kris (1975, p. 3), Rapaport (1959, p. 140), Margolin (1964, p. 44), and Wallerstein (1988, p. 27).

In a cognate vein, Glymour (1974, p. 304) maintains that Freud's theory is "strong enough to be tested on the couch," and according to Meehl (1978, p. 829), "the best place to study [i.e., test] psychoanalysis is the psychoanalytic session itself." Yet, more recently, Meehl (1983, p. 410) allowed that "it remains problematic just what *is* the state of our evidence from the best source, the analytic session." In like fashion, Luborsky and Spence (1978, p. 356) argue that "Freud was probably right" in his (1934) response to Rosenzweig. These authors maintain that *"Far more is known now* [in psychoanalysis] *through clinical wisdom than is known through quantitative* [i.e., controlled] *objective studies"* (p. 358). Despite an initial emphatic disclaimer that "Psychoanalysts, like other psychotherapists, literally *do not know* how they achieve their results," they conclude in the same sentence that analysts "possess a unique store of clinical wisdom" (1978, p. 360). More generally, one influential tradition among analysts is quite skeptical, if not outright hostile, toward attempts to test Freudian theory *outside* the clinical setting of the psychoanalytic interview. The argument is that as a depth psychology, this theory must rely on the psychoanalytic method to first uncover or even to first *generate* some of the very processes and phenomena to which Freud's hypotheses pertain. As Freud (1933, p. 174) himself put it, "In analysis, however, we have to do without the assistance afforded to research by experiment."

For anyone concerned with the evidential merit of psychoanalysis, the clinical validation of its theory and therapy poses a spate of challenging epistemological problems. For we have been told that the validation or discreditation of psychoanalytic hypotheses is vouchsafed by the *investigative value* of the particular clinical techniques employed in the psychoanalytic interview. But this thesis has been gainsaid by the ominous, if not deadly, reproach leveled by Wilhelm Fliess against Freud in 1900 (Freud, 1954, p. 334; Meehl, 1983, pp. 349, 410), that clinical observations are irremediably *contaminated* epistemologically and hence *probatively* unavailing *for that reason alone.* It is to be understood at the outset that when I impugn the *probative* value of clinical findings further on, I do not thereby cast any aspersions on their heuristic merits. It is to be clearly understood that this challenge is as follows (Grünbaum, 1984, p. 172): ". . . the major pillars of the theory of repression will turn out to be [clinically] ill-founded, *even if clinical data could be taken at face value as being uncontaminated epistemically,*" which they are not.

The persistence of this dispute, the results reported in Garfield and Bergin (1978), and some very important experimental investigations in cognitive psychology all prompt me to address the following question here: What is the probative value, if any, of data from the psychoanalytic interview for the evidential appraisal of Freudian theory? This assessment is a natural complement to my critical scrutiny in chapters 2 and 8, and in Grünbaum (1977, 1979a, 1984), of various charges of nontestability against the mere scientific entertainability of that body of hypotheses.

Let me begin with a very concise account of the received theoretical rationale for the procedures of administering psychoanalytic treatment. This rationale is traditionally offered by those who espouse this kind of intervention as being at least educative and presumably also emotionally corrective. But note that the enshrined theoretical rationale of treatment may well *not* be implemented in actual psychoanalytic practice (Fisher and Greenberg, 1977, chap. 7). Indeed, Freud (1912c) avowedly took liberties in the published reports he gave on his case histories and declared soothingly: "a reader who is willing to believe an analyst at all will give him credit for the touch of revision to which he has subjected his material" (p. 114). But as was documented by Mahoney (1986) and in chapter 4, this reassurance is not reliable. Thus there is reason to believe that Freud's published advocacy of how psychoanalysis should be carried out diverged from his own practice. Today the hiatus may well be even greater.

I should stress that there is no general consensus among those present-day analysts who have modified one or another of Freud's therapeutic tenets or even some facet of his theory of personality, while remaining his disciples for the most part. Indeed, the proliferation of their rather discordant modifications has eluded unification into a systematic and coherent body of "present-day psychoanalytic theory" (Eagle, 1984b; Reppen, 1985). Hence I deem it useful rather than anachronistic (Grünbaum, 1984, chap. 7) to take Freud's own classical views on both personality *and* therapy as the basis for the construal of "Psychoanalysis," which was also done for the same reason in the treatise by Fisher and Greenberg (1977). Moreover, I should emphasize that my scrutiny of the clinical validation of psychoanalytic theory focuses on the *distinctly Freudian* tenets as to the *identity* of the unconscious determinants of our mental life.

But it must not be forgotten that the much weaker generic thesis of determination by unconscious factors has had many exponents before Freud. This intellectual ancestry has been depicted by Whyte (1960), Ellenberger (1970), and Rauhala (1969). Indeed, the legacy of this tradition was bequeathed to Freud in Johann Herbart's philosophy of the unconscious via a psychology textbook that Freud used during his last year of Gymnasium. As Whyte points out, according to Herbart, ideas that become unconscious by inhibition "continue to exert their pressure against those in consciousness" (p. 143). There has likewise been a series of pre-Freudian champions of effecting *psychotherapy* by means of tapping the "pathogenic secrets" that were hypothesized to be hidden in the unconscious, a generic thesis of mental healing that is the hallmark of "dynamic psychiatry" (cf. Ellenberger, 1970).

THE THEORETICAL RATIONALE OF PSYCHOANALYTIC PROCEDURES

According to Freud's theory of personality, there is an ingression into adult interpersonal relations of unconscious conflict-laden attitudes, needs, and strivings which have been unwittingly *carried over* from originally infantile dispositions entertained toward important figures during childhood, e.g., a parent (Kubie, 1950). No wonder that, unbeknownst to the patient, the latter reacts to others during adulthood as if they were persons from his distant early past, thereby often misattributing alien motives and traits to them. The originally childish *transferred* feelings and aspirations are thus *inappropriate* to the patient's adult life situation. Hence the so-called transference phenomena which they generate distort or disrupt his interpersonal relations. It is the tyranny of these unconscious and conflict-laden mechanisms which is at the heart of the patient's neurosis. In his essay-review of my book (1984), Eagle (1986) points out instructively that, when challenged to substantiate this etiologic theory of transference, analysts such as Luborsky et al. (1985) impermissively weaken its content in the service of spurious substantiation.

On Freud's conception of psychoanalytic treatment, the crux of that procedure is the analyst's attempt to assist the patient in achieving deep *insight* into unconscious mechanisms that are held to generate the patient's neurosis. In order to enable the analysand to attain such insight, the analyst *interprets* to him the putative disguises of these surreptitious mechanisms in the following diverse contexts: the patient's purportedly free associations; transference phenomena that focus on the analyst and on other significant contemporary persons (e.g., a spouse); resistances to the elucidation of his repressions, waking fantasies, dreams ("the royal road to the unconscious"); slips of the tongue; and of course in his overt neurotic symptoms both inside and outside the analytic setting. While drawing on these sources of information, the analyst relies on the full range of Freud's etiological hypotheses to arrive at his interpretations or "constructions." In this way, the early repressed events that are conjectured to be the pathogens of the patient's adult neurosis are brought to light.

But the mere presentation of such an interpretative construction by the analyst does not at all issue automatically in the patient's acquisition and integration of the *insight* it can afford. Freud found in his clinical experience that the patient's repressions could not be removed by merely conveying the unconscious significance of his symptoms to him (1913a, pp. 141-143; 1909a, pp. 120-121). The patient must also penetrate the *resistances* he musters to obstruct access to his unconscious, resistances his ego has originally enlisted to repress the presumably pathogenic events uncovered by the analyst's constructions. If the analyst's interpretational excavations are to impart *insight* to the analysand, the latter's resistances must first be overcome. Only then can he expect to benefit therapeutically from the analyst's interpretations by understanding the *role* of the repressed experiences in the pathogenic conflicts. But this therapeutic gain would be aborted if the patient were to "allow what had been brought up into consciousness to slip back again into repression. At this point what turns the scale in his struggle [against his resistances] is not his intellectual insight—which is neither strong enough nor free enough for such an achievement—but simply and solely his relation to the doctor" (Freud, 1916-17, p. 445).

Soon after the analyst has begun to depict the previously unrecognized psychological linkages he hypothesizes between the patient's free associations, the analyst is not only faced with the patient's resistances but also becomes very much the focus of the latter's *emotionally charged* transference phenomena. The *transference* mechanism, which issues in the reemergence of infantile prototypes, operates especially in the patient's relationship with the analyst. In that interaction, the analysand recreates or models the cardinal conflictual features of his neurosis. While this so-called *transference neurosis* lasts, the analyst is assigned the roles of all the major figures from the patient's life. This emotional response occurs despite and perhaps partly because of the traditional analyst's purported ideal to maintain an impersonal, reserved stance of *non*moralizing neutrality, the so-called "analytic incognito" (Laplanche and Pontalis, 1973, pp. 271-272). But the transference phenomena evoked by the analyst will jeopardize therapeutic progress in the analysis, unless the analyst interprets these manifestations as such to the patient once adequate rapport has been established between them (Freud, 1913a, pp. 139-140).

While seeking to resolve the transference neurosis, the analyst controls the analysand's regression to early life events that are the presumed pathogens of the patient's adult neurosis. These events include an arrestive fixation that obstructed subsequent personal growth and emotional maturation. Utilizing the transference phenomena, the psychoanalyst explains to the patient, over and over again, just how the analyst interprets these occurrences as manifestations of the causal factors identified in his constructions. This "analysis of the transference" is an important component of the process of steadfast repetition of analytic interpretations. Thus assisted, the analysand "works through" his resistances, repressions, and other defenses with a view to acquiring *lasting* insight from the analyst's interpretations (see Laplanche and Pontalis [1973] on "Working Through").

We can now characterize the *aims* of analytic treatment more specifically. To do so, we shall first distinguish *genetic* considerations from so-called "dynamic" ones, as analytic writers are wont to do. Let us note that although the psychoanalytic theory of adult personality endows the early events of infancy and childhood with considerable causal significance (1914b, pp. 10, 17), it *allows* for later determinants. It does so by emphasizing (Freud, 1954, p. 176; Laplanche and Pontalis, 1973, pp. 111-112) that the pathogenic efficacy of a memory can depend on its being *subsequently* tainted further by a similar experience as follows. The later experience first turns the original memory into a *pathogen* (Freud, 1914b, p. 10). In such cases a memory is first held to *acquire* the etiological role of a trauma when infected by newly impinging experiences. Freud (1918) referred to this dependence of pathogenicity on a later experience as *Nachträglichkeit*. But its English rendering by "deferred action" can *mislead*, since it wrongly suggests that the role of the later experience is just to trigger the action of an already stored pathogen. By ruling out such merely delayed discharge by a later precipitant, Freud renounces the stereotype that depicts him as confining the causal determinants of the life of an individual to the earliest infantile period of his ontogeny. By the same token, present dispositions may encapsulate the effects of past history, and yet these current dispositions may serve to explain essentially co-present behavior that manifests them. It is therefore convenient, largely for the sake of temporal emphasis, to draw a rough distinction between those determinants of a patient's personal life that are practically nearly co-present with their effects on the one hand, and the distantly past determinants that exert long-term influences upon him, on the other.

While the latter early formative causes are quite naturally classified as "developmental" or "genetic," the quasi co-present causes are classified as "dynamic" (Kris, 1947, p. 15). The same temporal criteria are used to distinguish between Freud's developmental *hypotheses* and his dynamic ones. For instance, it is a genetic hypothesis of his so-called "theory of psychosexual development" that the adult male disposition of castration anxiety is attributable to oedipal childhood events prior to age 6. But the hypothesis of present adult castration anxiety, when used to explain an inordinate adult fear of competing with other males (Brenner, 1976, pp. 43-44), would count as a "dynamic" proposition. Dynamic hypotheses are further exemplified by the postulates of the theory of defense against dangerous impulses (e.g., reaction formation, projection). By the same token, the etiology of the "actual" neuroses is dynamic, though not unconsciously so, whereas the etiology of the "psychoneuroses" is genetic (Laplanche and Pontalis, 1973, pp. 10, 38, 265). We can now employ the distinction between genetic and dynamic factors or hypotheses.

The success of an analysis is traditionally held to require that the patient's principal conscious acts, thoughts, and feelings be traced to their *actual* unconscious determinants, both genetic and dynamic. A successful analysis is claimed to comprise a *veridical reconstruction* of the causally relevant events in the patient's early and current life. Therefore, we must ask: What reason does the orthodox analyst offer for expecting that his intraclinical procedures can attain such a veridical reconstruction of the pathogenesis of the patient's affliction? His reason is none other than that the general genetic and dynamic hypotheses of Freudian etiologic theory, which he invokes at every turn in his interpretations, are either true or well supported.

Spence (1982) has forsaken the endeavor of veridical reconstruction as largely utopian. It is integral to his rival account of psychoanalytic interpretations that the analyst's therapeutic hopes rest on the remedial potency of presumably mythic narrative constructions, coherently tailored to strike the patient as believable and as providing a persuasive rationale for future conduct. Though Spence fully allows that the explanatory segments of these avowedly *non*archaeological narratives are likely to be largely fancied, he nevertheless misleadingly and pretentiously baptizes them as containing "narrative truth." In short, as will become apparent from my discussion of Freud's definitive "Analytic Therapy" lecture (1916-17), Spence's account *severs* the traditionally fundamental bond between the "archaeologic" Freudian etiologies of the neuroses on the one hand, and psychoanalytic treatment on the other.

It would seem that, in Spence's view, the psychoanalytic enterprise cannot even realistically *aspire* to furnish well-supported general accounts of the actual dynamics of pathogenesis,
dream formation, and slip generation. After all, these hypotheses are typically "archaeologic." Yet as I argue in chapters 4 and
6, once we have resolutely sprung the stultifying epistemological confines of the clinical setting—a cognitive enclave that is
the arena for Spence's entire case!—the archaeologic *aspirations*
of the theory of repression can be legitimately retained. For
this reason alone, I shall hereafter disregard Spence's notion
of psychoanalytic therapy. Instead, I shall resume discussing
the received "archaeologic" one, in which the term "truth" is
never employed in Spence's misleading manner. Indeed,
Spence offers no good reason at all for using *psychoanalytic* notions to equip the patient with a coping strategy. He gives no
evidence that his version of therapy issues in better *outcome* than
rival therapies, let alone that psychoanalytic ingredients of it
deserve the credit for such putative outcome. As chapter 3
above has shown, the provision of the latter evidence is an even
taller order than the comparative demonstration of superior
treatment outcome.

It is fundamental to appreciate that the truth, or at least
the warranted credibility of Freud's theory of personality, is
deemed to underwrite the *traditional* promise that the analysand
can acquire genuine rather than only fancied self-knowledge
from psychoanalytic treatment. Just such knowledge is taken to
be the effective ingredient of the therapy. A good analysis is
regarded to be *educative* in the specific sense of furnishing verid-
ically insightful self-knowledge via the cognitive devices of interpretation and memory retrieval (see Marmor, 1962, pp.
286-299; Redlich and Freedman, 1966, p. 277). This presumed educative function has an important consequence for
gauging the degree of ambitiousness of the aims of an analysis.
Suppose the avowed goal of the analytic encounter were parsi-
monious by modestly abjuring the expectation of symptom relief as a causal concomitant of the achievement of educative
insight. Even such an explicit disclaimer of emotional benefit,
which is issued by some analysts, does not lessen the inordinate

ambitiousness of Freud's proclaimed goal of imparting self-knowledge to the patient. Indeed, Freud (1930) wrote: "The future will probably attribute far greater importance to psychoanalysis as the science of the unconscious than as a therapeutic procedure" (p. 265). Unless and until the bold psychoanalytic theory of personality on which the acquisition of self-understanding is predicated does have good epistemic credentials, this avowed objective is pretentious to the point of being a snare and a delusion for the unwary.

This cardinal caveat is often blithely overlooked by analysts. Thus, Cooper and Michels (1978, p. 376) first tell us that "the development of self-knowledge and self-potential is a value held dearly by a significant subgroup within the culture." Yet when acknowledging the legitimacy of the social "pressure for psychoanalysis to demonstrate therapeutic efficacy" in future treatment outcome studies, they are undaunted by epistemic hesitations about its theory of personality and declare: "There will always be individuals who want to undertake personal analysis in order to expand self-awareness, even if studies show it not to have significant therapeutic effect" (p. 377).

But *if* Freud's psychogenetics and psychodynamics are accepted, the psychoanalytic scenario of free versus enslaved behavior unfolds with nearly impeccable logic and great persuasiveness. Even theories of unconscious motivations that reject all the distinctly Freudian assumptions of the substance and generation of unconscious contents would presumably subscribe to the general schema of this scenario: Precisely insofar as thoughts, feelings, behavior, and personality traits are *primarily* a function of unconscious mental processes, their long-term patterns are rigidly inflexible and hence maladaptive. Neither rational argument nor emotional exhortations, nor perhaps even rewards or punishments can fundamentally alter neurotically engendered dispositions, although such inducements may determine whether these dispositions will become manifest in given situations. And if, as in Freudian theory, unconscious influences are held to generate the symptomatic manifestations of unattainable and unknown goals, the cravings generated by these influences are insatiable. These yearnings repeatedly give rise to behavior which is largely insensitive to ensuing unhappiness or happiness, and oblivious to errors of judgment. There is little scope for learning from experience, change, or growth; instead, there is considerable enslavement to unconscious dictates.

Yet processes of which we are conscious can be affected by rational argument, emotional exhortation, success or failure, the satiation of a need, and by rewards or punishments. Mental processes that are predominantly determined by consciously operating factors can be flexibly adaptive to external or intradermal signals. In the psychoanalytic picture of the human condition, these conscious processes are the hallmark of human freedom, for to the extent that they do govern our lives, there is freedom or scope for learning, change, and growth. As Freud put it epigrammatically: "Where id was, there ego shall be" (1933, p. 80).[1] Incidentally, this conception of freedom of action is clearly part of an essentially *deterministic* conception of human thought, feeling, and behavior: It makes the freedom of an act contingent *not* on *whether* it is causally determined but only on the *particular character* of its causal determinants (Freud, 1901, pp. 253-254; Grünbaum, 1972, pp. 610-617). So much for the rationale of the promise of a psychoanalysis to furnish self-knowledge that will rid the analysand of irrational shackles.

Traditionally, the function of being an emotional *corrective* in specified ways has often been claimed for Freudian treatment over and above the stated educative one. When such emotional efficacy has been asserted as well, we are told that an *otherwise unattainable* quality and durability of target symptom reduction (or elimination) will be a frequent causal byproduct of the resolution of complexes, which is effected by the achievement of conscious insight (Freud, 1923c, p. 251). For if neurotic behavior is indeed engendered by unconscious conflicts, then nothing better than relapse or symptom substitution can be expected from any treatment that leaves these pathogenic agencies intact

---

[1] Brandt (1966) has cautioned against the misleading overtones of this rendition of "Wo Es war soll Ich werden." For an illuminating discussion of the two distinct ways in which Freud's dictum can be understood, see Eagle (1984b). As he points out (p. 203), these two ways are "a function of how one conceptualizes the terms 'ego' and 'id.' "

(Freud, 1916-17, p. 436). In this vein, Anna Freud (1969) declared: "In competition with the psychotherapies they [analysts] are justified to maintain that what they have to offer is unique, i.e., thoroughgoing personality changes as compared with more superficial symptomatic cures. Unfortunately, the former is not always aspired to by the patients, who aim above all at immediate relief from suffering" (p. 131). On this basis, analysis is held to have a uniquely superior capability to counteract both relapse and symptom substitution, when effecting therapeutic outcome such as anxiety reduction (Freud, 1916-17, pp. 444-445, 451; 1940a, p. 179; cf. Brenner, 1976, p. 146).

As we saw, even with regard to producing desired *emotional* effects on the patient, the orthodox account of psychoanalytic treatment is *cognitivist* to the extent of assigning *causal indispensability* to insight generated from interpretations (see Laplanche and Pontalis, 1973, p. 229, *sub.* "Interpretation"). But just this essential role of insight in effecting positive therapeutic change has been denied by Alexander (1935; 1963, p. 287; Alexander and French, 1946, p. 20; Christiansen, 1964, p. 61).

Speaking historically, Alexander (1966) maintains that "the classical technique [of psychoanalysis] was originally devised for research and not treatment. . . . [The] apparent parallelism between the aims of research and treatment has proved a grave overstatement" (pp. 247-248). Indeed, Alexander forsakes the neutrality of the analytic incognito in favor of *deliberately* adopting at the outset a role-playing attitude tailored to each particular patient. He manipulates the patient's transference by assuming specific roles unfamiliar to the patient from prior important interpersonal relations. Alexander then attributes corrective efficacy to the patient's ensuing *emotional* experience of his rapport with the analyst to the extent that even when this experience is not infused with enhanced insight, he deems it capable of being durably remedial.

In this way, he stresses the less ratiocinative facets of the patient's emotional reactions to the analyst. According to this more "emotivist" account, both insight and the recovery of repressed memories, which are primarily cognitive, are mere manifestations of therapeutic progress rather than its cause. But Alexander offers this claim as an *ipse dixit*. In this sense, he downgrades the *causal* relevance of the very ingredients of analytic treatment to which Freud (1937b) still assigned fundamental therapeutic indispensability two years before his death. By demoting interpretations relating to the patient's remote past, as well as the latter's responses to such interpretations, Alexander seems to lessen significantly any promise the clinical findings were traditionally claimed to have for validating Freud's *genetic* theory.

But I am concerned with that validation, and also mindful of the paramount influence of Freud's rival view. Hence I shall take his predominantly cognitivist account as the basis for my assessment of the probative value that has been claimed for therapeutic findings obtained within the psychoanalytic interview. Note that I speak of Freud's conception of the dynamics of therapy as "predominantly" cognitivist. For as we saw above, he explicitly acknowledged that the patient's positive transference *feelings* toward the analyst would safeguard the fruition of therapeutic success from a resurgence of the repressions laboriously uncovered by the analysis (1916-17, p. 455). Because Freud held that therapeutically the patient's emotional attachment to the analyst is *also* essential initially as an ice-breaker or catalyst, he qualified the connection between the patient's insight and recovery when declaring: "understanding and cure almost coincide" (1933, p. 145).

According to Freudian theory, the clinical data furnished by analytic sessions are of significantly wider compass than those deemed to be indices of therapeutic progress, standstill, or even retrogression. Instead of being confined to such therapeutic findings, the clinical data from analysis comprise the full range of the patient's verbal and nonverbal communications concerning his past and present experience as well as observations relating to the analyst's own overt to covert conduct. Nonetheless, observed therapeutic gain has avowedly been assigned an important place by Freud and other analysts among the clinical data held to validate the developmental and dynamic hypotheses of the Freudian corpus. Here, let us focus our scrutiny on the probative significance of the genus of clinical evidence on the particular species of psychoanalytic observations that relate to therapeutic gain or loss.

Is the Attribution of Therapeutic Gain to Veridical Psychoanalytic Insight Warranted?

In his lecture on "Analytic Therapy," Freud (1916-17) enunciates his thesis that telling clinical support for his general theory of personality is furnished by his *therapeutic success*. Speaking of the analysand's "illness," he declares:

> After all, his conflicts will only be successfully solved and his resistances overcome if the anticipatory ideas [i.e., interpretative depictions of analytic meaning] he is given tally [both objectively and subjectively] with what is real in him. Whatever in the doctor's conjectures is inaccurate drops out in the course of the analysis; it has to be withdrawn and replaced by something more correct [p. 452].

This is Freud's reply to what he considers "the objection that is most often raised against psychoanalysis." He formulates this objection as follows:

> . . . there is a risk that the influencing of our patient may make the objective certainty of our findings doubtful. What is advantageous to our therapy is damaging to our researches [i.e., damaging to the clinical validation of the general psychoanalytic theory of personality].

In other words, the serious criticism Freud is anxious to *undermine* here and elsewhere (e.g., in 1923c, pp. 250-251) is: Epistemologically, therapeutic success is *non*probative because it is achieved *not* by imparting veridical insight, but rather by the persuasive suggestion of fanciful pseudo insights that merely ring verisimilar to the docile patient. As we noted above, Freud was really stung and became indignant when his intimate friend Wilhelm Fliess charged him with *projecting* his own thoughts *into* those of his patients instead of *reading* their thoughts and abstaining from tailoring them to his expectations by suggestion (Freud, 1954, pp. 334, 337). Yet in his lecture on "Transference," which immediately preceded the one dealing with "Analytic Therapy," Freud not only explains how the patient's positive feeling ("positive transference") toward the analyst safeguards therapeutic success, but also points out that "In so far as his transference bears a 'plus' sign, it clothes the doctor with authority and is transformed into belief in his communications and explanations" (p. 445). Precisely because the analysand's ensuing credulity renders him intellectually docile, it has been objected that his compliant responses furnish only *spurious* confirmations of the therapist's theoretical inferences, no matter how successful the therapy.

The cardinal importance Freud attaches to refuting such disparagement can be gauged from his account of the devastating import that this objection would have if it were not disarmed:

> If it were justified, psycho-analysis would be nothing more than a particularly well-disguised and particularly effective form of suggestive treatment and we should have to attach little weight to all that it tells us about what influences our lives, the dynamics of the mind or the unconscious. That is what our opponents believe; and in especial they think that we have 'talked' the patients into everything relating to the importance of sexual experiences—or even into those experiences themselves—after such notions have grown up in our own depraved imagination [p. 452].

Let us look in more detail at just how Freud appealed to the requirements he postulated for therapeutic success to rebut the criticism that analysts talk their patients into producing the very clinical data they need to validate Freud's theory of personality, and psychoanalysis acts as an emotional corrective by mere suggestion rather than by imparting veridical self-knowledge.

It is an avowed goal of psychoanalytic intervention to effect a durable remission of the patient's neurosis. But just what constitutes the successful conquest of the analysand's neurosis? Ideally, this conquest consists in an adaptive restructuring of the intrapsychic personality dispositions so that there is concomitant lasting overt symptom relief without symptom substitution. The intrapsychic restructuring is deemed crucial to safeguard the quality and durability of overt symptomatic improvement. Yet it needs to be borne in mind that Freud deemed only the so-called "psychoneuroses" (Laplanche and Pontalis, 1973, p. 369) amenable to psychoanalytic treatment and investigation, as distinct from the "actual neuroses" (p. 10). He postulated a purely somatic and indeed toxic etiology for the latter, while attributing the former to infantile conflicts. Just for brevity, I shall omit the qualification "psycho" when speaking of the former neuroses and their therapeutic requirements.

For many years, Freud (1916-17, pp. 255, 438-439; 1925b, p. 42) insisted that unlike the "transference" neuroses, the "narcissistic" ones, e.g., paranoia and schizophrenia, are recalcitrant to psychoanalytic treatment. But in a widely overlooked 1924 addendum to Freud's Three Essays (1905b, p. 218, n. 1) to which Zvi Lothane called my attention, Freud allowed that the psychoses "have become to a greater extent accessible to psychoanalysis." Indeed, Harold Searles (1963) claims to have shown that schizophrenics can form a transference *psychosis* no less than nonpsychotic neurotics can produce a transference neurosis.

As I have stressed (chap. 1), Freud enunciated a conjection of causally necessary conditions for the analysand's conquest of his neurosis, a cardinal thesis that I there dubbed "Freud's Master Proposition." Here, let me restate it equivalently as follows: (1) Only the psychoanalytic method of interpretation and treatment can yield or mediate to the patient correct insight into the unconscious pathogens of his psychoneurosis; and (2) the analysand's correct insight into the etiology of his affliction and into the unconscious dynamics of his character is, in turn, *causally necessary* for the therapeutic conquest of his neurosis. In order to remain mindful that this Master Proposition is, in fact, an affirmation of two necessary conditions, I shall hereafter also call it Freud's "Necessary Condition Thesis" or, for brevity, just "NCT." Let me recall here that, as I pointed out in chapter 1, Sachs's (1989) exegetical challenge to my attribution of the Master Proposition to Freud completely trivializes the central thesis of Freud's (1916-17) "Analytic Therapy" lecture (see also Grünbaum, 1984, pp. 270-275; Erwin, 1992).

As we saw, Freud invoked his NCT to infer from actual therapeutic success in any given case that the pertinent psychoanalytic interpretations had been both objectively correct *and* subjectively verisimilar for the patient. In so doing, he described *such* interpretations by saying that they "tally with what is real" in the client. (In the German original, Freud (1940-52, vol. 11, p. 470) speaks of such interpretations as "Erwartungsvor-

stellungen . . . die mit der Wirklichkeit in ihm übereinstim-
men.") In view of Freud's use of the phrase "tally with what is
real," I shall use the designation "Tally Argument" to refer to
the following kind of inference:

Premise 1: The analysis of patient X was therapeutically successful
Premise 2: NCT (Freud's Master Proposition)
Conclusion: The psychoanalytic interpretations given to X were
veridical and seemed verisimilar to X

Incidentally, Freud was usually loath to attribute his therapeutic *failures* to the incorrectness of his interpretations, blaming the patient's resistance instead. Thus he tells us (1920b,
p. 164) that the very psychogenesis he had inferred for the
lesbianism of a patient likewise explained why she clung to her
"perversion" by resisting his therapeutic efforts. Yet in 1897,
he abandoned his seduction etiology of hysteria *partly* because
of some of his therapeutic failures with hysterical patients
(1954, pp. 215-216, Letter 69).

The reader is asked to recall from chapter 1 the three sets of
consequences Freud was able to deduce by means of his NCT.
Here let me partly recapitulate these results in order to elaborate on them.

It is of capital importance to appreciate that Freud is at pains
to employ the Tally Argument in order to justify the following
epistemological claim: Actual *durable* therapeutic success guar-
antees *not only* that the pertinent analytic interpretations *ring*
true to the analysand, *but also* that they *are* indeed veridical, or
at least quite close to the mark. Freud then relies on this bold
intermediate contention to conclude nothing less than the following: Collectively, the successful outcomes of analyses do constitute *cogent* evidence for all that general psychoanalytic theory
tells us about the influences of the unconscious dynamics of the
mind on our lives; see the somewhat less categorical earlier
claims made in Freud's case history of Little Hans (1909a, pp.
104-105, 120-121). In short, psychoanalytic treatment successes
vouch for the truth of the Freudian theory of personality. Near
the end of his life, he (1933) wrote:

I have told you that psycho-analysis began as a method of treatment; but I did not want to commend it to your interest as a method of treatment but on account of the truths it contains, on account of the information it gives us about what concerns human beings most of all—their own nature—and on account of the connections it discloses between the most different of their activities. As a method of treatment it is one among many, though, to be sure, *primus inter pares*. If it . . . [were] without therapeutic value it would not have been discovered, as it was, in connection with sick people and would not have gone on developing for more than thirty years [pp. 156-157].

As we saw, Freud tended to deem therapeutic *failure* compatible with the correctness of the analyst's interpretations, if only because of the patient's resistance. But he claimed further that, by prolonging the gathering of *potentially heuristic* further data from the patient, even a *therapeutic fiasco* can positively contribute to the *scientific* fruitfulness of the analysis. Thus, in the case history of the Rat-Man (1909b, pp. 207-208), he maintained that remedial success curtails scientific exploration by shortening analytic treatment, whereas therapeutic failure is positively inducive to such discovery, a fact that was misinvoked by Cioffi against my exegesis (Grünbaum, 1986, p. 272). He concluded (p. 208): "The scientific results of psycho-analysis are at present only a by-product of its therapeutic aims, and for that reason it is often just in those cases where treatment fails that most discoveries are made." In a similar vein, he admonished in 1927, "I only want to feel assured that the therapy will not destroy the science" (p. 254), a theme vigorously taken up by Holzman (1985).

Consequently, to the extent that Freud placed less stock in analytic treatment success as compared to his theory of the unconscious, which he did in his later years—for example, in a 1930 statement cited at the beginning of this chapter—he lessened the availability of his Tally Argument for vindicating clinical findings epistemologically against the charge of contamination by suggestion. Indeed, the *first* premise of this argument would hardly ever be satisfied if his later therapeutically pessimistic paper (1937a) were taken to be his *final* evaluation of analytic therapy.

More recently, leading analysts have also espoused NCT and have countenanced his invocation of the Tally Argument. For instance, Kubie (1950) tells us: "It is the discovery of the reasons for the patient's unconscious need tenaciously to cling to error that alone makes lasting correction of the error possible" (p. 54). And he maintains further that "the analyst knows that unless he succeeds the patient will remain sick indefinitely" (p. 179). In 1952, Kubie listed "alterations of symptoms" on the client's part as one of the principal bases for testing the accuracy of an interpretation, amid emphasizing that "Analysis stands or falls by the validity of its specific interpretations in specific instances." On the other hand, in the revised edition of his (1950) book, published in 1975, Kubie seems to have had second thoughts at least about his 1952 claim and presumably even about his espousal of NCT. There he wrote:

> . . . therapeutic successes or failures do not provide dependable evidence for the accuracy or inaccuracy of a theory . . . there is no constant or easily predictable correlation between the accuracy of a theory and the therapeutic results achieved by its applications. . . . One could cite countless . . . examples . . . from psychoanalysis, where success and failure of our therapeutic efforts seem at times to bear only an accidental relationship to the accuracy or inaccuracy of theoretical constructions [p. 353].

Much more unequivocally than Kubie, Malan (1976) noted that NCT had been a pillar of Freudian therapeutic doctrine, but called on his analytic colleagues to abandon it in the face of "conclusive evidence" that "all-pervading" psychic improvements or cures can be effected by theoretically rival treatment modalities such as behavior therapy and even by extraclinical life events (pp. 147, 173, 269). Hence the label "spontaneous remission" for the *latter* gains of course does *not* signify that they were uncaused, but only that *therapists* did not cause them.

The stubborn evidence acknowledged by Malan makes it more imperative than ever to address the serious challenge to clinical validation posed by it. The several fundamental doubts it raises as to the probative value of data from the psychoanalytic interview can now be formulated by means of the following sets of questions:

1. Can analytic data warrant at all the causal attribution of gains made by patients *after* their analyses to their having received professional treatment? Or is the inference of such therapeutic efficacy vitiated by the fallacy of *post hoc ergo propter hoc*, much like speciously crediting coffee drinking with curing colds?

2. If analytic data are able to license giving therapeutic credit to the intervention of professional treatment at all, do these data furthermore corroborate the stated *superiority* of treatment outcome that analysts have been wont to claim, especially for chronically and severely ill patients? It will be recalled that such superiority of outcome has been claimed for an analysis *vis-à-vis* the results attained by treatment modalities based on a rival theoretical rationale of therapeutic change.

3. For the purpose of the next set of questions, assume that—for specified diagnostic categories—analytic treatment outcome exceeds any gains ordinary life events produce in untreated neurotics belonging to those nosological categories. Then we must ask a so-called process question, which is crucial: Can analytic clinical data justify crediting the surplus gains supposedly exhibited by analyzed patients to those *particular factors* within the psychoanalytic *process* to which Freud attributes its remedial efficacy? It is imperative to learn how, if at all, this attribution of remedial efficacy to the analytic insight factors singled out by Freud can be upheld in the face of the following reportedly impressive evidence (Luborsky and Spence, 1978, p. 338; Bergin and Lambert, 1978, p. 179-180): Clearly positive treatment results in excess of spontaneous remission are achieved by therapists guided by quite contrary therapeutic theories, who do not impart "insights" licensed by the psychoanalytic etiologies. This sanguine report has been firmly corrected by Prioleau et al. (1983) in regard to the superiority of *professional* psychotherapy. But granted the latter rival achievement in regard to *parity* with psychoanalysis, is it not incumbent upon analysts to tell us just why we should hesitate to attribute the gains assumedly made by their patients to treatment factors *other than* those singled out by Freud's account of favorable therapeutic change?

The challenge posed by the *last* group of questions threatens to undermine the Tally Argument by impugning Freud's NCT as causally spurious. If the Tally Argument is thus undercut, any therapeutic successes scored by analysts become probatively unavailing to the clinical validation of Freud's theory of personality via that argument. Yet he had avowedly relied on only that argument to *counter* the mortal charge from Fliess and others that suggestion is the epistemologic bane of the psychoanalytic method of investigation, no less than it is the decisive agency in his therapy (1916-17, pp. 446-447). In view of our current concern with the therapeutic validation of the cornerstone theory of psychopathology, the last (third) group of questions above is more fundamental to our epistemologic concerns than the two earlier ones. I shall therefore tackle these more basic questions while deferring the others.

The gravamen of the objections implicit in these questions needs to be articulated more sharply. This logical refinement can be given by drawing on the important *generalization of the traditional pharmacological concept of placebo* now employed in the leading literature of both medicine and psychiatry. In the preceding chapter 3, I offered a detailed explication of this generalized notion of placebo treatment and "placebo effect." I shall avail myself of that clarification here, and I ask that the reader bear it well in mind in the sequel, rather than operate with whatever intuitive notion of placebo he or she may have harbored previously. In particular, recall from chapter 3 that I do *not* rely on the rather vague notion of suggestion at all to characterize a placebo effect. Instead I speak of a treatment gain as a "placebo effect" with respect to a particular target disorder, therapeutic *theory*, and type of patient, just when that positive effect is produced by treatment factors *other than* those designated as the efficacious ones by the given therapeutic theory.

As we shall see shortly, it is still *arguable* that psychoanalytic treatment is *not* a generic placebo. But for the moment, just *posit* that analysis is actually such a placebo after all. This would mean that if psychoanalysis does yield therapeutic benefits, these are not, in fact, due to any remedial efficacy on the part of the presumed insight engendered by the application of Freud's etiologic hypotheses to the analysis of the client's transference and resistance. In the posited case, analysts are advocating their modality for the *wrong* reason, having miscredited causally irrelevant characteristic treatment factors with being therapeutic, while overlooking or even explicitly discounting the actually remedial incidental ones. As we saw in chapter 3, Frank (1973, 1974) denies that the *characteristic* factors of analytic treatment are therapeutic. Yet he credits psychoanalysis with being placebogenically beneficial for stated types of patients, with yielding gains beyond those associated with so-called "spontaneous" remission, a conclusion that needs to be qualified (Prioleau et al., 1983).

On his general account of the remedial dynamics of psychotherapy, the arousal of hope and the mobilization of a sense of mastery in the patient constitute key causal factors in the healing process. Frank considers the diverse specific techniques of intervention enjoined by various rival views of the therapeutic process to be causally immaterial for the most part. Indeed, he hypothesizes (1973, p. xvi), "when therapies have a differential effect, it may depend on the differential ability of the technique to mobilize certain features common to all" competing therapies. In the same vein, Kiev (1978, pp. 579-581) points out that these common features are mobilized by primitive witch doctors no less than by modern psychotherapists and include the following culturally accepted trappings of the healing role: well-practiced rituals, a special jargon, a knowledgeable and systematic manner, and more generally the therapist's charisma. If psychoanalytic treatment is actually a placebo, as posited, then in the parlance of chapter 3 above, it is, of course, an *inadvertent* placebo relatively to Freud's therapeutic tenets, but *avowedly* a generic placebo with respect to Frank's reckoning of remedial relevance. Note, however, that if analysis *is* a placebo, this does not, in practice, preclude a situation as follows: An analyst who administers Freudian treatment, in the presumably mistaken belief that its characteristic factors are actually therapeutic, may be more successful than a less credulous and more cynical analytic colleague who would dispense it as an intentional placebo.[2]

---

[2]For a discussion of possible placebos and placebo stimuli ranging from different kinds of suggestion, to patient aversion, to cognitive dissonance, see Shapiro and Morris (1978, pp. 375, 379, 385, 387-388, 390-391, 394). For

The explication of the notion of placebo given in chapter 3 can now serve to appraise the clinical validation of the Freudian corpus. We can now focus on the details of the challenge posed for Freud's Tally Argument by the hypothesis that analytic treatment success is *placebogenic*. The nub of the threat to the Tally Argument from the latter placebo hypothesis is this: The remedially efficacious factors belong to the class of *incidental* treatment constituents, instead of being the postulated characteristic ones, as claimed by Freud in that argument. The particular *identity* of the remedial factors *within* the class of *incidental* constituents is immaterial here. Thus, Frank may not have picked them out. What matters is that, assumedly, analytic treatment success is a placebogenic effect at all with respect to Freud's avowed dynamics of therapy. As long as that putative therapeutic success derives from the remedial potency of *incidental* rather than of the declared characteristic factors in the treatment process, veridical psychoanalytic insight is hardly causally necessary for the successful outcome of that process. In that case, Freud's NCT is false.

For, according to that premise, veridical insight *is* causally necessary for the conquest of the patient's neurosis, *and only psychoanalysis* can supply the requisite insight. But once NCT has become untenable, even regular therapeutic triumphs cannot redound to the credibility of Freud's theory of personality via the Tally Argument, since NCT is a premise of that argument. In short, if the presumed therapeutic outcome success of analysis is indeed placebogenic, then this remedial success is *probatively unavailing* for sustaining Freud's theoretical edifice via the Tally Argument.

While the posited placebogenic character of psychoanalytic outcome success is *sufficient* to discredit NCT, it is hardly necessary. NCT is likewise invalidated by the treatment-outcome gains from *non*analytic therapies for the following reason: Either the successful *non*analytic therapies do *not* supply veridical insight or they do. In *either* case, their success refutes NCT by

additional discussions of the use of placebos in *psychiatric* treatment, see Bourne (1971), Uhlenhuth et al. (1959), Malitz and Kanzler (1971), Hankoff et al. (1960), and Gliedman et al. (1958).

refuting *one* of its conjuncts *without requiring* analysis to be a placebo. Though NCT may be false even when analytic therapy is *not* a placebo, the specific challenge to Freud's NCT posed by the putative placebogenic success of his therapy is important. Suppose analysis is just an inadvertent placebo, but succeeds therapeutically. This placebo status would *abort* a *new* attempt to deduce the conclusion of Freud's Tally Argument via the following *modified* version of NCT. It would now be conceded that each of several rival therapies can succeed no less than analysis amid stoutly contending, however, that the conquest of the neurosis by any patient receiving *only* psychoanalytic treatment does depend causally on veridical Freudian insight.

This altered version of NCT collapses in the face of the posit that analytic outcome success is inadvertently placebogenic, for such placebogenesis *discredits* Freud's attribution of remedial efficacy to analytic insight, no matter how successful the actual outcome of analysis. If analysis *is* a placebo, his far-ranging epistemic tribute to clinical findings cannot be vindicated even via the *modified* Tally Argument in question!

Just what reasons are adduced by those who categorize Freud's modality as a placebo while fully allowing that it *is* therapeutic? More fundamentally, how cogent are their reasons? In dealing with these questions, comparisons of the results from psychoanalytic treatment with those yielded by "rival" treatments will be relevant. It should be pointed out that treatment modalities are held to be "rivals" of one another in the sense that there is a divergence between their *theories* of the rationale, strategy, methods, or techniques of the therapeutic process. That there is a plethora of such rival therapeutic modalities is clear enough. Sloane et al. (1975) report:

> In 1959 Harper described thirty-six different kinds of psychotherapy. His list was not exhaustive even at that time, and since then many new therapies have emerged, each with a different name, underlying theory, and set of therapeutic strategies. Advocates of each believe its novel approach is far superior to others if not in fact the final answer to the problem [p. 7].

Wolberg (1977) reports that there are no less than 200 purportedly distinct psychotherapies!

Luborsky and Spence (1978) are very mindful of this profusion of rivals when they address the bearing of treatment outcome comparisons on placebogenesis:

> Controlled comparisons of psychoanalytic with other forms of treatment are almost nonexistent . . . because proper studies of this type are difficult, there are also relatively few of them. The implication of this conclusion is obvious: it is impossible to say that one type of psychotherapy is better than another. . . . For those comparisons for which a sufficient number of studies exist, there is usually a nonsignificant difference in percentage of patients improving with each treatment (with only a couple of nonimpressive exceptions). One strong implication is that treatment effects are mainly a product of nonspecific [i.e., incidental] factors that those treatments have in common. . . . No good studies exist dealing with differences in the *quality* of the outcomes [p. 338].

This state of affairs clearly impugns Freud's NCT. Furthermore, it makes it incumbent on Freudians to try to show by future controlled treatment-process research that the remedial efficacy of their modality is not placebogenic after all, but due to its characteristic treatment factors. But Bergin and Lambert (1978) actually affirm that the successes attained by a broad range of rival verbal psychotherapies are indeed placebogenic in *each* case:

> A growing number of controlled outcome studies are analyzing a wide variety of therapies. These findings generally yield clearly positive results when compared with no-treatment, wait-list, and [*intended*] placebo or pseudotherapies. . . .
>
> Although there is a growing body of knowledge that confirms the value of psychotherapy, differences in outcome between various forms of intervention are rare. Although behavior therapies, and their cognitive variations, sometimes show superior outcomes, this is by no means the general case. Even where it is the case, the criteria of change are often biased in the direction of being sensitive mainly to behavioral changes. . . .
>
> Interpersonal and nonspecific [i.e., incidental] or nontechnical factors still loom large as stimulators of patient improvement. . . .
>
> It appears that these personal factors are crucial ingredients even in the more technical therapies. . . . This is not to say that techniques are irrelevant but that their power for change pales

when compared with that of personal influence. Technique is crucial to the extent that it provides a believable rationale and congenial *modus operandi* for the change agent and the client.

These considerations imply that psychotherapy is laden with non-specific [incidental] or placebo factors [references omitted]: but these influences, when specified, may prove to be the essence of what provides therapeutic benefit [pp. 179-180].

In short, Bergin and Lambert adduce the apparent absence of significant differences in treatment outcome from rival modalities to opt for the view that all these modes of intervention are inadvertent placebos relative to the therapeutic beliefs of their advocates. On this view, psychoanalysis as well as its nonanalytic rivals achieves positive results only placebogenically. Clearly *if* the evidence from comparative outcome studies and other controlled investigations sustains such placebogenesis, then not only is Freud's Tally Argument devastatingly undermined, but his account of the remedial efficacy of insight is actually *discredited*, no matter how successful the actual outcome of an analysis. Thus, the doctrinal threat from placebogenesis is far more serious than the concession by such analysts as Kris and Kubie that *too many variables* are involved in the therapeutic process to permit validation of analytic interpretations by means of successful treatment outcome.

Bergin and Lambert articulate their thesis of placebogenesis by conjecturing quite precisely that the *incidental* factors from which the rival therapies derive their remedial efficacy are the *same* in each case: An "interpersonal relationship" with the therapist "that is characterized by trust, warmth, acceptance, and human wisdom" (p. 180).

Similarly, though confining himself to rival schools of *psychoanalytic* treatment, Marmor (1962) discounts the therapeutic value of "the theoretical inclination of the analyst" in favor of the remedial relevance of the latter's "personal characteristics, experience, and empathic capacity" (p. 288). Marmor contends that "interpretations that put the patient's material within one frame of reference [which is associated with *one* of the rival analytic schools] seem to be just as effective for the patient as interpretations that put it within another frame of reference" (p. 290), and he offers telling reasons:

But what *is* insight? To a Freudian it means one thing, to a Jungian another, and to a Rankian, a Horneyite, an Adlerian or a Sullivanian, still another. Each school gives its own particular brand of insight. Whose are the correct insights? The fact is that patients treated by analysts of all these schools may not only respond favorably, but also believe strongly in the insights which they have been given [p. 289].

Indeed, as early as 1931 Glover admitted that interpretations which subsequently turn out as "inexact" (false)—as distinct from merely "incomplete"—can be held to have effected "improvement in the symptomatic sense" no less warrantedly than ("exact") (veridical) interpretations. As he concedes, even a "glaringly inaccurate interpretation" that is "backed by [the analyst's] strong transference authority" may well have this kind of therapeutic value (pp. 400-401). But Glover appeals only to Freudian *therapeutic theory*—instead of marshaling clinical findings—to salvage the situation: Insights afforded by exact interpretations genuinely cure in depth by resolving underlying conflicts, he tells us, whereas inexact interpretations effect a mere redressing of the balance of *unresolved* conflicts by means of "pseudo-analytical suggestion." In other words, pseudointerpretations can issue in nothing better than a shallow and ephemeral "transference cure." And only Freudian theory can furnish the allegedly needed veridical, exact interpretations, despite occasional lapses into inexact ones in practice. Glover thought he could dispose of all the *non*-Freudian analytic therapies by characterizing "all pseudo-Freudian analysis as essentially pseudo-analytic suggestion" (p. 406). In short, any beneficial results from *pseudo*-Freudian analysis are inadvertently placebogenic and just cosmetic symptomatically.

Glover sought to dispose of a therapeutic challenge posed by the positive treatment outcome attained by two groups of practitioners: (1) orthodox Freudians who unwittingly used interpretations that turned out to be inexact only after completion of the analysis, because the purported memories elicited from patients were later unmasked as mere fantasies; and (2) renegade analysts whose interpretations were based on a rival theoretical framework. Yet Glover's handling of this unexpected challenge dismissively begs the crucial question posed by Marmor some 30 years later: How can *any* of the *rival* schools invoke therapeutic success and patient assent to claim that *its* particular interpretations are "exact" or correct? In 1977, Fisher and Greenberg lent added poignancy to this question in reporting:

> Research evidence has consistently indicated that a patient's be-lief in interpretations and his consequent anxiety reduction do not depend on the accuracy of the interpretations. Investigators have found that individuals will enthusiastically accept bogus interpretations as accurate descriptions of their own personalities [p. 364].

Yet *if* the remedially efficacious ingredient in Freud's treatment is not the distinctive brand of insight authenticated by his the-ory of personality, then his therapeutic successes are just place-bogenic. And, in that case, these successes are devoid of the probative significance he claimed for them. In a 1952 paper, Glover admitted that the use of interpretations in psychoana-lytic investigations "is the Achilles heel of psychoanalytical re-search" mainly because of "suggestion through interpretation" (p. 405). But, undaunted by this cardinal concession, he then blithely ignored it when speaking of "our proven etiological systems" (p. 408).

The jeopardy in which placebogenesis places the program of validation by positive treatment outcome was put into bold re-lief by Freud himself. Very late in his life, he wrote plaintively (1933): "I do not think our cures can compete with those of Lourdes. There are so many more people who believe in the miracles of the Blessed Virgin than in the existence of the un-conscious" (p. 152). The crunch from being upstaged by Lourdes is not lessened merely because, reportedly, "no native of Lourdes was ever cured at Lourdes; it is difficult to partici-pate in a miracle at the shrine where one once played hop-scotch" (Fish, 1973, p. 5).

But how compelling is the evidence for deeming orthodox analytic treatment an inadvertent placebo? Is the lack of evi-dence for the superiority of this treatment over its nonanalytic and pseudo-Freudian rivals actually *best* interpreted by postulating that all these modalities alike succeed only placebogenically? As against such an epistemological preference for placebogenesis, a Freudian partisan might maintain that the stated lack of evidence for the therapeutic superiority of orthodox analysis is rather insignificant. The basis for his retort might be the paucity of controlled outcome studies *directly* comparing the results from Freudian treatment with those from the many rival therapies (see Luborsky and Spence, 1978, p. 338). He might urge that the unavailability of evidence for therapeutic superiority need not bespeak essential *parity* of remedial efficacy between the rival therapies. In this vein, Fisher and Greenberg (1977, p. 337) have conjectured that analysis first really comes into its own and could prove its superior mettle in the treatment of *chronic* severe neuroses, as contrasted with *acute* but less severe ones. They suggest (p. 337) that this hypothesized qualitative or percentage rate superiority of analysis may well have escaped detection partly because studies comparing analysis to rival therapies "have tended to focus on more acute cases of lesser severity." On this basis, they say "one could argue that the less severe the disturbance, the more likely it is that any treatment will result in favorable change."

Heartened by this line of reasoning, a Freudian may then point out that the therapeutic preeminence of analysis conjectured by Fisher and Greenberg comports with the tenet that Freud's modality derives *unmatched* remedial potency from its own *characteristic* treatment ingredients rather than placebogenically, whereas rival therapies fail to mobilize these same unique ingredients. But as a partial concession to those who charge placebogenesis, this defender of Freud might allow that some therapeutic gains can issue from a disjunctive plurality of remedial causes in the sense of Mill (1887). Indeed, this concession was made explicitly by Malan (1976, p. 269).

Yet Fisher and Greenberg's unproven posit that analysis is the paragon of therapies comports not only with its being a *non*placebo, but also with its being an inadvertent placebo along with its rivals, as contended by Frank. According to Frank's version of placebogenesis even the conjectured, peerless remedial performance by analysis would be explained by an auxiliary hypothesis: Any differential effects of rival therapies are due to the differential abilities of their respective techniques to actuate remedial *incidental* factors, i.e., placebo agencies *common* to all of them. Hence, the moral of Frank's thesis is that even the posited therapeutic uniqueness of analysis need not militate against its being a placebo.

Like Frank, Eysenck believes in a unified account of the therapeutic ingredients of behavior therapy, verbal psychotherapy, and those life events that issue in so-called "spontaneous" remission. But he differs from Frank in regard to the particular *identity* of the hypothesized common remedial factors. Eysenck rests his proposed identification of the single agency of favorable therapeutic change on his *new* version of the conditioning theory of neurosis, which is based on recent developments in learning theory. This revised theory diverges from the original conditioning paradigm that Mowrer (1939) had put forward to explain the genesis of neurotic disorders. Eysenck (1980) writes:

> . . . little effort has been made by behaviour therapists to explain the apparent success of spontaneous remission and psychotherapy in alleviating the distress of the neurotic patient.
>
> If our theories are correct in essence, then we should be able to deduce from them a unified theory of treatment which would explain the apparent successes of spontaneous remission (which may be regarded as the baseline against which all other methods of treatment must be measured); the various types of psychotherapy which, while on the whole they have not been shown to do better than spontaneous remission, nevertheless probably also are no worse, and consequently require an explanation of such effectiveness as they possess; and the many different types of behaviour therapy. . . . It is suggested that not only can the success of all these methods of treatment be predicted from a particular theory of the nature and development of neurosis, but it is also claimed that the relative effectiveness of these methods can also be predicted in terms of this theory . . . which may therefore be said to possess considerable explanatory power [pp. 43-44].

In the briefest terms, the nub of Eysenck's proposed unified account is that neurotic symptoms "can be eliminated by a process of ordinary Pavlovian extinction, which takes place under

certain specified conditions such as those obtaining in spontaneous remission, psychotherapy and in particular behaviour therapy" (p. 44). According to Eysenck's unified view, the successes
of behavior therapy are *not* placebogenic, whereas any positive
results from theoretically rival treatment modalities are *inadvertently* placebogenic.

Whatever the merits of either Frank's or Eysenck's views on
the particular *identity* of the putatively common therapeutic
agents, successful analytic treatment *outcome* can hardly serve
to underwrite the probative value Freud attributed to it. It
cannot do so *at least* unless and until there is actual evidence,
from controlled studies of treatment *process*, that *presumed* analytic insight is the remedially efficacious *ingredient* of Freudian
intervention. But even such evidence is a long way from showing that veridical, rather than merely presumed Freudian insight is the causally efficacious factor in the therapy. If we *assume* the therapeuticity of *plausible*, subjectively believable
analytic interpretations, and even posit, for argument's sake,
the *superiority* of analytic treatment *outcome*, we still are unable
to vouchsafe that such outcome was actually wrought by *correct,
veridical* insight. In fact, despite their optimistic conjecture that
analytic insight might well be the *primus inter pares* among therapeutic agents for stubborn neuroses, Fisher and Greenberg
(1977) disavow the cardinal premise NCT of Freud's Tally Argument:

> Are therapist interpretations the only means of securing lasting
> beneficial changes? Obviously not, since there is a wealth of evi-
> dence that many kinds of experiences and therapeutic tech-
> niques have led to meaningful and enduring changes. Is it neces-
> sary that a patient understand the relationship between his past
> and present in order to decrease his anxieties and change his
> behavior? Again, there are strong indications that there are many
> roads to change that may be differentially effective and efficient,
> depending upon the problem, the patient, and the therapist.
> Apparently, for many patients, self-understanding may follow
> making changes, while for others initial preparation and self-
> exploration may facilitate taking the risk of trying new solutions
> to old problems [p. 372].

Moreover, in the face of having posited the qualitative therapeutic superiority of analysis, Fisher and Greenberg themselves

call attention to major lacunae in the validation of Freud's therapeutic theory, for example:

> Our general conclusion, in reviewing the data, is that there is very little evidence in the experimental literature even suggesting that the results of therapies called "psychoanalysis" are in any way different from the results obtained by treatments given other labels. This finding is in marked contrast to our conclusion that psychoanalysis appears to achieve results significantly different from no-treatment [p. 324].
>
> There is virtually no evidence that psychoanalysis generally results in more long-lasting or profound patient change than other therapies. . . . Indeed, both Pfeffer and Deutsch have found evidence of unresolved neurotic conflicts in successfully analyzed patients years after their treatment [p. 341].
>
> In looking back over the literature we have reviewed, we must conclude that Freud's ideas concerning the relationship between insight and [therapeutic] change have not been adequately tested [p. 361].

This untestedness was emphasized by Kubie (1950). Speaking of "the generally accepted concept of the role of insight in the therapeutic process," he declared:

> Unfortunately, this most fundamental of all elements in psychoanalytic therapy has never been adequately tested and verified experimentally [p. 59]. . . . Indeed, it is fair to say that this cornerstone of the modern conception of a dynamic psychotherapeutic process confronts us with many complex and unsolved problems [p. 60].

In the same vein, Stewart (1978) addresses the question: What is the evidence that patients in whom "restoration of insight" is achieved by lifting their repressions have a different therapeutic outcome from those in whom this analytic goal is not attained? But his answer does no more than echo Sherlock Holmes's remark to Dr. Watson: "It was easier to know it than to explain why I know it" (p. 561). To fill this particular epistemological gap, Fisher and Greenberg propose the application of controlled inquiry akin to Mill's (1887) method of concomitant variations. They suggest ascertaining the existence of any causal dependence of outcome variables on the characteristic psychoanalytic treatment variables:

At the least, more direct tests of Freud's ideas would seem to require comparative studies using different operationalized levels of working through with chronic *neurotic* patients and experienced therapists in *individual* therapy. They would also require an independent measure of insight defined in terms of the patient's ability to conceptualize the relationship between his past and his present [Fisher and Greenberg, 1977, p. 362].

Prima facie, it might appear that this controlled causal inquiry might be carried out *within* the confines of the psychoanalytic interview if enough stable standardization can be affected by any one therapist over individual patients and also over other analysts. By the same token, this proposal seems to lend some credibility to the contention that the analytic setting itself provides the analyst with an *experimental* environment for testing Freud's hypotheses, at least if the analyst pools the findings from various patients (Christiansen, 1964, p. 53). But this *prima facie* epistemic capability of the analytic interview to test the remedial potency of psychoanalytic insight will dissolve, unless the clinical setting can accommodate a key requirement: An interpretation that *rings* true to the analysand can qualify as insightful for Freudian therapy only if it is also actually "exact" or veridical. Therefore, the veridicality of the purported insights must be ascertained.

Failing this, the envisioned concomitant variations of outcome attributes with characteristic treatment factors cannot serve to validate the presumed causal dependence of therapeutic success on *veridical* insight. In turn, the authentication of the insights as *bona fide* relies on the presumed truth of Freud's developmental and dynamic hypotheses. Yet in Fisher and Greenberg's proposed testing design, we are not told just how the investigating analyst assures the fulfillment of their insight requirement, as measured by "the patient's ability to conceptualize the relationship between his past and his present." As we shall see (chapter 8), if the analyst is to document in the treatment setting that *bona fide* insight is at hand, he would have to use the retrospective psychoanalytic method in an endeavor (1) to authenticate the actual past occurrence of the events P retrodicted by Freud's etiologies; and (2) to show that these past events were *pathogenically relevant* to the patient's present problems.

We have patently come full circle in the quest for a viable surrogate for the discredited NCT that might still yield the sanguine conclusion of the Tally Argument, and would thus vindicate the psychoanalytic method of inquiry as well as the hypotheses evolved by means of it. The Freudian's program is now reduced to seeking a validation of these hypotheses that is devoid of reliance on a vestigial version of the Tally Argument. Here we need not rehearse the telling reasons already given in chapter 4, or to be given in chapters 6 and 8, for doubting seriously that such validation can be secured within the clinical confines of the psychoanalytic interview. But let us just *amplify* our prior statement of some of these reasons.

Recall first that Freud's developmental postulates assert long-term causal connections between the patient's infantile experiences and his adult psyche. How is the historical occurrence of the initial childhood conditions, deemed pathogenic by these etiological principles, to be certified *clinically*? It would seem that clinical authentication of such early history must rely largely on the adult patient's *memories* of *very early* experiences. Requirements of consistency or at least overall coherence do, of course, afford the analyst *some* check on what the patient alleges to be *bona fide* memories. But when Freud repudiated his childhood seduction etiology of adult hysteria in 1897, one of the reasons he gave was that he had become aware of the general unreliability of purported adult memories of early childhood episodes that had presumably been repressed in the interim and then retrieved by the analysis. As he wrote to his friend Fliess: " . . . there is no 'indication of reality' in the unconscious, so that it is impossible to distinguish between truth and emotionally-charged fiction" (1954, p. 216, letter 69). Indeed, Freud concluded that the seemingly vivid memories of childhood seductions reported by the hysterics—though only after some very vigorous prodding from him—had often been only wishful fantasies (Freud, 1898, p. 269; 1905a, pp. 58-59).

Moreover, in his 1918 account of the Wolf-Man case, he acknowledged Jung as follows: The Wolf-Man's supposed memory of having witnessed his parents engaged in *a tergo* intercourse, when he was a mere infant of 18 months, was just a retrospective fantasy stemming from that patient's adult problems and/or products of *phylogenetic* rather than ontogenetic inheritance.

Yet Freud (1918) had given credence to that inferred memory of his phobically obsessed 25-year-old patient (pp. 44-45). How could Freud certify *intraclinically* that this supposed memory was not first *induced*—rather than merely retrieved—by the effects of his verbal and nonverbal communications to the patient? He avowedly could not. As we saw in chapter 4, very late in life the Wolf-Man reenforced this doubt (Obholzer, 1982). Under the pressure of Jung's challenge, Freud grudgingly conceded (pp. 57-60, 95-97) that the patient may well have manufactured the alleged memory by fusing the recollection of an innocuously routine copresence of his parents with a veridical memory of having witnessed *animals* engage in *a tergo* copulation. Nevertheless, Freud used his analysis of the Wolf-Man as a basis for maintaining "how unjust it is to attribute the results of analysis to the physician's imagination and suggestion." He said this on the heels of noting "how inadequate the physician's constructive efforts usually are for clearing up questions that arise" (pp. 89-90). Worse yet, decades later, he conceded that even reliance on the slender reed of patient recall is frequently unavailable as a means of historical authentication of initial conditions. Two years before his death, he wrote:

> The path that starts from the analyst's construction ought to end in the patient's recollection; but it does not always lead so far. Quite often we do not succeed in bringing the patient to recollect what has been repressed. Instead of that, if the analysis is carried out correctly, we produce in him an assured conviction of the truth of the construction which achieves the same therapeutic result as a recaptured memory [1937b, pp. 265-266].

Clearly, the achievement of an equally good therapeutic result *without* recall of the repressed memory can hardly supply the historical authentication that was to have been furnished by just such recall. I conclude that, at least insofar as there is to be reliance on memory, the veridicality of the purported insights into the influence of the patient's infancy on his adulthood cannot be attested within the clinical confines of the psychoanalytic interview. Yet suppose the patient's recollection could reliably certify the actual occurrence of the appropriate childhood events. Even then, there remains the even more serious problem of whether the clinical findings could also validate the alleged *causal* role of these early happenings (see chapters 4 and 8).

Faced with the array of objections I have marshaled, the exponent of clinical validation might counter that just this causal inference can be warranted by the following special device: Once the intrapsychic restructuring of the analysand has been successfully completed—though *not* until such completion of the analysis!—introspective self-observation affords the quondam neurotic *reliable access* to causal connections between his early formative experiences, which are now reconstructed, and their psychic repercussions (Waelder, 1960, pp. 22-23). It behooves us to examine this rejoinder carefully in the light of fairly recent experimental demonstrations whose import is this: The extent of the *poverty* of introspective access to the *causal dynamics* of our mental processes is far greater than earlier general doubts about the veridicality of introspection would have led one to expect. And I shall be concerned to point out that these new experimental findings show this poverty to be indeed far worse than psychoanalytic theory emphasized, when Freud maintained that *"the ego is not master in its own house"* (1917, p. 143).

CAN PSYCHOANALYTICALLY RECTIFIED INTROSPECTION SAFEGUARD THE CLINICAL VALIDATION OF FREUDIAN THEORY?

Freud characterized his advocacy of the psychoanalytic quest overall as a "call to introspection" (1916-17, p. 285). And the analysand's quest, whose objective he epitomized by "Where id was, there ego shall be" (1933, p. 80), avowedly requires free association. But Freud paid high epistemic tribute (1923c, p. 238; 1925b, p. 41) to the stream of free association from patients who follow his "fundamental rule of analysis." He claimed probative reliability for these introspective data (1940a, p. 174).

In this vein, he asserted confirmation for his theory of para-praxes on the basis of introspective *self*-observations made by Storfer, by himself, and by Lou Andréas Salomé (1901, pp. 118, 162-163, 168). Indeed, as he put it: "you shall grant me that there can be no doubt of a parapraxis having sense [i.e., having been caused by a hypothesized repression] if the subject himself admits it" (1916-17, p. 50).

It is an utter commonplace that while the patient's motiva-tions are still being obfuscated by repressed conflicts, his analyst will place little credence in his purported introspective account of the promptings of his own actions. Yet Freudians hold that improved introspection goes hand in hand with the patient's progress toward their therapeutic goal of insight. No wonder that, in the case of one's own dreams, Freud rated the "trust-worthiness" of a *self*-analysis so highly: "In my judgement the situation is in fact more favourable in the case of *self*-observa-tion than in that of other people" (1900, p. 105). Furthermore: "In that way one acquires the desired sense of conviction of the reality of the processes described by analysis and of the correctness of its views" (1916-17, p. 19). The superego is the special agency Freud credits with the capability for veridical self-observation of the ego (1919, p. 235; 1933, pp. 58, 60).

As Robert Fliess (1948) emphasizes, the patient has, by enter-ing the analysis, "committed himself to an alteration of his per-sonality that will ultimately . . . enable him to verify introspec-tively the hitherto unacceptable statement about himself" (p. xv). Once the analysand has overcome his neurotic resistances, he is put into the position of "confirming it through improved introspection" (p. xvi). Rycroft (1968)—when defining "intro-spection"—explicitly applies the label "self-observation" honor-ifically to convey "objective self-scrutiny." And he points out that the term "introspection" is sometimes reserved "to describe worried or narcissistic self-preoccupation." He then says: "Ac-cording to this distinction, one of the aims of psycho-analytical treatment is to decrease introspection and to increase the capac-ity for self-observation" (p. 78).

But if there is to be reliable introspective confirmation of interpretations relating to the influences on the patient's psy-che, the introspective verdicts of well-analyzed patients must attest reliably to the *causal dynamics* of mental processes that appear consciously accessible to such patients. According to some analysts, in the case of causally relevant *early* experiences, even experiences whose occurrences were not disclosed via a recovered *bona fide* memory, can be introspectively certified to be thus relevant. Indeed, Gedo (1979) tells us that "the capacity of most patients to reach valid conclusions about the introspective data they produce in analysis has been generally underestimated," because the work of *interpreting* the patient's free associations has been unduly assigned to the analyst by the traditional authoritarian view of the division of labor between them (p. 253).

He contends that understanding "the *meaning*" (effects, in this case) of some covert wish, for example, is "a process for which the analysand may often be better equipped than is the analyst." And having claimed (p. 255) "the childhood experiences that mold the human personality are not objective happenings but the child's subjective perceptions of them," he deems the patient's introspections capable of furnishing insight into just what experiences did play the causal role of such molding: "Preferably, analysands should arrive at as many of these insights as possible through their own introspective efforts, for in the world of subjective meanings no outside observer, however empathic he may be, is really competent to judge the relative importance of various determinants" (p. 262). Notice that Gedo goes well beyond the view that psychoanalytically enlightened introspections can be *trustworthy* or reliable. He maintains that, on some occasions, self-observation affords the patient *privileged* cognitive access to truths about himself or herself.

As I turn again to Freud himself, note the account he gave us of the capabilities of "self-observation" in the epistemically honorific sense when he wrote (1933):

> We wish to make the ego the matter of our enquiry, our very own ego. But is that possible? After all, the ego is in its very essence a subject; how can it be made into an object? Well, there is no doubt that it can be. The ego can take itself as an object, can treat itself like other objects, can observe itself, criticize itself, and do Heaven knows what with itself. In this, one part of the ego is setting itself over against the rest. So the ego can be split;

it splits itself during a number of its functions—temporarily at least. Its parts can come together again afterwards [p. 58].

I might simply say that the special agency which I am beginning to distinguish in the ego is conscience. But it is more prudent to keep the agency as something independent and to suppose that conscience is one of its functions and that self-observation, which is an essential preliminary to the judging activity of conscience, is another of them. And since when we recognize that something has a separate existence we give it a name of its own, from this time forward I will describe this agency in the ego as the '*super-ego*' [p. 60]. . . . We have allotted it the functions of self-observation, of conscience [p. 66].

Nearly two decades earlier, Freud (1914c) had declared:

The complaints made by paranoics [of being observed by an agency they delusionally displace into external reality but which is actually their own superego] also show that at bottom the self-criticism of conscience coincides with the self-observation on which it is based. Thus the activity of the mind which has taken over the function of conscience has also placed itself at the service of internal research, which furnishes philosophy with the material for its intellectual operations. . . . It will certainly be of importance to us if evidence of the activity of this critically observing agency—which becomes heightened into conscience and philosophic introspection—can be found in other fields as well [pp. 96-97].

Yet at the very end of his career, Freud (1937b, pp. 257-269) held that a patient's assent to a psychoanalytic interpretation does *not* guarantee its correctness. At that late stage, he clearly weakened his earlier probative tributes to the analysand's introspective confirmations (Grünbaum, 1984, chap. 10).

Leading present-day analysts keep telling us that the psycho-analytic edifice rests almost entirely on the findings obtained in the treatment setting. Thus, Wallerstein (1982, p. 10) speaks of "the verbal interchanges of the consulting room upon which our total enterprise, clinical, educational, and, even to a large extent, research is made to rest." As I noted in chapter 4, he reiterated this thesis most recently (1988, p. 27) in emphatic terms. On being confronted by the arguments I have deployed against the probity of clinical validation, its defenders may well

be tempted to *stretch* Gedo's thesis so as to claim *privileged epistemic access for the patient's introspection*. That is, they may claim
that the objective self-scrutiny afforded by analytically rectified
introspection is not only epistemologically trustworthy, but
could provide the *otherwise elusive* clinical validation of two contentions: (1) Hitherto repressed material that qualifies as etiologically relevant according to Freudian theory was in fact a
contributory pathogen of the analysand's affliction; (2) analyst
constructions that qualify theoretically as authentic insights
were actually the remedial factors in the therapy, once the patient had integrated them consciously.

As envisaged by the putative defender of confirmations from
the couch, the introspective validation of these two assertions
would serve to corroborate Freud's psychogenetic theory and
would also discredit the rival therapeutic hypothesis of placebogenesis. It would then become plausible that the hypothesized privileged access furnished by introspective self-observation is indeed the source of the strong conviction of well-
analyzed patients that the interpretations yielded by their analyses are veridical rather than just ring verisimilar.

These hopeful speculations are fundamentally impugned by
Nisbett and Wilson (1977) in their paper on experimental demonstrations of unexpectedly gross limitations on introspective
access to the causal dynamics of mental processes. But they
make no mention at all of the bearing of their results on the
epistemological liabilities of the introspective validation of
Freudian causal hypotheses. The statement of this bearing that
I shall give below is *not* redundant with the later account given
by Nisbett and Ross (1980, pp. 242-247) of their reasons for
rejecting Freud's thesis that prior repression is responsible for
the lack of unaided introspective access to the causes of our
affective judgments. Hence neither Nisbett and Wilson nor Nisbett and Ross have any responsibility for the epistemological
import I shall derive from their theses.

The upshot of the work of Nisbett, Wilson, and Ross for our
concerns is essentially the following: The purported deliverances of the analyzed patient's introspection, besides not actually being obtained introspectively, are often not even trustworthy, let alone are they the products of the subject's privileged

epistemic access to the validation of psychoanalytic interpretations. But before reporting on the evidence for this conclusion, I should mention some objections at the outset, beginning with a recent charge of overstatement against Nisbett and Wilson by Smith and Miller (1978). The latter authors argue that *algorithmic* problem-solving in mathematics, explicitly rule-governed mental processes relevant to challenging tasks, and perhaps some specified other kinds of mentation, need to be exempt from Nisbett and Wilson's generalization. Smith and Miller may well have made a plausible case for their complaint of *some* overstatement. But they acknowledge that, for any given sort of mental process, Nisbett and Wilson have succeeded in placing the burden of proof squarely on those who would claim introspective access to the causal dynamics of the given kind of process. In any case though, their critique of Nisbett and Wilson was implicitly restricted to such cognitively dominated situations as algorithmic problem-solving and thus did not include such affective processes as traumatic experiences. Moreover, the two currently live theories of affect and cognition in social psychology have the following import relevant to our concern with introspective access:

1. A theory of emotion proposed by Schachter and Singer (1962) holds that people have no introspective access to the content of their emotions. Building on physiological evidence that all emotions (elations, fear, excitement, etc.) have similar physiological properties, Schachter and Singer claim that we label this physiological state with an emotion name based on cues we observe in our environment. Hence if it is Halloween and a fearsome witch is before us, we decide we must be scared; if we are at a closely fought World Series game, we decide we are excited. So this theory would put emotion in general outside the reach of introspection—we observe the undifferentiated emotional state and label it rather than being directly aware of which emotion we are experiencing.

2. Recent work by Zajonc and his colleagues (see Wilson, 1979) argues that certain conditions (repeated exposure to novel stimuli) can modify affective reactions *without* any mediation by cognitive processes such as recognition. This claim, if

true, would imply that the roots of certain affects are in principle inaccessible to introspective awareness because they need not even have been cognitively noticed or recognized at the time of exposure!

Furthermore, it emerges from the replies given by Nisbett and Ross (1980, pp. 215-223) to four groups of critiques of Nisbett and Wilson's work that the mental processes of concern to psychoanalysis apparently fall within the purview of the latter's *warranted* denial of introspective access to the causal dynamics of mental processes.

Nonetheless, it might be asked whether the following sorts of affective processes do not constitute genuine counterexamples to Nisbett and Wilson's downgrading of introspection after all; e.g., when we attribute sudden grief to learning that a loved one has died, or a sudden joy to receiving the verdict "benign" from a biopsy, or even a sudden elation to an unexpected huge windfall from a lottery. At least *prima facie*, these cases seem to be "commonsense" cases in which causal connections between ideational and affective states are certified introspectively.

To this I say: Even if these particular affective processes did pose some challenge to Nisbett and Wilson's generalization, they cannot *also* serve to vindicate the analyst's appeal to the patient's introspective verification of psychoanalytic causal claims. That the allegedly introspective verdicts of "common sense" cannot thus be adduced by Freudians is clear precisely because it is their theory which tells that such "truths" are *not* to be taken at face value: According to psychoanalytic theory, these judgments are often falsehoods, misleading, or are actually shallow. The example of a grief reaction to hearing that a loved one has died is a poignant illustration. As Freud (1954, p. 170, letter 50) wrote to Fliess, it is true enough that the news of the death of his own father, though expected, made him feel as if he "had been torn up by the roots."[1] But his analysis then revealed that he was so very greatly shaken by the event largely from repressed guilt resulting from having wished his father dead (Fancher, 1973, p. 140).

Indeed, as Eagle has suggested, it would be open to Nisbett and Wilson to point to one or another theory of unconscious motivations—it need not be Freud's—to *impugn* commonsense introspections of the causal dynamics of affective processes. But these authors do *not* need to resort to the invocation of unconscious motives to deal with the affective processes in question. Nor, as we shall see, are they driven to claim that the stated commonsense verdicts on the cognitive causes of the specified affective states are generally false or shallow. Instead, what they do assert is that, even when true, such verdicts are *not* certified by introspective *observation* of causal connection: Just as we *infer*—rather than merely observe—a causal connection between the motions of Hume's two colliding billiard balls, so also we do not just observe causal connections between mental states introspectively. Indeed, it will turn out that, in their account, claims about causal connections between mental states are no less fallible than corresponding assertions about physical states. And their reason is precisely that we do not directly observe—introspectively or otherwise—any kind of *causal connection*, be it between mental events or external physical occurrences, although the mental events themselves are accessible to introspection.

Nisbett (private communication) illustrates this point by reference to a person who is *unaware* of receiving demorol intravenously and who is then asked to what he attributes the ensuing euphoria. In search of plausible causes, such a person might well credit this joy to suddenly having seen a gorgeous robin on the window ledge or to the sudden realization that a much desired holiday is impending. The mental events of cognition and joy were themselves observed introspectively, but the *inference* concerning a *causal connection* between them was mistaken, even if the subject insists that this connection is warranted introspectively.

As we turn to the above "commonsense" cases, Nisbett hardly gainsays our *inference* that unexpected good news ordinarily causes us to feel elated or that shock and grief experienced after hearing tragic news are attributable to that news. What he does deny instead is that *introspection* furnishes the epistemic warrant for asserting a causal connection in those instances in which we do correctly affirm such a linkage between cognitive and affective states, or between other mental states. He issues that denial while maintaining that the cognitive and affective states themselves are introspectively observable as such. More-over, he points out that an outside observer is no more likely to misjudge the actual causes of my affective states than I am, a conclusion which is fundamentally at odds with Gedo's afore-mentioned contentions.

Nisbett replies to some of the main criticisms that have been made of the theses in his and Wilson's (1977) paper. He con-cludes (Nisbett and Ross, 1980, p. 223) that introspection does *not* afford people reliable knowledge as to "what makes them happy and what makes them unhappy." Yet this epistemic de-motion of introspection in regard to *causal* accounts of our own behavior fully allows scope for privileged access to some other sorts of information via introspection: "each of us is privy to a wealth of data pertinent to the generation of such accounts" (p. 203). And when we have access to such data while outside observers do not, we *may* well enjoy a potential advantage over them in arriving at a causal analysis of our behavior in some circumstances, while suffering a disadvantage in others (pp. 223-226).

As Nisbett and Wilson point out (1977, p. 255), "we do indeed have direct access to a great storehouse of private knowledge" about our respective selves. Each of us is aware of a host of personal historical facts, the object of his attention at the given instant, the contents of his momentary sensations, his current plans, etc. It is patent that we sometimes have at least relatively privileged access to such information through introspection. For example, I am surely not the only person who ever knew the first name of my deceased maternal grandfather, yet at present very few people besides myself have that information. However, the moment we consider access to even such basic *processes* as remembering and sensory perceiving, we confront a quite different cognitive situation: "Recent research has made it increasingly clear that there is almost no conscious awareness of perceptual and memorial processes" (Nisbett and Wilson, 1977, p. 232). For instance, people who can swiftly recall their mother's maiden name are quite helpless to tell *just how* they managed to come up with that name. Similarly, someone who has made a perceptual judgment of spatial depth would just make a gesture of futility if asked for an introspective report on the extent to which he had relied on parallel line convergence in arriving at that judgment.

But introspection lets us down in other ways as well. Creative geniuses ranging from Henri Poincaré to Pablo Picasso

> . . . describe themselves almost universally as bystanders, dif-
> fering from other observers only in that they are the first to
> witness the fruits of a problem-solving process that is almost
> completely hidden from conscious view. The reports of these
> workers are characterized by an insistence that (a) the influential
> stimuli are usually completely obscure—the individual has no
> idea what factors prompted the solution; and (b) even the fact
> that a process is taking place is sometimes unknown to the indi-
> vidual prior to the point that a solution appears in consciousness
> [p. 240].

Thus, the *processes* of problem-solving or creative artistic production leave the great minds in which they transpire no less
stumped than memorial and perceptual processes are hidden
from the ordinary people in whom they occur.

On the other hand, people often claim to be drawing on self-
observation when they readily answer questions as to *why* they
behave as they do. They likewise purport to know introspectively whether a given stimulus influenced them or not in contexts such as deciding to take action, changing their conduct or
their feelings, making a particular evaluation of another person, or finding a solution to a mundane problem of daily life.
Note that in the case of these cognitively mediated responses,
people avow the ability to give a correct introspective account
of the mediating causal *processes* that issue in these responses.
They claim direct access to the very workings of their own
minds, instead of maintaining that only the *products* of these
mental processes are directly available to consciousness.

Two major questions are posed by the prevalent conviction
that there is such introspective knowledge of causal dynamics:
(1) Is there any empirical justification for crediting introspective
self-observation with access to reliable knowledge of the psychic
processes in question; and (2) if this purported access is mythi-
cal, how is one to account for the fact that people report so
much more than they can actually know introspectively about
the causal workings of their own minds?

With a view to resolving these issues, Nisbett and Wilson adduce experimental results obtained over four decades from a variety of sometimes ingenious experimental designs. They marshal telling empirical support for their conclusions whose upshot for our concerns can now be summarized.

1. Far from justifying the prevalent belief in privileged access to the dynamics of our psychic responses, the findings strongly indicate a different conclusion: Purportedly introspective self-perception of causal connections between one's own mental states is just as liable to *theory-induced* errors as is drawing causal inferences about connections between purely external events from apparent covariations among their properties (p. 248). This liability to error takes multiple forms.

Sometimes people are unable to report even the very existence of stimuli that have a demonstrably critical influence on their higher-order responses, let alone correctly identify the former as such a cause (pp. 233, 240-241). In other cases, people are unaware of the existence of their responses to particular stimuli, and *a fortiori* unable to identify the effects of these stimuli. And "even when subjects are thoroughly cognizant of the existence of the relevant stimuli, and of their responses, they may be unable to report accurately about the influence of the stimuli on the responses" (p. 242). Indeed, the accuracy of the introspective reports of self-observation is so poor as to suggest that if there is any introspective access at all, it is insufficient to yield generally reliable reports (p. 233).

2. When asked how, if at all, a particular stimulus influenced a given response, the persons in the experimental studies, and ordinary people in their daily lives, did not and do not even attempt to interrogate the memories they may have of the mediating causal process. *Although it may feel like introspection, what they actually do is draw on the causal theories provided by their culture or pertinent intellectual subculture for a verdict as to the effect, if any, of that kind of stimulus on that kind of response.*

If no such verdicts are supplied by the culture either explicitly or implicitly, people will generate a theory yielding such a verdict. But they will do so *not* by introspection but rather "by searching their networks of connotative relations surrounding the stimulus description and the response description. If the stimulus is connotatively similar to the response, then it may be reported as having influenced the response" (p. 248). In this way, people may be able to generate causal hypotheses linking even novel stimuli and novel responses.

In short, they make a theoretical judgment of the plausibility of a causal linkage by consulting causal schemata endorsed or deemed plausible by a prevailing belief system, instead of founding their answers on introspective self-observation (pp. 233, 248-249). This class of causal schemata is employed to make *a priori* assessments, that is, depending on whether a given stimulus-response pair does or does not belong to this class, the stimulus in question will be reported to have or not to have influenced the particular response.

3. "Subjective reports about higher mental processes are sometimes correct, but even the instances of correct report are not due to direct introspective awareness. Instead, they are due to the incidentally correct employment of a priori causal theories" (p. 233).

It is *vital* to bear in mind that Nisbett and Wilson do *not* assert the *universal* falsity of purportedly introspective reports on the causal dynamics of the mind. What they *do* assert is that purportedly introspective reports on these causal dynamics are *not* warranted *introspectively*. Thus, even if *actual* introspection *were* reliably veridical when it does take place, this would be *unavailing* for sustaining theoretical claims as to the causal operation of our minds.

As we know, psychoanalytic theory not only emphatically discounts the deliverances of analytically unaided introspection, but also denies that even the best analyzed persons have introspective access to *all* of their mental processes. But now recall our account of the epistemic scope this theory nonetheless accords to the operation and probative value of analytically rectified introspection. We shall see below that even the circumscribed credence thus given to self-observation is fundamentally impugned by Nisbett and Wilson's experimentally supported conclusions. It will then become clear that the still missing validation of Freudian psychogenetic postulates, and the discreditation of the rival therapeutic hypothesis of placebogenesis, cannot be supplied by recourse to the purported findings of introspection.

In view of the nature, range, and diversity of the experimental studies adduced by Nisbett and Wilson, their stated devastating import for epistemic reliance on introspection to validate causal claims is hardly limited to those contexts in which psychoanalysis likewise discounts introspection: mental processes that are subject to unconscious neurotic distortions or of which we remain permanently unaware willy-nilly. Just one set of studies invoked by these authors will serve to illustrate the wider compass of this damaging import.

The latter studies pertained to mundane problem-solving activities of daily life and showed the following experimentally. When people were asked to tie some widely separated suspended cords together, their reports on the causal features of the mental processes by which they solved this problem were quite unreliable. Experimental subjects who were presented with both a helpful cue and a demonstratedly useless or "decoy" cue "reported that the useless cue had been helpful and denied that the critical cue had played any role in their [problem] solution" (p. 241). But if introspective self-observation is untrustworthy even for such a prosaic causal process of problem-solving, how can it be deemed reliable for those intrapsychic affect-laden contexts in which Freud actually invokes it?

Moreover, Nisbett and Wilson's dismal assessment of the epistemic role of introspection is supported not only by the experimental evidence they marshal, but also by certain *clinical* findings they do not mention. Indeed, these clinical findings will now turn out to be very embarrassing to Freud's thesis of validation by data from the psychoanalytic interview. As we saw, Nisbett and Wilson deny that we actually have reliable introspective access to the causal workings of our minds, *and* they affirm that culturally supplied causal schemata ingress *a priori* to furnish the verdicts of purported introspective self-observation. One of the clinical findings that seem to me to support the latter affirmation is acknowledged to be an embarrassment to Freud by Marmor (1962). Speaking of the gamut of "radically divergent theories" of psychoanalysis (p. 288), he says:

> The fact is that patients treated by analysts of all these schools . . . believe strongly in the insights which they have been

given . . . depending upon the point of view of the analyst, the patients of each school seem to bring up precisely the kind of phenomenological data which confirm the theories and interpretations of their analysts! Thus each theory tends to be self-validating. Freudians elicit material about the Oedipus Complex and castration anxiety, Jungians about archetypes, Rankians about separation anxiety, Adlerians about masculine strivings and feelings of inferiority, Horneyites about idealized images, Sullivanians about disturbed interpersonal relationships, etc. [p. 289].

Yet when Freud's rivals obtained responses from patients, including avowals of introspective insight, that were discordant with his own theoretical expectations, he dismissed them. Thus Freud (1925a) declared sarcastically:

. . . one hears of analysts who boast that, though they have worked for dozens of years, they have never found a sign of the existence of a castration complex. We must bow our heads in recognition of the greatness of this achievement, even though it is only a negative one, a piece of virtuosity in the art of overlooking and mistaking [p. 254].

But in the light of the results noted by Marmor, it would seem instead that Freud *persuaded* his male patients they harbored a fear of castration dating back to infancy. Then they furnished *spurious* introspective validation of the putative insight he had given them into the supposed origins and later *effects* of their hypothesized castration anxiety. Hence the ring of verisimilitude that interpretations have for patients cannot justly be claimed to have probative value. For example, in the case of interpretations that pertain to processes whose duration was confined to infancy, we can apply the remark of Nisbett and Wilson (1977) that "the vagaries of memory may allow the invention of factors presumed to be present at the time the process occurred. It is likely that such invented factors would be generated by use of causal theories" (p. 252).

One important moral I draw from their work in cognitive psychology is: Even if a patient can claim veridical recall of an episode as having been emotionally painful, we have no good reason to give credence to any *etiologic* role the analysand may assign to this trauma on purportedly introspective grounds. Furthermore, Nisbett and Wilson's account can serve to explain not only the docile patient responses reported by Marmor, but also the aforementioned enthusiastic acceptance of intentionally bogus interpretations by those to whose personality they pertain (Fisher and Greenberg, 1977, p. 364).

As for purportedly introspective confirmations by patients of the *remedial efficacy* of Freudian insight, Martin (1978) summarizes a pertinent investigation as follows:

> Heine, in a study of the reports of patients in psychoanalytic, non-directive, and Adlerian therapy about the changes that took place within them during therapy found that patients explained the changes along the 'school' lines of their therapist [p. 314].

Moreover, Heine's (1953) results suggested that the purported insight achieved by the patient is not the product of a process of veridical *self-discovery*, but rather reflects the patient's *conversion* to the therapist's interpretation: Knowledge of the therapist's theoretical system allowed a far more accurate prediction of the patient's presumed insights and emergent "unconscious" than information about his actual developmental history.

This finding accords with Nisbett and Wilson's contention that the verdicts of purported introspective self-observation are reached *a priori* via the causal schemata supplied by the pertinent intellectual subculture. In this case, that subculture endorses the particular brand of therapeutic theory avowed by the therapist to whom the patient has turned for treatment. And thus each patient is a docile receptacle—almost a Lockean *tabula rasa*—for the tenet that his therapeutic gains were wrought by the characteristic treatment factors singled out as being remedial by the therapeutic theory in question. Furthermore, in the mistaken belief that the patient is *independently* confirming this tenet by direct introspection, the therapist obtains spurious support for his theory.

When coupled with Heine's findings, Nisbett and Wilson's thesis of *a priori* subjective reporting on intrapsychic causal processes has a clear methodological corollary (p. 247) for *psychotherapeutic process research*: It is largely pointless and indeed quite misleading to ask people just *why* they improved. Even after a successful psychoanalysis, for example, the patient has no privileged epistemic access to the actual causal mechanisms involved in his changes. This is not to deny, of course, that answers given by people to therapeutic questions may have relevance to the *sociological* study of therapeutic belief systems *per se*.

In this chapter, I have dealt with some facets of the inadequacy of clinical observations as probative evidence for psychoanalytic theory and therapy. But there are still other epistemological liabilities that beset at least the clinical methods typically employed by analysts. Let me just mention *some* of the fair number of other such pitfalls.

1. Clinical studies that purport to validate *causal* claims often rely heavily on reasoning akin to Mill's (1887) method of agreement. But the latter has essentially heuristic rather than probative value. However great that heuristic value, it provides quite inadequate safeguards against the ravages of *post hoc ergo propter hoc*. To guard against inductive fallacies of causal inference, methods of *controlled* inquiry or their equivalents from relevant background knowledge are important. Such inquiry often employs reasoning akin to that of Mill's joint method of agreement and difference, or of the method of concomitant variations, not to speak of the utopian method of difference, as we saw in the *Postscript* for chapter 4. But, *by and large*, the controls required by these methods either have not or just cannot be instituted within the confines of the psychoanalytic interview.

For instance, as we shall see (chap. 8), long-term controlled *prospective* studies are very probably needed to test Freud's theory of psychosexual development and its associated etiologic hypotheses. The traditional reliance of analysts on the uncontrolled *retrospective* studies of the clinical interview setting just will not do. A case in point is furnished by the alleged purely clinical ascertainment of the *causal* bearing of family constellations during childhood on becoming a homosexual adult (Freud, 1922, pp. 230-232; 1920b, pp. 147-172; 1910, p. 99; 1905b, p. 144). But, as we shall see (chap. 9), psychoanalysts

have rightly cautioned that the experimental conditions of controlled studies must not be contrived to the point of rendering
these inquiries irrelevant to Freud's theories.

The evaluation of treatment outcome furnishes a further
example of the poverty of the traditional clinical validation of
causal hypotheses. It is unavailing to claim that if the patient
exhibits durable improvement such as anxiety reduction *after*
completing treatment, this gain is causally attributable to the
intervention, let alone to the veridical insight allegedly mediated by that intervention, let alone to the veridical insight allegedly mediated by that intervention (chap. 6 and Grünbaum,
1977). The patient's pretreatment history of affliction *alone* cannot serve as an adequate control to justify such an attribution.

Nor can that earlier history itself alternatively justify blaming
the analysis if there is no discernible improvement after, say, 5
years of steady treatment. Indeed, the absence of any detectable
change for better or worse does not entitle the critic of psychoanalytic treatment to infer that this treatment had no therapeutic effect on the analysand. The reason is that one cannot tell
from that outcome how the patient would have fared *without*
the analysis. Evidently, *one* possibility is that the patient would
have gotten *worse*. If so, the treatment prevented deterioration
and hence was beneficial, even though there was no *discernible*
change.

Another possibility is that the analysand might have improved if he had been left untreated. If such a patient then
shows no improvement, the analysis can be presumed to have
aborted the gains that would otherwise have occurred. But one
cannot justify this dismal presumption from facts gleaned in
the clinical setting alone. Just as one does not know on that
basis how the patient would have turned out if he had not
undergone psychoanalysis, so also one typically does not know
how the patient would have fared if he had received treatment
from therapists belonging to *rival* schools.

Indeed, without a long-term follow-up, the analyst cannot
even vouch for the *durability* of any "cure" that his treatment
may seemingly have achieved on termination. This patent un-
dependability of reported therapeutic successes is poignantly

illustrated by Freud's own assessment of the outcome of his 4-year analysis of the Wolf-Man from 1910-1914. Though Freud was typically less sanguine than many of his followers, he declared that at the end of this period there had been a "final clearing up" of the patient's symptoms, and reported he "parted from him, regarding him as cured" (1918, pp. 84, 121). Yet in 1919, Freud recommended an additional psychoanalysis. And ever since the latter rather brief treatment by Freud himself, the Wolf-Man (now deceased) has been *interminably* analyzed by a succession of analysts, beginning in 1926, when he suffered from a paranoid delusion (Gardiner, 1971; Obholzer, 1982)! How then can this series of analysts warrantedly claim to know what therapeutic credit, if any, should be given to his having been chronically seen by them, let alone to the purported analytic insights he acquired via the doctrines that animated their efforts?

Some recognized analysts have dealt with these troublesome considerations in a puzzlingly inconsistent and even evasive manner. Nemiah (1975, p. 180) tells us, on the one hand, that "the difficulty in . . . establishing adequate controls" as well as other obstacles "make the task of evaluating the effectiveness of analysis a Herculean if not impossible one." On the other hand, this concession comes on the heels of his astonishing declaration (p. 179) that "the striking effectiveness of analysis in many clinical situations" was such that it was "quite understandably" tried even on disorders "such as psychoses . . . for which it was generally felt to be contraindicated." And this assertion presumably rests on the unavailing fact that, unencumbered by the avowed difficulties of documentation, the power of analytic treatment to effect positive therapeutic change is "emotionally and experientially convincing" (p. 180) to both patient and analyst, both of whom patently have a great stake in believing in the treatment. Deplorably the latter remark is introduced by the probatively altogether disanalogous story that bumble bees do plainly fly even though some version of aerodynamic theory allegedly rules it out!

Alas, a like blithe indifference to elementary methodological safeguards for the evaluation of treatment outcome is displayed in a very recent 55-page report, claiming that "patients suitable for psychoanalysis derive substantial therapeutic benefit" (Bachrach, Galatzer-Levy, Skolnikoff, & Waldron, Jr., 1991). These authors admit that their outcome study does "not enable meaningful comparisons of the effectiveness of psychoanalysis with that of other forms of treatment for specific kinds of patients experiencing specific kinds of illnesses" (p. 911). To rationalize their self-validating procedure, they even misinvoke Thomas Kuhn's notion of "normal science," apparently unaware that a like misinvocation could even legitimate exorcism and other forms of sheer quackery.

An even stranger evasive twist is given to the question of therapeutic efficacy by Shands (1978) who writes:

> Whatever the reason, the lack of demonstrability of results has been widely admitted by psychotherapists.
>
> On the other hand, a conspicuous positive "result of psychotherapy" when such "therapy" has the specific *educational* purpose of training "candidates" (who freely admit to being at least "sick enough" to become psychotherapists) is demonstrated . . . to be a remarkable *upward social mobility*. Psychotherapists regularly move from a childhood Class IV level to an adult Class I or II level. Thus, all one has to do to demonstrate the tangible benefits of psychoanalysis and psychotherapy is the simple maneuver of changing the definition from *treatment to training*, therapy to education, and to use *income* criteria [p. 387].

2. A different major defect of clinical validation derives from the aforementioned typical inability of analysts, so far at any rate, to decontaminate their findings epistemologically from the effects of their theoretical stance on the patient's responses (Grünbaum, 1986, pp. 275-277). It is not that they have not *tried* to do so. As will be recalled from my appraisal of Freud's Tally Argument (this chap.), he no less than other eminent analysts, like Glover (1931), certainly did *address* the problems of epistemic contamination. They spelled out how, in their view, the role played by suggestion in effecting therapeutic change psychoanalytically *differed fundamentally* from its role in the avowedly suggestive treatment modalities, such as hypnosis or autosuggestion. With that focus, Freud discussed the charge of epistemic contamination by suggestion repeatedly (1909a, pp.

104, 120; 1912a, pp. 105-106; 1913a, p. 143; 1916-17, pp. 448-453; 1923b, p. 117), but after the demise of his Tally Argument, he never came to adequate grips with the range and depth of the difficulty it poses for clinical validation of his theory of personality. In chapter 8, we shall have the occasion to discuss Freud's one-paragraph appeal to the productions of allegedly contrasuggestible psychotics (1916-17, p. 453) to vindicate his theory of the transference neuroses. This appeal was unavailingly invoked by Sachs (1989, pp. 353-354), as explained there.

Incidentally, since Freud, Jones and Glover, for example, did explicitly *face* the challenge of suggestion; Popper (1962, p. 38) was uninformed as well as unfair when he accused psychoanalysts of not even having shown any interest in it. Their failure to *resolve* the difficulty in their own favor is hardly tantamount to having *ignored* it! Popper compounds his exegetical sleight-of-hand by saying the alleged failure of Freudians to show concern for the issue occurred "perhaps not accidentally." He hints that analysts are being characteristically evasive here or are even repressing an uncomfortable challenge. As I have shown elsewhere (1984, chap. 11), there is further telling evidence against this claim. And such textual evidence as Popper (1962, p. 38) gives from Freud is demonstrably misleading.

Furthermore, the critique of Popper I gave in chapter 2 did not use the conjecture of the sexual etiology of phobias offered by Abraham (1922) and Freud (1933, p. 24) to illustrate that psychoanalytic theory makes some predictions that qualify as "risky" by Popper's standards. The success of some of these predictions *would* serve, by Popper's standards, to corroborate the psychoanalytic theory of phobias, no less than to support that theory by neo-Baconian criteria of eliminative inductivism.

As elaborated by Freud's close collaborator, Abraham, the theory tells us, for example, that *all* manifest fears of spiders and of snakes are defenses against latent sexual fears, which are unconsciously transformed into the more acceptable manifest fears. If this is so, then the elimination of the manifest fears by behavioristic techniques such as desensitization eliminates this defense and ought to actuate a substitute defense in the form of some other psychological disturbance. But, contrary to this psychoanalytic prediction, a 1978 report from the Institute of

Psychiatry at the University of London shows: "In the over-whelming number of cases the reduction or elimination of a circumscribed fear is not followed by untoward effects" (Rachman, 1978, p. 221). So much for Popper's allegation that psychoanalytic theory is only *spuriously* testable empirically.

The challenge posed by the unsolved if not altogether insoluble problem of epistemological contamination of data from the psychoanalytic interview likewise impugns the aforementioned contention of Luborsky and Spence that analysts possess "a unique store of clinical wisdom" (1978, p. 360), notwithstanding the aforementioned *caveat* issued by these authors: They tempered the latter tribute in the same sentence by the disclaimer that analysts—like other psychotherapists—are literally ignorant of just *how* they achieve their results. How can Luborsky and Spence tell that the alleged wisdom is not replete with spuriously validated beliefs? As will be recalled, when Luborsky and Spence (1978, p. 358) endorsed Freud's generic encomium to clinical findings, they explicitly deemed these data *epistemologically* superior to the products of experimental, analogue, or other controlled studies in psychoanalysis. By contrast, I have impugned the probative value of data from the psychoanalytic interview, though without prejudice to their heuristic utility. In being skeptical, I hardly condoned probatively unenlightening experiments, let alone evidentially irrelevant ones. Yet I reject Luborsky and Spence's generic downgrading of experimental studies which they depict as intrinsically less pertinent probatively than clinical findings.

Freud addressed his theory of personality to the *in situ* events of man's psychic life. *Vis-à-vis* these life events, the interpersonal transaction in the psychoanalytic interview has emerged as a hothouse of contrivances, not only suffused with epistemological contamination but also beset by a whole array of other cognitive liabilities (Grünbaum, 1984, p. 172). Therefore, I maintain that whatever the *heuristic* superiority of the clinical setting to the psychological laboratory, the epistemological liabilities of the clinical transaction interdict its probative elevation above the laboratory or other extraclinical investigative settings. Indeed, it was none other than the leading British analyst Glover

(1952) who applied the "hothouse" metaphor to the psychoanalytic interview when discussing *training* analyses (p. 403). A like concession was made by Kohut (1978, p. 796).

The sobering moral I draw is that the obstacles to probative cogency confronting so-called clinical wisdom tend to be *different* but often still more formidable than those faced by controlled inquiries. For example, as we saw, the decontamination of clinical data from the effects of suggestion is an unsolved if not insoluble problem (Grünbaum, 1986, pp. 275-277). But as Wolitzky and his pro-Freudian colleagues stressed in their 1975 *experimental* study of repression (p. 216), their study was able to take pains to *control* for the effects of their *expectancy* upon their results. More generally, Shames (1979) argued that "the expectancy effect is neither inexorable nor unquestionably general in [experimental] psychological research" (p. 387). Maser and Seligman's book on models of psychopathology (1977) explicitly addresses the need to *demonstrate* probative relevance when offering experimentally based accounts of psychopathology that have (or have the potential for) applicability to the clinical setting (p. 4). Luborsky and Spence (1978, p. 357) even seem to concede that some such recent work, notably the paper by Sackeim and Gur (1978), "has been able to answer objections about its cogency for clinical concepts." Yet despite the "hothouse" nature of psychoanalytic research conducted within the clinical setting, Cooper and Michels (1978) tell us that "increasingly this [psychoanalytic] inquiry has recognized the analytic situation itself as paradigmatic for all human interactions" (p. 376).

This brings me to Meehl's aforementioned claim "that the best place to study [i.e., validate] psychoanalysis is the psychoanalytic session itself" (1978, p. 829). His defense of this contention essentially consists of three considerations, the second of which antedates the other two:

> 1. *None of us has bothered to carry out some relatively simple-minded kinds of analyses on a random sample of psychoanalytic protocols collected from essentially naive patients to whom no interpretations have as yet been offered.* This . . . category is, in my view, a category of research studies that we could have done, but have not done. *Example*: We can easily ascertain whether manifest dream content of

a certain kind is statistically associated (in the simple straightforward sense of a patterned fourfold table) with such and such kinds of thematic material in the patient's subsequent associations to the dream [p. 830].

2. We should at least be able to apply crude counting statistics, such as theme frequencies, to the verbal output during the later portions of the hour when these are predicted (by psychoanalytically skilled persons) from the output at the beginning of the hour. I look in this direction because of my clinical impression that one's ability to forecast the *general theme* of the associative material from the manifest content of the dream plus the initial associations to it, while far from perfect, is nevertheless often good enough to constitute the kind of clinical evidence that carries the heaviest weight with those who open-mindedly but skeptically embark upon psychoanalytic work. Let me give a concrete example (one on which I myself would be willing to lay odds of 90 to 10, and not on a mere "significant difference" but on an almost complete predictability within the limits of the reliability of thematic classification). If a male patient dreams about fire and water, or dreams about one and quickly associates to the other (and here the protocol scoring would be a straightforward, objective, almost purely clerical job approaching perfect interscorer reliability), the dominant theme in the remainder of the session will involve *ambition* as a motive and *shame* (or triumph) as an affect. In 25 years as a psychotherapist I have not found so much as a single exception to this generalization. This kind of temporal covariation was the essential evidential base from which Freud started, and I suggest that if sufficient protocols were available for study, it is the kind of thing which could be subjected to simple statistical test. Since there is no obvious phenotypic overlap in the content, a successful prediction along these lines would strongly corroborate one component of psychoanalytic theory, namely that concerning the urethral cluster [pp. 109-110].

3. I have found my own experience on the couch, and my clinical experience listening to the free associations of patients, far more persuasive than any published research purporting to test psychoanalytic theory. I do not assert that this is a good or a bad thing; I just want to have it down in the record. . . .

The inventor of psychoanalysis took the same view, and it might be good research strategy to concentrate attention upon the verbal behavior of the analytic session itself. If there is any strong empirical evidence in support of Freud's ideas, that is perhaps the best place to look, since that is where he hit upon them in the first place [pp. 106-107].

Let me now comment critically, in turn, on these three sets of remarks.

1. I take him to be making the following intriguing proposal. To circumvent epistemological contamination of patient responses by interpretations from the analyst, psychoanalytic protocols would be collected "from essentially naive patients to whom no interpretations have as yet been offered." I am unclear how many patients who seek out psychoanalysts or are referred to them *and* who are intelligent enough to be accepted for analysis are "naïve" in the intended sense: Before being given any interpretations, their clinical responses are not otherwise contaminated by prior knowledge of the general theoretical framework used by analysts. But, for argument's sake, let me assume that there is no such other prior epistemological contamination, even in the very production of "thematic material in the patient's subsequent associations to the dream." Then Meehl's proposal does not tell us whether any significant portion of psychoanalytic theory (e.g., the theory of repression) is testable in this way *without* begging the question of unconscious determinants *and* of their specifically Freudian contents. Doubts concerning both the scope and probative cogency of such testability arise, if only because—under the test conditions posited by Meehl—no dent in the patient's resistance to the disclosure of unconscious material can as yet have been made by the analyst. Given the difficulties raised in the other chapters here, how, for example, are etiologic or other genetic hypotheses pertaining to repressed contents to be tested in the way envisioned by Meehl?

2. Meehl tells us the clinical generalization he reports here from his 25 years as a psychotherapist constitutes "the kind of clinical evidence that carries the heaviest weight with those who open-mindedly but skeptically embark upon psychoanalytic work." But I am dumbfounded that a distinguished scientific psychologist of Meehl's sophistication and stature should not have addressed at all in this context the whole range of contaminations eloquently set forth by such Freudian partisans as Marmor (1962) and Christiansen (1964), not to speak of the pertinent import of the Nisbett and Wilson paper (1977). Meehl gives no hint of any safeguard against the persuasive effects of

the analyst's theoretical stance regarding the urethral cluster on the dominant theme of the remainder of the session, once the patient has reported a dream about fire and water. Nor does he tell us whether Adlerians, Jungians, Sullivanians, and other non-Freudian analysts confirm his generalizations. But he does allow (Meehl, 1983, p. 410) that "Fliess's Achsee question [concerning vitiation by suggestibility] deserves a better answer than it has yet received."

3. Meehl's initial personal disclaimer here does not prevent him from giving the appearance of perhaps drawing the inference that since the analytic session itself was the heuristic source of Freud's hypotheses, it is also likely to have been the prime testing ground for them, and potentially a major source of such strong empirical support as may exist. Yet it is the *justification* for this inference that is first at issue. Neither does Holt's sympathetic portrayal of the methods of clinical psychology (1978, pp. 140-141, 230-243) claim to gainsay the kinds of doubts I have urged against inferring probative promise from heuristic value.

The liabilities of data from the psychoanalytic interview that I am engaged in discussing apply at least to claims of validation of Freud's major causal hypotheses by clinical findings already in hand. These liabilities pertain not only to the evidential value of clinical data qua data (contamination issue), but also to their failure to support his cardinal causal hypotheses even if they could be taken at face value (Grünbaum, 1984, p. 172). Yet, as documented in these chapters, it is on this contaminated and *non*probative evidence that Freud and many of his adherents have relied to claim validation. But this skeptical assessment should *not* be taken to suggest that I confidently predict a generally unfavorable outcome across the board from genuinely probative future evidence. In fact, it is even conceivable, if not likely, that imaginative future clinical study designs will alter the bleak picture of clinical validation I have drawn. True, we must keep an open mind for that possibility as well—but, as the logician Alan Ross Anderson used to say, not so open that our brains fall out!

6

EPISTEMIC DEFECTS IN THE CLINICAL VALIDATION OF CAUSAL HYPOTHESES

A Reply to Marshall Edelson's Defense of Intraclinical
Testability of Causal Hypotheses in Psychoanalytic Theory

Let us now turn to the arguments offered by Edelson (1984) in his endeavor to claim that psychoanalytic hypotheses *can* be cogently tested within the treatment setting. He articulates this claim by telling us that, for the most part, "psychoanalysis . . . must depend" epistemically on "single subject research" (p. 56). He elaborates on the phrase "for the most part" by *rejecting* Freud's view that "extraclinical or experimental testing of psychoanalytic hypotheses" (p. 122) is *superfluous.*

In one of my publications (1982, pp. 404-406), which is cited by Edelson, I had given an account of recent single-subject research designs, presented my reasons for regarding these otherwise important designs to be unavailing for vindicating the thesis that psychoanalytic hypotheses are soundly testable *within* the clinical setting. In his 1984 book, Edelson disputed my 1982 appraisal of single-subject research. In order to deal with his objections, let me first recapitulate my earlier views on the matter from chapter 3.

SUMMARY OF MY EARLIER VIEWS ON SINGLE-SUBJECT RESEARCH DESIGNS

As I noted then, experimental validations of therapeutic efficacy have been carried out by using the response history of single individuals *without* controls drawn from other individuals to whom the given therapy is *not* administered (Hersen and Barlow, 1976; Kazdin, 1981, 1982). Thus, in these validations, the *causal* claims inherent in the pertinent assertions of therapeutic efficacy have been validated by single-case experimental designs. I asked whether these "*intra*subject" validations could become prototypic for using a given analysand to test *intra*clinically the causal assertions made by the long-term etiologic hypotheses of psychoanalytic theory and by such claims of efficacy as are made for its avowedly slow therapy. To answer this question, I first looked at situations in physics in which the *probative equivalent* of controlled experiments is furnished by other means.

When a billiard ball initially at rest on a billiard table suddenly acquires momentum upon being hit by another billiard ball, we are confident that the acceleration of the first ball results from the impact of the second. Even more strikingly, astronomers made sound causal claims about the motions of planets, binary stars, etc., before they were able to manipulate artificial earth satellites, moon probes, or interplanetary rockets. What took the probative place of control groups in these cases? In the case of the billiard ball, Newton's otherwise well-supported first law of motion gives us background knowledge as to the "natural history" of an object initially at rest that is not exposed to external forces: Such an object will remain at rest. This information, or the law of conservation of linear momentum, enables us to point the finger at the moving second billiard ball to furnish the cause of the change in the momentum of the first. A similar reliance on otherwise attested background knowledge supplies the probative equivalent of experimental controls in the astronomical cases.

Turning to the *single*-case validation of therapeutic efficacy, I emphasize that they pertain to the following sort of instance:

> A seven-year old boy would beat his head when not restrained. His head was covered with scar tissue and his ears were swollen and bleeding. An extinction procedure was tried: The boy was allowed to sit in bed with no restraints and with no attention given to his self-destructive behavior. After seven days, the rate of injurious behavior decreased markedly, but in the interim the

boy had engaged in over ten thousand such acts, thus making the therapists fearful for his safety. A punishment procedure was subsequently introduced in the form of one-second electric shocks. In a brief time, the shock treatment dramatically decreased the unwanted behavior [Erwin, 1978, pp. 11-12].

Here the dismal prospects of an untreated autistic child are presumably known from the natural history of other such children. In the light of this presumed background knowledge, the dramatic and substantial behavior change ensuing shortly after electric shock allowed the attribution of the change to the shock without control groups. The reason is that, under the circumstances, the operation of *other* causal agencies seems very unlikely. More generally, the *paradigmatic* example of an *intra*subject clinical validation of the causal efficacy of a given intervention is furnished by the following *variant* of using the single patient as his own "historical" control: (1) The natural history of the disorder is presumably otherwise known; *or* (2) the therapist intervenes only in on-off fashion, and this intermittent intervention is found to yield alternating remissions and relapses with dramatic rapidity.

Can the causal validation designs employed in these intrasubject clinical tests of therapeutic efficacy become prototypic for using an individual analysand to validate Freud's *long*-term etiologic hypotheses, or to furnish evidence that an analysis whose typical duration extends over a good many years deserves credit for any therapeutic gain registered by the patient after, say, four years? I claimed that the answer is negative. The natural history of a person *not* subjected to the experiences deemed pathogenic by Freudian theory is *notoriously* unknown! As for crediting therapeutic gain to analytic intervention on the basis of an intrasubject case history, I asked: How could such an attribution possibly be made in the face of Freud's own (1926a, p. 154) acknowledgment of the occurrence of *spontaneous* remissions? In short, I averred, the stated intrasubject validation by means of dramatic therapeutic gains can hardly be extrapolated to underwrite the single-case evaluation of slow analytic therapy, let alone to vindicate the testing of a Freudian etiology in the course of an individual analysis.

In my 1980 essay in the journal *Nous* (chap. 5, this monograph), which is also cited by Edelson, I had expressed specific doubts as to why a single-case design using Mill's method of concomitant variations is incompetent to test the purported *insight dynamics* of analytic therapy. According to Freudian theory, the patient achieves insight by *working through* or overcoming his resistances to the recognition of the actual unconscious pathogens of his affliction. Hence the etiologic *authenticity* of the presumed pathogens needs to be warranted. Otherwise *presumed* insight runs the serious risk of being pseudoinsight. And it is a cardinal tenet of psychoanalytic theory that only *bona fide veridical* insight is dependably therapeutic. But as I argue in other places herein, free association does not have the epistemic capability to certify pathogenicity, because it cannot warrant *causal* relevance. Therefore, the etiologic authenticity of a presumed pathogen in the patient's early life needs to be warranted, if at all, by the application of the pertinent *general* etiologic hypotheses of the theory to the personal life history of the patient. Edelson acknowledges (pp. 124, 151) that the challenge to his program of intraclinical validation by single-subject designs includes these etiologic hypotheses.

With this understanding of the prerequisites for psychoanalytic insight, let us turn to the research design offered by Fisher and Greenberg (1977), with a view to investigating whether insight is the therapeutically operative *ingredient* of psychoanalytic treatment, as claimed by Freudian theory? They outline their envisioned investigative design as follows:

> At the least, more direct tests of Freud's ideas would seem to require comparative studies using different operationalized levels of working through with chronic *neurotic* patients and experienced therapists in *individual* therapy. They would also require an independent measure of insight defined in terms of the patient's ability to conceptualize the relationship between his past and his present [p. 362].

At first glance, this proposal makes it appear as if the treatment setting itself provides the psychoanalyst with a quasi-experimental environment for testing the *dynamics* of his therapy via concomitant variations of therapeutic *outcome* attributes with various levels of insight. But this *prima facie* epistemic capability of the clinical arena to test the remedial potency of psychoanalytic insight will dissolve, unless that setting has the resources to vouch for the *veridicality* of presumed insights. The mere ring of verisimilitude to both analyst and patient is not enough: As we saw, according to Freudian therapeutic theory, presumed insights are not *dependably* remedial, unless they are, in fact, correct.

In Fisher and Greenberg's proposed testing design, we are not told just how the investigating analyst assures the fulfillment of their insight requirement, as measured by "the patient's ability to conceptualize the relationship between his past and his present." But, as is now clear, to document *in the treatment setting* that *bona fide* insight is at hand would require two things: (1) the retrospective clinical authentication of the *actual* past occurrence in the patient's early life of the events retrodicted via Freud's etiologies; and (2) the validation of the *general* etiologic hypotheses invoked to reconstruct the pathogenesis of the analysand's affliction. Note that the mere historical authentication of retrodicted episodes is *not* enough to furnish the required certification of their *pathogenic role*. This then is the challenge to single-subject research in psychoanalysis I issued to which Edelson wishes to respond in his 1984 book.

CRITIQUE OF EDELSON'S CASE FOR INTRACLINICAL TESTABILITY

The core of his lengthy attempt in that volume to neutralize my doubts consists of slightly more than one page. The passage on which he essentially rests his entire case follows:

> . . . typically, data obtained in the psychoanalytic situation are nonexperimental. Causality can be argued, according to the canons of eliminative inductivism, from nonexperimental data by using, for example, causal modeling and statistical controls (Asher, 1976; Blalock, 1961, 1969; Cook and Campbell, 1979; Watson and McGaw, 1980).
>   Causality can be argued, according to the canons of eliminative inductivism, from single subject data, if, for example, multiple measurements under baseline (no-treatment) and treatment conditions, or multiple measurements under different treatments or

conditions, are obtained for comparison (Hersen and Barlow, 1976).

Grünbaum, when he refers to single subject research, argues as if the only possibility is an "on-off" intervention-baseline—intervention-baseline kind of design. He then supposes that this design is irrelevant to evaluating the efficacy of psychoanalysis because the long duration of the intervention makes it very difficult to eliminate alternative explanatory candidates that might be supposed to account for any effect observed. Other designs are available, however, including the time-series design (designs 7 and 9 described by Campbell and Stanley, 1963); as well as the multiple baseline design (which Grünbaum clearly sees is the prototype for cases like [Breuer's patient] Anna O., where it implicitly serves as the basis for the argument that one is justified in eliminating a general placebo effect as an alternative explanation of the effects of the "talking cure" on different symptoms, because these symptoms are affected separately or independently).

That a multiple baseline design is not in principle inapposite to hypothesis testing in the psychoanalytic situation, despite changes in the theory since the case of Anna O. was written, is suggested by the following characteristics of psychoanalytic treatment, among others. For long periods anyway, a particular focal conflict may be the focus of analytic work (Luborsky and Mintz, 1974). "Working through" (roughly, interpreting the manifestations of the same conflict in one context after another) is an important aspect of psychoanalytic treatment.

There is every reason to believe that such designs as these can be used in single subject research to test psychoanalytic hypotheses in the psychoanalytic situation, although not necessarily those hypotheses focused on etiology or therapeutic efficacy with which Grünbaum appears to be especially concerned. Even with respect to these hypotheses, it is possible that etiologic hypotheses can be tested indirectly, by testing hypotheses deduced from them. If, for example, variations in the intensity of an unconscious conflict result in variations in severity or frequency of a symptom, that could be argued to be indirect though incomplete evidence for the role of unconscious conflicts in the *genesis* of neurotic symptoms. The work of Luborsky (1967, 1973) and Luborsky and Mintz (1974) is especially important with respect to this point [Edelson, 1984, pp. 124-125].

But, as I shall now argue, not even one of the single-subject designs enumerated by Edelson sustains his thesis that psychoanalytic *causal* hypotheses can be *cogently* tested in the treatment setting.

1. Edelson notes that the pertinent clinical data are "nonexperimental." Thereupon he tells us that "causality can be argued, according to the canons of eliminative inductivism, from nonexperimental data by using . . . causal modeling and statistical controls." At this point, his references include Cook and Campbell (1979), among others. In this way, Edelson's reader gets the misleading impression that the testing arrangements countenanced by these authors can be made serviceable in Edelson's cause by being adaptable to the psychoanalytic clinical situation. Cook and Campbell (p. 308) *explicitly indict* the *probative* invocation of their so-called "causal pathway maps" as illegitimate. Indeed, they point out the probative *inferiority* of these maps to the experimental evaluation of causal hypotheses. What they do aver is that such maps do have *heuristic* value in such fields as sociology. But *heuristic* capability was never at issue. Far from having denied the heuristic merits of the psychoanalytic treatment setting, I have emphasized them all along.

2. Edelson's recourse to the so-called "time series design with single intervention" also boomerangs. In this treatment scheme, a single intervention that turns out to have a lasting therapeutic effect on the target disorder is given credit for the remedial gain. Yet, as Hersen and Barlow stress (1976, p. 169), this causal attribution is tempered by *"some major reservations."* First, the design *does nothing* to rule out the *rival* hypothesis that the target disorder would have remitted anyway, without a therapist's intervention, as a matter of so-called "spontaneous remission." Though Edelson cites Campbell and Stanley (1963) regarding the single intervention scheme, he overlooks that they too emphasized—under the rubric of history—this failure to control for spontaneous remission. And they point to some six other *inferential liabilities* that bedevil the given design. Second, even if the positive treatment outcome *is* credited to the intervention, this attribution is still a far cry from showing that some particular ingredient of the therapy—such as Freudian insight—produced the improvement. This intervention blueprint clearly *fails to rule out* the rival hypothesis that the positive outcome is a *placebo effect*, wrought by treatment ingredients *other than those* deemed remedial by the therapist's theory.

To appreciate the issue of spontaneous remission, consider a typical psychoanalysis, which can last for five to ten years. Assume that a hypothetical patient has clearly recovered, in specified respects, upon termination of the therapy. Suppose further that the patient's gains turn out to be *permanent* upon follow-up. If the Freudian intervention is to earn the credit for this welcome result, there needs to be evidence that, after all these years, the improvement would *not* have occurred anyway, *or* that—if it had set in spontaneously—it would *not* have been equally *durable* or as good. But how is Edelson going to demonstrate that analytic patients fare better—in these respects—than their untreated counterparts? Surely, in order to carry out the requisite inquiry, he needs to spring the confines of the single intervention schema by going *outside* the analytic treatment framework.

As Hersen and Barlow point out (1976, p. 176), one can *extend* the previous, simple, time-series design so as to obtain evidence *against* spontaneous remission, if indeed the therapy can produce short-term improvement. Let "A" represent the patient's troubled state, a state serving as the *baseline* against which any subsequent improvement (or deterioration) during or after treatment is to be measured. And let "B" be the treatment phase. Now consider an initially troubled patient who improves during the therapy, but then relapses, once it is discontinued. In the stated A-B notation, such a case history takes the form "A-B-A."

With reference to this history, Hersen and Barlow (1976) argue persuasively that it convincingly tells *against* the attribution of the patient's *temporary* improvement to spontaneous remission:

> If after baseline measure (A) the application of a treatment (B) leads to improvement and conversely results in deterioration after it is withdrawn (A), one can conclude with a high degree of certainty that the treatment variable is the agent responsible for observed changes in the target behavior. Unless the natural history of the behavior under study were to follow identical fluctuations in trends, it is *most improbable* that observed changes are due to any influence (e.g., some correlated or uncontrolled variable) other than the treatment variable that is systemically

changed. Also, replication of the A-B-A design in different subjects strengthens conclusions as to power and controlling forces of the treatment [p. 176].

Thus, the A-B-A design does succeed in discrediting spontaneous remission.

But, as Freud himself rightly explained by reference to cathartic treatment, even an *indefinite* prolongation of this design, containing *repeated* cycles A-B-A, does *not* impugn the rival hypothesis of placebo effect. Let us recall the account I gave in chapter 1:

> Soon after Freud had begun to practice without Breuer, it became devastatingly plain that they had been all too hasty in rejecting the rival hypothesis of placebo effect. The remissions achieved by additional patients whom Freud himself treated cathartically turned out *not* to be durable. Indeed, the ensuing pattern of relapses, additional treatment, ephemeral remissions, and further relapses gainsaid the attribution of therapeutic credit to the lifting of those repressions that Freud had uncovered. Ironically, he began to be haunted by the triumph of the hypothesis of placebo effect over the fundamental therapeutic tenet that Breuer and he had originally enunciated, for he recognized that the vicissitudes of his personal relations to the patient were highly correlated with the pattern of symptom relapses and intermittent remissions. In his view, this correlation "proved that the personal emotional relation between doctor and patient was after all stronger than the whole cathartic process" (1925b, p. 27).

It is, I submit, unavailing that Edelson repeatedly adduces the case of Breuer's first hysterical patient, Anna O., as support for his thesis (pp. 50, 124, 150). As he sees it, this case history illustrates that the placebo hypothesis can be cogently discredited by positive therapeutic outcome from a single patient in a protopsychoanalytic treatment scenario. He believes the design embodied in Breuer's celebrated case history is capable of lending credence to the insight dynamics purportedly operative in Freudian therapy. I aim to show that Edelson's view is ill-founded. In order to do so, let me first highlight the relevant features reported by Breuer *before* Freud became disenchanted with hypnotic treatment.

Besides a phobic aversion for drinking water, Anna O.'s symptoms included a severe nervous cough, visual disturbances, paresis of the neck muscles, and a host of other disturbances (Breuer and Freud, 1893-95, pp. 23-34). When Breuer put her under hypnosis, it turned out that, for *each* of her *distinct* sorts of symptoms *S*, she had *repressed* the memory of a trauma that had closely preceded the onset of *S* and was thematically cognate to *S*. And when she achieved *cathartic recall* of the pertinent trauma, *S* disappeared dramatically. Thus, Breuer's hypnotic technique yielded such success for *each* of her various symptoms.

When Freud still believed in hypnotic treatment, Breuer and he contended (p. 7) their symptom removals were *not* placebo effects, wrought by suggestion. The treatment gains made by Anna O. and others, they reasoned, were wrought by *cathartic memory retrieval*. And their grounds were that *distinct* kinds of symptoms had been removed *separately*, one at a time, so that any one symptom disappeared only after lifting a corresponding *particular* repression.

Yet as we saw before, *à propos* the cyclically repeated A-B-A design, Freud subsequently *repudiated* the claim that cathartic *recall* was the therapeutically efficacious *ingredient* of Breuer's method. He adduced the *impermanence* of the ensuing remissions as his grounds for this disavowal. But even if the therapeutic gains made by Anna O. and others had turned out to be durable as well as splendid, the *separate* symptom removals would *not* have eliminated the placebo hypothesis. As I noted in chapters 1 and 3, even such impressive results may not be due at all to the lifting of pathogenic repressions; instead, they may be a *placebo effect*, generated by the patient's awareness that the therapist was *intent* on uncovering a thematically particular episode *E* when focusing the former's attention on the initial appearance of the distinct symptom *S*. Thus, it was communicated to the patient that Breuer and Freud attached potential therapeutic significance to the recall of *E* with respect to *S*. To discredit the hypothesis of placebo effect, it would have been essential to have comparisons with treatment outcome from a suitable control group whose repressions are *not* lifted. If that control group were to fare equally well, treatment gains from psychoanalysis would then be placebo effects after all. Hence the attribution of remedial efficacy to the abreactive lifting of repressions was devoid of adequate evidential warrant.

In short, to rule out placebo effect, the analyst must provide a comparison with outcome from treatment *in which there is no lifting of repressions!* But to the detriment of Edelson's thesis, just that latter sort of intervention is, *by definition, not* confined to the framework of *analytic* therapy, even if administered by an analyst in his usual consulting room.

In the vocabulary of current single-subject research, the term "baseline" refers to a particular sort of symptom. Hence a *"multiple* baseline design" is one in which there are *at least two distinct kinds* of target symptoms at whose removal the intervention is aimed, one at a time. As Hersen and Barlow point out (1976, p. 9), the case of Anna O. is a classic instance of a multiple baseline schema. Yet as our scrutiny of that case showed, this type of multiple attack on the target disorder is just as *incompetent* to rule out placebo effect as the earlier single-intervention A-B design.

Edelson supposes that merely because distinct symptoms are removed, one at a time, the therapeutic agency that effects the removal should be presumed to be psychoanalytic insight, rather than a placebo component of the therapy. But he does not tell us *why* we should deem the likelihood that the removal is placebogenic to be *lower* when *several* symptoms are wiped out seriatim, than in the case of getting rid of only one. Instead, he repeatedly (pp. 50, 124, 150) brings up the multiple baseline feature in Anna O.'s therapy to make the following erroneous claim for her case: "one is justified in eliminating a general placebo effect as an alternative explanation of the effects of the 'talking cure' on different symptoms" (p. 124). As is now apparent, Edelson has failed to establish the intraclinical testability of the hypothesized insight dynamics of analytic treatment by means of the multiple baseline blueprint.

It is odd that, in his endeavor to support such testability, Edelson (p. 67) calls attention to Hersen and Barlow's mention of the Anna O. case as a pioneering instance of the multiple baseline design. Ironically, he is unaware that just these authors credited Breuer with having appreciated the *inability* of his own method to decide between the rival hypotheses of placebo effect and of insight-cure. As they put it:

> In a series of treatment sessions, Breuer dealt with one symptom at a time through hypnosis and subsequent "talking through," where each symptom was traced back to its hypothetical causation. . . . One at a time, these behaviors disappeared, but only when treatment was administered to each respective behavior. This process of treating one behavior at a time fulfills the basic requirement for a multiple baseline experimental design . . . and the clearly observable success indicated that Breuer's treatment was effective. Of course, Breuer did not define his independent variables in that there were several components to his treatment (e.g., hypnosis, [etiologic] interpretation [of the repressed trauma], etc.); but, in the manner of a good scientist as well as a good clinician, Breuer admitted that he did not know which component or components of his treatment were responsible for success. He noted at least two possibilities, the suggestion inherent in the hypnosis or the interpretation [Hersen and Barlow, 1976, p. 9].

But what is the textual basis for this exegesis of Breuer? After all, as we know from the "Preliminary Communication" (Breuer and Freud, 1893), he explicitly rejected the rival explanation of placebo effect. Furthermore, just before the very end of Breuer's own case history of Anna O., he made a point of giving his "assurance" that the symptom removals by means of cathartic recall were "not an invention of mine which I imposed on the patient by suggestion" (Breuer and Freud, 1893-95, p. 46). Yet, only a few pages earlier, he contradicted his other assertions as follows: "As regards the symptoms disappearing after being 'talked away', I cannot use this as evidence; it may very well be explained by suggestion" (p. 43). Presumably, this dissonant averral of Breuer's was the basis for Hersen and Barlow's tribute that he was "a good scientist as well as a good clinician."

Yet, after all is said and done, the Anna O. case does not deserve the place it received above in the debate on placebogenic gain: As we know from Ellenberger (1972) and Hirschmüller (1989), Breuer's treatment of her soon turned out to be a therapeutic fiasco.

Besides multiple baseline designs, Edelson also recites others cryptically in his effort to document the *bona fides* of clinical testing. He quotes Hersen and Barlow (p. 124) to the effect that: "Causality can be argued, according to the canons of eliminative inductivism, from single subject data, if, for example, multiple measurements under . . . different treatments or conditions, are obtained for comparison." But how, I must ask, is a psychoanalyst going to carry out such treatment *comparison*? If the research analyst is to fulfill Edelson's methodological promise, this researcher must evaluate the causal efficacy of analytic treatment by means of single-subject data from a patient undergoing *only* psychoanalysis. How then can the findings secured by an analyst while *dispensing Freudian treatment* possibly show that his own therapy is more efficacious for the patient's target disorder than, say, behavior therapy?

Indeed, imagine the actually utopian scenario of finding a Freudian who is equally skilled at administering either behavior therapy or psychoanalysis, despite his *disbelief* in the value of the former. And now suppose that in order to vindicate his belief in the remedial superiority of his own modality, the analyst takes a single patient *P* and does the following: First, he administers *behavior* therapy to *P*, using any requisite paraphernalia of treatment in his own consulting room, whereupon he evaluates the outcome, as is his wont with his usual analytic patients. For argument's sake, posit that the result is less than satisfactory. Next, the research analyst treats *P*, using the Freudian techniques that constitute his customary stock-in-trade. Imagine further that thereupon he assesses *P* as having been cured.

Even on these rather utopian assumptions, I submit, this design would not serve at all to sustain Edelson's thesis, for at least two reasons. First, though the behaviorist segment of this successive treatment design is carried out by a supposedly most versatile analyst, it would obviously be a mere abuse of language to count it as meeting Edelson's requirement of being research *within* the framework of the analytic setting. Equally obviously, in this context, the analyst cannot tell whether the posited final cure is due only to the *analytic* portion of the design, rather than being the *cumulative* effect of the successive interventions.

By contrast, when different sorts of treatment are administered to *different* individuals in therapeutic *group* research, the
ensuing effects may be cogently compared, because they are
causally *independent* of one another. But such independence can
hardly be assumed in the scenario of dispensing different kinds
of treatment *successively* to a single patient. In fact, Edelson
appreciates this point, as shown by his critical remarks (pp. 61-
62) on Kohut's two consecutive, doctrinally different psychoanalyses of Mr. Z. More generally, he also acknowledges
further on (p. 69) that, in single-subject research, the problem
of independence of effects does pose a methodological hurdle
for the single-case research design.

Let us suppose, however, that the challenge of *internal* validity
can be met by this design. In that event, there would still be the
following question of *external* validity: How can the results from
a single-subject investigation be warrantedly generalized to
populations of other subjects? By way of reply, Edelson advocates "systematic replication of the single subject study . . . with
other subjects." And, as an elaboration, he offers pie in the sky:
"With each replication, the subject . . . is [qualitatively] the same
with the exception of one property or feature; properties of
the subject . . . are considered then to be systematically varied"
(p. 66).

But it is *utterly chimerical* to predicate a research design on a
situation in which two people differ *only* with respect to the
property that the investigator *conjecturally* deems relevant to
the outcome! The utopianism of *such* a construal of systematic
replication has long been familiar from the critique of Mill's
(1887) experimental method of difference. Contrary to his own
sanguine depiction of this canon, it fails to assure that the two
different instances to which it is applied differ *only* in a *causally
relevant* respect (Cohen and Nagel, 1934, p. 257). If other, overlooked factors that may be causally relevant are to be neutralized by *increasing* the *number* of single-subject replications, then
the individual case research advocated by Edelson would
merge, in principle, with group research.

Thus, in order to vouch for the generalizability of results
from *individual* psychoanalytic patients, Edelson paints an illusory, methodologically idyllic picture of systematic replication.

By contrast, he is relentlessly down-to-earth and scientifically streetwise in his tally of the problems of probity that beset *group*-comparison research designs (pp. 63-65). Indeed, in the course of that tally, his bias becomes blatant, because he charges against group research precisely the difficulty of *extraneous* causes, to which he was oblivious when he depicted the systematic variation of just one property in the replication of a single-subject study. He gives the following description of the pertinent liability of *group*-comparison research:

> It is not easy to obtain truly random samples in clinical practice and settings. But then the effects of extraneous variables cannot be assumed to be randomized and equivalent in the compared groups, and these groups cannot be assumed to be similar with respect to all relevant variables other than the explanatory variable(s) [p. 63].

Hence, he expresses regret that "the group-comparison method . . . unfortunately is held up by Grünbaum among others as *the* way to satisfy the canons" of scientifically sound inference (p. 65).

Yet, I submit, what is sauce for the goose is sauce for the gander. Any methodological dispensation that is granted to single-subject replication ought to be likewise explicitly accorded to group comparisons. What then entitles him to deplore that I am beholden to the group-comparison method for psychoanalytic research? In addition, as Erwin has noted (private communication), when Edelson (p. 63) cites Kazdin (1980), he creates the misleading impression that Kazdin considers single-subject blueprints to be investigatively superior to group designs. Furthermore, Edelson fails to mention Kazdin's discussion of standard strategies used to overcome the defects of comparative group studies. Thus, it is Kazdin, not Edelson, who is even-handed when drawing up a balance sheet of merits and demerits for the different designs.

In all, when Edelson lists a series of single-subject designs in rapid succession on a single page (p. 124), he gives the reader every impression that, in his view, they can all be used for "hypothesis testing in the psychoanalytic situation." Indeed, in the light of his immediately preceding page, his reader gets the impression that he offers this array of designs as a refutation of my doubts concerning the intraclinical testability of psychoanalysis—and, the designs discussed by Cook and Campbell (1979) and by Campbell and Stanley (1963) loom large in his enumeration, as we saw. Thereupon (p. 125), Edelson elaborates on Campbell and Stanley's proposal to use a number of independent and different kinds of studies as tests of a particular hypothesis. His own amplification of that proposal then shows clearly, however, that the Campbell and Stanley designs cannot serve to impugn my doubts. As Edelson himself puts it:

> Of course, the converging studies must be independent and different in some way (different investigators, methods, settings, subjects). If one adopts this strategy, one accepts that a psychoanalytic hypothesis cannot be tested in the psychoanalytic situation alone [p. 125].

But he is unaware that, as I showed, precisely the same concession of having to go outside the analytic treatment setting needs to be made for essentially all the designs he discusses.

Edelson (chap. 11) offers two purported counterexamples to my thesis that, on present evidence, it appears very unlikely that the causal hypotheses of psychoanalytic theory—which are its lifeblood—can be cogently tested intraclinically. His first example is a study by Luborsky and Mintz (1974). The second is Glymour's (1974, 1980) account of the Rat-Man case which I have already discussed in chapter 3. I shall now examine *Edelson's own gloss* (pp. 144-146) on the work of Luborsky and Mintz. Thus, when I make attributions to Luborsky and Mintz, it is to be understood that these refer to Edelson's account of their study, not necessarily to that study itself.

Luborsky and Mintz investigated a certain Miss X who exhibited 13 instances of momentary forgetting during about 300 sessions of psychoanalysis. In Edelson's version of their research design, she is postulated to instantiate Freudian theory. On the strength of this postulate and of her episodes of forgetting, Edelson deduces a hypothesis c, and then d and e. But thereupon he makes the crucial claim that a conclusion f, which purportedly states the expected empirical outcome of Luborsky and Mintz's study, "follows" from the hypotheses c, d, and e. Finally, he reports (p. 146) they confirm the alleged prediction f.

As Edelson sees it, Luborsky and Mintz's confirmation of his conclusion f qualifies as a test of the conjunction of psychoanalytic hypotheses c, d, and e, because f "follows" from this conjunction (p. 145). I submit, however, this is a *non sequitur*. Edelson provides no grounds that his conclusion f is *validly* deducible from some other set of psychoanalytic hypotheses. Therefore, he is not entitled to claim that the testing of his ill-founded conclusion f qualifies as an intraclinical test of psychoanalysis.

To exhibit the logical structure of his fallacious deduction, I shall use $>$ for *causal implication*, and capital letters for the pertinent propositions as follows:

N   = Neurotic symptoms or parapraxes either occur or become more severe.

F   = Focal psychic conflict intensifies.

M   = Momentary forgetting occurs.

E   = Emotional involvement with an analyst increases (from zero or otherwise).

It is to be understood, of course, that the various states, such as forgetting, are states of a *person*, who happens to be Miss X in Luborsky and Mintz's study. The reader is asked to bear in mind that my use here of the symbol ">" for *causal implication* is not to be confused with its familiar use in arithmetic to denote the relation of "greater than."

In this notation, Edelson's premises c, d, e, and his conclusion f become—in requisitely polished form—respectively:

Premises
$$\begin{cases} c\colon N > F \\ d\colon M > N \\ e\colon E > F \end{cases}$$

Conclusion $f\colon M > E$

The argument is an endeavor to deduce a causal linkage between M and E via a linkage of *each* of them to F. From c and d, it follows validly, by the transitivity of implication, $k\colon M > F$. But, to the detriment of Edelson's case, it is a patent fallacy to deduce the conclusion f from the conjunction of e and k. Merely because memory lapses and emotional involvement with an analyst *each* intensify conflict, it does *not* follow that memory lapses enhance the propensity for emotional involvement with the analyst.

In the paperback edition of Edelson's book (1984), he has changed his reconstruction (pp. 144-146) of the Luborsky and Mintz study. But in the new version, no less than in the old, the conclusion f simply does not follow from his psychoanalytic premises, because his deduction relies on a fallacious hypothetical syllogism.

If the premise e could be replaced by its *converse*, l: $F > E$, then f would indeed follow from the conjunction of k with that converse l. But l asserts that whenever a person's focal psychic conflict intensifies, there is an increased emotional involvement with an analyst. This assertion is clearly not countenanced by Freudian theory, if only because conflict intensifications are *also* presumed to occur in neurotics who never see an analyst, let alone become emotionally involved with one.

Hence Edelson's (1984) reconstruction of Luborsky's symptom-context method has offered no valid grounds for believing that Luborsky's empirical confirmation of the ill-founded conclusion f qualifies as an intraclinical test of a psychoanalytic causal hypothesis.

Edelson (pp. 101ff.) digresses into a sketch of the definition of the predicate ". . . is a Freudian system," as applied to the domain of the psychological states of an individual person X. And the defining property of being a Freudian system is that the given domain of X's psychic states satisfies a specified set of hypotheses enunciated in Freud's theory. This way of reformulating the theory by means of a theoretical predicate is called the *"non*statement" form of the theory, because the predicate—". . . is a Freudian system"—is not *itself* a statement, though the definition in which it occurs is a statement. Moreover, in the definiens, the Freudian hypotheses asserted about the given psychological domain are also statements.

Edelson concerns himself with such a predicate recasting of psychoanalytic theory in the expressed hope that it will yield a series of purported benefits. One such presumed gain is the systematization and articulation of psychoanalytic hypotheses, with a view to knowing just what claims are to be tested (pp. 84, 157). But I find nothing in his account of the supposed heuristic virtues of the predicate version of Freud's theory that cannot be accomplished by a disciplined rigorization of psychoanalytic hypotheses *qua* statements, as well as of their domain of application. For example, if there actually are good grounds for separating discourse about the human brain from discourse about the mind, then such a separation could be just as neatly effected by *distinct* statement versions of brain theory and psychology respectively, as by following Edelson's advice to define two distinct predicates ". . . is a mind system," and ". . . is a brain system." On the other hand, if it is a heuristic *handicap* to work respectively with mindless brains and brainless minds, then one can draw up hypotheses about *mind-brain* systems in the definiens of a complex predicate ". . . is a mind-brain system," no less than in the received statement form of the postulates. Yet Edelson writes:

> The nonstatement view of theory suggests, at least to me, that development of a theoretical predicate about mind and a theoretical predicate about brain, each with intended applications in its own quite different set of possible and actual domains, can and should be carried on independently, at least at this point in history [p. 110].

Qua assertion about *Edelson himself*, I certainly take his word for it. But, *qua* claim that the nonstatement viewpoints to *parallel* research strategies on the mind-body problem, as against a unified one, it is clearly false. It is false, if only because nothing in the nonstatement construal *as such* militates against the definability of a complex predicate ". . . is a mind-brain system," as I have already noted. Indeed, if the nonstatement view did have the import Edelson claims for it, that view could discourage potentially fruitful research on the mind-body problem. Besides, the heralding of this view as portending a promising scientific future for psychoanalysis may have other unfortunate consequences that Edelson himself would deplore. It may encourage the psychoanalytic community to *temporize* even further, instead of pooling resources to devise cogent tests of those hypotheses that much of it does endorse, in word and deed. It is now over 90 years since the publication of Freud's *Studies on Hysteria*. The hour is late, and the bell is tolling.

Let me now turn to my doubts concerning Edelson's recipe for handling the problem of epistemic contamination by suggestion and its ramifications.

He begins his chapter on clinical data in psychoanalysis (chap. 9) with the noncontroversial remark that any theoretical endeavor needs to take some sort of evidence for granted provisionally in order to test its hypotheses. Then he tells us that, in the analytic setting, these presumed data do *not* have to include what the analysand purports to *remember*. But such dispensation with the analysand's *early* memories *exacerbates* the problem of validating those key interpretations that take the patient to be *reenacting*, toward the analyst, actual childhood responses to authentic and purportedly pathogenic episodes.

Clearly, the use of the term "transference" to speak of the doctor-patient relationship, and of the "transference neurosis" developed by the patient in that interaction, is *predicated* on the assumption that the patient's unwholesome adult dispositions are indeed *carry-overs* or *repetitions from childhood*. And it would beg the question of the etiology and pathogenesis of the patient's affliction to evade it by just *decreeing* the stated loaded use of the term "transference." Yet, though having forsaken reliance on early memories, Edelson tells us reassuringly:

> . . . in fact, in psychoanalysis the pathogen is not merely a remote event, or a series of such events, the effect of which lives on. The pathogen reappears in all its virulence, with increasing frankness and explicitness, in the transference—in a new edition, a new version, a reemergence, a repetition of the past pathogenic events or factors [p. 150].

I examined this argument in detail in chapter 4 as part of my critique of the theory of the transference neurosis. But suffice it to say for now that it begs several questions. If *even* the thin reed of *malleable* patient recall is forsaken, as Edelson suggests, how can the analyst ascertain clinically, in *typical* circumstances, that each of the following conditions is satisfied? (1) The hypothesized remote event E actually occurred, be it an experience of an external event or a childhood fantasy; (2) assuming such occurrence, E was the original pathogen; (3) E's alleged current thematic *replica* is *presently* responsible for the patient's neurosis and indeed "virulent," as Edelson says. What does Edelson offer toward the fulfillment of these conditions?

1. With regard to the problem of providing historical authentication of the event E, Edelson offers nothing. Even if supposed memories of early childhood *are* invoked, this difficulty is trenchantly and graphically illustrated by Freud's case history of the Wolf-Man. In that account, Freud (1918, pp. 57-60, 95-97) had to address the following challenge from Jung: The Wolf-Man's purported memory of having witnessed his parents engaged in *a tergo* intercourse when he was a mere infant of 18 months was just a *retrospective adult* fantasy stemming from that patient's adult problems. Faced by this Jungian thesis of regressive symbolism, Freud grudgingly concedes that the alleged memory may well have been a *current* fantasy. We must be mindful of all we have learned as to the pitfalls of reliance on the *childhood* memories of adult patients *undergoing psychoanalysis*. Alas, it therefore strikes me as hollow hand-waving, when Edelson states, under the rubric of "The Fallibility of Memory":

> In general, I believe that Grünbaum's justifiable emphasis on the fallibility of memory does tend to underestimate the autonomous functioning of memory—that aspect of memory which, in Piaget's sense, is accommodative—and the possibility of detecting which aspects of memory are the results of accommodation to reality as it is and which are the outcome of distortion or fictive construction. . . . Psychoanalysts often feel that they can intuitively distinguish between effects of what "really happened to the analysand"—when an outcome is an adjustment to a noxious reality—and effects of what the analysand imagined, where "what happened" was merely used as material in his imagining [p. 137].

As for the accommodative function of memory in adult recall from early childhood, it is ironic that Edelson invokes Piaget. After all, it was Piaget who epitomized in his own life the malleability of later memories from childhood by suggestion. Reportedly (Loftus, 1980, pp. 119-121), he vividly recalled the *minute details* of being in his baby carriage in Paris, when his heroic nurse saved him from being kidnapped by an assailant. Yet the nurse confessed years later that she had self-servingly fabricated the entire story, which Piaget had then internalized mnemonically as authentic. In the court of science, credence should not be given to the unsubstantiated beliefs of analysts that they have an intuitive ability to discriminate pseudo memories from authentic ones—the less so, since their intuitions are bound to be steered and regimented by the theoretical exigencies of their craft in the context of their therapeutic objectives.

2. Our second issue was how the analyst can attest clinically that E was the pathogen, even if it were known to have occurred. Toward this objective and indeed toward demonstrating the current virulence of E, Edelson offers the following:

> The pathogen together with its pathological effects are, therefore, under the investigator's eye, so to speak, in the psychoanalytic situation, and demonstrating the causal relation between them in that situation, by nonexperimental or quasi-experimental methods, surely provides support, even if indirect, for the hypothesis that in the past the same kind of pathogenic factors were necessary to bring about the same kind of effects [p. 151].

To this, I say, let us be specific.

The classical psychoanalytic etiologies are sexual. And the *uncashed promissory note* in Edelson's declaration here is the articulation of a concrete research design, comprising an analyst and a single patient, cogently attesting to a *causal relation* between the allegedly *reappearing sexual pathogen* and the neurosis for which the patient is being treated. The claim of *reappearance* needs to be justified in the sense of supplying evidence that an *oedipal* conflict was the original pathogen. Mere backward extrapolation by speaking vaguely of "the same kind of pathogenic factors" as having been operative in the past will not do; such extrapolation does more to *presuppose* the Freudian theory of psychosexual development than to *vindicate* it retrospectively.

Indeed, the extrapolation favored by Edelson is insensitive to just the sorts of empirically inspired doubts raised by Kagan (1984), who urges a skeptical attitude toward the widespread, psychoanalytically endorsed doctrine that the developmental link between the infant and the adult is like "a journey in which the mind absorbs each new experience, never discarding any of its acquired treasures" (p. xiv).

But Edelson thinks the skeptics should be swayed epistemically, because both the patient and his analyst give "special weight" to "the emergence of circumstantial detail, having an astonishing degree of specificity and idiosyncratic nuance, in reports of fantasies and interpretations of experience" (pp. 136-137). His grounds are that beforehand the patient had no focal awareness or memory of these emerging specifics; nor is it usual that the analyst anticipates them, since they often come as a surprise. In this same vein, Edelson had stressed a few pages earlier, "The disciplined use of psychoanalytic technique . . . focuses on interpreting defense [as being present], rather than providing the analysand with suggestions about what [unconscious thought] he is defending against" (p. 130).

By way of amplification, he explains that some interpretations of the patient's productions merely "point to the contexts in which the analysand is having difficulty saying what is on his mind, without telling him just what he is censoring." Furthermore, he legislates rather *a priori* that "the psychoanalyst must also be able to argue that suggestion does not determine the analysand's responses to an interpretation, especially if that response is to be taken at face value as both true and a 'confirmation' of the psychoanalyst's inference" (p. 131).

But, I submit, serious doctrinal epistemic contamination does not require that all the *minutiae* of a patient's emerging associations be suggested to him; it is enough that the key *thematic context* within which hidden motives are expected to be found is suggested. And Edelson admits that the context prompts the interpretations. How, other than by thematic regimentation, does he explain Freud's complaint that doctrinally heterodox analysts failed to turn up male castration anxiety, which clearly emerged in his own Viennese consulting room? Besides, how—I ask—does Edelson reason that an adult patient's highly specific reports of his fantasies or idiosyncratic conceptualizations of experience attest reliably to childhood events? To this key question, Edelson, in effect, offers a mere possibility, if not a forlorn hope, as an answer, saying: "It is these data that may in the end prove to be most relevant to the search in the psychoanalytic situation for probative evidence providing support for psychoanalytic hypotheses" (p. 137). Yet for the uncommitted, this possibility is no reason to think that it will materialize.

Let me return to Freud's complaint that other analysts over-looked castration anxiety themes in the associative output of their patients. This divergence alone raises the question as to the criteria used by analysts to comb the patient's associations. I have objected (Grünbaum, 1982, p. 350; 1984, p. 210) that analysts use a causally *question-begging* antecedent *bias* to effect a thematic selection among the patient's associations. Freud picked out sexual themes as pathogens from the associations to neurotic symptoms, wishes as motives of dreams from associations linked to the manifest dream content, and "motives of unpleasure" as the causes of slips from the associative chains initiated by parapraxes. "Yet, qua method of causal identification and certification, the psychoanalytic method of investigation provides no [justificatory] basis for effecting such a selection" (Grünbaum, 1984, p. 210). In the context of dream theory, Glymour (1983) likewise objects to the baselessness of the selection bias by saying: "by Freud's method [of free association] every dream could be made out to be an expression of a wish just as every dream could, with almost equal ease, be made an expression of disgust or regret or fear or . . ." (1983, p. 66). To this Edelson says, at complete cross purposes with Glymour and me: "What Grünbaum suggests is certainly not true—that the psychoanalyst has no prior criteria for selecting among associations" (p. 134).

But my objection was *not* that analysts have no criteria of selection; it was that the ones they *do* have are causally question-begging! I had leveled this charge of *petitio principii* after making the following point: When therapeutic failure discredited the repression etiology that Freud had inferred from earlier therapeutic gain *via the use of free association*, this method was robbed of its claim to being a means of causal certification. To this, Edelson replies by begging the question in yet another way: "What appears to me to be presupposed instead by the method of free association (in the sense that laws of physics are presupposed in the use of a microscope or telescope), as far as

Freud was concerned, is that mental processes are purposive" (pp. 134-135). The comparison with physics is not viable, I contend, because there is *independent evidence* for the optical laws presupposed in claiming that the images produced by microscopes and telescopes respectively betoken small and remote objects as the *causes* of these images. Yet there is no corresponding independent evidence that a sexual conflict was the pathogen of hysteria, for example. *On the contrary*, as Freud's 1896 paper on its etiology makes clear, precisely that etiologic claim is purportedly validated on the strength of the associative emergence of sexual childhood memories.

Finally, I turn to Edelson's attempt to harness Glymour's account of the Rat-Man case to his own cause. Here he complains that my methodological reproach of epistemic adulteration of clinical data "ignores Glymour's basis for regarding as reasonable the selection of the analysand's reports of certain conscious thoughts and feelings as nontheoretical facts, since these do not require knowledge of psychoanalytic hypotheses to obtain or evaluate as true or false" (p. 149). On the contrary, I have *affirmed* rather than denied that, at least *prima facie*, the analyst is entitled to accept as "nontheoretical" data the patient's responses to such questions as, "What are you thinking about now? What comes to mind?" (1984, p. 29). What I do claim is that this data base is *far too narrow* to carry out Edelson's program of cogent testing in single-subject research on analytic patients.

In the absence of those *other* data that are now highly suspect, how does Edelson expect to test the hypotheses he tentatively refers to as "Major Theoretical Ideas in Psychoanalysis" (pp. 78-83)? It would be foolhardy to declare it *impossible* that some future psychoanalytic researchers might come up with as yet unimagined clinical research designs capable of cogently testing Freud's major clinical hypotheses. As I noted in chapter 4, I am no more inclined to put a cap on the ingenuity of *intra*clinical investigators than on that of extraclinical ones. But as I have been at pains to argue, Edelson has not supplied good grounds for expecting the development envisioned by him.

In conclusion, let me say specifically under what sorts of conditions I would be prepared to acknowledge that cogent testability within the psychoanalytic situation is feasible. Perrez

(1979) gives an explicit statement of the array of hypotheses invoked by Freud in the single case history of the Wolf-Man. I would change my view on intraclinical testability if, for example, someone were to envision cogent research designs within the treatment setting, capable of testing even a fraction of this elaborate set of hypotheses. Until and unless such research plans are worked out, I shall deplore the insistence of analysts, including Edelson and Wallerstein (1988, p. 27), on shackling themselves with the do-or-die demand that their clinical arena *must* carry the probative burdens of their enterprise, over and above the heuristic ones. As Edelson put it: "Psychoanalysis must be prepared to argue that adherence to the canons of eliminative inductivism is to varying degrees possible in single subject research" (p. 59). Alas, there is much reason to expect that most analysts will continue to saddle themselves with the hamstringing legacy bequeathed by Freud in 1933, when he declared: "In analysis, however, we have to do without the assistance afforded to [other] research by experiment" (p. 174).

In Edelson's more recent book (1988), he devotes chapters 12 and 14 to giving his most recent systematic assessment of my views. As emerges from my qualifications above, quite limited though they are, he somewhat overstates my skepticism when he speaks of my "conclusion that any reliance by psychoanalysis on data obtained from the psychoanalytic situation to support its causal inferences according to . . . [the] canons [of eliminative inductivism] is by the very nature of things doomed to failure and that psychoanalysis must turn instead entirely to epidemiologic and experimental research for such support" (p. 275). Yet, besides saying "of course, I would have no problem agreeing with Grünbaum that epidemiologic and experimental studies should be attempted" (p. 275), he writes:

> There can be little question about the cogency of Grünbaum's detailed demonstrations that psychoanalysts have argued fallaciously when they have concluded that data obtained in the psychoanalytic situation provide scientific support for inferences that a particular causal event (whether situational or intrapersonal) has occurred and furthermore (assuming one is willing to grant that this event has occurred) that it bears a causal relation—is causally relevant—to the clinical phenomenon of interest [1988, p. 274].

This much prompts Edelson to conclude (p. 276):

> In short, I am not inclined to quarrel with Grünbaum's diagnosis,
> whatever quibble we may have over details, but I am prepared
> to question his remedy. I have made my own proposal for dealing
> with the problems he has so compellingly identified (Edelson,
> 1984, especially pp. 157-160).

Yet he concedes the reasonableness of my residual reservations
(p. 276):

> Grünbaum has every right (and perhaps from his point of view
> every reason) to remain skeptical that such a program can or will
> be carried out and that taking such a direction will ever remedy
> the defects in the foundation of psychoanalysis he has identified.
> Here, of course, only time will tell.

With a view to a hopeful beginning he urges his psychoanalytic colleagues to adopt a minimal set of eight standards to be
met by clinical case studies that he itemized in the conclusion
of his preceding chapter 11. Yet he issues the important *caveat*
(p. 277, n. 7) that "while conformity to these eight canons is
a minimal requirement for testing empirical generalizations,
conformity to them will not suffice in attempts to establish the
scientific credibility of complex theoretical causal explanations."

Edelson's summary of his appraisal of my views is generous
even by the standards of our personal friendship (1988, p.
313):

> My own view of Grünbaum's critique is that, because of the ex-
> plicitness and utter lucidity of his argument, and the thorough
> scholarship with which he has documented his depiction of psy-
> choanalysis, the critique can function as a powerful stimulus to
> hard thinking about the issues he has raised. I do not know for
> what more one could ask from a philosopher of science [footnote
> omitted].

In this vein, he concludes his chapter 14 in a section "Responses
to Grünbaum's Critique," which includes poignant rebuttals to
ill-conceived objections to my views from some segments of the
psychoanalytic community.

7

PSYCHOANALYSIS AND THEISM

INTRODUCTION

The topic of "Psychoanalysis and Theism" suggests two distinct questions. First, what is the import, if any, of psychoanalytic theory for the truth or falsity of theism? And furthermore, what was the attitude of Freud, the man, toward belief in God? It must be borne in mind that *psychological* explanations of any sort as to why people believe in God are subject to an important *caveat*. Even if they are true, such explanations are not entitled to beg the following *different* question: Is religious belief *justified* by pertinent evidence or argument, whatever its motivational inspiration? Freud's usage, as well as stylistic reasons of my own, prompt me to use the terms "religion" and "theism" more or less interchangeably, although in other contexts the notion of religion is, of course, more inclusive.

Freud declared himself to be an atheist. But I submit that when he offered his psychological account of religious allegiances, he did *not* succumb to the temptation of arguing for atheism by begging the question. He understood all too well that a purely psychological explanation—however unflattering—of why people embrace Judaism, Christianity, or Islam does not itself suffice to discredit theism. Therefore, I claim, he did *not* fall prey to the well-known genetic fallacy, which is often called "the reductionism of nothing but." As he himself pointed out, those who commit this error overlook that the validity or invalidity of a doctrine as well as its truth or falsity

257

are still left open by the psychological causes of its espousal. Thus, in a section on "The Philosophical Interest of Psychoanalysis," Freud wrote:

> . . . psycho-analysis can indicate the subjective and individual motives behind philosophical theories which have ostensibly sprung from impartial logical work. . . . It is not the business of psychoanalysis [itself], however, to undertake . . . criticism [of these theories] . . . for . . . the fact that [the acceptance of] a theory is psychologically determined does not in the least invalidate its scientific truth [1913d, p. 179].

Like Nietzsche before him, Freud had become an atheist in his student days.[1] Then, in 1901, at the age of 45, he offered his first published psychiatric diagnosis of religion as an obsessional neurosis. He did so in order to illustrate his psychological account of superstition (1901, pp. 258-259). As for the credibility of theism, he had reached a dismal verdict: "it is precisely the elements . . . which have the task of solving the riddles of the universe and of reconciling us to the sufferings of life—it is precisely those elements that are the least well authenticated of any" (1927b, p. 27). But note how careful he was to stress the logical priority of his atheism *vis-à-vis* his psychology of theism:

> Nothing that I have said here against the truth-value of religions needed the support of psycho-analysis; it had been said by others long before analysis came into existence. If the application of the psycho-analytic method makes it possible to find a new argument against the truths of religion, *tant pis* [so much the worse] for religion; but defenders of religion will by the same right make use of psycho-analysis in order to give full value to the affective significance of religious doctrines [1927b, p. 37].

In the same vein, he declared: "All I have done—and this is the only thing that is new in my exposition—is to add some psychological foundation to the [evidential] criticisms of my great predecessors" (1927b, p. 35).

---

[1]As a young student in Vienna, Freud took a course on the existence of God from Franz Brentano. For details, see W. J. McGrath (1986).

Apparently, Freud will be walking a tightrope. As we saw, he was very much aware that it is one thing to provide a *psychogenesis* of religious belief, and quite another to appraise that belief epistemologically, with a view to estimating its truth value. Yet, as he just told us, he also claimed that, after all, the *psychogenesis* of theism can have a *supplementary* philosophical bearing on the question of the truth or falsity of religion. And he sees his own contribution to the debate as being one of elucidating precisely that supplementary import. Hence, if we are to examine the philosophical case that Freud tries to make for atheism, we must first consider the evidential merit of the explanatory psychological hypotheses on which his psychogenetic portrait of religion relies.

My first task will be to develop the purely psychological content of Freud's theory of religion, but with a view to passing an epistemological judgment on its major psychological assumptions. These pivotal hypotheses are of three main sorts. Yet, only *two* of these sorts are *psychoanalytic* in the technical sense. Thus, only two-thirds of Freud's psychology of religion depends on the epistemic fortunes of his psychoanalytic enterprise. Later, I shall endeavor to articulate *and* appraise his sophisticated effort to harness his psychogenetic account of theism in the service of his irreligious philosophical agenda.

FREUD'S PSYCHOGENESIS OF RELIGION

A short book entitled *The Future of an Illusion* (1927b) is one of Freud's several major writings on religion. Just what claims did he make about belief in God by characterizing it as an "illusion"? As he tells us, "we call a belief an illusion when a wish-fulfilment is a prominent factor in its motivation, and in doing so we disregard its relation to reality, just as the illusion itself sets no store by verification" (p. 31). Thus, this sense of the term "illusion" is both psychogenetic and epistemological. It requires that the wish-fulfilling character of the belief content be an important motivating factor in its acceptance, whereas the availability of supporting evidence played no such psychogenetic role. In brief, Freud calls a belief an illusion, just when it is inspired by wishes *rather than* by awareness of some evidential warrant for it. Hence, as he uses the label, it is psychologically descriptive but epistemologically derogatory.

Yet clearly, it is then still an empirical question of actual fact whether any given illusion, thus defined, is true or false. Someone's wish-inspired belief to have bought a winning ticket to the Pennsylvania lottery may well be pathetically ill-founded, but just may turn out to be true after all. Christopher Columbus's conviction that he had discovered a new, shorter sea route to the orient was at once wish-inspired and false. In the vast majority of cases, middle-class girls who have believed that a prince charming will come and marry them were concocting mere fantasies. Yet, in a few instances, this hope was not dashed. Hence Freud points out (pp. 30-31) that an illusion is not necessarily false. Nor is a false belief necessarily illusory. For example, the belief that the earth is flat may be induced mainly by inadequate observations, rather than by wishes. To qualify as an illusion, even a false belief needs to have been prompted mainly by a wish, rather than by known evidence.

There is an important subclass of false illusions whose generating wishes are complex enough to include unconscious desires. For example, according to Freud's theory of paranoia, the false notions of persecution entertained by a paranoiac are held to be inspired by repressed homosexual wishes, and by the operation of two unconscious defense mechanisms. Freud uses the term "delusion" to refer to such psychogenetically complex false illusions (1927b, pp. 31, 81; 1911, pp. 59-65; 1915a; 1922). Thus, he also speaks of delusions of jealousy, delusions of grandeur, and the delusions associated with heterosexual erotomania (Laplanche and Pontalis, 1973, p. 296). In brief, every delusion is a false illusion, generated by requisitely complex wishes. Thus, a false illusion can fail to qualify as a delusion, if the desires that inspire it lack the stated psychogenetic complexity. But how do both illusions and delusions matter in Freud's philosophy of religion? They do, because the nub of his own philosophical argument for atheism will turn out to be the attempt to demonstrate the following: The theistic religions are delusions, rather than just illusions; in fact, they are mass delusions in important parts of the world.

It is to be borne in mind that these two technical notions differ importantly from the senses of "illusion" and "delusion" encountered in the *Psychiatric Dictionary* published by the Oxford University Press in 1981 (pp. 307-308). By contrast to Freud's wish-laden notion of "illusion," the Oxford *Psychiatric Dictionary* uses the same term to denote a false sense perception produced by a real external stimulus, as in the case of some mirages. Thus, when a straight pencil or glass tube is partially immersed in water, we have the so-called visual illusion that the submerged portion has bent and forms an angle with its free upper part, though it is actually still straight. In virtue of thus being induced by a real stimulus, an illusion in Oxford parlance differs from a *hallucinatory* sensation, which has no source in the subject's environment, but is produced endogenously.

Evidently, the Oxford sense of "illusion" requires that the perceptually induced belief be false, whereas Freud's wish-laden notion does not insist on a generic attribution of falsity. And instead of requiring a particular external physical object to be the eliciting cause, his concept calls for a psychological state. Later, when we address Freud's philosophical aim, we shall see just how the definition of "delusion" in the Oxford *Psychiatric Dictionary* (p. 157) seriously diverges from his, no less than its notion of illusion does. In Oxford parlance, it is a matter of definition that there cannot be any mass delusions, but only idiosyncratic ones.

By saying that Freud's psychogenetic portrait of theism depicts it as a collection of "illusions," we have so far merely scratched its surface. That portrayal has at least two other major features.

1. The relevant illusions pertain to the fulfillment of those time-honored and widely shared human yearnings that the theologian Paul Tillich dubbed "ultimate concerns." Thus, in this context, Freud's accent was not on illusions—however strong—that are entertained only temporarily, or by only a relatively small number of people, let alone on more or less idiosyncratic ones. A purely wish-inspired belief that your favorite team will win the Super Bowl does qualify as an illusion in the Freudian sense. But this illusion is both demographically and temporally parochial. By contrast, his theory of religion

claims importance for evidentially ill-founded beliefs that envision actual "fulfilments of the oldest, strongest and most urgent wishes of mankind" (1927b, p. 30). As he tells us, these beliefs, though still widespread today, were already held by "our wretched, ignorant, and downtrodden ancestors" (p. 33). These forbears, we know, did not have the joys of American football. Therefore, we can refer to the sort of illusion already entertained by our ignorant, primitive ancestors as "archaic," if not as venerable.

2. A further, even more important psychological earmark of theism, in Freud's view, is that this doctrine is engendered by the cooperation or synergism of three significantly different sorts of powerful, relentless wishes. And for each of this trio of wishes, he offers a distinct scenario that specifies their content and mode of operation. Hence let us consider the relevant triad of hypotheses in turn.

As he points out (p. 33), the first set of these psychogenetic assumptions features wish motives that are largely conscious or "*manifest*," instead of being the repressed wishes postulated by psychoanalytic theory. Accordingly, this component of Freud's triadic psychology of religion does not rely on any of his technical psychoanalytic teachings. But what are the relevant archaic conscious wishes? He explains eloquently:

> ... the terrifying impression of helplessness in childhood aroused the need for protection—for protection through love—which was provided by the father; and the recognition that this helplessness lasts throughout life made it necessary to cling to the existence of a father, but this time a more powerful one. Thus the benevolent rule of a divine Providence allays our fear of the dangers of life; the establishment of a moral world-order ensures the fulfilment of the demands of justice, which have so often remained unfulfilled in human civilization; and the prolongation of earthly existence in a future life provides the local and temporal framework in which these wish-fulfilments shall take place. Answers to the riddles that tempt the curiosity of man, such as how the universe began or what the relation is between body and mind, are developed in conformity with the underlying assumptions of this system [p. 30].

Understandably, therefore, the protector, creator, *and* lawgiver are all rolled into one. No wonder, says Freud (1933, pp.

163-164), that, in one and the same breath, Immanuel Kant coupled the starry heavens above, and the moral law within as both being awe-inspiring. After all, Freud asks rhetorically, "what have the heavenly bodies to do with the question of whether one human creature loves another or kills him?" And he answers: "The same father (or parental agency) which gave the child life and guarded him against its perils, taught him as well what he might do and what he must leave undone" (p. 164).

Therefore, Freud deems it to be quite natural that man is receptive to the psychological subordination inherent in compliance with authority, especially authority that is claimed to derive from God. In this vein, Freud would presumably say that the Roman Catholic clergy astutely potentiates the religious fealty of its faithful by requiring them to call its priests "Father," to refer to the Pope as "the Holy Father," and to the Church itself as "Holy Mother Church." Again, Freud might adduce that when parents are asked by their children to give a reason for their commands, many an exasperated, if not authoritarian, mother or father will answer with finality: "Because!" No wonder, then, that religious systems too can secure the acquiescence of their believers, if they teach that the will of God is mysterious or inscrutable, and that some of their tenets transcend human understanding. In sum, it is one of Freud's recurrent psychological contentions that theism *infantilizes* adults by reinforcing the childish residues in their minds (1927b, p. 49; 1930, p. 85).

But even the liberal Catholic theologian Hans Küng goes so far as to say: "All religions have in common the periodical *childlike* surrender to a Provider or providers who dispense earthly fortune as well as spiritual health" (1979, p. 120, my italics).[2]

The motivational account cited from Freud thus far is not predicated on psychoanalytic theory. Small wonder, therefore, that it was largely anticipated by earlier thinkers. At about age 18, Freud studied philosophy with Franz Brentano. Thereby he was exposed to the ideas of the early nineteenth-century German atheist-theologian Ludwig Feuerbach,[3] whose writings

---

[2]For a critique of Hans Küng's theological views, see Albert (1979).
[3]Reported in Stepansky (1986, pp. 231-232).

made a lasting impression on him. According to Feuerbach's psychological projection theory, it was man who created God in his own image, rather than conversely. Being dependent on external nature, and beset by the slings and arrows of outrageous fortune, man projects his cravings and fantasies outward onto the cosmos into a figment of his own imagination.

Feuerbach took it to be the task of his atheistic theology to *demystify* religious beliefs by showing in detail how God was an object "of the heart's necessity, not of the mind's freedom" (quoted in Stepansky, 1986, p. 223). Freud (1927b, pp. 35, 37) used psychoanalysis to yield a further demystification by specifying additional, repressed feelings of human dependency on a father figure that would enhance the substance and credibility of Feuerbach's psychological reconstruction of religious history.

Likewise strongly influenced by Feuerbach, Karl Marx wrote:

> Religion . . . is . . . the *protest* against real distress. Religion is the sigh of the oppressed creature, the heart of a heartless world, just as it is the spirit of an unspiritual situation. It is the *opium* of the people [Feuer, 1959, p. 523].

In Marx's time, opium was the most available painkiller and could be bought without any prescription. As he uses the name of this drug, its meaning is largely descriptive rather than pejorative. But Marx appreciated insufficiently that an impoverished nineteenth-century industrial proletariat and peasantry are not the only groups in society that crave supernatural consolation for the trials and tribulations of life. Freud took into account, much more than Marx did, that a good many of the rich and privileged in society also seek religious refuge from the blows of existence. At least to this extent, Freud was closer to Feuerbach's view than Marx was. Recently, Sidney Hook (1985) drew a germane comparison between Feuerbach and Marx, declaring Feuerbach to have been "more profound":

> . . . when Marx says, "Religion is the opium of the people," he is really echoing Feuerbach. In Feuerbach's day it wasn't a disgrace to take opium. It was a medicine, an anodyne. It was the only

thing people had to relieve their pain. Feuerbach was really implying that under any system there will be tragedy, heartache, failure, and frustration. Religion, for him (he regarded humanism and even atheism as a religion), serves that function [of relieving distress] in every society. Marx ridiculed this view because he was more optimistic than Feuerbach. He believed that science would solve not only the problem of economic scarcity but all human problems that arise from it. He ignored other human problems. Feuerbach seems to me to be more realistic about most human beings [p. 33].

Insofar as Freud's psychogenetic portrayal of religion depicts it as the product of *conscious* wishes, his account draws, I submit, not only on Feuerbach, but also on commonsense psychology. After all, at least *prima facie*, it is rather a commonplace that people seek to avoid anxiety, and that they therefore tend to welcome the replacement of threatening beliefs by reassuring ones. Hence, for brevity, we can refer to this component of Freud's triadic psychology of religion as "the commonsense hypothesis," which is not to say, however, that it is obviously true. Each of the other two components of his trinity is a set of *psychoanalytic* claims, asserting the operation of repressed motives. And yet they differ from each other, because one of them relies on Freud's theory of the psychosexual development of the human individual, while the other consists of *ethno*psychological and psychohistorical averrals pertaining to the evolution of our species as a whole. Accordingly, we shall label the psychoanalytic assumptions relating to the individual as "ontogenetic," but will refer to the ethnopsychological ones as "phylogenetic."

As previously emphasized, the legitimacy of any psychogenetic portrait of religious creeds depends on the *evidential merit* of the explanatory psychological hypotheses adduced by it. Even the commonsense component of Freud's triad is subject to this *caveat*. Invoking the criticisms of his great predecessors, he took it for granted that there is no cogency in any of the arguments for the existence of God offered by believers. But he coupled this philosophical judgment with the daring motivational claim that the faithful who nonetheless adduce such proofs had not, in fact, themselves been decisively moved by them, when giving assent to theism. Instead, he maintained, psychologically this assent is emotional or affective in origin:

> Where questions of religion are concerned, people are guilty of every possible sort of dishonesty and intellectual misdemeanour. Philosophers stretch the meaning of words until they retain scarcely anything of their original sense. They give the name of 'God' to some vague abstraction which they have created for themselves; having done so . . . they can even boast that they have recognized a higher, purer concept of God, notwithstanding that their God is now nothing more than an insubstantial shadow and no longer the mighty personality of religious doctrines [1927b, p. 32].

In brief, he is telling us that motivationally, the dialectical excogitations offered as existence proofs are *post hoc* rationalizations in which an elaborate intellectual façade takes the place of the deep-seated wishes that actually persuaded the theologians. Speaking epigrammatically in another context, Freud quotes Falstaff as saying that reasons are "as plenty as blackberries" (1914b, p. 24). Hence, Freud could not have disagreed more with Edward Gibbon, who reversed the order of motivational priority as follows, though perhaps only tongue-in-cheek:

> Our curiosity is naturally prompted to inquire by what means the Christian faith obtained so remarkable a victory over the established religions of the earth. To this inquiry an obvious but satisfactory answer may be returned; that it was owing to the convincing evidence of the doctrine itself, and to the ruling providence of its great Author. But as truth and reason seldom find so favourable a reception in the world, and as the wisdom of Providence frequently condescends to use the passions of the human heart, and the general circumstances of mankind, as instruments to execute its purpose, we may still be permitted, though with becoming submission, to ask, not indeed what were the first, but what were the secondary causes of the rapid growth of the Christian church? [1899, p. 523].

It would seem to be basically a matter of empirical psychological fact whether the commonsense constituent of Freud's psychogenetic portrait of religion is sound. Yet, it is not clear how to design a cogent test even of this hypothesis. For note that the required design needs to have two epistemic capabilities as follows: (1) It needs to yield evidence bearing on the validity of the functional explanation of religious belief as being anxiety-reducing; presumably this explanation postulates some kind of stabilizing psychic servomechanism that reacts homeostatically to psychological threat. Furthermore, (2) the required test needs to be at least able to rank-order the intensity of the wish to escape from anxiety, as compared to the motivational persuasiveness of the theological existence proofs. Perhaps oscillating anxieties of believers who went through cycles of doubt and belief have already gone some way toward meeting the first condition by Mill's method of concomitant variations. In any case, it would seem that an explicitly *fideist* belief in the existence of God—which avowedly is *not* based on any arguments—calls for *psychological* explanation in terms of wish motives! The second requirement, however, seems to be a tall order indeed, although it does not warrant putting a cap on the ingenuity of potential empirical investigators. It too must be met, because of Freud's bold claim that even the best of the arguments for the existence of God would not have convinced the great minds who advanced them, unless stronger tacit wishes had carried the day, or had prompted these intellects to prevaricate. But note that, so far, Freud's portrayal of the motives for religious belief has studiously refrained from claiming that this belief is false.

Hence whatever the empirical difficulties of validating his psychogenetic portrait, they are hardly tantamount to his commission of the hackneyed genetic fallacy, a mode of inference that he explicitly rejected by means of disclaimers and qualifications, as we saw. Yet this state of affairs is completely overlooked in Philip Rieff's very influential book (1959). There Rieff offers a combination of intellectual history, sociology of knowledge, and philosophy of culture. As he would have it, Freud's psychology of religion refurbishes the inveterate genetic fallacy (p. 292) "by which animus is sanctified as science," with the aid of some "scientistic name calling" (p. 268). Moreover, as indicated by the title of Rieff's book, he sees the entire monumental psychoanalytic corpus as a thinly veiled system of moralisms.

To be sure, as we shall see, Freud deemed religion an undesirably arrestive childish fixation. And avowedly, he did *advocate* (1927b, p. 48)—as an "experiment" worth making—that children be given an irreligious education. But he took pains to say at once: "Should the experiment prove unsatisfactory I am ready to give up the reform and to return to my earlier, purely descriptive judgement that man is a creature of weak intelligence who is ruled by his instinctual wishes" (pp. 48-49). How then does Rieff reason that, throughout his theoretical system, Freud "can always get from description to judgment in a single step" (p. 293) such that *all* of psychoanalytic theory is moralistic? Rieff explains, "because in his case histories Freud never *reported* the facts but *interpreted* them, what passes for description in the Freudian method is already judgment" (p. 293).

But when Freud spoke of possibly having to retract his plea for an atheistic education in favor of returning to his "earlier, purely descriptive judgement" of human nature, he was using the term "descriptive" in contrast to "normative" to characterize a claim as being devoid of *moral* advocacy. And he was fully alert to the truism that the psychoanalytic method generated theory-laden interpretations. Indeed, Freud had emphasized, in a Kantian vein, that even a purportedly observational description of phenomena is already theory-laden (1915b, p. 117). Yet when Rieff uses the term "judgment" to refer to an interpretation, he slides from the fact that the latter is theory-laden to its also necessarily being *value*-laden. Thus, he reckons speciously that all psychoanalytic interpretations are tantamount to moral judgments, simply because they are theory-laden.

Apparently, Freud's psychology of religion is exonerated from Rieff's reproach that it incurred the genetic fallacy and was part of a *globally* moralistic theoretical enterprise (pp. 257, 263, 265). Ironically, it is Rieff himself who begs the question in regard to the evidence against theism (p. 269). For example, he diagnoses the appeal of atheism during the Enlightenment as depending on religious illiteracy, such as unfamiliarity "with the lines of self-criticism laid down by the theologians themselves" (p. 272). Thus Rieff endeavors to garner support for religion by offering a psychological discreditation of atheism.

Yet the imperative to avoid the genetic fallacy cuts both ways. Just as the psychogenesis of religious belief cannot itself refute theism, so also the emotional gratifications it affords cannot support it *epistemically*. The dissident psychoanalysts Carl Jung and Alfred Adler appreciated this point, although they did claim *psychological* value or even emotional necessity for belief in God (Küng, pp. 62-63). Jung saw God as man's projection, manufactured from human emotions and from archetypes that he believed to have excavated psychoanalytically from an untamed collective unconscious. But, as a therapist, he thought that we court psychological disaster, if we do not give conscious expression to unconscious religious feelings. All the same, he stressed that the purportedly necessary psychological function of the idea of God has "nothing whatever to do with the question of God's existence" (quoted in Stepansky, 1986, p. 227).

Let us turn to the two psychoanalytic ingredients of Freud's triad, consisting of his ontogeny and phylogeny of theism. In their case, we must ask, I claim, even whether there is good evidence for the existence of the repressed wishes postulated by them. Insofar as even the very existence of these hidden desires is questionable, one remains less than convinced, when told that they contributed significantly to the initial genesis and later persistence of religious creeds.

It is a major tenet of Freudian theory that psychopathology is rooted in the psychic conflict created by unsuccessfully repressed desires. Guided by this model of mental disorder, his ontogeny and phylogeny diagnose religion as a mixture of syndromes, featuring oedipal, paranoid, and obsessional elements. Yet he explicitly allowed that there are several interesting differences between, say, the illusions of a paranoiac and religious beliefs. For example, the specifics of the former are idiosyncratic, while the latter are usually shared, sometimes even widely (1907, pp. 119-120; 1927b, p. 44). Let us now consider, in turn, some of the highlights of the ontogeny and the phylogeny.

In 1901, in his *Psychopathology of Everyday Life*, Freud traced superstitions to unconscious causes (pp. 258-260). The psychological mechanism operative here, we are told (1913c, p. 92), is that of transmuting feelings and impulses into external agencies by *projection* or displacement.

> . . . psycho-analysis can also say something new about the *quality* of the unconscious motives that find expression in superstition. It can be recognized most clearly in neurotics suffering from

obsessional thinking or obsessional states—people who are often
of high intelligence—that superstition derives from suppressed
hostile and cruel impulses. Superstition is in large part the expectation of trouble; and a person who has harboured frequent evil
wishes against others, but has been brought up to be good and
has therefore repressed such wishes into the unconscious, will
be especially ready to expect punishment for his unconscious
wickedness in the form of trouble threatening him from without
[1901, p. 260].

Obsessional neurosis features relentlessly intrusive, anxiety-
producing thoughts, rumination, doubt, and scruples as well as
repetitive impulses to perform such acts as ceremonials, counting, hand washing, checking, etc. One might include here perhaps the reported practice of a world-famous logician to cover
his handwritten address on envelopes with transparent nail pol-
ish as prophylaxis against moisture. The hypothesized causes
of a disorder X are said to be the "etiology" of X. Derivatively,
the term "etiology" is also used to refer to the pertinent causal
hypothesis, rather than to the presumed causes themselves.

In Freud's 1907 paper "Obsessive Actions and Religious Practices," he employed his etiology of obsessional neurosis to diagnose religious *rituals*, no less than obsessive-compulsive secular
acts. According to his etiologic hypothesis, these repetitive acts
result from the conflict between a repressed forbidden instinct
and the repressing forces of consciousness. *Qua* being a species
of obsessive-compulsive acts, the religious rites are seen etiologically as *exorcistic defenses* against evil wishes, and against the
disasters that such forbidden desires are feared to engender by
sheer magic. Precisely by fearing that *mere* desires or thoughts
can magically produce calamities, the obsessive's overvaluation
of the power of mental processes betrays the mind-set of sav-
ages, who believe in just such an omnipotence of thoughts (see
Freud's case history of the Rat-Man [1909b, pp. 229ff.; 1913c,
p. 86]). And by performing the supposedly protective rituals,
the obsessive wards off a crescendo of anxiety, the qualms of
conscience brought on by their neglect (1907, p. 119). Here
then, Freud's psychogenetic accent is on religious ceremonials
or sacramental *acts*, rather than on theoretical religious doctrine.

But what of the important differences between religious practices or doctrine, on the one hand, and obsessive-compulsive acts or thoughts, on the other? He addresses these differences head on, only to proceed to neutralize them diagnostically by psychoanalytic argument. Speaking of the "obvious" differences, he declares:

> . . . a few of them are so glaring that they make the comparison a sacrilege: the greater individual variability of [neurotic] ceremonial actions in contrast to the stereotyped character of rituals (prayer, turning to the East, etc.), their private nature as opposed to the public and communal character of religious observances, above all, however, the fact that, while the minutiae of religious ceremonial are full of significance and have a symbolic meaning, those of neurotics seem foolish and senseless. In this respect an obsessional neurosis presents a travesty, half comic and half tragic, of a private religion. But it is precisely this sharpest difference between neurotic and religious ceremonial which disappears when, with the help of the psycho-analytic technique of investigation, one penetrates to the true meaning of obsessive actions.
>   . . . Those who are familiar with the findings of psycho-analytic investigation into the psychoneuroses will not be surprised to learn that what is being represented in obsessive actions or in ceremonials is derived from the most intimate, and for the most part from the sexual, experiences of the patient [1907, pp. 119-120].

Diagnostically, therefore, Freud rejects the objection that he has ridden roughshod over the differences between neurosis and religion, when he "psychopathologized" religion. This charge was leveled in 1983 by the psychoanalyst E. R. Wallace. According to Wallace, Freud "overlooked an important distinction between symptom and ritual: the *ego-dystonic* nature of the former versus the *ego-syntonic* [nature] of the latter" (p. 277).[4] This means that, subjectively, the compulsive hand washer finds his repetitive need disagreeable, whereas the religious worshipper finds his observances congenial. It is less than clear, however, that—for example—Roman Catholics typically find it ego-syntonic, when they are asked to say so many "Hail Marys" or

---

[4]For his most recent account, see Wallace (1985).

Lord's Prayers for penance. To be sure, these repetitive acts may relieve the anxiety induced by the priest's admonition. But let us grant Wallace that all religious observances are ego-syntonic. Even then, according to standard psychoanalytic theory, which Wallace accepts (p. 276), the ego-syntonic character of feelings and behavior does not necessarily militate against their etiologic status as a neurotic manifestation: The so-called "character neuroses" are distinguished, within the theory, from the "symptom neuroses" by precisely the fact that the former are ego-syntonic, while the latter are not (Laplanche and Pontalis, 1973, pp. 67-68). Thus, having the narcissistic personality syndrome need not militate against the self-satisfaction of its exemplar, and the paranoiac afflicted by delusions of grandeur need not find them ego-dystonic.

Qua neurotic manifestations, Freud sees religious rituals as typically conducing to psychological intimidation, uniformity and dependence, if not to outright infantilization. Hans Küng, the liberal Roman Catholic theologian, is a vigorous champion of psychoanalysis as a scientific theory (pp. 93, 95, 98, and esp. 102-109). Yet, in this 1979 book, he claims, *contra* Freud, that "religious rites . . . foster man's individuation and self-discovery . . . and [can] . . . contribute to creativity" (p. 119). Freud himself does emphasize, however, that sharing in the glorified, enlarged obsessional neurosis of religion with other people can obviate an idiosyncratic one: "Devout believers are safeguarded in a high degree against the risk of certain neurotic illnesses; their acceptance of the universal neurosis spares them the task of constructing a personal one" (1927b, p. 44). This sort of trade-off is a theme that Freud strikes time and again, starting in 1907 and ending with his *Moses and Monotheism*, which appeared in 1939, the year of his death (see 1907; 1910, pp. 123, 146; 1921, p. 142; 1930, pp. 84-85, 144; 1939, pp. 72-80).

It would seem that within the ranks of religious psychoanalysts, Wallace's critique of Freud's psychopathology of religion has failed to carry conviction. A notable case in point is the Roman Catholic Jesuit priest William Meissner, who is a practicing psychoanalyst and professor of psychiatry at Harvard. In his 1984 book, he paints a sobering psychological picture of religion. True, Meissner tells us that religious experience can occur at different levels of development, and can include at its apex, "mature, integrated, and adaptive levels of psychic functioning." And, if so, then "Freud was able to envision only a segment of the broader developmental spectrum" (p. 14). But, unlike Wallace, Meissner does make a major concession as follows: "the psychology of religious experience . . . overlaps, and to a significant degree is intertwined with mental processes that, from a clinical perspective, can be described as pathological" (pp. 9-10). Referring to one of Freud's famous case histories, Meissner says: "the Wolf Man's obsessive religiosity was a vehicle for his instinctual pathology" (p. 60). Indeed, Meissner's verdict is rather dismal:

> A caricature of [ideal] religion, which Freud himself employed as an analogy to obsessional states, is not infrequently found among religious people in whom blind adherence to ritual and scrupulous conscientiousness, as well as conscience, dominate religious life. In fact, we can safely say that the great mass of believers lend credence to Freud's formulations.
> More mature and integrated forms of religious experience are modestly distributed among the people of God. Those who reach the highest level of religious experience and achieve the maximum expression of religious ideals are very rare indeed. . . . Unfortunately, to study the religious experience of those more advanced and saintly souls who have gained a high level of religious maturity, we must rely on the secondhand historical accounts that leave many questions unanswered and unapproachable. . . . the theologian directs his attention to a more or less idealized, rarely attained level of religious maturity [p. 15].

Freud's psychopathological ontogeny of theism is not confined to obsessional neurosis. He thought that the Oedipus "complex constitutes the nucleus of all neuroses" (1913c, pp. 157, 129). Thus, we learn, the pathogens of obsessional neurosis are interwoven with those of the Oedipus complex. In its so-called "complete" form of ambivalence toward *each* parent, that complex is produced by the conflict between affectionate sexual feelings, on the one hand, and hostile aggressive feelings of rivalry, on the other, which are entertained toward both parents in the psyche of all children between the ages of 3 and 6 (Laplanche and Pontalis, 1973, pp. 282-286). The special focus of these affects is the powerful, protective, and yet threatening father, who has replaced the mother in her initial role of providing food and protection (1927b, p. 24). Being too disturbing to be entertained consciously, these emotions are repressed (Fenichel, 1945, pp. 91-98). It may be asked at once how the oedipal conflict can be deemed pathogenically relevant, if *all* people experience it in childhood, while only *some* become strikingly neurotic. The Freudian answer is that people do differ in regard to their success in *resolving* the infantile Oedipus complex (1925b, pp. 55-56). But some ambivalence toward the father figure lingers on into adulthood.

Hence the cosmic projection and exaltation of this authority figure as a Deity in publicly approved fashion has an enormous appeal. As Freud (1927b) puts it: "It is an enormous relief to the individual psyche if the conflicts of its childhood arising from the father-complex—conflicts which it has never wholly overcome—are removed from it and brought to a solution which is universally accepted" (p. 30). By the same token, a true child-father relationship is achieved, once polytheism yields to monotheism after man "creates for himself the gods whom he dreads, whom he seeks to propitiate, and whom he nevertheless entrusts with his own protection" (p. 24).

Indeed, the psychoanalytically fathomed, unconscious wishes of the adult's residual Oedipus complex are held to combine *synergistically* with the urgent desire for relief from the *conscious* fears of enduring vulnerability, fears which are lifelong intensifications of the child's dread of helplessness (1927b, pp. 23-24). The product is the belief in an omnipotent God, who is thought to love any of us, even if no one else does.

Apparently, the apotheosis of the father does fit Judaism, Christianity, and Islam. But Freud seems to have neglected Hinduism, Buddhism, and Taoism. And at least one writer (Erdelyi, 1985, p. 207) has claimed that as between the two parents, the mother seems to be the more important figure in these religions. Yet Freud did say: "the creator is usually a man, though there is far from being a lack of female deities; and some mythologies actually make the creation begin with a male God getting rid of a female deity, who is degraded into being a monster" (1933, p. 162).

It is a measure of the current influence of psychoanalytic oedipal theory that Hans Küng peremptorily takes this hypothesis to be an empirically well-established body of knowledge. Nay, he vigorously champions it in the face of criticisms (pp. 93, 98, and esp. 102-109). Indeed, Küng (p. 95), no less than Meissner (pp. 213, 216), explicitly endorses the method of psychoanalytic investigation as a *natural science* mode of inquiry. True, both of these two Roman Catholic writers repeatedly contend that the *full dimensions* of religious experience elude capture by Freud's theory of psychopathology. Yet, despite their denial of such complete explanatory subsumption, they regard psychoanalytic *ontogeny* as a viable and illuminating part of the psychology of religious belief. More generally, the Protestant theologian Paul Tillich opted for the use of psychoanalysis, along with Marxism, to offer unflattering motivational explanations of what he regarded as much false consciousness in Western society (see Shinn, 1986).

But what are the actual empirical credentials of Freud's sexual etiology of obsessional neurosis, and of his oedipal *ontogeny* of theism? In the context of the conjugal family, this oedipal plot calls for not only an erotic love-hate triangle prior to the age of 6, but also a redemptive denouement of the guilt-laden parricidal wish by projective exaltation of the father into God. It is a clear moral of my recent book (1984) that, far from having good empirical support, at best these obsessional and oedipal hypotheses have yet to be adequately tested, even prior to their use in a psychology of religion. *A fortiori*, the psychoanalytic ontogeny of theism still lacks evidential warrant, with the possible exception of the psychogenesis of the doctrine of the Virgin Birth of Jesus, as we shall see below. Until and unless there is more warrant for the ontogeny, it is surely at least the better part of wisdom to place little explanatory reliance on it, brilliantly suggestive though it may be.

But Freud was not content to confine himself to explanatory reliance on the conscious quest for anxiety reduction, and on his ontogeny of theism. Rather, he went on to develop a psychoanalytic *phylogeny* of theism (1913e, essay IV). In his view, this historical ethnopsychology is a valid extension of psychoanalysis. He reasoned as follows:

> The obscure sense of guilt to which mankind has been subject since prehistoric times, and which in some religions has been condensed into the doctrine of primal guilt, or original sin, is probably the outcome of a blood-guilt incurred by prehistoric man. In my book *Totem and Taboo* (1912-13) I have, following clues given by Robertson Smith, Atkinson and Charles Darwin, tried to guess the nature of this primal guilt, and I believe, too, that the Christian doctrine of to-day enables us to deduce it. If the Son of God was obliged to sacrifice his life to redeem mankind from original sin, then by the [Mosaic] law of talion, the requital of like by like, that sin must have been a killing, a murder. Nothing else could call for the sacrifice of a life for its expiation. And if the original sin was an offence against God the Father, the primal crime of mankind must have been a parricide, the killing of the primal father of the primitive human horde, whose mnemic image was later transfigured into a deity [1915d, pp. 292-293; see also 1939, pp. 130-131].

Yet there is still the question of how Freud conjectured the *motive* for the inferred parricide. As he tells us: "Darwin deduced from the habits of the higher apes that men, too, originally lived in comparatively small groups or hordes within which the jealousy of the oldest and strongest male prevented sexual promiscuity" (1913e, p. 125). In each of these hordes or families, the dominant male imposed such erotic restraint on his younger and subordinate male rivals by controlling their sexual access to the women of the clan. But this prohibition did not sit well with these rivals. Freud speculates that, driven by their ensuing hostility, and being cannibals, they banded together into a brother clan to *kill and eat* their own father (1913e, pp. 141-142). Yet they soon began to quarrel over the sexual spoils of his harem. Thus, they became highly ambivalent about their parricidal achievement. The memory of the homicide itself was repressed, and thereby generated guilt.

The resulting filial remorse, in turn, issued in two major developments: (1) The delayed enforcement of the father's original edict against incestuous sex within the clan made exogamy mandatory, thereby generating the incest taboo (1913e, pp. 5-6); and (2) the prohibition of parricide turned into the expiatory *deification* of the slain parent. As Freud put it: "the primal father, at once feared and hated, revered and envied, became the prototype of God himself" (1925b, p. 68).

Freud assumed that over the millennia, our primitive ancestors reenacted the parricidal scenario countless times (1939, p. 81). And, as a convinced Lamarckian, he believed that racial memories of it, cumulatively registered by our primitive ancestors—but subsequently repressed by them—were transmitted to us by the inheritance of acquired characteristics (Sulloway, 1977, pp. 274-275, 439-442). Thus, at least each male has supposedly stored this phylogenetic legacy in his unconscious, including the resulting sense of collective guilt over the primal crime (1939, p. 132). Hence, shortly before Freud's death, he confidently announced that "men have always known (in this special [Lamarckian] way) that they once possessed a primal father and killed him" (1939, p. 101). He explicitly credits the Scottish biblical scholar Robertson Smith and the anthropologist J. G. Frazer with the recognition that Christian Communion is a residue of the eating of the sacred totem animal, which in turn appeared to Freud to hark back to the eating of the slain primal father (1925b, p. 68).

As he sees it, by combining ethnography with psychoanalysis, he has discerned a third set of strong wishes that unite synergistically with the other two classes of his triad, and make the psychogenesis of belief in God the Father the more imperative. Therefore he proclaimed: "We now observe that the store of religious ideas includes not only wish-fulfilments but important historical recollections. This concurrent influence of past and present must give religion a truly incomparable wealth of power" (1927b, p. 42).

Moreover, the *ontogeny* of the Oedipus complex is, at least in its earlier stages, developmentally similar to its conjectured *phylogeny*. And this psychogenetic parallelism seemed all the more credible to Freud because he saw it as the psychological counterpart of Ernst Haeckel's biogenetic law. According to Haeckel, the embryonic ontogeny of each animal, including man, *recapitulates* the morphological changes undergone by the successive ancestors of the species during its phylogeny. No wonder that Freud felt entitled to regard the early *ontogenetic* development of moral dispositions like remorse and guilt in each of us as both a replica and a phylogenetic residue of the primal father complex of early man (1923a, p. 37).

At this point, standing at the portal of death in 1939, Freud is ready to deploy his repression etiology of neurosis, together with his ethnopsychological retrodictions. And he joins them to explain the characteristic irrationality of traditional theism as follows:

> A tradition that was based only on communication could not lead to the compulsive character that attaches to religious phenomena. It would be listened to, judged, and perhaps dismissed, like any other piece of information from outside; it would never attain the privilege of being liberated from the constraint of logical thought. It must have undergone the fate of being repressed, the condition of lingering in the unconscious, before it is able to display such powerful effects on its return, to bring the masses under its spell, as we have seen with astonishment and hitherto without comprehension in the case of religious tradition [1939, p. 101].

As we learn on the same page, the "return" of the religious tradition refers to the *reawakening* of the repressed memory of ancestral totemistic parricide. And this reanimation was supposedly effected by two epoch-making episodes, each of which Freud claimed to be historically authentic: First, the murder of Moses by the ancient Hebrews, who rebelled against his tyrannical imposition of the intolerable prescriptions of monotheism; thereafter, "the supposed judicial murder of Christ."

Daring and ingenious though it is, Freud's psychoanalytic phylogeny of theism is dubious, if only because it assumes a Lamarckian inheritance of repressed racial memories. Furthermore, contrary to the uniform evolution of religions required by his account, more recent historical scholarship seems to call for developmental pluriformity (Küng, p. 67). And if there are such differences of religious history, it becomes more difficult to sustain the historical authenticity of the common parricidal scenario postulated by Freud's phylogeny. Overall, Küng (1979, pp. 70-71) emphasizes that hitherto no primordial religion has been found. Indeed, "the sources necessary for a historical explanation of the origin of religion are simply not available." Meissner devotes chapter 5 to the scrutiny of Freud's psychoanalytic phylogeny of Mosaic monotheism. Writing from the standpoint of biblical archeology, exegesis, and anthropology, Meissner reaches the following verdict: "Subsequent years have subjected the whole area of biblical studies and criticism to a radical revision that makes it clear that the fundamental points of view on which Freud based his synthetic reconstruction were themselves faulty and misleading" (p. ix).

FREUD'S ARGUMENT FOR ATHEISM

Having maintained that, psychogenetically, theistic beliefs are illusions, Freud deploys the following dialectical strategy on behalf of atheism: He aims to show that religious illusions, in particular, are very probably *false*. For that purpose, he deems it relevant—rather than *ad hominem*—to point out that religious illusions, though still widespread, were already commonly held by our ignorant, primitive ancestors. We shall designate *any* beliefs of such primitive vintage as "archaic," for brevity.

Freud makes only very cursory mention of the dread of the "evil eye" (1919, p. 240). But this belief is presumably archaic and still rampant. According to its adherents, the covetous glances of some persons have the malignant power to injure or kill people and animals, even involuntarily. Among the Greeks and Romans, as well as in the musical *Fiddler on the Roof*, spitting was used as a supposed antidote to the poison of the evil eye. Other gestures too—often intentionally obscene ones—were regarded as prophylactics on meeting the dreaded poisonous individual. By extension, praise for one's possessions or good fortune was thought to be an omen of bad luck. Thus, when I was a boy in Germany, even educated people who reported being in good health would *protectively* hasten to add the German word "unberufen," which literally means "uncalled for" or "unauthorized." Not to be outdone by Germans, Americans say "knock wood" with equal prophylactic efficacy. Presumably, no one has ever run a controlled study to determine whether envious glances have the pernicious effects envisaged in the evil eye doctrine. But it is safe to say that if there were any such dire effects, the wealthy and successful of this world, who have been known to dread evil eyes, would not fare nearly as well as they actually do. Hence we may conclude that the archaic belief in the evil eye doctrine is false.

How then does Freud invoke the *archaic* character of theism as a means of discrediting religious belief? He puts it as follows:

> To assess the truth-value of religious doctrines does not lie within the scope of the present enquiry. It is enough for us that we have recognized them as being, in their psychological nature, illusions. But we do not have to conceal the fact that this discovery also strongly influences our attitude to the question [of truth-value] which must appear to many to be the most important of all. We know approximately at what periods and by what kind of men religious doctrines were created. If in addition we discover the motives which led to this, our attitude to the problem of [the truth of] religion will undergo a marked displacement. We shall tell ourselves that it would be very nice if there were a God who created the world and was a benevolent Providence, and if there were a moral order in the universe and an after-life; but it is a very striking fact that all this is exactly as we are bound to wish it to be. And it would be more remarkable still if our wretched, ignorant and downtrodden ancestors had succeeded in solving all these difficult riddles of the universe [1927b, p. 33].

In context, the opening disclaimer in this statement as to the scope of his inquiry is an ellipsis for his aforecited tribute to his atheistic predecessors. Presumably, by "religious doctrines," Freud means here beliefs, including totemism and polytheism, that *eventuated* in theism. And, in view of the phylogenetic history he postulated for theism, that religious belief qualifies as "archaic." Though the *word* "theism" was apparently coined in a book by Cudworth as recently as 1678, the belief itself antedates the birth of Christ by nearly a millenium, at least among the Jews. In its traditional form, it asserts the existence of an omnipotent, omniscient, and omnibenevolent paternal creator—at once immanent and transcendent—who is accessible to personal communion with us. This divine being is to be respected, loved, and feared. In fact, normally, compliance with His ethical demands holds out the promise of heaven, though there have been theists who disbelieved in personal immortality. On this construal, at least some forms of Buddhism and Taoism do not teach belief in the existence of God, as was noted by

Supreme Court Justice Hugo L. Black in a decision he wrote in 1961 (see Safire, 1986).

To reconstruct the logical framework of Freud's own case for atheism, we can encapsulate his argument in the following syllogism (1933, p. 168; 1927b, p. 33):

> Premise 1:   All archaic, evidentially ill-supported illusions are very probably false.
>
> Premise 2:   Anyone's belief in theism is an archaic, evidentially ill-supported illusion.
>
> ---
>
> Conclusion: Anyone's belief in theism is very probably false.

Note that since Freudian illusions are, by definition, evidentially unwarranted, the modifying adjective "evidentially ill-supported" in the two premises is redundant. But it is there for the sake of emphasis. Furthermore, observe that by talking about the belief states of all theists, both the second premise and the conclusion are, in effect, making claims about *all known versions* of theism, except those that no one ever took seriously enough to believe them. Formally speaking, this syllogism is deductively valid, if we can regard probable falsity as a property of some beliefs. Hence the warrant for presuming its conclusion to be true depends, of course, on the epistemic merits of the two premises. In effect, the first premise says that the world being what it is, archaic illusions are, so to speak, too good to be true. The second premise, however, is a terse assertion of Freud's psychogenetic and epistemological thesis that religious beliefs are indeed archaic illusions; it states that these creeds were prompted not by cogent evidence, but by the need to fulfill a trio of "the oldest, strongest, and most urgent wishes of mankind" (1927b, p. 30). Freud is making use of the fact that a belief state can be characterized motivationally, while its content can be appraised as to the evidence for it, if any, and also as to its truth value.

Consider the first premise. It would seem that he took it to be a legitimate induction from the discreditation of various archaic illusions by scientific advances. But *prima facie*, one might think that an example of his own from the history of alchemy furnishes evidence against the universal claim of Premise 1, which is that all archaic illusions are probably false. As he points out: "Examples of illusions which have proved true are not easy to find, but the illusion of the alchemists that all metals can be turned into gold might be one of them" (1927b, p. 31). When Freud allowed that the wish-inspired guess of the alchemists might perhaps be redeemed after all, he was presumably referring to the transmutation of elements known from the radioactive decay of metals of high atomic weight, such as uranium and thorium. Though relevant, let us ignore questions of practical and economic feasibility, and suppose that all base metals can be turned into noble ones, as desired by the alchemists. Then this state of affairs would not refute Freud's first premise, which claims only that any archaic illusion is very likely to be false, rather than that it *is* categorically false. Besides, even the Greek and Egyptian alchemists of old probably towered in intellectual sophistication over the members of Darwin's primal hordes. Hence even these early alchemists presumably do not qualify as primitive and wretched ancestors by Freud's standards. And if not, then the belief in alchemy—though psychogenetically and evidentially an "illusion" for centuries—does not count as an "archaic" illusion.

Anyone who is still inclined to quarrel with Premise 1 will find it sobering to bear in mind how very difficult even science finds it to come up with true theories. Indeed, the history of science—both ancient and modern—is largely the history of discarded theories. Hence even for scientific theories that are now well-supported by evidence, it is a reasonable induction from the past that they, too, will be found wanting in due course. Moreover, success has eluded Karl Popper and others who have tried to develop a technical notion of relative proximity to the truth or comparative verisimilitude, so that consecutive scientific theories would demonstrably get ever closer to being true. As we know, these bleak results have bedeviled the so-called "realist" philosophies of science. Thus, even the Australian aborigines of 12,000 years ago, if now alive, could be looking at Premise 1 undauntedly and say to Freud: "*Tu quoque.*" Therefore, the discreditation of archaic illusions by scientific advances, which presumably legitimates Premise 1, seems to pose a paradox: If the great scientific theories themselves eventually turn out to be false, by what right can Freud, or anyone, rely on *them* to scorn archaic illusory beliefs as sheer superstitions?

We have reason to think that Newtonian physics, and perhaps even general relativity theory, are partly wrong. But that does not prevent either from yielding otherwise unavailable, often stunningly accurate predictions of, say, the trajectory of the interplanetary Voyager 2, and of Halley's comet. Again, the current theories of neurotransmitters may well turn out to be wrong in some respects. Yet, the fact remains that dopamine and related medications—though of limited efficacy—control the symptoms of Parkinson's disease far more reliably than exorcistic rituals based on archaic illusions, such as shamanism, sorcery, occult art, thamaturgy, demonology, voodoo, hoodoo, incantation, mumbo-jumbo, hocus-pocus, and abracadabra. More often than not, the manifestly true *predictions* made by scientific theories—as distinct from their more speculative hypotheses—suffice to discredit archaic beliefs, such as that of the evil eye, which claims small amounts of visible light to be injurious, if not lethal. Thus, such discreditation does *not* stand or fall with the truth of the major scientific hypotheses themselves. Indeed, in striking contrast to the tenacity with which people cling to illusory beliefs, the methods of the scientific enterprise seem to have the following distinction: They are the only means of choosing theoretical beliefs that allow observational evidence to override, sooner or later, the appeal to wish fulfillment.

It emerges after all that, though the history of science is the history of abandoned theories, scientific advances redound to the credibility of Premise 1, instead of leaving it devoid of support. Therefore, we can permit that premise to stand.

As for Premise 2, however, we need to recall our earlier hesitations and doubts. Let us grant Freud that theists have produced no proofs for the existence of God that are cogent, either severally or even collectively. Then there still remains the motivational question whether some of the faithful, when giving assent to theism, had not, in fact, been decisively moved by supposed proofs, rather than by deep-seated wishes. To be sure, the existence of a conscious wish for anxiety reduction by reassuring beliefs is well attested. Yet it is not clear empirically that every case of religious belief can be attributed psychogenetically either to this wish or to the more speculative unconscious oedipal craving, let alone to the questionable repressed desire to expiate the parricidal guilt of Freud's Lamarckian phylogeny. Note that this *caveat* in regard to repressed oedipal wishes and parricidal guilt is not a matter of *generic* doubts as to the psychic operation of a mechanism of repression; instead, the doubts pertain to the existence of the *specific* sorts of repressed wishes invoked here by Freud, and to their explanatory role as the actual causes of the belief phenomena he claims to explain. For his part, Freud thought that precisely by being so strong and urgent, his trio of wishes were psychologically theogenic. Anyway, the second premise seems to be the weak link in Freud's deductively valid syllogism.

Still, we can *allow* that all cases of belief in God may perhaps be inspired by conscious favoritism for consoling beliefs over ominous ones, combined with any repressed wishes that do turn out to have such psychogenetic credentials.

The Bridge from Illusion to Delusion

Recall that Freud labels as a "delusion" a *false* illusion produced by wishes that are complex enough to include repressed desires or defense mechanisms. And suppose that one were to grant him both of the premises in his syllogism, including his triadic construal of the wishes that engender the illusions of the second premise. Then it would follow that theistic beliefs are indeed *very probably* delusions, rather than just illusions. As he reminds us: "In the case of delusions, we emphasize as essential their being in contradiction with reality," i.e., their falsity, whereas "Illusions need not necessarily be false" (1927b, p. 31). Moreover, Freud's psychogenetic, epistemological, and semantic concept of delusion allows that delusional beliefs be either idiosyncratic or socially shared. In fact, as he explains in *Civilization and Its Discontents*, he sees religion as an infantilizing mass delusion:

. . . one can try to re-create the world, to build up in its stead another world in which its most unbearable features are eliminated and replaced by others that are in conformity with one's own wishes. But whoever, in desperate defiance, sets out upon this path to happiness will as a rule attain nothing. Reality is too strong for him. . . . A special importance attaches to the case in which this attempt to procure a certainty of happiness and a protection against suffering through a delusional remoulding of reality is made by a considerable number of people in common. The religions of mankind must be classed among the mass-delusions of this kind. No one, needless to say, who shares a delusion ever recognizes it as such [1930, p. 81].

. . . by forcibly fixing them in a state of psychical infantilism and by drawing them into a mass-delusion, religion succeeds in sparing many people an individual neurosis [1930, pp. 84-85].

But Freud's concept of a *mass* delusion is strongly at odds with the notion of delusion encountered in the 1970 and 1981 editions of the Oxford *Psychiatric Dictionary*. First let us note the points of agreement between them. In its 4th edition of 1970, the Oxford *Dictionary* says, under the rubric of "hallucination," that the belief associated with a hallucinatory sensation is a "delusion" in the sense of being "obviously contrary to demonstrable fact." And the stated reason is that a hallucination is defined there as "a *sense perception* to which there is no external stimulus" (p. 333).

Thus, the 4th edition speaks of a delusion as "a belief engendered without appropriate external stimulation and maintained by one in spite of what to normal beings constitutes incontrovertible and 'plain-as-day' proof or evidence to the contrary." So far, there is no conflict with Freud's concept of delusion. But then comes the sociological demurrer: "Further, the belief held is not one which is ordinarily accepted by other members of the patient's culture or subculture (i.e., it is not a commonly believed superstition)" (p. 191). The 5th Oxford edition repudiates Freud's *supra*cultural notion of a "mass delusion" altogether in favor of an entirely intracultural concept of delusion. The later Oxford definition allows a false belief to qualify as a delusion *only* if it is held idiosyncratically, and it makes social consensus the *sole* arbiter of reality. It reads:

delusion A false belief that is firmly maintained even though it is contradicted by social reality. While it is true that some superstitions and religious beliefs are held despite the lack of confirmatory evidence, such culturally engendered concepts are not considered delusions. What is characteristic of the delusion is that it is *not* shared by others; rather, it is an idiosyncratic and individual misconception or misinterpretation. Further, it is a thinking disorder of enough import to interfere with the subject's functioning, since in the area of his delusion he no longer shares a consensually validated reality with other people [p. 157].

Evidently, no matter how inordinately primitive, superstitious or anthropomorphic the belief, it does not earn the Oxford label "delusion," if it is *shared* in its cultural milieu. Thus, even the paranoid beliefs of a hysterical lynch mob cannot count as deluded. But we are not told how many others in a given society need to share an idea, if it is to be part of what that Dictionary calls "social reality." Does it have to be a majority? And, according to the definition, what counts as "social reality" in a highly pluralistic society such as the United States, in which there are subcultures holding radically different, incompatible beliefs? The secular humanists, who allegedly dominate the public schools, and the self-styled "moral majoritarians" extolled by Vice-President [now President] Bush are only two such subcultures. To avoid misunderstanding, let me emphasize that to object to social reality as the sole arbiter of warranted belief is *not* to deny that consensus among independent observers does play a role in evidential corroboration. After all, the chances that five or more experimental physicists will hallucinate *in unison* are smaller than that only one physicist will hallucinate.

Alas, the Oxford notion of socially deviant thought as being delusional seems to be akin to the view of some Soviet psychiatrists that individual political dissent should be seen as a psychiatric problem. Furthermore, like the psychoanalyst Wallace, the 1981 Dictionary limits the concept of delusion to idiosyncratic thinking disorders that are socially maladaptive *within* a culture. Thus, it makes no psychiatric allowance for shared beliefs that may turn out to be highly maladaptive for the group as a whole, even biologically, such as in Jonestown. And what of internecine religious wars, either civil or external, as between Hindu India and Moslem Pakistan? As Mrs. Sadat has warned, Islamic religious fundamentalism threatens civil strife in Egypt, and Rabbi Kahane announced blithely on television that Israel is headed for civil war, because secular Israelis do not wish to yield to the undemocratic demands of the orthodox authoritarians. Finally, there is the Ayatollah Khomeini's theological diagnosis of President Carter as "Satan," which was undoubtedly shared by his mullahs and by some of the population in Iran. According to the Oxford definition, that belief is not delusional. By contrast, Freud depicted the belief in Satan as "nothing but a mass fantasy, constructed along the lines of a paranoid delusion" (quoted in Wallace, 1983, p. 271).

It is puzzling, therefore, that Philip Rieff (1959) has objected to Freud's notion of a mass delusion on the following grounds: "When large numbers of people share it, a delusion takes on a different meaning. . . . He [Freud] inclined to treat a public emotion like religion . . . simply as a multiple of private emotions—ignoring the fact that a belief or act is not simply enlarged but fundamentally altered by being shared" (p. 289). But how, one must ask, does the sharing of an avowedly delusional belief "fundamentally alter" its content? If a Protestant in Northern Ireland whips up a frenzied group of his coreligionists to have a hysterical fear of Irish Catholics, how is the agitator's phobic belief basically changed thereby? And was it not Freud himself who pointed out that "religion succeeds in sparing many people an individual neurosis" (1930, p. 85)? Did he not thus recognize that the *effects* of shared beliefs can differ from those of idiosyncratic ones, even if the shared beliefs are, in his view, delusional?

As against the Oxford and Rieff views, Freud does *not* relativize his notion of delusion to social reality, but is prepared to make an independent epistemological and psychiatric assessment of belief systems held by a subculture or even by a majority. Thus, in a section devoted to "The Analogy" between Judaism and neurosis, he speaks of both as featuring "the characteristic of compulsion, which forces itself on the mind along with an overpowering of logical thought" (1939, p. 72). And he elaborates:

... the symptoms ... have great psychical intensity and at the same time exhibit a far-reaching independence of the organization of the other mental processes, which are adjusted to the demands of the real external world and obey the laws of logical thinking. ... They [the symptoms] are, one might say, a State within a State, an inaccessible party, with which co-operation is impossible, but which may succeed in overcoming what is known as the normal party and forcing it into its service. If this happens, it implies a domination by an internal psychical reality over the reality of the external world and the path to a psychosis lies open [1939, p. 76].

Note Freud's stress here on the "far-reaching independence"—in one and the same person—of orthodox religious or neurotic thought processes from those of the individual's other modes of thought that, in Freud's view, are reality-oriented. What he seems to have in mind here is that just as true religious believers are often anything but credulous in their mundane pursuits in the business world, so also the paranoiac's intricate network of delusions are "typically isolated [thematically] from the rest of the personality and intellect."[5] For example, in the dual psychosis known as *"folie à deux,"* there can be a transfer of a *circumscribed* delusion from a psychotic individual to a non-psychotic one within the framework of a close relationship, so that the previously nonpsychotic individual may well internalize only *one* of the delusions of the psychotic one. Similarly, I know of a very intelligent mental patient who is amiable, good-natured, delusionally suspicious of the state police in this country, and yet seems to regard all other people as normally benevolent or neutral. When he claimed that New Jersey state troopers had punitively implanted tiny metal strips in his head, his psychiatrist suggested a cat-scan of his brain. Predictably, when the X-ray turned out negative, the patient's response was that tomography had inadequate resolving power to detect the tiny metal strips.

As both a Jesuit priest and a psychoanalyst, William Meissner is all too aware of the striking similarity between the manner in which religious believers, on the one hand, and paranoiacs, on the other, dispose of evidence contrary to their claims.

---

[5]Oxford *Psychiatric Dictionary*, 4th ed., p. 540.

Hence in 1978 he was prompted to say: "we must ask what it is that distinguishes systems of religious belief from paranoid delusions" (p. 92). He adds poignancy to this question by reference to Freud's (1911) case study of the paranoiac Schreber, whose autobiography was heuristic for the psychoanalytic etiology of paranoia. As Meissner puts it:

> How, then, does one draw a line between the theocosmological delusions of Schreber and the belief system of religious men? Schreber's *Memoirs* read in part like an elaborate theological tract. His delusional system is a highly evolved and systematized attempt to organize and understand his experience in terms of a coherent theory. Organized [religious] doctrine represents a similar attempt to interpret human experience and give it meaning in terms of a divinely instituted plan and guidance. Both delusional and [religious] belief systems reach certain untestable conclusions which cannot be contradicted by available evidences. How in fact would one go about disproving Schreber's delusion that he was being transformed into a woman? How would one disprove the Christian assertion of the real presence in the Eucharistic sacrifice [p. 93]?

Let us consider, therefore, Meissner's example of Communion in the Roman Catholic Mass. The Eucharist sacrament is supposed to repeat the action of Jesus at his last supper with his disciples, when he reportedly gave them bread, saying, "This is my body," and wine, saying, "This is my blood" (Matt. 26; Mark 14; Luke 22; 1 Cor. 11). According to Roman Catholic doctrine, as I have read it, when the sacrament is performed, the bread and wine miraculously undergo literal transsubstantiation into the body and blood of the crucified savior. But the doctrine comes equipped with an immunizing strategy to deal with the following natural question: If the consumption of bread and wine at the sacrament is, in fact, ontologically a cannibalistic act, as claimed, how is it that no such chemical change into flesh and blood, let alone into the flesh and blood of Jesus of Nazareth in particular, is detectable by taste or otherwise?

To parry this question, a peculiar version of Aristotle's distinction between the essential and accidental properties of an object is called to the rescue. Familiarly, for Aristotle, being a rational animal was an essential property of being human, whereas being a shepherd or a Greek was an accidental one. What is peculiar, in the Eucharist doctrine, about the invocation of Aristotle's distinction is that, after the purported transsubstantiation, any and every breadlike and winelike attribute of what is consumed is suddenly demoted to the status of being *only* "accidental." But the underlying substance purportedly bearing all the observationally accessible properties is that of the body and blood of Jesus. Despite this supposed "real presence" of these biological attributes in, with, and under mere bread and wine, the biological ones mysteriously elude detection, whereas the ontologically demoted accidental properties stubbornly do not go away. In short, while all appearances remain the same, the words of consecration by a priest at Mass purportedly transform the entire substance of the bread and wine literally into Christ's body and blood. As will be recalled, the Freudian phylogeny of religion postulated that the primal father was cannibalized by his rebellious sons after they had killed him. Hence Freud sees Christian communion as one means of perpetuating guilt, which the faithful then expiate by bowing to religious authority, both intellectually and emotionally (see Rieff, p. 276). But even numerous disciples of the apostle John balked at his teaching of transsubstantiation. As we read in the Gospel of John (VI.60, 66), "Many of them said: 'This is a hard saying. Who can accept it?' . . . From that time many of His disciples went back and walked no more with him."

It was hard not to agree with Meissner, when he noted the epistemological similarity between the Eucharist doctrine of the real presence, on the one hand, and Schreber's delusional belief in his own sex change, on the other. Some traditional religious apologetics feature other examples of built-in devices for begging the question and evading refutation by contrary evidence. The attempt made by the influential twentieth-century Jewish theologian Martin Buber to reconcile the existence of evil with the omnibenevolence of God is another case in point. As I have noted on another occasion, *qua* proposed solution of the problem of evil, Buber's is perhaps one of the lamest in the history of theodicy. And I heed Richard Gale's admonition that it would therefore be misleading to regard the defects of Buber's account as typical for theodicies. Though indeed not representative in this respect, Buber's solution is, I claim, not atypical of both theological and paranoid stratagems for evading falsification (Grünbaum, 1992).

Buber apparently thought that the Nazi holocaust challenged the benevolence of God in particularly acute form. To deal with it, he decided that God temporarily goes into eclipse. And this eclipse-of-God doctrine has since been championed by the Jewish philosopher Emil Fackenheim. Just why a benevolent God would go into eclipse to accommodate the likes of Adolf Hitler is not explained. Yet going into eclipse would seem to be a case of morally irresponsible absenteeism on God's part. Indeed, if Buber is to be believed, and one looks at the history of the societies that have embraced theism in one form or another, then it is difficult to find any time at all when God was not at least partially in eclipse. It will suffice to give two further illustrations of religious reasoning that seem to be simply indistinguishable from paranoid processes. Take, for instance, the question-begging claim that the existence of God is not impugned by *prima facie* contrary evidence, because He is merely *testing* us by means of such misleading data. Doesn't the Book of Job suggest that one of Satan's tasks is to test us in this way? Furthermore, as the Old Testament tells us, barren women who prayed to God secured his active intervention to become mothers: Sarah, Rebecca, and Rachel were each blessed in this way ("to make fruitful the barren woman"). Presumably, the orthodox would not allow that fertility clinics nowadays are more efficacious than prayer. Yet over 350 years ago, Francis Bacon questioned the efficacy of petitionary prayer in his *Novum Organum* (I, Section 46). Francis Galton (1872) did so again by special reference to the enormous number of prayers that are said in monarchies for the health of members of the royal families. To such doubts, it has been replied that God does not always give the supplicant what he or she seeks, but rather what he or the prayed-for person "really needs." Thus, if a victim of arthritis prays for relief from this affliction, but contracts pancreatic cancer to boot, even then the petitioner's prayer has purportedly been "answered." Is this reasoning not clearly as immunized against contrary evidence as the mind-set of the paranoiac who interprets any conduct by others, however cordial, in accord with his persecutory delusion?

Meissner (1978) makes several additional observations concerning the similarities between paranoid delusions and religious belief systems:

> . . . the degree of closedness and resistance to change by experience is a function of the degree to which the [religious] belief system serves a defensive function in preserving the believer from inner psychic insecurity and dread. Where the underlying anxiety is more intense [it] is reflected in an increased rigidity and dogmatism and a reluctance to even question any part of the complex of moral and speculative positions which compose the system [p. 93].

But turning in particular to the Roman Catholic rationale for communion, Meissner tries to snatch philosophical legitimacy from the jaws of psychopathological diagnosis:

> How would one disprove the Christian assertion of the real presence in the Eucharistic sacrifice? We can recognize that a delusional system is in conflict with reality as we interpret it, but how does one go about proving that our interpretation is sane and that the delusional one is insane and in contradiction to reality? Ultimately we cannot. We can resort to an appeal to consensus or to practical and adaptive exigencies that are consequent on our interpretation rather than the delusional one—but these are not matters of evidence [pp. 93-94].

Why—one must ask urgently—is it not a *matter of evidence* that the delusions of schizophrenics and paranoiacs are far less adaptive, even physically, than, say, belief in the principles of engineering accepted by the ancient Romans or Greeks? Disappointingly, Meissner completely dodges and sidetracks the imperative to *justify* his *obiter dictum* that the distinction between sanity and insanity is just not a matter of evidence. Thus, he immediately switches to claiming a common emotional psychogenesis for both psychotic delusions and religious belief systems: "The delusional system as well as the [religious] belief system is maintained on the basis of a prior emotional commitment, not on the basis of evidences. The illusion sets no store by verification" (p. 94). Here Meissner is, of course, echoing Freud and indeed, his second sentence is taken verbatim from Freud (1927b, p. 31).

But, unlike Meissner, Freud saw clearly that, though evidence may have played no role in the motivation of the believer, it is crucial for appraising the belief itself epistemically and semantically. How else can Meissner, the psychiatrist, ever reach the verdict of delusion, even if only fallibly? In the same vein, avowedly renouncing evidence for giving assent to the Bible, he says: "Apologetics must ultimately appeal to an acceptance through faith which lies beyond the reach of reason" (p. 94). But this characterization is an attempt to set such belief apart from a delusion. It does so by abandoning psychiatric vocabulary in favor of honorific language that gratuitously uses a spatial metaphor to elevate the illusion and to demote reason. Why not say instead that since the belief is avowedly ill-supported, it is *beneath* reason rather than beyond it? As for differences between religious tenets and psychotic delusions, Meissner lucidly elaborates on ideas that are vintage Freud (p. 94).

But in his most recent book (1984), Meissner does take issue with Freud by accusing him of misrepresenting the believer's own epistemic valuation of his faith:

> The believer does not regard his faith as a matter of wishful hallucination or of purely subjective implications. . . .
> The question we are addressing here is not that of the truth value of the believer's faith. The point, rather, is that to envision his faith solely in subjective terms, as essentially did Freud, is to do a disservice to the believer and actually to distort the substance of his belief [p. 178].

This complaint, however, seems misdirected. Freud never averred that his appraisal of the psychogenetic, epistemic, and semantic status of theism as both an illusion and a delusion (1930, pp. 81, 85; 1933, pp. 160-162, 166-168) is a *reconstruction* of the believer's own view of his creed. On the contrary, as he emphasized, "No one, needless to say, who shares a delusion ever recognizes it as such" (1930, p. 81). And Meissner is arguing at cross purposes with Freud, who was indeed addressing the question of truth value when he referred to Tertullian's declaration "Credo quia absurdum," and wrote: "But this *Credo* is only of interest as a self-confession. As an authoritative statement [vouching for the truth value of the faith] it has no binding force" (1927b, p. 28).

Nor does it impugn any of Freud's theses on religion to adduce, as Meissner does, D. W. Winnicott's 1971 theory of child development. As the child makes its first attempts to relate to the world outside its mother, we learn, it creates so-called "transitional objects" that are "neither totally subjective nor totally objective" (p. 16). Instead, these objects share elements contributed from objective reality no less than from the child's subjective inner world, a view akin to John Locke's notion of primary and secondary qualities of material objects. And to the extent that the subjective component distorts the representation of an externally existing object, yet is *not* just hallucinatory, Winnicott's notion of transitional object can be assimilated to the *Oxford* sense of "illusion." According to that construal of the term, we recall, illusions are false sensory perceptions, but—unlike hallucinations—they do originate from a real external stimulus.

When Freud proclaimed that the consolations of religion are delusional, he had alluded, just in passing, to the germ of Winnicott's idea. Thus he declared: "It is asserted, however, that each one of us behaves in some one respect like a paranoic, corrects some aspect of the world which is unbearable to him by the construction of a wish and introduces this delusion into reality" (1930, p. 81). Examples that come to mind at once include the practice of what psychoanalysts call "denial," even by highly knowledgeable medical experts, who invent farfetched diagnostic hypotheses to discount their own ominous symptoms of serious illness. Hence one may well grant Meissner the claim that none of us get through any stage of life without some reliance on Winnicott's transitional objects (pp. 165-171).

Yet the recognition of this state of affairs does not even begin to make a dent in Freud's case against theism. As Küng appreciates: "It does not follow—as some theologians have mistakenly concluded—from man's profound desire for God and eternal life that God exists and eternal life and happiness are real. . . . It is true that the wish alone does not contain within itself its fulfillment" (p. 79).[6] Indeed, for any particular wish-inspired belief, it must be asked anew whether it is not just delusional, being a mere projection in the sense of Feuerbach and Freud. And clearly, in the context of religious experience, this key question can hardly be answered by the existence of *some* objects that do qualify as a kind of admixture of objective elements with subjective projections.

It would seem, therefore, that—interesting though it is in its own right—Meissner's extrapolation of Winnicott's notion of transitional object does not adequately come to grips with Freud's epistemological challenge, or even begs the question.

UNACKNOWLEDGED MOTIVES AND RELIGIOUS BELIEF

So far, our treatment of Freud's philosophy of religion has emphasized the important gaps in its evidential support. But there are also a number of considerations that either lend substance to some of his contentions, or pose important questions to which we have been alerted by his notion of belief in theism as psychopathology.

It is remarkable that neither Hans Küng nor William Meissner discussed the doctrine of the Virgin Birth of Jesus *vis-à-vis* psychoanalytic theory. Freud makes only incidental, passing reference to the ancient fable of virgin births among vultures, which the Church Fathers took up eagerly as a plausibility argument, drawn from the natural order (1910a, p. 90). But it is an obvious psychological question to ask: Why is it thought to enhance Christ's moral or divine stature that he was supposedly born of a virgin? And what would Roman Catholic Maryology be without Mary's virginal status? She is venerated as the Mother of God by the Anglican, Eastern Orthodox, and Roman Catholic Churches. And the miracle of the Virgin Birth is reportedly that Christ was "conceived by the Holy Ghost and born of the Virgin Mary" (Luke 1:34-38). This asexual event is supposed to have occurred in response to her having asked the angel Gabriel how she, a virgin, should become the mother of the promised Messiah.

---

[6]See also Ricoeur (1966).

There are, of course, people in our culture who scoff at anthropological tales of asexual reproduction in humans, except for the Virgin Birth of Jesus. Yet they know very well that no one monitored Mary's encounters with Joseph, or with any other male. In fact, early Christian legends incorrectly described Joseph as an aged widower, presumably to discredit the idea that he was Jesus's biological father.[7]

It is clear that anyone who believes in the divinity of Jesus may presume that his conception and birth were not tainted in any way. But the question is why his birth would have been less exalted if his conception had been sexual? If Mary's ovum itself is presumed to be unblemished, why then would Joseph's sperm or prostatic fluid be a pollutant? Is it not perhaps the pleasure incident upon sexual conception that is held to detract from divinity? And, if so, why? Does it not bespeak a strong desire to *dissociate* motherhood from sexuality, a desire that is normally deemed unrealizable, because people know better? Is it not precisely the opportunity to fulfill this wish that makes otherwise hard-headed, worldly, and even street-wise Christians eager to suspend all disbelief? And even if one is prepared to postulate that Mary's pregnancy was asexual, would it not be more reasonable to see it as a very rare case of *spontaneous* parthenogenesis among humans, rather than to attribute it to the action of the Holy Ghost? After all, in some kinds of lower species, the development of eggs without fertilization is the normal means of reproduction, as in the case of male ants, bees, and wasps. Yet according to current genetic theory, only *females* could develop *among humans* from an ovum that divides parthenogenetically. The Y-chromosome that is needed to produce a male can come only from a sperm, since ova contain only X-chromosomes. But Jesus was male.

It might be objected that this whole line of reasoning is unsound. Instead, it might be argued, a *sexual* conception is held to detract from the divinity of the offspring, because Jesus's conception would then no longer be *miraculous*, rather than because it would make Mary's motherhood pleasurably sexual. Yet this alternative rationale for the willingness to believe in

---

[7]"Joseph," *The World Book Encyclopedia*, 11:132, 1966.

the virgin birth does not seem to capture its psychological motivation adequately. In the first place, it is the *purity* of Mary's motherhood—rather than *just* its miraculousness—that is being steadily celebrated in the adulatory references to her as the Virgin. And the very notion that the ASEXUAL motherhood of a married woman is purer than the normal sexual sort—by being morally superior to the latter—seems to militate in favor of our original motivational conjecture: Psychologically, the doctrine of the virgin birth provides a golden, sublime opportunity to fulfill the wish to dissociate motherhood from sexuality. In the second place, if the hypothesized role of the Holy Ghost in Mary's pregnancy was only to render Jesus's conception miraculous, would it not be more credible that God the father created his own son directly *ex nihilo*—as he had done with photons, for example—rather than that the *a*sexual story of the five Gospels is true? Hence let us proceed on the basis of our prior motivational interpretation.

But what accounts for the initial desire to dissociate sexuality from motherhood? Might it not be, after all, that this phenomenon is due to the existence of repressed oedipal conflicts? Let us assume with Freud that each child wishes to possess the parent of the opposite sex, and to eliminate the rival parent of the same sex. Then, at one stroke, the mother's supposed virginity fulfills the oedipal cravings of both boys and girls. The son has the satisfaction that the rival father did not possess the mother sexually; and the daughter gets her wish that the rival mother did not get her sexual tentacles on the father. If this is implausible, how much more implausible still is the belief in the virgin birth, whose ubiquity in Christendom cries out for psychological explanation, especially among those to whom you could never sell the Brooklyn Bridge. Again, if oedipal wishes are normally present, they might also be a contributory cause of the great frequency with which the Madonna and the Child are featured in the works of artists and musicians. Whatever the underlying psychological impetus, it seems very difficult to escape the conjecture that primarily a guilt-ridden, jaundiced view of sexuality inspires the strong feeling that Jesus's moral or theological stature is enhanced by his virgin birth.

The notion of an asexual reproduction in humans is intelligible, if implausible. But orthodox believers insist on making other religious utterances that are avowedly incomprehensible to themselves and to their fellows. To make this unintelligibility palatable, the pertinent linguistic pronouncements are sometimes said to express "mysteries." The renunciation of such mysteries and/or of their revelation is often a feature of eighteenth-century deism, insofar as it distances itself from theism. *Qua* being admittedly unintelligible, the so-called mysteries are not susceptible to evidential assessment in any ordinary sense, but are said to have the sanction of *special* revelation. Thus, Meissner (1984) strikes the theme of ultimate unintelligibility as follows: "faith is a response to revelation . . . and . . . revelation conveys a *content* that eludes human understanding" (p. 110; my italics). Yet, several considerations call for psychological explanation of why the faithful are eager to see themselves as giving creedal assent to beliefs whose very content is avowedly incomprehensible.

At least in our current state of biological evolution, our species may well be limited by intrinsic intellectual horizons of some sort, much as theoretical physics, for example, defies comprehension by dogs. Yet, whatever the extent of human inadequacy, the demand for creedal assent to an admittedly unintelligible declarative sentence seems to bespeak an altogether misplaced sense of intellectual humility. For, even if one is willing to accept such a claim on faith in the absence of evidence, it is impossible to do so, even with the best of intentions, since one can *believe* only a statement whose content one comprehends. Otherwise, what is it that is being believed? It would seem clear that assent, even on faith, requires prior understanding, if the assent is to be significant at all. But, if so, why do even the most highly intelligent among the faithful nevertheless affirm assent?

Recall that we allowed, in criticism of Freud, that arguments rather than mere wishes may have prompted *some* theists to believe in God. But spurious assent to avowedly incomprehensible utterances purely on faith is much more likely to be a matter of wish fulfillment. What else could motivate such would-be assent? What does it mean to say, as some have said, that God is transcendent to the point of being "wholly other"? And why does anyone want to say it?

In the same vein, if the very content of revelation does elude human understanding, how can it be conveyed in utterances? And why does the clergy not heed Wittgenstein's injunction: "Whereof one cannot speak, thereof one must be silent" in the wake of telling us about the intellectual horizons of our finite minds? How do ecclesiastics acquire greater expertise than others for discerning the limits of human cognition, say, in regard to so-called "ultimate causes"? As a further example, Yahweh, the god of Moses, was said to be even "above naming and beyond understanding" (Meissner, 1984, p. 119). How then can such an object be intelligibly loved, in addition to being feared and taken on faith? Indeed, how can love and fear of God be other than diffuse, if their very object eludes us? And why is this whole web of notions *not* a case of thought pathology?

Hans Küng's 1984 book on personal immortality unfortunately offers similar kinds of verbal fetish, which *evades* the substantial evidence against immortality. There he tells us in dozens of ways that eternal life is "beyond the dimension of space and time, in God's invisible, imperishable, *incomprehensible* domain" (p. 113; my italics). And, furthermore, that "The glory of eternal life is completely new, unsuspected and incomprehensible, unthinkable and unutterable" (p. 220). But, again, if the very domain of eternal life is avowedly "incomprehensible," what does it mean to *believe* in it? And how could Küng possibly take the "unutterable" on faith? In what sense does our personal identity survive in Küng's vision? Just what does the spatial metaphor "beyond" mean if the domain is "beyond space-time"? Indeed, as Küng would have it, eternity is devoid of temporal succession and consists instead of an endless "now." But what is to be understood by an "endless now"? And how can the prospect of it be consoling to a person who is reflective, rather than just verbally conditioned? Why would a believer not pray to God for the oblivion of death as deliverance from such excrutiating cosmic monotony? Moreover, this supposed eternal life is not even cold comfort as compensation for biological death. Is our fear of death not a matter of the impending loss of just those terrestrial joys that, we know, depend on the integrity of our physical brain? Would we not miss the embrace of someone we love, the fragrance of a rose, the satisfactions of work and friendship, the sounds of music, the panorama of a glorious sunrise or sunset, the biological pleasures of the body, and the delights of wit and humor? Hence, far from being blissful, the eternal beatitude held out by Küng, and by Pascal's wager, is at best stale, flat, and undeserving of our trust. Though well-intentioned, its vision of immortality seems to be largely an unintelligible myth. Yet none other than Martin Gardner (1986), the well-known science writer and debunker of pseudoscientific superstition, speaks *approvingly* of Reinhold Niebuhr's vision of a personal immortality that "will not destroy the essential unity of mind and body" (pp. 52-53). According to Gardner, Niebuhr took "Paul's symbol of the resurrection of the body as pointing to a transcendent realm, wholly beyond reason, where there would be no destruction of our essential nature, though in a manner about which we can know absolutely nothing." Alas, this is literally just nonsense!

One wonders, therefore, in what sense there can be a community of faith or belief, rather than of mere verbal utterance, in regard to those statements that are admittedly incomprehensible. And one is distressed by the intensity of the emotions engendered and the effort expended to secure from people an assent which, in the nature of the case, can be little more than parroting linguistic expressions. Man, it appears, is not only a symbol-using animal, but also a symbol-*abusing* being. To deplore the spurious assent orchestrated by linguistic regimentation is not to say, however, that it is ineffective as a means of securing the compliance of the faithful with concrete behavioral directives. On the contrary, precisely because the content of the purported mysteries is elusive, their utterance may enhance the psychological subordination needed for such compliance.

It has been said that these mysteries can perhaps be demystified, if they are seen as just allegorical expressions of the sense of awe felt by human beings in the face of the vastness and inexhaustible intricacy of the universe. But such awe can be and is felt by atheists too. As Freud observed: "what constitutes the essence of the religious attitude is not this feeling but only the next step after it, the reaction to it which seeks a remedy for it" (1927b, p. 32) from belief in God.

We have considered the critical response to Freud's psychology of religion by the theological partisans Küng and Meissner. This focus on them seemed warranted, not only because their writings are psychoanalytically informed and recent, but also because they criticized Freud in a spirit of intellectual comradeship and human brotherhood. Both Küng and Meissner see themselves as having salvaged what is valid in his psychological critique of religion without fundamental detriment to the essential tenets of theism, or even of Roman Catholicism. For our part, we have claimed that Freud's syllogistic argument for atheism relies on a premise whose warrant is open to question. But, as we saw, Küng's and Meissner's own insistence that the content of some cardinal religious utterances is incomprehensible renders belief in them meaningless. Thus, it becomes imperative to explain *psychologically* what stake such theists have in paradoxically demanding credulous assent to those utterances. Unintelligible utterances are neither true nor false. Therefore, they cannot qualify technically as either delusions or illusions. Delusions are, by definition, false beliefs. And Freudian illusions are either true or false.

Though assent to incomprehensible utterances is spurious, the aura of mystery surrounding the elusive content of such would-be beliefs may perhaps furnish welcome release for the faithful from doubt as to the more intelligible beliefs that are wish-fulfilling. The dogma of the *bodily* assumption of Mary into heaven may thus facilitate credulous acceptance of her virginal motherhood. Any attrition of our critical faculty in a given domain seems to make it easier to suspend its use even more in that domain. Thus belief in personal immortality may be made more acceptable to some by the view that the angels now have the technology to read each person's DNA, and therefore they can clone each of us in heaven. But these psychological conjectures are only suggestions of mine, inspired by questions to which Freud's theory of religion as psychopathology has alerted us. In short, despite the major evidential lacunae in his philosophy of religion, it is probably not without some substantive merit, over and above its heuristic value.

In striking contrast to Küng and Meissner, the psychoanalyst Gregory Zilboorg, a one-time Russian Jew who became a convert to Roman Catholicism, characterized Freud's philosophy of religion as a case of "megalomanic scientism" (1962, p. 243). Yet Freud had fully acknowledged both the epistemic fallibility and substantive incompleteness of the scientific enterprise:

> I know how difficult it is to avoid illusions; perhaps the hopes I have confessed to for science are of an illusory nature, too. But I hold fast to one distinction. Apart from the fact that no penalty is imposed for not sharing them, my illusions are not, like religious ones, incapable of correction. They have not the character of a delusion. If experience should show—not to me, but to others after me, who think as I do—that we have been mistaken, we will give up our expectations [1927b, p. 53].

And, in the wake of this concession, he says to the partisan of theism: "the weakness of my position does not imply any strengthening of yours." Thus, the capstone of these admonitions, which is the very last sentence of *The Future of an Illusion*, is the caveat: "But an illusion it would be to suppose that what science cannot give us we can get elsewhere" (1927b, p. 56). This assertion hardly promises pie-in-the-sky from science.

The accusation of megalomania continues to be leveled against the irreligious humanism espoused by Freud. A notable, more recent example is furnished by Alexander Solzhenitsyn's 1978 Commencement Address at Harvard University. Entitled "A World Split Apart," it contains the following lament: "There is a disaster which is already very much with us. I am referring to the calamity of an autonomous [despiritualized] and irreligious, humanistic consciousness. It has made man the measure of all things on Earth—imperfect man, who is never free of pride, self-interest, envy, vanity, and dozens of other defects. . . . Is it true that man is above everything? Is there no Superior Spirit above him?"

Prima facie, this declaration may sound ingratiatingly modest. But, as it stands, it is morally hollow and theologically question-begging. Whose revelation, one must ask, is to supplant man as the measure of all things? That of the Czarist Russian Orthodox Church? Or the edicts of the Ayatollah Khomeini, as enforced

by his mullahs? Those of the Dutch Reformed Church in apart-
heid South Africa? Or the teachings of Pope John Paul II,
who—amid starvation in Africa—is getting support from the
native episcopate for the prohibition of "artificial" birth control? The moral prescriptions of the Church of England? Or
yet those of the orthodox rabbinate in Israel, which prohibits
autopsies, for example? And, if the latter, which of the two
competing chief rabbis is to be believed, the Ashkenazi, or the
Sephardic one? If the ethical perplexity of modern man is to
be resolved by concrete moral injunctions, does Solzhenitsyn's
jeremiad not simply replace secular man by *clergymen*, who become the moral touchstone of everything? Indeed, was the invocation of divine Providence not a regular feature of Hitler's
speeches, illustrating anew that religion can also be the last
refuge of the scoundrel?

After all, even if one has no problem with the very concept
of divine omnibenevolence, this notion is itself altogether sterile
in regard to specific moral imperatives. Assuming omnibenevolence, it presumably follows that all divinely ordained conduct
is morally right. Yet we are left wholly in the dark as to whether
to share or abhor, for example, the Reverend Falwell's and
Rabbi Kahane's claim that a nuclear Armageddon is part of
God's just and loving plan for us. From Rabbi Kahane we learn:
"The Messiah will come. There will be a resurrection of the
dead—all the things that Jews believed in before they got so
damn sophisticated" (quoted in Friedman, 1986).

To an observer who is not already identified with one of the
contending theological revelations, it appears that the moment
a theology is to be used to yield ethical prescriptions, these rules
of conduct are obtained by deliberations in whose outcome
secular aims and thought are every bit as decisive as in the
reflections of secular ethicists who deny theism. And the perplexity of moral problems is not lessened by the theological
superstructure, which itself leaves us in an ethical quandary.
That this superstructure is at best logically superfluous for ethics or simply unavailing emerges further from the failure of
divine omnibenevolence to answer a key question, put by Socrates in Plato's *Euthyphro*: Is the conduct approved by the gods
right because of *properties of its own*, or *merely* because it pleases

the gods to command it? If God enjoins us to do what is desirable *in its own right*, then ethical rules do not depend for their validity on divine command, and they can then be independently adopted. But if conduct is good merely because God decrees it, then we are again faced with the cacophony of conflicting revelations as well as with the basic ethical disagreements existing even within the clergy of the same religious denomination.

No wonder that the Judaeo-Christian theology has been invoked as a sanction for such diverse ethical doctrines as the divine right of kings, the inalienable rights of life, liberty, and the pursuit of happiness, black slavery, "Deutschland über alles," the social Darwinism of Spencer, and socialism. Some religious sects in India would have us abstain from the surgical excision of cancerous growths in man, and Christian Scientists in the West reach somewhat similar conclusions from rather different premises. Roman Catholics, on the other ·hand, endorse the medical prevention of death but condemn interference with nature in the form of birth control, a position not shared by leading Protestant and Jewish clergymen. Indeed, both Mahatma Ghandi and Hitler saw themselves as serving God. And divine Providence was as frequent a feature of Hitler's speeches as it is of Ronald Reagan's. One believer's will of God is another's will of Satan, as illustrated by the exchange between the Ayatollah Khomeini and President Carter, a born-again Christian.

Solzhenitsyn's charge of moral inadequacy against an irreligious humanistic consciousness is of a piece with the point of his rhetorical questions, "Is it true that man is above everything? Is there no Superior Spirit above him?" Surely the assumption that man may well *not* be above everything hardly requires belief in the existence of God. As we know, NASA has been scanning the skies for signals from extraterrestrial and indeed extrasolar humanoids, whose intelligence may indeed be suprahuman. Thus Voyager 2 carries samples of our own intellectual productions to send a potential message from us. Yet theists and atheists alike know that if there are such mentally superior beings, they could be morally even worse than we are. For example, if they landed on earth, they might both bring the means and have the will to enslave our species beyond anything envisioned by George Orwell. By the same token, even if there were a disembodied spirit far superior to us intellectually, what is the evidence that it is not malevolent, allowing just enough good to exist to exacerbate the world's rampant evils (Russell, 1954, p. 590)?

POSTSCRIPT (1992)

Meissner (1992) has just published an article on "The Pathology of Belief Systems," which is a sequel to his (1984) and to his earlier psychoanalytic treatment of religious beliefs (Meissner, 1978, pp. 92-95, 810-813). It behooves me to deal with those claims in his (1992) that pertain to the present chapter 7, which he cites (1992, pp. 107-109) from its original publication (Grünbaum, 1987).

Yet he took account of only my conceptual comparison of Freud's notion of delusion with the conflicting one offered in the Oxford *Psychiatric Dictionary* (Campbell, 1981, 1989). Besides, Meissner's statement of my view as to the relative merits of these rival notions is, alas, simply topsy turvy.

As the reader saw above, I sided explicitly with Freud's epistemologically and semantically derogatory construal of delusions, and I noted his claim that their psychogenetic status allows them to be socially shared as such. By the same token, I clearly opposed the recent Oxford socio-cultural relativization such that a "delusion" is idiosyncratic, which is politicized and precludes, by definition, that delusions be shared.

Thus, I commended Freud for allowing that there can be *mass* delusions or mass psychoses, and I rejected the Oxford notion as unacceptably restrictive. Yet Meissner saddles me with precisely the opposite view: "He [Grünbaum] takes issue with Freud's concept of mass delusion, insofar as it is not at all congruent with the notion of delusion found in common psychiatric usage" (1992, p. 107).

More disappointingly, Meissner (1992) is silent in regard to the principal arguments I offered in my (1987) against his

(1978) and (1984) stance: He simply repeats (1992, pp. 123-124) almost verbatim contentions from his (1978) that I had clearly challenged. Indeed, his (1992) elaboration is even more vulnerable to my (1987) arguments than his earlier writings. Thus, now he tells us:

> Let us take one religious belief that is fairly widely accepted in Christian religions, namely that there will be a final judgment by God when an ultimate disposition will be made of all men assigning them for all eternity to the beatitude of heaven or the torment of hell.
> . . . We have no empirical tests to satisfy our need for verification. We also have no means for demonstrating the falsity of these assertions. On what basis would we deny their validity? . . . If we accept the ideas, we accept them on the basis of faith. If we do not accept the ideas, we reject them on the basis of no faith. From the perspective of scientific or psychoanalytic understanding, we have no resource that would allow us to solve the matter. We can say no more than that we simply do not know. [1992, p. 103].

Believing to have immunized religious belief systems in this way against any and all evidential scrutiny, Meissner claims nevertheless that they actually *explain* observable facts: "Religious belief systems are complex cognitive organizations which explain in a coherent fashion fundamental and existential questions involving the origin of the universe, . . ." (1992, p. 122).

As against these claims, I offer the following considerations.

1. Consider Meissner's example of the religious belief that, at the final judgment, men's souls will be assigned "for all eternity to the beatitude of heaven or the torment of hell." Insofar as the envisioned modes of the survival of personal identity are intelligible at all—rather than just gibberish—the given belief presupposes personal immortality.

But there is very strong evidence for the very dependence of consciousness—be it labeled "mind" or "soul"—on adequate brain function, and thus for the demise of personal identity upon the death of the brain (Edwards, 1992). For example, there are known mental and psychiatric effects of traumatic brain injury, brain tumors, Alzheimer's disease, degenerative dementias, toxic disorders (e.g. alcoholism), cerebro-vascular dysfunctions, and of endocrine disorders (Yudofsky and Hales, 1992, Part IV).

Just as personal immortality is discredited by adverse evidence, so also, contrary to Meissner, Schreber's belief that he was being transformed into a woman is gainsaid by refuting anatomical evidence. Of course, like other paranoiacs, Schreber might try to make his delusion irrefutable by tampering with its very content, such as modifying the criteria for being male or female. But such a gambit could hardly render his delusion of gender-transformation immune to evidential discreditation. Similarly, the belief in the purported efficacy of petitionary prayer to God by well-wishers of fatally ill people is statistically testable and thus disconfirmable by potential medical findings.

2. Both Pope John Paul II (Associated Press dispatch 5-24-1987) and Cardinal O'Connor of New York have endorsed exorcism, which is the therapeutic application of the demonic possession theory of insanity. This primitive animist theory has been adduced to "explain" hysteria, somnambulism and epilepsy. But it is discredited by the aforecited dependence of at least some psychiatric disorders on known sorts of neuroanatomical or neurochemical brain dysfunctions. Besides, in the Roman Catholic exorcist ritual, the very existence of death in the world is attributed to Satanic activity, despite the overwhelming evidence for the physiological causation of our demise. Thus, even if Satan were to exist, he would be *causally irrelevant* to both psychosis and death, despite his useful allegorical role as Mephistopheles in Goethe's *Faust*.

Undaunted by such caveats, the current Pope has told us that Lucifer or Satan is "a cosmic liar and murderer . . . [who] has the skill in the world to induce people to deny his existence in the name of rationalism." Thus, John Paul II tries to render the purported Satanic activity immune to evidential discreditation by precisely the sorts of reasoning featured in the arguments characteristically employed by paranoiacs in defense of their delusions.

These animadversions alone undermine Meissner's allegation that "The problem in evaluating religious belief systems is that not only is there no evidence for them, but that there is also no evidence contradictory to them" (1992, p. 109). By the

same token, the existence of cogent evidence against both personal immortality and demonic possession invalidates Meissner's charge that Freud "had no legitimate basis for declaring
religious beliefs delusional, that is violating reality" (1992, p.
107). Having drawn that unsound conclusion, Meissner infers
unjustifiably that Freud, *malgré lui*, had to base his assertion of
the delusional character of religious beliefs *solely* on their wish-
fulfilling character.

It appears that Meissner has fundamentally misportrayed the
epistemology of religious doctrines by his wholesale declaration
that "If we do not accept the ideas, we reject them on the basis
of no faith. From the perspective of scientific or psychoanalytic
understanding, we have no resource that would allow us to
solve the matter" (1992, p. 103). Does Meissner himself really
believe that his psychoanalytic account of the paranoid process
is not evidentially superior to that offered by demonic possession? And is his preference for the psychoanalytic explanation
merely a matter of his sheer lack of faith in the demonic one?

As he would have it, disbelievers can never have any grounds
for rejecting religious doctrines other than the unavailability
of supporting evidence. But, as I have argued, for at least a
significant subclass of religious beliefs, there is telling evidence
against them (Grünbaum, 1992).

Just as Popper erred seriously—as we saw in chapter 2—when
he asserted the empirical untestability of psychoanalytic theory
tout court, so also Meissner's sweeping fideist denial of the evidential scrutibility of religious beliefs is wide of the mark.

His claim that a religious belief, though eluding both evidential confirmation and disconfirmation, can "explain . . . the origin of the universe" (Meissner, 1992, p. 122) fares no better.
In a famous 1951 address to the Pontifical Academy of Sciences,
Pope Pius XII claimed that the "big bang" model of the origin
of the universe, which has been in vogue among astrophysicists
for three decades, vindicates the Christian doctrine of creation
ex nihilo, which is familiar since the second century. In the fifth
century, Augustine even taught that God created both matter
and time out of nothing.

But, as I have contended in some of my cosmological writings
(Grünbaum 1990b; 1991; in press), in the big bang model based

on Einstein's theory of general relativity, physical processes or states already existed in some form or other *at every actual past instant of time,* because there simply was no time at all during which the physical world did not already exist in some form or other.

Furthermore, Augustine's notion that *time itself* "was made" by God, along with matter, presupposes a fictitious super-time. And it literally makes no sense to treat time itself as being on a par with objects like stars or atoms that come into existence in the course of time. On the other hand, the concept of temporally simultaneous divine creation of time itself is either nonsensical or uselessly circular as an explanation.

As against Meissner's explanatory tribute to theological creationism, it emerges from the big bang cosmogony that Augustine's creation *ex nihilo* offers only a *pseudo*-explanation of the existence of the universe. Yet Meissner's observations on the role of psychopathology in rigid adherence to religious dogma and related behaviors are not impugned by these criticisms. On the other hand, I do not think that Meissner's (1990) elaborate critique of my (1984) really comes to grips with the problems I have posed, let alone offers a viable resolution of them.

8

RETROSPECTIVE VERSUS PROSPECTIVE TESTING OF ETIOLOGIC HYPOTHESES IN PSYCHOANALYSIS

INTRODUCTION

The repression etiology of neurotic disorders is, as we saw, the cornerstone of the psychoanalytic theory of unconscious motivations. Repressions are held to be not only the pathogens of the psychoneuroses but also the motives of dream construction and the causes of various sorts of bungled actions (parapraxes) in which the subject is normally successful (e.g., slips of the tongue or pen). Thus, even in the case of "normal" people, Freud saw manifest dream content and various sorts of "slips" as the telltale symptoms of (temporary) *mini*neuroses, engendered by repressions.

Having modified Breuer's cathartic method of investigation *and* therapy, Freud arrived at the purported sexual etiologies of the psychoneuroses, as well as at the supposed causes of dreams and parapraxes, by lifting presumed repressions via the patient's allegedly "free" associations. At the same time, excavation of the pertinent repressed ideation was to remove the pathogens of the patient's afflictions. Scientifically, Freud deemed the psychoanalytic method of investigation to be both heuristic *and* probative, over and above being a method of therapy.

311

Yet he and his disciples have not been alone in maintaining that the *clinical* setting of the psychoanalytic treatment sessions provides cogent epistemic avenues for testing his etiologies *retrospectively*. The scrutiny of this thesis has highly instructive import for adjudicating the general polemic waged by critics against the clinical validation that Freudians have claimed for their theory. But the examination of the purported cogent testability likewise helps us assess the merits of prospective versus retrospective testing of etiologic hypotheses in psychiatry. I shall focus this chapter on the scrutiny of issues of clinical testability of the Freudian etiologies beyond those treated in chapter 6.

STATEMENT OF THE CONTROVERSY AS TO CLINICAL TESTABILITY

Eysenck (1963) maintains "we can no more test Freudian hypotheses 'on the couch' [used by the patient during psychoanalytic treatment] than we can adjudicate between the rival hypotheses of Newton and Einstein by going to sleep under an apple tree" (p. 220). In Eysenck's view, only suitably designed *experimental* studies can perform the *probative* role of *tests*, while the clinical data from the couch may be heuristically fruitful by suggesting hypotheses. Glymour (1974) argues that "the theory Sigmund Freud developed at the turn of the century was strong enough to be tested [cogently] on the couch" (p. 304). Glymour proposes to illuminate Eysenck's disparagement of clinical data but then to discount it by the following dialectical give-and-take:

> It stems in part, I think, from what are genuine drawbacks to clinical testing; for example, the problem of ensuring that a patient's responses are not *simply* the result of suggestion or the feeling, not without foundation, that the "basic data" obtained from clinical sessions—the patient's introspective reports of his own feelings, reports of dreams, memories of childhood and adolescence—are less reliable than we should like. But neither of these considerations seems sufficient to reject the clinical method generally, although they may of course be sufficient to warrant

us in rejecting particular clinical results. Clinicians can hopefully be trained so as not to elicit by suggestion the expected responses from their patients; patients' reports can sometimes be checked independently, as in the case of memories, and even when they cannot be so checked there is no good reason to distrust them generally. But I think condemnations like Eysenck's derive from a belief about clinical testing which goes considerably beyond either of these points: the belief that clinical sessions, even cleansed of suggestibility and of doubts about the reliability of patients' reports, can involve no rational strategy for testing theories.

I think that Eysenck's claim is wrong. I think there is a rational strategy for testing important parts of psychoanalysis, a strategy that relies almost exclusively on clinical evidence; moreover, I think this strategy is immanent in at least one of Freud's case studies, that of the Rat Man. Indeed, I want to make a much bolder claim. The strategy involved in the Rat Man case is essentially the same as a strategy very frequently used in testing physical theories. Further, this strategy, while simple enough, is more powerful than the hypothetico-deductive-falsification strategy described for us by so many philosophers of science [pp. 287-288].

Despite this epistemological tribute to Freud's couch, Glymour issues a *caveat*:

I am certainly not claiming that there is good clinical evidence for Freud's theory; I am claiming that if one wants to test psychoanalysis, there is a reasonable strategy for doing so which can be, and to some degree has been, effected through clinical sessions [p. 288].

Glymour (1980) tells us more explicitly why we should countenance the rationale that animated Freud's (1909b) clinical investigation of psychoanalytic hypotheses during the treatment of the Rat-Man. Glymour points to at least three important specific episodes in the history of physical science in which he discerns just the logical pincer-and-bootstrap strategy of piecemeal testing he also teased out from Freud's analysis of the Rat-Man. He states, "unlikely as it may sound . . . the major argument of the Rat Man case is not so very different from the major argument of Book III of Newton's *Principia*" (Glymour, 1980, p. 265). He stresses that this argument employs a logical *pincer* strategy of more or less *piecemeal* testing *within* an overall theory, instead of the completely global theory appraisal of the hypothetico-deductive method, which altogether abjures any attempt to rate different components of the theory individually as to their merits in the face of the evidence.

Besides commending Freud's clinical study of the Rat-Man for its rationale, Glymour attributes a fair degree of scientific rigor to a *few* of Freud's other investigations. But he couples these particular appreciative judgments with a largely uncomplimentary overall evaluation, after deploring the very uneven logical quality of the Freudian corpus. Indeed, Glymour thinks he is being "gentle" (p. 265) when he deems Freud's (1909a) case study of Little Hans to be "appalling." He finds that "on the whole Freud's arguments for psychoanalytic theory are dreadful," marred by the frequent—though by no means universal—substitution of "rhetorical flourish" for real argument, and of a "superabundance of explanation" for cogent evidence (p. 264). Yet clearly these quite fundamental dissatisfactions with Freud's all-too-frequent lapses do not militate against Glymour's espousal of the clinical testability of such central parts of psychoanalytic theory as the specific etiologies of the psychoneuroses, at least in the etiological versions Freud enunciated before 1909.

Just this championship of the *probative* value of data from the analytic treatment sessions is philosophical music to the ears of those who echo Freud's own emphatic claim that the bulk of psychoanalytic theory is well founded empirically. As Jones (1959) reminded everyone in his Editorial Preface to Freud's *Collected Papers*, the clinical findings are "the real basis of Psycho-analysis. All of Professor Freud's other works and theories are essentially founded on the clinical investigations." Most advocates of this theoretical corpus regard the analyst's many observations of the patient's interactions with him in the treatment sessions as the source of findings that are simply *peerless* not only heuristically but *also* probatively. We are told that during a typical analysis, which lasts for some years, the analyst accumulates a vast number of variegated data from each patient that furnish evidence relevant to Freud's theory of personality no less than to the dynamics and outcome of his therapy. The so-called psychoanalytic interview sessions are claimed to yield genuinely probative data because of the alleged real-life nature of the rich relationship between the analyst and the analysand.

Even an analyst who just declared it to be high time that Freudians "move from overreliance on our hypothetical discoveries to a much needed validation of our basic theoretical and clinical concepts" (Kaplan, 1981, p. 23) characterizes "the naturalistic observations within the psychoanalytic treatment situation" as "the major scientific method of psychoanalysis" (p. 18). Hence the clinical setting or "psychoanalytic situation" is purported to be the arena of *experiments in situ,* in marked contrast to the contrived environment of the psychological laboratory with its superficial, transitory interaction between the experimental psychologist and his subject. Cooper and Michels (1978) tell us that "increasingly this [psychoanalytic] inquiry has recognized the analytic situation itself as paradigmatic for all human interactions" (p. 376). Indeed, the psychoanalytic method is said to be uniquely suited to first eliciting some of the important manifestations of the unconscious processes to which Freud's *depth* psychology pertains.

This superior *investigative value* of the analyst's clinical techniques is held to make the psychoanalytic interview at once the prime testing ground and the heuristic inspiration for Freud's theory of personality as well as for his therapy. Some leading orthodox analytic theoreticians have been concerned to *exclude* the so-called metapsychology of Freud's psychic energy model, and *a fortiori* its erstwhile neurobiological trappings from the avowed purview of clinical validation. Therefore it is to be understood that the term "psychoanalytic theory of personality" is here construed to *exclude* the metapsychology of psychic energy with its cathexes and anticathexes. In any case, most analysts have traditionally been quite skeptical, if not outright hostile, toward attempts to test Freudian theory experimentally *outside* the psychoanalytic interview.

Just such an assessment was enunciated again fairly by Luborsky and Spence (1978). They do issue the sobering caveat that "psychoanalysts, like other psychotherapists, literally *do not know* how they achieve their results" (p. 360), but they couple this disclaimer with the tribute that analysts "possess a unique store of clinical wisdom." Moreover, Luborsky and Spence emphasize that *"far more is known now* [in psychoanalysis] *through clinical wisdom than is known through quantitative* [i.e., controlled] *objective studies"* (p. 350). In short, they claim that—in this area—clinical confirmation is presently superior to experimentally obtained validation. They deem findings from the psychoanalytic session to have such epistemic superiority not only therapeutically but also in the validation of Freud's general theory of unconscious motivations (pp. 356-357). This view is also held by those who purport to have validated Kohut's currently influential variant of psychoanalysis, which supplants Freud's oedipal conflict by the child's *pre*oedipal narcissistic struggle for a cohesive self as the major determinant of adult personality structure (Ornstein in Kohut, 1978).

Despite their strong differences, both parties to the above dispute about the probative value of *clinical* data for the empirical appraisal of psychoanalytic theory do agree that at least part of the Freudian corpus is indeed cogently testable by empirical findings of *some* sort: The Freudians have the support of Glymour, for example, in contending that observations made within the confines of the treatment setting do or can afford sound testability, while such anti-Freudian protagonists as Eysenck make the contrary claim that well-conceived tests are possible, at least in principle, but *only* in the controlled environment of the laboratory or in other *extra*clinical contexts. Clearly the assumption of empirical testability shared by the disputants is likewise affirmed by someone who maintains that *both* clinical and extraclinical findings are suitable, at least in principle, for testing psychoanalysis.

This shared assumption of testability has been repeatedly denied *simpliciter* by Popper (1974) in his reply to his critics (pp. 984-985) and in his (1983, chap. II). There he reiterates his earlier claim that Freud's theory, as well as Adler's, are "simply non-testable, irrefutable. There was no conceivable human behaviour which would contradict them" (Popper, 1962, p. 37). It is then a mere corollary of this thesis of nontestability that *clinical* data, in particular, likewise cannot serve as a basis for genuine empirical tests.

CAN POPPER'S INDICTMENT OF FREUDIAN THEORY BE SUSTAINED?

In chapter 2 and in earlier publications, I have argued that neither the Freudian theory of personality nor the therapeutic tenet of psychoanalysis is untestable in Popper's sense (Grünbaum, 1976, 1977, 1979a, 1984, chap. 1, sec. B, and chap. 11). Furthermore, there I contended in detail that Popper's portrayal of psychoanalysis as a theory that is entitled to claim good *inductivist* credentials is predicated on a caricature of the requirements for theory validation laid down by such arch inductivists as Bacon and Mill. I pointed out that Freud's theory is replete with *causal* hypotheses and that the evidential conditions that must be met to furnish genuine inductive support for *such* hypotheses are very demanding. But I emphasized that precisely these exacting inductivist conditions were pathetically *unfulfilled* by those Freudians who claimed ubiquitous confirmation of the psychoanalytic corpus, to Popper's fully justified consternation.

Therefore, it will suffice here to supplement the critique I gave in chapter 2.

Being a strict determinist, Freud's etiologic quest was for *universal* hypotheses (1915a, p. 265), but he believed he had empirical grounds for holding that the development of a disorder N after an individual I suffered a pathogenic experience P depended on I's hereditary vulnerability. His universal etiologic hypotheses typically asserted that exposure to P is *causally necessary* for the development of N, *not* that it is causally sufficient.

Indeed, by claiming that P is the *specific* pathogen of N, he was asserting not only that P is causally necessary for N, but also that P is never, or hardly ever, an etiologic factor in the pathogenesis of any other nosologically distinct syndrome (Freud, 1895b, pp. 135-139). Robert Koch's specific etiology of tuberculosis, i.e., the pathogenic tubercle bacillus, served as a model. By the same token, Freud pointed to the tubercle bacillus to illustrate that a pathogen can be quite explanatory, although its mere presence does not guarantee the occurrence of the illness (1896, p. 209). And Freud was wont to conjecture *specific* etiologies for the various psychoneuroses until late in his career (1925b, p. 55). As illustrated by the above example of paranoia, these etiologies evidently have a high degree of empirical falsifiability, whenever empirical indicators can attest a differential diagnosis of N, as well as the absence of P. The hypothesis that P is the specific pathogen of N entails the universal prediction that every case of non-P will remain a non-N, and equivalently, the universal retrodiction that any N suffered P, although it does not predict whether a given exposure to P will issue in N. Thus Glymour's (1974) account of Freud's case history of the Rat-Man makes clear how Freud's specific etiology of the Rat-Man's obsession was impugned by means of disconfirming the retrodiction Freud had based on it. But, as I explained in chapter 4, this disconfirmation is predicated on specific auxiliary assumptions.

Let us return to our paranoia example of chapter 2. As I pointed out in earlier papers (Grünbaum, 1979a, pp. 138-139; 1986, pp. 266, 268) and mentioned briefly in chapters 1 and 2, Freud's etiology of paranoia likewise makes an important "statistical" prediction that qualifies as "risky" with respect to any rival "background" theory that denies the etiologic relevance of repressed homosexuality for paranoia. By Popper's standards, the failure of this prediction would count against Freud's etiology, whereas its success would corroborate it. I remind the reader that the epidemiologic testability I am about to claim pertains to *Freud's* theory of paranoia, not to the modified etiologies of other analysts, such as Gill, who bear the onus of showing that their versions are cogently testable at all. Hence it surely will not do to dismiss my avowal of epidemiologic testability as logically naïve on the irrelevant ground that Freud's etiology is held to be empirically "naïve."

To be specific, Freud (1911) originally hypothesized the etiology of (male) paranoia (Schreber case) along the following lines. Given the social taboo on (male) homosexuality, the failure to

repress homosexual impulses may well issue in feelings of severe anxiety and guilt. The latter anxiety could then be eliminated by converting the love emotion, "I love him," into its
opposite, "I hate him," a type of transformation Freud labeled
"reaction formation." The pattern of reaction formation is that
once a dangerous impulse has been largely repressed, it surfaces in the guise of a far more acceptable *contrary* feeling, a
conversion that therefore serves as a *defense* against the *anxiety*
associated with the underlying dangerous impulse. When the
defense of reaction formation proves insufficient to alleviate the
anxiety, however, the afflicted party may resort to the further
defensive maneuver of "projection" in which "I hate him" is
converted into "He hates me." This final stage of the employment of defenses is the full-blown paranoia. This rather epi-
grammatic formulation depicts reaction formation and projection as the repressed defense mechanisms that are actuated by
the postulated *specific* pathogen, i.e., repressed homosexuality.
But if just such repression is indeed the causally necessary etiologic factor in paranoia, then the decline of the taboo on homosexuality in our society should be accompanied by a decreased
incidence of (male) paranoia. For, on Freud's view and on that
of others, such as Herbert Marcuse, sociocultural prohibitions
and penalties also engender repressions. By the same token,
there ought to have been relatively less male paranoia in those
ancient societies in which male homosexuality was condoned
or even sanctioned, for the reduction of strong anxiety and
repression with respect to homosexual feelings would contribute to the removal of Freud's *conditio sine qua non* for this syndrome.

Incidentally, as Freud explains (1915a, p. 265), before he
enunciated universally that homosexuality is the specific pathogen of paranoia, he had declared more cautiously that it is
"perhaps an invariable" etiologic factor (1911, pp. 59-63).
When I first drew the above "statistical" prediction from
Freud's etiology (Grünbaum, 1979a, p. 139), I allowed for
Freud's more cautious early (1911) formulation. There I predicated the forecast of decreased incidence as a concomitant of
taboo decline on the *ceteris paribus* clause that no other potential

causes of paranoia become operative. By then avowing repressed homosexuality to be the *conditio sine qua non* of the syndrome (1915a), Freud's specific etiology clearly enables the prediction to go through *without* any such provision (Grünbaum, 1984, p. 111).

On the other hand, even assertions of pathogenic causal relevance that are logically *weaker* than the specific etiologies can be empirically disconfirmable. They can have testable (disconfirmable) predictive import, although they fall short of declaring P to be causally necessary for N. When pertinent empirical data fail to bear out the prediction that P positively affects the incidence of N, they bespeak the causal *irrelevance* of P to N. Consequently the currently hypothesized causal relevance of heavy cigarette smoking to lung cancer and cardiovascular disease is disconfirmable. So is the alleged causal relevance of laetril to cancer remission, which was reportedly discredited by recent findings in the United States.

The etiology Freud (1920b) conjectured for one of his female homosexual patients furnishes a useful case in point. He states its substance as follows:

> It was just when the girl was experiencing the revival of her infantile Oedipus complex at puberty that she suffered her great disappointment. She became keenly conscious of the wish to have a child, and a male one; that what she desired was her *father's* child and an image of *him*, her consciousness was not allowed to know. And what happened next? It was not *she* who bore the child, but her unconsciously hated rival, her mother. Furiously resentful and embittered, she turned away from her father and from men altogether. After this first great reverse she forswore her womanhood and sought another goal for her libido [p. 157].

But later on he cautions:

> We do not, therefore, mean to maintain that every girl who experiences a disappointment such as this of the longing for love that springs from the Oedipus attitude at puberty will necessarily on that account fall a victim to homosexuality. On the contrary, other kinds of reaction to this trauma are undoubtedly commoner [p. 168].

Thus he disclaims the predictability of lesbianism from the stated pubescent disappointment *in any one given case*. Yet the frustration does have disconfirmable predictive import, although its causal relevance is not claimed to be that of a specific pathogen, for by designating the stated sort of disappointment as *an* etiologic factor for lesbianism, Freud is claiming that occurrences of such disappointment *positively affect* the incidence of lesbianism.

This predictive consequence should be borne in mind, since Freud's case history of his lesbian patient occasioned his general observation that the etiologic explanation of an already existing instance of a disorder is usually not matched by the predictability of the syndrome *in any one given case* (1920b, pp. 167-168). An apologist for Popper was thereby led to conclude that the limitation on predictability in psychoanalysis avowed by Freud is tantamount to generic nonpredictability and hence to nondisconfirmability. But, oddly enough, this apologist is not inclined to regard the causal relevance of heavy smoking to cardiovascular disease as wholly nonpredictive or nondisconfirmable, although chain smoking is not even held to be a specific pathogen for this disease, let alone a universal predictor of it.

The comments I made so far in response to Popper should be completed by dealing with Freud's 1933 "Revision of the Theory of Dreams," which presents an acknowledged falsification by the recurrent dreams of war neurotics. The significance of that revision is discussed in chapter 10.

These are mere illustrations of falsifiability, but I trust they have prepared the ground for my claim that Popper's refutability criterion is too insensitive to reveal the genuinely egregious epistemic defects that indeed bedevil the clinical psychoanalytic method and the etiologies based on it. As I shall argue, time-honored inductivist canons for the validation of causal claims do have the capability to exhibit these cognitive deficits.

DOES NEO-BACONIAN INDUCTIVISM SANCTION THE TESTABILITY OF PSYCHOANALYTIC ETIOLOGIES BY CLINICAL DATA?

I should remind the reader that "clinical data" are here construed as findings coming from *within* the psychoanalytic treatment sessions. When I am concerned to contrast these data from the couch with observational results secured from *outside* the psychoanalytic interview, I shall speak of the former as *intra*clinical. Freud gave a cardinal epistemological defense of the psychoanalytic method of clinical investigation that seems to have gone entirely unnoticed in the literature, as far as I know, until I recently called attention to its significance. I have dubbed this pivotal defense the "Tally Argument" (Grünbaum, 1979b), and I shall use this designation hereafter (see also chap. 5 and Grünbaum, 1984, chap. 2).

As I pointed out in chapter 1, Erwin (1992) has discredited Sachs's (1989) objection that my attribution of the Tally Argument is exegetically unwarranted. Indeed, in my view, Sachs unwarrantly offers a reading that trivializes Freud's central thesis (Freud, 1916-17).

1. It was Freud's "Tally Argument"—or its bold lawlike master proposition—that was all at once his basis for five claims, each of which is of the first importance for the legitimation of the central parts of his theory. These claims are the following: (a) The denial of an irremediable epistemic contamination of clinical data by suggestion. (b) The affirmation of a crucial difference, in regard to the *dynamics* of therapy, between psychoanalytic treatment and all rival therapies that actually operate entirely by suggestion. (c) The assertion that the psychoanalytic method is able to validate its major causal claims—such as its specific sexual etiologies of the various psychoneuroses—by essentially *retrospective* methods without vitiation by *post hoc ergo propter hoc*, and without the burdens of prospective studies employing the controls of experimental inquiries. (d) The contention that favorable therapeutic outcome can be warrantedly attributed to psychoanalytic intervention *without* statistical comparisons pertaining to the results from untreated control groups. (e) The avowal that, once the patient's motivations are no longer distorted or hidden by repressed conflicts, credence can rightly be given to his or her introspective self-observations, because these data then do supply probatively significant information (cf. Waelder, 1962, pp. 628-629; Kohut, 1959).

Yet recent evidence has been accumulating that makes the principal premise of the Tally Argument well-nigh empirically untenable, devastatingly undermining the conclusions Freud drew from it. Indeed, no empirically plausible alternative to that crucial discredited premise capable of yielding Freud's desired conclusions seems to be in sight.

2. Without a viable replacement for Freud's Tally Argument there is woefully insufficient warrant to claim the intraclinical *validation* or, even to vindicate the intraclinical testability of the cardinal tenets of psychoanalysis—especially its ubiquitous causal claims—a testability espoused traditionally by analysts, and more recently by Glymour on the strength of the pincer-and-bootstrap strategy. This unfavorable conclusion is reached by the application of inductivist standards whose demands for the validation of causal claims can generally not be met intraclinically, unless the psychoanalytic method is buttressed by a powerful substitute for the defunct Tally Argument. In the absence of such a substitute, the epistemic decontamination of the bulk of the patient's productions on the couch from the suggestive effects of the analyst's communications appears to be quite utopian.

But even if the patient's clinical responses *could* be taken at face value as epistemologically uncontaminated, the moral of several chapters in this monograph would remain: Freud's principal clinical arguments for his cornerstone theory of repression are fundamentally flawed.

3. Insofar as the credentials of psychoanalytic theory are currenty held to rest on clinical findings, as most of its official spokesmen would have us believe, the dearth of acceptable and probatively cogent clinical data renders these credentials quite weak. And without a viable alternative to the aborted Tally Argument having comparable scope and ambition, the future validation of Freudian theory, if any, will have to come very largely from *extra*clinical findings.

4. Two years before his death, Freud (1937b) invoked the *consilience* or convergence of clinical inductions to determine the probative cogency of the patient's assent or dissent in response to interpretations presented by the analyst. But such a reliance on consilience is unavailing unless and until there emerges an as yet unimagined trustworthy method for epistemically decontaminating each of the *seemingly* independent consilient pieces of clinical evidence. For the methodological defects of Freud's "fundamental rule" of free association (1923c,

p. 238; 1925b, p. 41; 1940a, p. 174) ingress *alike* into the interpretation of several of these *prima facie* independent pieces of evidence (e.g., manifest dream content, parapraxes, waking fantasies). This multiple ingression renders the seeming consilience probatively spurious. Yet, even if clinical data could furnish genuinely consilient evidence for the prior operation of certain repressions in the patient's early life, this consilience would hardly show that these repressions *engendered* neuroses, dreams, or slips.

6. Given this dismal inductivist verdict, traditional inductivist methodology of theory appraisal no more countenances the *clinical* validation of psychoanalysis than Popper does (1962, p. 38). Hence, as noted in chapter 2, the specifically clinical confirmations claimed by many Freudians, but abjured as spurious by inductivist canons, are unavailable as a basis for Popper's charge of undue permissiveness against an inductivist criterion of demarcation between science and nonscience. The actual falsifiability of psychoanalysis demonstrated in chapters 2 and 10 undercuts his reliance on Freud's theory as a basis for claiming greater stringency for his falsifiability criterion of demarcation.

Now I shall focus solely on the major remaining issue posed by the *third* of these six theses. In chapters 4, 6 and 9, I argue in detail that there are fundamentally damaging flaws in the actual *clinical* arguments given by Freud and his disciples for the very foundation of his entire edifice: the theory of repression. I have contended that the actual clinical evidence adduced by Freudians provides no cogent basis for the repression etiology of neuroses, for the compromise model of manifest dream content, or for the causal attribution of parapraxes to repressed ideation. Elsewhere (Grünbaum, 1984, chap. 6), I canvassed solid evidence for the considerable epistemic contamination and hence lack of probative value on the part of three major kinds of clinical findings that Freud deemed either initially exempt from such adulteration or certifiably not marred by it because of due precautions: the products of "free" association, the patient's assent to analytic interpretations initially resisted, and memories recovered from early life.

Indeed, the epistemic adulteration I documented there seems to be *ineradicable* in just those patient responses that are supposed to lay bare his repressions and disguised defenses after his resistances have been overcome. Yet Freud attributed pride of place to these very data in the validation of his theory of repression, a doctrine that is avowedly "the corner-stone on which the whole structure of psycho-analysis rests . . . the most essential part of it" (1914b, p. 16). Generally speaking, clinical findings—in and of themselves—forfeit the probative value Freud claimed for them, although their potential heuristic merits may be substantial. To assert that the contamination of intraclinical data is *ineradicable* without extensive and essential recourse to *extra*clinical findings is *not*, of course, to declare the automatic falsity of any and every analytic interpretation which gained the patient's assent by means of prodding from the analyst. But it *is* to maintain—to the great detriment of intraclinical testability!—that, in general, the epistemic devices confined to the analytic setting cannot reliably *sift* or decontaminate the clinical data so as to *identify* those that may be adduced probatively (Grünbaum, 1986, pp. 275-277). Clearly all of these liabilities apply fully as much to the purported clinical validation of modified post-Freudian versions of his theory, such as Heinz Kohut's "self psychology" version of psychoanalysis, which places the major determinants of adult personality structure into an even earlier phase of childhood than Freud did (see Meyers, 1981; Basch, 1980, chap. 11).

One must admire the strenuous and ingenious efforts made by Freud (1923c) to legitimate his psychoanalytic method by arguing that it had precisely such an identifying capability. These efforts included the attempt to vouchsafe the probity of free associations by secluding their *contents* in the bastion of *internal* causal relatedness. Freud's dialectical exertions culminated in the generic underwriting of clinical investigations by the Tally Argument. But the empirical untenability of the cardinal premise of the Tally Argument that I have documented (see chaps. 1 and 5) has issued in the latter's collapse, leaving intraclinical validation defenseless against all the skeptical inroads from the substantial evidence for the distortion and tailoring of its data by such mechanisms as suggestion. Hence it is *unavailing* to take contaminated findings from the psychoanalytic interview more or less at face value, and then try to employ them probatively in some testing strategy whose *formal* structure is rational enough as such, and whose application to *other* contexts may be unproblematic—all the more so, since no viable substitute for the Tally Argument appears to be in sight. Indeed, the seeming ineradicability of epistemic contamination in the clinical data adduced as support for the cornerstones of the psychoanalytic edifice may reasonably be presumed to doom any prospects for the cogent intraclinical testing of the major tenets espoused by Freud.

These considerations can now be brought to bear on the scrutiny of Glymour's defense of clinical testability, outlined above. Glymour gives an illuminating reconstruction of Freud's account of the Rat-Man case by means of the logical pincer-and bootstrap strategy that Glymour had teased out of that account. I have no reason to gainsay this strategy in general, as far as it goes—but with or without it strong reasons militate against the intraclinical testability of the specific etiologic hypothesis that was at issue in the case of the Rat-Man, who suffered from an obsessional fear of rats. The present chapter supplements the treatment of the Rat-Man case given in chapter 4 by focusing on facts of the case relevant to *intraclinical testability*. In chapter 4, I also justified some simplifications that I employed in the current chapter.

At the time of the Rat-Man case, Freud had postulated that premature sexual activity such as excessive masturbation, subjected to severe repression, is the specific cause of obsessional neurosis. As will be recalled, in his carefully defined usage of "specific cause," the claim that X is the specific cause of Y entails unilaterally that X is causally *necessary* for Y. And the latter asserts that being an X *makes a difference* to being a Y *at least* to the extent that (a) any non-X has to be a non-Y, *and* (b) the (nonempty) class of X's is to have a positive incidence of Y's. This conjunction, in turn, unilaterally entails that all cases of Y were X's. Thus if this *particular consequence* of the conjectured sexual etiology is to get confirmation from the Rat-Man's psychoanalysis, the intraclinical data yielded by it need to be able to certify the following: The Rat-Man, who was an adult victim of obsessional neurosis, engaged in precocious sexual activity, which was then repressed. Let us inquire first whether intraclinical data produced by the adult patient can *reliably* attest the actual occurrence of a childhood event of the stated sort. Even if the answer to this question were positive, this much would be quite insufficient to support Freud's etiologic hypothesis that repressed precocious sexual activity is *causally relevant* to adult obsessional neurosis.

As Glymour (1980) notes, "Freud had . . . arrived at a retrodicted state of affairs, namely, the patient's having been punished by his father for masturbation" (p. 272). And indeed, "the crucial question is whether or not the Rat-Man was in fact punished by his father for masturbation" (p. 273). But Freud's specific etiology of adult obsessional neurosis as such calls only for an early childhood event in which precocious sexual activity was repressed. Why then should it be probatively "crucial" whether it was the patient's *father* who was involved in the sexual event required by the hypothesized etiology?

As is clear from Freud's account, the elder's involvement became probatively weighty because of the unconscious significance that psychoanalytic theory assigns to the patient's recollection of recurring fears of his father's death, at least after the age of 6. While having these fears, the child bore his father deep conscious affection. Freud derived the presumed unconscious origin of the fears from a theoretical postulate of so-called precise contrariety, which he took pains to communicate to the patient, who then became "much agitated at this and very incredulous" (1909b, p. 180). Freud both explains his reasoning and revealingly relates his indoctrination of the patient:

> . . . he was quite certain that his father's death could never have been an object of his desire but only of his fear.—After his forcible enunciation of these words I thought it advisable to bring a fresh piece of theory to his notice. According to psycho-analytic theory, I told him, every fear corresponded to a former wish which was now repressed; we were therefore obliged to believe the exact contrary of what he had asserted. This would also fit in with another theoretical requirement, namely, that the unconscious must be the precise contrary of the conscious.—He was much agitated at this and very incredulous. He wondered how

he could possibly have had such a wish, considering that he loved his father more than any one else in the world. . . . I answered that it was precisely such intense love as his that was the necessary precondition of the repressed hatred [1909b, pp. 179-180].

Having thus theoretically inferred the patient's deep childhood grudge against his father from the recurring fears of losing the father, Freud also conjectured that the grudge remained so durably unconscious only because it was a response to the father's interference with the patient's sensual gratification.

This conclusion was, then, serendipitous in suggesting that there had been an early event satisfying the specific etiology Freud had hypothesized for the Rat-Man's obsessional neurosis. Since this etiology required precocious masturbation events, Freud retrodicted that the patient had been punished by his father for masturbation "in his very early childhood . . . before he had reached the age of six" (p. 183). Clearly the actual occurrence of an event having these attributes would *simultaneously* satisfy the initial condition of the postulated etiology and explain the Rat-Man's early dread of his father's death via Freud's principle of precise contrariety.

Let us now suppose, just for argument's sake, that Freud's avowedly *well-coached* adult patient had actually reported having a memory of the very early childhood event Freud had retrodicted. Then I ask: Could such a clinical event have reliably attested the actual occurrence of the distant event? I have framed this question hypothetically because it so happened that the Rat-Man actually had no *direct* memory of any physical punishment by his father, let alone of a punishment for a *sexual* offense. He did remember having been *told* repeatedly by his *mother* that there had been *one* incident of angry conflict with his father at age 3 or 4, when he was beaten by him. And when the mother was asked whether this beating had been provoked by a misdeed of a sexual nature, her answer was negative. Furthermore, this was apparently the *only* beating the child had ever received from the father. In chapter 4, section II, item 2, I noted the discrepancy between Freud's published case history and his own original record of the case, where mention is made of a *further* paternal punishment.

But for the purpose of our inquiry, we are positing that, at some point in his analysis, the patient had claimed to remember just the kind of early childhood event Freud had retrodicted via his specific etiology of obsessional neurosis. Then I am concerned to show that, taken by itself, such a finding would be insufficient to lend any significant support to the hypothesized etiology of obsessional neurosis. And my reasons for this claim will then enable me to argue quite generally for the following conclusion: Given the demise of the Tally Argument, the intraclinical testing of the causal assertions made by Freud's specific etiologies of the psychoneuroses, and by his ontogenetic developmental hypotheses, is *epistemically quite hopeless*.

Let N (neurosis) denote a psychoneurosis such as the syndrome of obsessional neurosis, while P (pathogen) denotes the kind of sex-related antecedent event that Freud postulated to be the specific cause of N. Thus I shall say that a person who had a sexual experience of the sort P is a P. And if that person was then afflicted by N, I shall say that he was both a P and an N. It is taken for granted, of course, that *there are* both N's and non-N's, as well as P's and non-P's. To support Freud's etiologic hypothesis that P is causally necessary for N, evidence must be produced that being a P *makes a difference* to being an N. But such causal relevance is *not* attested by *mere* instances of N that were P's, i.e., by patients who are both P's and N's. For even a large number of such cases does not preclude that just as many *non-P*'s would also become N's, if followed in a longitudinal study from childhood onward! Thus instances of N that were P's may just *happen* to have been P's, whereas being a P has no etiologic role at all in becoming an N.

A telling, sobering illustration of this moral is given by the following conclusion from a review of 40 years of research (Frank, 1965):

> No factors were found in the parent-child interaction of schizophrenics, neurotics, or those with behavior disorders which could be identified as unique to them or which could distinguish one group from the other, or any of the groups from the families of the [normal] controls [p. 191].

Hence it is insufficient evidence for causal relevance that any
N who turns out to have been a P does instantiate the retrodiction "All N's were P's," which is entailed by Freud's specific
etiology. To provide evidence for the causal relevance claimed
by Freud, we need to *combine* instances of N that were P's with
instances of non-P who are *non-N's*. Since he deemed P to be
causally necessary for N—rather than just causally relevant—his
etiology requires that the class of non-P's should not contain
any N's whatever, whereas the class of P's is to have a positive
(though numerically unspecified) incidence of N's.

Although Hempel's (1965, chap. 1) paradox has taught us
otherwise, just for the sake of argument, let us grant that since
"All N's are (were) P's" is logically equivalent to "All non-P's
are (will be) non-N's," any case of an N who was a P will support
the latter to whatever extent it supports the former. But this
fact is unavailing to the support of Freud's etiology, for the
issue is *not* merely to provide evidential support for "All non-
P's are (will be) non-N's," or for its logical equivalent, by some
instances. The issue is to furnish evidential support for the
(strong kind of) *causal relevance* claimed by Freud. For the reasons I have given, the fulfillment of that requirement demands
that there be cases of non-P's that are non-N's no less than
instances of N's that were P's. Yet *at best*, the Rat-Man could
furnish only the *latter* kind of instance. In other words, if we
are to avoid committing the fallacy of *post hoc ergo propter hoc*,
we cannot be content with instances of N's that were P's, no
matter how numerous. Analogously, suppose it were hypothesized that drinking coffee is causally relevant to overcoming the
common cold. And consider the case of a recovered cold suf-
ferer who retrospectively turns out to have been drinking coffee while still afflicted with the cold. Such an instance, taken by
itself, would hardly qualify as *supportive* of the hypothesized
causal relevance.

Advocates of psychoanalytic theory and therapy (e.g., Luborsky et al., 1985) have often encouraged the disregard and even
flouting of the elementary safeguards against the pitfalls of
causal inference familiar since the days of Francis Bacon, not
to speak of J. S. Mill (Grünbaum, 1986, pp. 278-279). Yet even
informed laymen in our culture are aware that such safeguards

are indeed heeded *in medicine* before there is public assent to
the validity of such etiologic claims as "heavy tobacco smoking
causes cardiovascular disease." This double standard of evidential rigor in the validation of etiologic hypotheses even makes
itself felt in current criminal law. Legal prohibitions—and so-
called expert psychiatric testimony in courts of law—are sometimes predicated on such hypotheses even when the empirical
support for the pathogenicity they allege is no better than that
blithe repetition has turned them into articles of faith.

The recently publicized reiteration of the purported pathogenicity of child molestation in opposition to its decriminaliza-
tion is a case in point. In our society, such sexual molestation
is often alleged to be pathogenic, even when it is affectionate
and tender rather than violent. And this allegation has been
invoked to justify making it illegal and fraught with substantial
penalties. Yet recently a number of sexologists have maintained
that very young children should be allowed, and perhaps even
encouraged, to have sex with adults, unencumbered by interference from the law. In their view, such activity itself is harmless to the child and becomes harmful only when parents raise
a fuss about it. Indeed, *some* of these advocates have made
the daring and quite unfashionable etiologic claim that unless
children do have early sex, their psychological development will
go awry. And even the less daring champions of harmlessness
are opposed to jailing affectionate pedophiles.

Reasons of elementary prudence and also of humaneness
make it a good policy, in my view, to put the burden of proof
on those who maintain that affectionate and tender child molestation is *not* even distressing to the child, let alone pathogenic.
But a cautionary basis for a legal prohibition is a far cry from
the confident assertion of demonstrated pathogenicity. The difference between mere caution and authenticated causation of
neurosis may, of course, be relevant to the severity of the punishment appropriate for violations of the interdiction.

In a 1981 issue of *Time* magazine, John Leo inveighed etiologically *against* the demand to legalize tender pedophilia, which
he sees as a thinly disguised manifesto for child molesters' liber-
ation. He offers the following justification for his indictment:

Unfortunately, few responsible child experts have reacted . . . so far to the radical writing on child sex. One who has is Child Psychiatrist Leon Eisenberg of Children's Hospital Medical Center, Boston: "Premature sexual behavior among children in this society almost always leads to psychological difficulties because you have a child acting out behavior for which he is not cognitively or emotionally ready. . . .
Psychotherapist Sam Janus, author of a new book, *The Death of Innocence*, says that people who were seduced early in life "go through the motions of living and may seem all right, but they are damaged. I see these people year after year in therapy."
U.C.L.A. Psychiatrist Edward Ritvo also says that much of his work is with children who have been involved in catastrophic sexual situations. His conclusion: "Childhood sexuality is like playing with a loaded gun" [September 7, 1981, p. 69].

But the etiologic reasoning of those whom *Time* cites to document the pernicious effects of child molestation is just as shoddy as the causal inferences of those advocates of pedophilia who claim dire psychological consequences from the *failure* of infant boys to act on their erections, and of infant girls to utilize their vaginal lubrications, for the findings adduced by *Time* do not answer either of the following two questions: (1) Is the occurrence of childhood seduction not equally frequent among those who are well enough never to see a psychotherapist? In the parlance of John Stuart Mill, this question calls for the use of the *joint* method of agreement and difference, rather than just the heuristic method of agreement. (2) Would a representative sample of those who were *not* seduced in childhood have a significantly *lower* incidence of adult neurosis than those who *were* seduced? By the same token, we must ask those who claim seduction to be *beneficial* psychologically to show that those who were indeed seduced *fared better* psychologically than those who were not sexually active in this way. Without the appropriate answers to these questions, the respective assertions of causal relevance remain gratuitous.

Thus we must ask those who *condemn* childhood seduction the foregoing questions, because it may be that childhood seduction just *happens* to be quite common among neurotics, even though it has no etiologic role in the production of neurosis. In that case, the same people would have become neurotics anyway, in the absence of early seduction. Without answers to these questions, the evidence given by those whom *Time* invokes as authorities merely suggests the bare *possibility* that childhood seduction is pathogenic. By the same token, certain analysts have overlooked the fact that repressed homosexual feelings cannot be shown to be the pathogen of adult paranoia, by merely pointing to the frequency of homosexually tinged themes in the associative output of paranoiacs during analysis. This finding does not tell us whether homosexual themes would not likewise turn up to the same extent in the so-called free associations of nonparanoiacs who lead well-adjusted lives and never see a therapist. Here no less than in the case of the Rat-Man, the invocation of J. S. Mill's heuristic method of agreement is not enough to lend support to the hypothesis of etiologic relevance.

Even if the Rat-Man did in fact have the sexually repressive experience *P* retrodicted via Freud's etiology of obsessional neurosis, this alone would hardly qualify as evidential support for that etiology. And there is a further reason for concluding that even if the Rat-Man as a child had actually been punished by his father for masturbating, as retrodicted via Freud's etiology, this putative occurrence would confer little, if any, support on this etiology. As Ronald Giere has remarked (in a private communication), the occurrence of this sort of event is to be routinely expected in the Victorian child-rearing culture of the time on grounds *other than* psychoanalytic theory.

Moreover, Freud had made the adult Rat-Man patient well aware, as we saw, of the inferences that Freud had drawn about his childhood via psychoanalytic theory. Given the substantial evidence adduced in chapter 5 for the notorious docility of patients in analysis, I submit that one ought to discount the Rat-Man's *putative* early childhood memory as too contaminated to attest reliably the actual occurrence of the retrodicted early event (see also Grünbaum, 1984, chaps. 2, 4-6).

It can be granted, of course, that requirements of consistency or at least overall coherence afford the analyst *some* check on what the patient alleges to be *bona fide* memories. But Freud's own writings attest to the untrustworthiness of purported adult memories of early childhood episodes that had presumably been repressed in the interim and then retrieved by the analysis. Indeed, the malleability of adult memories from childhood is epitomized by a report from Jean Piaget (Loftus, 1980, pp. 119-121), who thought he remembered vividly an attempt to kidnap him from his baby carriage along the Champs Elysées. He recalled the gathered crowd, the scratches on the face of the heroic nurse who saved him, the policeman's white baton, the assailant running away. However vivid, Piaget's recollections were false. Years later the nurse confessed she had made up the entire story, which he then internalized as a presumed experience under the influence of an authority figure.

The discounting of the Rat-Man's putative early childhood memory is hardly a general derogation of the reliability of adult memories in ordinary life. But in the clinical context, the *posited* memory is simply not sufficiently dependable to qualify as evidence for the retrodicted event. Thus the retrospective intraclinical ascertainment of the actual occurrence of the retrodicted distant event is just too unreliable. The patient's memory may simply fail to recall whether the pertinent event did occur, as Freud himself stressed (1920a, p. 18; 1937b, pp. 265-266). Even in survey studies of lung cancer patients who are asked about their prior smoking habits, and of heroin addicts who are questioned about previous use of marijuana, the retrospective ascertainment of the actual occurrence of the suspected causal condition is epistemically flawed (Giere, 1979, pp. 216, 265).

Have I provided adequate grounds for maintaining that long-term *prospective* studies, which employ control groups and spring the clinical confines of the usual psychoanalytic setting, must supplant the *retrospective* clinical testing of etiology defended by Glymour? Not just yet. Suppose analysts could secure reasonable numbers of patients who, though presumed to need analysis for a neurotic affliction, are certifiably free of the *particular* neurosis N (say, obsessional neurosis) whose etiology is currently at issue. Since neuroses usually occur in mixed rather than pure form, this is a generous assumption. All the same, let us operate with it. Now postulate, *merely for argument's sake*, that, though retrospective, psychoanalytic inquiry *were* typically able to ascertain *reliably* whether a given case of non-N was indeed a non-P or a P.

What then is the probative value of patients who are *neither* N's nor P's? Would such people, together with other persons who are both N's and P's, jointly bespeak that P is pathogenic for N (*obsessional* neurosis) *within the class of all persons*?

Note that the intraclinical testing design I have envisaged for scrutiny had to be *confined* to the class of neurotics, for even the non-N's of this design are presumed to be afflicted by some neurosis other than N. The reason is that persons who have practically no neuroses of any sort are hardly available to analysts in sufficient numbers to carry out the putative retrospective determination of whether they were non-P's or P's. But the confinement of this retrospective clinical determination to the class of neurotics has the following consequence: Even if every observed non-N (nonobsessive neurotic) is a non-P while every observed N is a P, these combined instances lend credence only to the hypothesis that, *within the class of neurotics*, P is etiologically relevant to N. But these putative combined instances do not support the Freudian claim of such etiologic relevance within the wider class of persons, which comprises both neurotics and nonneurotics.

In short, the Freudian clinical setting does *not* have the epistemic resources to warrant that P is *neurosogenic*. And this unfavorable conclusion emerges even though it was granted, for argument's sake, that the retrospective methods of psychoanalytic inquiry can determine *reliably* whether adult neurotics who are nonobsessives were non-P's in early life.

But is it reasonable to posit such reliability? It would seem not, for clearly, even if the patient believes to have the required memories, the retrospective clinical ascertainability of whether a given non-N was actually a non-P is epistemically on a par with the psychoanalytic determination of whether a given N was a P. And, as we saw, the latter is unreliable. Moreover, as Freud himself acknowledged, "the patient cannot remember the whole of what is repressed in him, and what he cannot remember may be precisely the essential part of it" (1920a, p. 18). Thus, even if—contrary to my argument—*reliable* intraclinical data *could* cogently validate etiologic relevance, their sheer unavailability negates the feasibility of such validation.

Now contrast the stated epistemic liabilities of the retrospective psychoanalytic inference that a given adult patient was or was not a *P* during his early childhood with the assets of *prospective* controlled inquiry: A *present* determination would be made, under suitably supervised conditions, that children in the experimental and control groups are *P*'s and non-*P*'s respectively; again, during long-term follow-ups, later findings as to *N* or non-*N* would also be made in what is then the present.

Although Freud's specific etiologies did not specify numerically the percentage of *P*'s who become *N*'s, it is noteworthy that only prospective investigation can yield the information needed for such a statistical refinement. Let us suppose that retrospective data confirm the retrodiction of Freud's specific etiology that the incidence of *P*'s within the sample group of *N*'s is 100 percent. This percentage incidence clearly would not permit an inference as to the percentage incidence of *N*'s within the class of *P*'s. Yet such information is clearly desirable, if only in order to estimate the probability that a child who was subjected to *P* will become an *N*. More generally, when *P* is not deemed causally necessary for *N*, but merely causally relevant, retrospective data simply do not yield any estimates of *P*'s degree of causal effectiveness (Giere, 1979, pp. 274, 277).

Our inquiry into the Rat-Man case so far has operated with a *counterfactual* posit in order to discuss the reliability of clinical data by reference to this case. The *hypothetical* clinical datum we used was that the patient *had* reported having a memory of the early childhood event retrodicted by Freud. As against Glymour's generic thesis that the specific psychoanalytic etiologies can be cogently tested "on the couch," I have argued that, at least typically, such testing is epistemically quite hopeless. Hence it would seem that the Rat-Man's psychoanalysis would have failed to furnish adequate evidential support for the *etiologic relevance* of childhood sexual repression to obsessional neurosis, even if the Rat-Man's father had reliably reported having repeatedly punished his young son for masturbation. Incidentally, when Waelder defended the clinical confirmation of the psychoanalytic etiologies, he overlooked precisely that their substantiation requires evidential support for the *causal relevance* of the purportedly pathogenic experience, and not merely the historical authentication of the bare occurrence of that experience (1962, pp. 625-626).

Let us return to Glymour's account of the testing strategy in the Rat-Man's analysis, which was predicated on his failure, in actual fact, to have any *direct* recall of receiving a punishment from his father, let alone a castigation for a sexual offense. Let us now see how Glymour evaluated the probative significance of this finding. I shall be concerned to stress the scope that Glymour gives to *essential* reliance on *extra*clinical data for probative purposes. Indeed, it will turn out that the entire testing procedure in the Rat-Man case comes out to be probatively *parasitic* on an extraclinical finding. Hence I wonder how Glymour can see himself as rebutting Eysenck's denial of intraclinical testability, although he does succeed in impugning the demand that all extraclinical disconfirmation be *experimental*.

By Glymour's own account of the Rat-Man case, the probatively "crucial" data came from the *extra*clinical testimony of the patient's mother. On Glymour's reading of Freud, at the time of the Rat-Man's analysis, Freud still postulated *actual* rather than fancied early sexual experiences to be the pathogens of obsessional neurosis (Glymour, 1980, pp. 274-275). As Glymour explains lucidly, what made the Rat-Man's case a *counterexample* to this etiology was *not* the mere failure of the patient to recall the event retrodicted by Freud. Instead, it was the *extra*clinical testimony from the *mother* that had this negative probative import (p. 273). It was her testimony that supplied the probatively crucial datum by contravening Freud's retrodiction, when she answered the question Glymour characterized as "the crucial question." He himself characterizes "the memory of an adult observer"—in this case that of the mother—as "the most reliable available means" for answering this decisive question as to the character of the offense for which the child had been punished (p. 273). How, then, in the face of the *extra*clinical status of the *decisive* datum, can Glymour justify his description of the testing rationale used in the Rat-Man case as "a strategy that relies almost exclusively on clinical evidence"? (Glymour, 1974, p. 287).

It is true enough that, as we know from the case history of the Wolf-Man, Freud (1918) regarded stories told by other

members of the family to the patient about his childhood to be
"absolutely authentic" and hence admissible data (p. 14 n.).
Other analysts, however, are far more skeptical (Meissner,
1978, p. 155). But even Freud completes his assertion by cau-
tioning that responses by the patient's relatives to pointed inquiries from the analyst—or from the patient *while in analysis*—may well be contaminated by misgivings on their part:

> So it may seem tempting to take the easy course of filling up the
> gaps in a patient's memory by making enquiries from the older
> members of his family; but I cannot advise too strongly against
> such a technique. Any stories that may be told by relatives in
> reply to enquiries and requests are at the mercy of every critical
> misgiving that can come into play. One invariably regrets having
> made oneself dependent upon such information; at the same
> time confidence in the analysis is shaken and a court of appeal
> is set up over it. Whatever can be remembered at all will anyhow
> come to light in the further course of analysis [Freud, 1918, p.
> 14 n.].

Even if one were to discount Freud's caveat against distorted
responses from the family, several facts remain: (1) It is misleading to claim intraclinical testability if, as in the Rat-Man
case, the avowedly crucial datum does *not* come from "the
couch." (2) What makes the reliance on extraclinical devices
important is that, far from being marginal epistemically, its
imperativeness derives from the typically present probative defects of the analytic setting, defects insufficiently acknowledged
by Glymour. In my view, it does not lessen the liabilities of
intraclinical testing that the compensations for some of its deficits from *outside* the clinical setting *may occasionally* be available
in situ (e.g., from family records) and thus do not necessarily
require the experimental laboratory. Even when supplemented
by such nonexperimental, extraclinical devices, the thus enlarged "clinical" testing procedure is not adequate or *epistemically autonomous*. For example, when it becomes necessary to
resort to extraclinical information for the sort of reason that
was operative in the Rat-Man case, it will be a matter of mere
happenstance whether suitable relatives are even available, let
alone whether they can *reliably* supply the missing essential information. As Freud himself pointed out (1909b, p. 207): "It is

seldom that we are in the fortunate position of being able, as in the present instance, to establish the facts upon which these tales of the individual's prehistoric past are based, by recourse to the unimpeachable testimony of a grown-up person." Why then dignify as a "clinical testing strategy" a procedure of inquiry that depends on such contingent good fortunes and, when luck runs out, cannot dispense with experimental or epidemiologic information? (3) The issue is whether the clinical setting *typically*—rather than under contingently favorable circumstances—does have the epistemic resources for the cogent testing and even validation of the etiology at issue in the Rat-Man case, and of other analytic etiologies. In dealing with that issue, Glymour's otherwise illuminating account has not demonstrated the existence of such a cogent intraclinical testing strategy, even if he succeeded in showing that extraclinical compensations for its lacunae need not be experimental.

Indeed, the extent of his essential epistemic reliance on extraclinical findings can now be gauged from his view of the effect that Freud's modifications of the specific sexual etiology of obsessional neurosis (and of other neuroses) had on the *testability* of these evolving etiologic hypotheses. Glymour (1980) recounts this evolution:

> After the turn of the century and before 1909, . . . there is no statement of the view that sexual phantasies formed in childhood or subsequently, having no real basis in fact, may themselves serve *in place of* sexual experiences as etiological factors. . . . Yet after the Rat Man case the view that either infantile sexual experiences *or* phantasies of them may equally serve as etiological factors became a standard part of Freud's theory. In *Totem and Taboo*, four years after the Rat Man case appeared, Freud emphasized that the guilt that obsessional neurotics feel is guilt over a happening that is psychically real but need not actually have occurred. By 1917 Freud not only listed phantasies themselves as etiological factors alternative to real childhood sexual experiences, but omitted even the claim that the former are usually or probably based on the latter. The effect of these changes is to remove counterexamples like that posed by the Rat Man case, but at the cost of making the theory less easily testable. For whereas Freud's theories, until about 1909, required quite definite events to take place in the childhood of a neurotic, events that could be witnessed and later recounted by adults, Freud's

> later theory required no more than psychological events in child-
> hood, events that might well remain utterly private [pp. 276-
> 277].

Thus Glymour attributes the diminishing testability of Freud's
modified etiologies quite rightly to the lessening *extra*clinical
ascertainability of the sorts of events Freud successively postulated as etiologic. But if the testability of the psychoanalytic
etiologies is in fact "almost exclusively" intraclinical, as Glymour
told us, why should it be *vital* for their testability that the etiologic events required by Freud's later theory are just mental
states of the patient to which only the patient himself and his
analyst become privy in the treatment setting?

Incidentally, the problem of testing Freud's sexual etiology
of the neuroses—either clinically or extraclinically—became less
well defined after he gave up the quest for qualitatively *specific*
pathogens of nosologically distinct psychoneuroses in favor of
a generic oedipal etiology for all of them. In fact, he used the
analogy of explaining the great qualitative differences among
the chemical substances by means of quantitative variations in
the proportions in which the same elements were combined.
But having thus dissolved his prior long-standing concern with
the problem of "the choice of neurosis," he was content to
leave it at vague metapsychological remarks about the constant
intertransformation of "narcissistic libido" and "object libido"
(Freud, 1925b, pp. 55-56).

What of Glymour's reliance on *intra*clinical data? In that context, he seems to have taken much too little cognizance of even
the evidence furnished by such analysts as Marmor (1962, p.
289) that intraclinically the suggestibility problem is radically
unsolved, if not altogether insoluble, a difficulty put into bolder
relief by the lack of a viable substitute for the defunct Tally
Argument.

Sachs (1989, pp. 353-354) has adduced Freud's (1916-17, p.
453) appeal to the alleged *total nonsuggestibility* of psychotics, and
the purported support of their productions for his hypotheses
concerning neurotics. But, as I document in detail in my forth-
coming reply to Sachs, and as shown by Erwin (1992), Freud's
allegation of utter nonsuggestibility of psychotics is untenable.

Indeed, catatonic schizophrenics exhibit several forms of *hyper*-suggestibility *alongside* their negativism or contrasuggestibility. Thus, the Oxford *Psychiatric Dictionary* (Campbell, 1989, p. 112) points out that "Catalepse [the maintenance of imposed postures] is regarded as a high degree of suggestibility and is often also cited [in catatonic schizophrenics] with other forms of suggestibility, such as echopraxia [repetition of actions seen], echolalia [repetition of words heard], command automatisms." Nary a word from Freud concerning these phenomena; just the pretense, in a single sweeping paragraph, that there is nothing but contrasuggestibility. And evidently Sachs did not know better.

Can we place any stock in Glymour's aspiration that clinicians can be "trained so as not to elicit by suggestion the expected responses from their patients"? In view of the evidence for the *ineradicability* of suggestive contamination, it would now seem that this hope is sanguine to the point of being utopian. Glymour (1982) has reacted to some of these particular doubts as follows:

> I do not see . . . that the experimental knowledge we now have about suggestibility requires us to renounce clinical evidence altogether. Indeed, I can imagine circumstances in which clinical evidence might have considerable force: when, for example, the clinical proceedings show no evident sign of indoctrination, leading the patient, and the like; when the results obtained fall into a regular and apparently lawlike pattern obtained independently by many clinicians; and when those results are contrary to the expectation and belief of the clinician. I do not intend these as *criteria* for using clinical evidence, but only as indications of features which, in combination, give weight to such evidence.

To this I reply:

1. I do *not* maintain that any and all clinical data are altogether irrelevant probatively. Instead, I hold that such findings cannot possibly bear the probative burden placed on them by those who claim, as Glymour did, that psychoanalysis can *typically* be validated or invalidated "on the couch," using a clinical strategy that is essentially confined to the analytic setting.

2. The existence of *some* circumstances which would warrant not renouncing clinical evidence "altogether" is surely not

enough to sustain clinical testing as a largely cogent and essentially autonomous scientific enterprise. As for Glymour's illustrations of such circumstances, I cannot see that absence of evident indoctrination, or regular concordance among the results obtained independently by many clinicians, exemplify circumstances under which "clinical evidence might have considerable force." Apart from contamination by covert or unwitting suggestion from the analyst (Grünbaum, 1984, p. 212), it seems to me that the utopian character of Glymour's illustrations here as a step toward solving the compliance problem is epitomized by the sobering results reported by Marmor (1962):

> . . . depending upon the point of view of the analyst, the patients of each [rival psychoanalytic] school seem to bring up precisely the kind of phenomenological data which confirm the theories and interpretations of their analysts! Thus each theory tends to be self-validating. Freudians elicit material about the Oedipus Complex and castration anxiety, Jungians about archetypes, Rankians about separation anxiety, Adlerians about masculine strivings and feelings of inferiority, Horneyites about idealized images. Sullivanians about disturbed interpersonal relationships, etc. [p. 289].

3. I do not deny at all that *now and then* clinical results "are contrary to the expectations and belief of the clinicians," but as a step toward vindicating clinical inquiry *qua* epistemically autonomous testing strategy, I can only say, "One swallow does not a summer make."

What seems to emerge from Glymour's interesting reconstruction is that, on the whole, data from the couch *acquire* probative significance when they are independently corroborated by extraclinical findings, or inductively concur with such findings by pointing to the same hypothesis. I do not maintain that any and all clinical data are altogether irrelevant probatively, but this much only conditionally confers *potential* relevance on intraclinical results beyond their heuristic value. Surely this is not enough to vindicate testability on the couch in the sense claimed by its Freudian exponents (e.g., Brenner, 1982, p. 5).

9

THE LOGICAL FOUNDATIONS OF THE CLINICAL THEORY OF REPRESSION

Freud (1924) has emphasized that Breuer's "cathartic method (of therapy and clinical investigation) was the immediate precursor of psycho-analysis; and, in spite of every extension of experience and of every modification of theory, is still contained within it as its nucleus" (p. 194). Breuer used hypnosis to revive and articulate the patient's memory of a *repressed* traumatic experience which had presumably occasioned the first appearance of a particular hysterical symptom. Thereby Freud's mentor induced a purgative release of the pent-up emotional distress that had been originally bound to the trauma. Since such cathartic reliving of a previously repressed trauma seemed to yield relief from the particular hysterical symptom, Breuer and Freud hypothesized that repression is a causal *sine qua non* for the pathogenesis of the patient's psychoneurosis (Breuer and Freud, 1893, pp. 6-7; Freud, 1893, pp. 29-30).

This *etiologic* role of repressed ideation then became prototypic for much of Freud's own theory of unconscious motivations. Repressed *wishes* were postulated to be the motives of *all* dreaming, and sundry repressed mentation was deemed to cause the bungling of actions at which the subject is normally successful—"parapraxes" such as slips of the tongue or pen; instances of mishearing or misreading; cases of forgetting of words, intentions, or events; and mislaying or losing of objects

(Freud, 1916-17, pp. 25, 67). Thus, even in the case of "normal" people, Freud saw manifest dream content and various sorts of "slips" as the telltale symptoms of (temporary) *mini*neuroses, engendered by repressions.

He arrived at the purported sexual repression etiologies of the psychoneuroses, as well as at the supposed causes of dreams and parapraxes, by lifting presumed repressions via the patient's allegedly "free" associations. At the same time, excavation of the pertinent repressed ideation was to remove the pathogens of the patient's afflictions. Scientifically, Freud deemed the psychoanalytic method of investigation to be both heuristic *and* causally probative, over and above being a method of therapy. By the same token, he declared that "the theory of repression is the cornerstone on which the whole structure of psychoanalysis rests. It is the most essential part of it" (1914b, p. 16), and he claimed that clinical evidence furnishes compelling support for this theoretical cornerstone. Therefore, we can scrutinize the logical foundations of psychoanalytic theory by examining Freud's clinical arguments for the repression etiology of the psychoneuroses and for the cardinal causal role of repressed ideation in committing "Freudian slips" and in dreaming. An *overview* of such a scrutiny was given in chapter 1.

This chapter will develop in some detail the sketch of Freud's theory of psychopathology given in that initial overview. Its upshot will be that the reasoning by which Freud sought to justify the very foundation of his theoretical edifice was grievously flawed. The same verdict applies to the principal post-Freudian formulations insofar as they are psychoanalytic in substance, rather than mainly in name (Eagle, 1984a, 1984b; Grünbaum, 1984, chap. 7).

In the next chapter, I shall offer a novel scrutiny of the three major stages of Freud's theory of dreams, which will be a considerable extension of my earlier criticisms (Grünbaum, 1984, chap. 5). It was the burden of my previous strictures to show that the dream theory was evidentially ill-founded. But in chapter 10 below, I shall contend that it should be deemed false.

I do not know of any viable challenge to the animadversions on the psychoanalytic theory of slips I presented in my earlier book (Grünbaum, 1984, chap. 4). Erwin (1992) has shown that Sachs's (1989) objections to my account are without merit, and elsewhere I shall give further reasons for denying their cogency. Therefore, I stand by my earlier arguments and need not deal with parapraxes here.

THE REPRESSION ETIOLOGY OF THE PSYCHONEUROSES

Breuer and Freud explicitly adduced the separate *therapeutic* removal of particular neurotic symptoms, by means of undoing repressions having a thematic and associative affinity to these very symptoms, as their *evidence* for attributing a cardinal *causal* role in symptom formation to the repression of traumatic events. Let us look at the intermediate reasoning on which the founders of psychoanalysis relied to claim therapeutic support for their etiologic identification of an original act of repression as the specific pathogen initially responsible for the formation of the neurotic symptom.

They extrapolated this account of the first origination of the symptom backward from the dynamics they had postulated for the subsequently continuing existence of the symptom. Breuer and Freud (1893) had been led to attribute the *maintenance* of the symptom, in turn, to a *coexisting* ongoing repression of the traumatic *memory* which "acts like a foreign body which long after its entry must continue to be regarded as an agent that is still at work." But what is their basis for this attribution? As they tell us at once: "we find the evidence for this in a highly remarkable phenomenon," which they describe in italics as follows: "*each individual hysterical symptom immediately and permanently disappeared when we had succeeded in bringing clearly to light the memory of the event by which it was provoked and in arousing its accompanying affect*" (p. 6).

What then is the evidence they give for their etiologic identification of the repressed experience of a particular traumatic event E as the pathogen—avowedly *not* as the mere precipitator!—of a given symptom S that first appeared at the time of E? Plainly and emphatically, they predicate their identification of the repression of E as the pathogen of S on the fact that the abreactive lifting of that repression issued in the durable *re-moval* of S. And, as their wording shows, they appreciate all too well that *without* this symptom removal, neither the mere painfulness of the event E, nor its temporal coincidence with S's first appearance, nor yet the mere fact that the hysteric patient had *repressed* the trauma E could justify, even together, blaming the pathogenesis of S on the repression of E. Thus, the credibility of the repression etiology is crucially dependent on the reportedly durable separate removal of various symptoms, a therapeutic outcome deemed supportive because it appears to have been wrought by *separately* lifting particular repressions!

This epistemic dependence of the repression etiology on the presumed carthartic dynamics of effecting positive therapeutic outcome is further accentuated by the pains Breuer and Freud (1893) take promptly to argue that their symptom removals are due to the lifting of repressions rather than to expectancy suggestion: "It is plausible to suppose that . . . the patient expects to be relieved of his sufferings by this procedure, and it is this expectation . . . which is the [therapeutically] operative factor. This, however, is not so . . . the symptoms, which sprang from separate causes, were separately removed" (p. 7). Thus the separate symptom removals are made to carry the vital probative burden of discrediting the threatening rival hypothesis of placebo effect, wrought by mere suggestion.

Believing to have met this challenge, Breuer and Freud at once reiterate their epoch-making repression etiology. Let us now recapitulate the essential steps of the reasoning that prompted them to postulate this etiology. First they attributed their positive therapeutic results to the lifting of repressions. Having assumed such a *therapeutic connection*, they wished to *explain* it. Then they saw that it would indeed be explained deductively by the following etiologic hypothesis: The particular cognitive repression and/or affective suppression whose undoing removed a given symptom S is *causally necessary* for the initial formation *and* maintenance of S (Grünbaum, 1984, pp. 180-181). Therefore, the nub of their inductive argument for inferring a repression etiology can be formulated in simplified form as follows: The *removal* of a hysterical symptom S by means of *lifting* a repression R is *cogent evidence* that the repression R was *causally necessary* for the formation of the symptom S. After all, if an ongoing repression R is causally necessary for the pathogenesis *and* persistence of a neurosis N, then the removal of R must issue in the eradication of N. Hence the inferred etiology yielded a deductive explanation of the supposed remedial efficacy of undoing repressions.

Clearly, the attribution of *therapeutic* success to the undoing of repressions—rather than to mere expectancy or suggestion—was the foundation, both logically and historically, for the general dynamic significance that unconscious ideation acquired in psychoanalytic theory: Without reliance on the presumed *dynamics* of their *therapeutic* results, Breuer and Freud could never have propelled clinical data into repression etiologies.

As we saw, they had argued pointedly that the therapeutic gains made by their cathartically treated patients were *not* wrought by suggestion. Instead, they attributed these remedial results to the abreactive recall of *repressed* traumata during which the distressing symptoms had first presented themselves. Since these traumata occasioned the onset of the hysterical symptoms, I shall refer to them as "occasioning" traumata. Hence we can say that Breuer and Freud had credited the patient's improvements to the *lifting* of the particular repression by which he had sequestered the memory of the *occasioning* trauma in his unconscious. And yet, when Freud himself treated additional patients by Breuer's cathartic method, this treatment failed to achieve *lasting* therapeutic gains. Indeed, the ensuing correlation of symptom relapses and intermittent removals, on the one hand, with the vicissitudes of his personal relations to the patient, on the other, led him to *repudiate* the *decisive* therapeutic role that Breuer and he had attributed to undoing the repression of the *occasioning* trauma!

The evidence and reasoning that had driven Freud to this repudiation by 1896 are poignantly recalled by him in his 1925 "Autobiographical Study":

> . . . even the most brilliant [therapeutic] results were liable to be suddenly wiped away if my personal relation with the patient

became disturbed. It was true that they would be re-established if a reconciliation could be effected; but such an occurrence proved that the personal emotional relation between doctor and patient was after all stronger than the whole cathartic process [1925b, p. 27].

Freud's therapeutic repudiation of abreactively retrieving the memory of the *occasioning* trauma also had a momentous corollary: He likewise renounced the major *etiologic* significance that he and Breuer had originally attributed to the *repression* of *this* trauma (Freud, 1896, pp. 194-195). Yet he adhered undauntedly to the research program of seeking the pathogens of neuroses among *some* repressed traumata *or other* (pp. 195-199). And, though the disappointments of cathartic treatment outcome had undercut the very basis for giving decisive remedial credit to the lifting of repressions, he unflinchingly clung to the therapeutic view that the excavation of *some* repression or *other* would remove the pathogen of the patient's affliction. But as I shall now argue, the empirical rationale that Breuer and Freud had used for postulating a *repression* etiology *at all* was altogether undermined by just the findings that induced Freud himself to repudiate the attribution of therapeutic gain to the undoing of the repression of the occasioning trauma.

The aforementioned symptom *relapses*, which ensued after Freud had lifted the patient's repression of the occasioning trauma, showed him that the undoing of this repression failed to uproot the *cause* of the neurotic symptoms. Moreover, the fragile, ephemeral symptom remissions achieved by patients who received Breuer's cathartic treatment could hardly be credited to the lifting of this repression. By Freud's own account, giving such therapeutic credit had very soon run afoul of a stubborn fact: "The personal emotional relation between doctor and patient was after all [therapeutically] stronger than the whole cathartic process' (1925b, p. 27). Freud means that even *after* the patient's repression of the occasioning trauma had indeed been undone cathartically, the alternation between his remissions and relapses still depended *decisively* on the ups and downs of how well he got along emotionally with his doctor.

Yet, as we saw earlier, the 1893 postulation of a repression etiology of neurosis in Breuer's and Freud's foundational communication had rested *crucially* on the premise that the patient's symptom removals had actually been wrought by lifting his repression of the memory of the occasioning trauma. And thus Freud's own abandonment of just this therapeutic premise completely negated the very reason that Breuer and he had invoked for postulating the pathogenicity of repression at all. In short, I claim that *the moral of Freud's therapeutic disappointments in the use of the cathartic method after 1893 was nothing less than the collapse of the epoch-making 1893 argument for the repression etiology of neurosis*, which Breuer and he had propounded.

Why, I ask, did Freud adamantly retain the generic repression etiology instead of allowing that this etiology itself had simply become baseless? And why, in the face of this baselessness, was he content with his mere etiologic demotion of the repressed *occasioning* trauma, while clinging to the view that the pathogen is bound to be some other earlier repressed trauma of a sexual nature, to be excavated via free associations (1896, pp. 195-199)? Whatever his reason, he seemingly did not appreciate that the etiologic fiasco suffered by Breuer's account in the wake of the disappointingly fragile therapeutic results had made a shambles of the very cornerstone of this psychoanalytic edifice. Such an appreciation would have been tantamount to his realization that the etiology of neurosis still posed the same fundamental challenge as it had *before* Anna O. enabled Breuer to stumble on the alleged "talking cure." Instead, Freud avowedly committed himself to a "prolonged search for the traumatic experiences from which hysterical symptoms appeared to be derived" (1923c, p. 243), just when the initially plausible traumatic etiology had been found to be baseless after all.

I have stressed the collapse of the 1893 therapeutic argument on which Breuer and Freud rested their originally hypothesized repression etiology of neurosis. Yet I need to forestall a possible misunderstanding of my methodological complaint against Freud's tenacious search for evidence that might warrant the *rehabilitation* of the repression etiology in a *new* version. Hence let me emphasize that I do *not* fault the pursuit of this research program *per se* after the demise of the cathartic method. What I do find objectionable, however, is Freud's all-too-ready willingness—once he was no longer collaborating with Breuer—to claim pathogenicity for purported childhood repressions on evidence *far less cogent* than the *separate* symptom removals that Breuer and he had pointedly adduced in 1893. In short, having embarked on the program of retaining the repression etiology *somehow*. Freud was prepared to draw etiologic conclusions whose credentials just did not live up to Breuer's initial 1893 standard. And even that higher original standard, I contend, was still not high enough.

Indeed I maintain that the repression etiology of neurosis would have lacked adequate empirical credentials, even if the therapeutic gains from cathartic treatment had turned out to be both durable and splendid. For, even such impressive results may well not be due at all to the lifting of pathogenic repressions; instead they may be a *placebo effect* (see chap. 3), generated by the patient's awareness that the therapist was *intent* on uncovering a thematically particular E when focusing the former's attention on the initial appearance of the distinct symptom S. Thus, it was communicated to the patient that Breuer and Freud attached potential therapeutic significance to the recall of E with respect to S. Indeed, it is far from clear that the likelihood of placebo effect is lower when several symptoms are wiped out separately—one at a time—than in the case of getting rid of only one symptom. Yet, as we saw, Breuer and Freud invoked just that likelihood. To discredit the hypothesis of placebo effect, it is essential to have comparisons with treatment outcome from a suitable control group whose repressions are *not* lifted.

The attribution of remedial efficacy to the abreactive lifting of repressions was therefore devoid of adequate evidential warrant. Moreover, as has clearly emerged from chapter 8, the retrospective validation of repression as the *initial* pathogen lacks the sort of controls needed to attest its *causal relevance*, even if the evidence had sufficed to attribute the current *maintenance* of S to the ongoing repression. There also is doubt about the reliability of purported memories elicited under the suggestive conditions of hypnosis (Dywan and Bowers, 1983). Incidentally, despite the replacement of hypnosis by free association in psychoanalytic treatment, Freudian therapy has retained an important tenet of its cathartic predecessor: "Recollection without affect almost invariably produces no [therapeutic] result" (Breuer and Freud, 1893, p. 6).

As outlined in chapter 1, à propos Freud's "Master Proposition," and as shown in detail in chapter 5, Freud's own subsequent (1916-17) *therapeutic* defense of his sexual version of the repression etiology—a defense I dub the "Tally Argument"—has fared no better empirically than the original reliance on cathartic treatment success as evidence for the pathogenicity of repression. Whatever his own evidential or personal motivations for retaining the repression etiology, I claim that it should now be regarded as *generically* devoid of clinical evidential support, no less than Breuer's particular version of it, which Freud repudiated as clinically unfounded. By the same token, I maintain that the demise of the therapeutic justification for the repression etiology fundamentally impugns the *investigative cogency* of lifting repressions (via "free" associations) in the conduct of etiologic inquiry. In short, *the collapse of the therapeutic argument for the repression etiology seriously undermines the purported clinical research value of free associations*, which are given pride of place as an epistemic avenue to the identification of presumed pathogens as such. After all, Freud had enunciated his fundamental rule of free association as a maxim of clinical research because he thought on *therapeutic* grounds that associations governed by it had *reliably identified* the unconscious pathogens of the neuroses (1900, p. 528).

Though the repression etiology of psychoneurotic disorders was thus itself in grave jeopardy from lack of cogent clinical support, Freud extrapolated its compromise model by postulating that repressions engender "slips" (parapraxes) and dreams no less than they spawn full-blown neuroses. For example, he assimilated a slip of the tongue to the status of a minineurotic symptom by viewing the slip as a *compromise* between a repressed motive that crops out in the form of a disturbance, on the one hand, and the conscious intention to make a certain utterance, on the other. Thus, he tells us that parapraxes committed by "healthy people . . . may easily be shown [by free association] to depend on the action of strong unconscious ideas in the same way as neurotic symptoms" (1912b, p. 263). As against this generalized explanatory reliance on repressed mentation, I shall argue for the following thesis: Even if the original *therapeutic* defense of the repression etiology of neuroses had actually turned out to be empirically viable, Freud's compromise models of parapraxes and of manifest dream content would be *misextrapolations* of that etiology, precisely because they lacked any corresponding therapeutic base or any evidential *counterpart* to that base at the outset. For his defense of free association in the Irma dream (1900, chap. II) fails (Grünbaum, 1984, chap. 5), and in 1900 Freud also defended the heuristic and probative use of free association in *interpreting dreams* by pointing to its primary use in *etiologic* inquiry. Indeed, he explicitly adduced *therapeutic* results, in turn, to legitimate free association as a reliable means of certifying the pathogens etiologically. In a passage I discussed in chapter 1 (pp. 24-26), he wrote:

> We might also point out in our defence that our procedure in interpreting dreams [by means of free association] is identical with the procedure by which we resolve hysterical symptoms; and there the correctness of our method is warranted by the coincident emergence and disappearance of the symptoms [1900, p. 528].

Saul Rosenzweig (1934) sent Freud experimental results that Rosenzweig (1986) took to be supportive of Freud's theory of repression. Though Freud was then in his late seventies and ill with cancer, he took only a short time to react to this unsolicited claim of confirmation. Quite soon thereafter, he wrote Rosenzweig with almost patronizing disenchantment:

> I have examined your experimental studies for the verification of the psychoanalytic assertions with interest. I cannot put much value on these confirmations because the wealth of reliable observations on which these assertions rest make them independent of experimental verification. Still, it can do no harm [quoted in MacKinnon and Dukes (1964, p. 703); the German original is reproduced on p. 702].

Just what was Freud's rationale for feeling entitled to dismiss Rosenzweig's experimental investigation in the way he did?

Note at once that Freud's dissatisfaction was *not* that Rosenzweig's experiment failed to qualify logically as a genuine test of the psychoanalytic conception of repression. Thus, Freud's objection was *not* that sheer evidential *irrelevance* rendered the experimental results probatively unavailing. Nor did he level the weaker charge that Rosenzweig's findings failed to pass muster *logically* as confirmations. On the contrary, he did refer to them as "confirmations" (*Bestätigungen*). Rather what disenchanted Freud was that, in his view, these results were *probatively superfluous* or *redundant*, albeit harmless as such. But *why* did Freud look upon them as superfluous? As he stated, he regarded psychoanalytic hypotheses as already abundantly well established clinically by "a wealth of reliable observations." Hence, he saw no need for further substantiation by experiments conducted outside the psychoanalytic situation (1933, p. 174).

Some psychoanalysts dissented from Freud's appraisal of Rosenzweig's claim of experimental confirmation. But while doing so, these other analysts *indicted* rather than endorsed Rosenzweig's contention that his findings support Freud's theory of repression. For they objected vehemently that, far from yielding harmlessly superfluous confirmations, Rosenzweig's (1986) work was fundamentally unsound, because his experiment simply did not qualify logically as a test of the *psychoanalytic* notion of repression (MacKinnon and Dukes, 1964, pp. 703-709). I concur completely with these other analysts that whatever relevance Rosenzweig's findings may have to *non*psychoanalytic accounts of forgetting, they patently have no evidential bearing on Freudian repression as that notion is articulated in Freud's classic 1915 papers (1915c, pp. 146-158). Indeed, it is most puzzling that this fact was not evident to Rosenzweig before others pointed it out. For in the aforecited 1934 article, Rosenzweig himself states explicitly at the outset (p. 248) what he takes to be the pertinent construal of Freud's 1915 paper. And I submit that the probative *irrelevance* of Rosenzweig's laboratory findings is immediately perspicuous from that very formulation.

Conclusion

Freud told us that the theory of repression is the cornerstone of the entire psychoanalytic theory of unconscious motivations, and he claimed that his clinical evidence furnishes compelling support for this cornerstone. Thus, I was able to scrutinize the logical foundations of the psychoanalytic edifice by examining Freud's clinical arguments for the repression etiology of the psychoneuroses. The upshot of this scrutiny was that the reasoning by which he thought to justify the very foundation of his theory was grievously flawed.

Plainly, this conclusion leaves quite open whether some other, genuinely probative evidence will turn out to lend significant support at least to the repression etiology of psychoneuroses, which is *the* major pillar of the Freudian structure.

Though I have given a critique of the basic pillars of psycho-analysis, it might be asked, why its anachronistic focus on Freud's reasoning to the exclusion of the modifications and elaborations by those post-Freudians whose doctrines are recognizably psychoanalytic in content rather than only in name? Latter-day psychoanalytic theoreticians who come to mind are Heinz Kohut, who pioneered "self psychology," and the "object relations" theorists, who include not only Otto Kernberg, but also Harry Guntrip, W. R. D. Fairbairn, D. W. Winnicott, and others. Kohut, for example, downgrades Freud's oedipal, *instinctual* factors in favor of preoedipal, *environmental* ones as the sources of the purported *unconscious* determinants of personality structure. More generally, insofar as these post-Freudian theories are indeed recognizably psychoanalytic, they do of course embrace some version of the repression etiology. Furthermore, they rely epistemically on free association in the clinical investigation of purported pathogens and other unconscious determinants of behavior, while lifting repressions as one means to effecting therapy.

Precisely to the extent that these outgrowths of Freud's ideas are thus recognizably psychoanalytic in content as well as in method of inquiry and therapy, my epistemic critique of Freud's original hypotheses applies with equal force to the etiologic, developmental and therapeutic tenets of these successors.

How, for example, can Kohut possibly claim better validation for his species of unconscious determinants than Freud can for the sexual ones? Moreover, it is just ludicrous to pretend with Flax (1981, p. 564) that my focus on Freud in appraising psychoanalytic theory epistemically is akin to the anachronistic procedure of "throwing out physics because there are unresolved problems in Newton's theory." This purported analogy suggests misleadingly that the epistemic difficulties that beset Freud's original formulations have been overcome by the much vaunted post-Freudian formulations of self psychology and object relations theory. Besides, it overlooks the logical incompatibility of the most influential of these versions: As Robbins (1980, p. 477) points out, Kohut's and Kernberg's views are "fundamentally antagonistic" to one another, being rooted in a schism between Melanie Klein and Fairbairn (Grünbaum, 1983).

True, there are elements in some of the post-Freudian theories that give less emphasis to repression, both etiologically and therapeutically, than the received doctrine. But I must emphasize anew that exactly to the extent that there is such divergence from the very cornerstone of psychoanalysis, these post-Freudian theories are only nominally rather than substantively "psychoanalytic." For example, self psychology gives significant etiologic weight to the absence of empathic mirroring in early childhood. Yet, as Eagle (1984a) has shown, these ingredients of the post-Freudian theories are *at least* as flawed epistemologically as the repression model that was found seriously wanting above. It is futile to adduce these modifications, as the disciples of self psychology and object relations theory are wont to do, *qua* improvements on Freud's original hypotheses, whose articulation was more lucid and more amenable to scrutiny (Grünbaum, 1984, chap. 7). Indeed, Holt (1985, p. 289) has argued persuasively: "Object relations and self psychology have had a large vogue but do not address the fundamental theoretical problems. Those threaten the survival of psychoanalysis, but are being complacently ignored."

Indeed, as I stressed at the outset of chapter 4, the alteration in the *content* of Freud's original hypotheses hardly makes their *validation* more secure. This point is overlooked by Meissner

(1990, p. 526), who questions the relevance of my animadversions to post-Freudian formulations.

There is not even agreement among the post-Freudians in regard to the probative value that may be assigned to *one and the same case study material*. While Kohut claimed clinical support for his theory from his reanalysis of Mr. Z.—a patient whose prior analysis had been a traditional one—Gedo (1980) harshly discounts the scientific quality of Kohut's case study material. He concludes (p. 382) that the "theoretical inferences" drawn by Kohut from his clinical observations "fail to carry scientific conviction." A similarly negative assessment is reached by Levine (1979), an ardent exponent of psychoanalytic methods of investigation and therapy. On the other hand, Ferguson (1981, pp. 135-136) believes that Kohut's case history of Mr. Z. is "a crystalline example of the *fact* that a progressive theory change has taken place in psychoanalysis." But Ferguson then seems to damn it with faint praise, saying "the case of Mr. Z. provides something of a 'confirming instance' of the new theory." No wonder that Fisher and Greenberg (1977) reached the verdict: "The diversity of the secondary elaborations of Freud's ideas is so Babel-like as to defy the derivation of sensible deductions that can be put to empirical test" (p. ix).

10

TWO NEW MAJOR DIFFICULTIES FOR FREUD'S THEORY OF DREAMS

INTRODUCTION

Before 1920, Freud's wish-fulfillment theory of dreams asserted two universal major theses, which he encapsulated in the following conjunction: The manifest dream *"content was the fulfilment of a wish* [first thesis] *and its motive was a wish"* [second thesis] (1900, p. 119). As Freud recognized, neither of these two theses is redundant with the other. But in his 1933 "Revision of the Theory of Dreams" (pp. 28-30), he explicitly retracted the *first* claim that the manifest dream content universally *displays* the fulfillment of a wish, though in a more or less defensively disguised form. On the other hand, there he continued to uphold his second thesis that the *dream motive* is *always* a wish, rather than, say, a fear. Moreover, that wish was purportedly always, at bottom, a *repressed infantile* one. But in his earlier 1920 revision in *Beyond the Pleasure Principle*, he had even retracted this second thesis in favor of the notion that the so-called "compulsion to repeat," rather than a wish, was the motive of dreams that reenact traumatic experiences. Examples of such dreams are produced by war-ravaged soldiers who recapitulate the horrors of combat in their dreams. And their dreams were the ones that prompted Freud in 1933 to acknowledge an exception to his *first* thesis of wish-fulfillment.

As we know, the evidence Freud offered for his theory of dreaming depended crucially on his method of free association.

357

But in my (1984) book *The Foundations of Psychoanalysis*, I argued that Freud's celebrated Irma dream completely failed to vindicate free association as a method of reliably fathoming dream motives. Nor was he successful in his other efforts to show that free associations are causally probative. As I pointed out, Freud (1900) simply had no warrant for making the following major investigative assumption (pp. 279-280): If we associate to a given manifest dream element, then the emerging associations *recapitulate* in *inverse temporal order* the original unconscious dream thoughts, so that at least the great bulk of these thoughts was *causally relevant* to the very formation of the manifest dream content by means of the defensive operations of the dream work.

A fortiori, Freud had no good grounds for picking out repressed infantile wishes from the emerging glut of diverse unconscious dream thoughts as the principal motive forces of our dreams, nor for inferring that "each individual element . . . of the dream" (p. 280) is the product of a large-scale condensation of the purported dream thoughts.

In a reconstruction of an articulation of Freud's neurobiology of dreaming by Raymond Fancher and Frank Sulloway, Patricia Kitcher (in press) offers a deductive argument by which Freud could well have derived the wish-fulfilling character of dreaming from his account of endogenous biological needs. But his pre-1914 drive theory featured not only the sexual instinct; it also gave a major role to the "ego instinct," which strives for the self-preservation of the individual in the face of danger. And just as wishes are associated with the former instinct, so also *fears* of threats to the individual's survival are associated with the latter.

It would seem, therefore, that Freud ought to have countenanced fears as dream motives for some dreams, no less than wishes for others. Thus, he appears to have been gratuitously selective in favor of wish-motives from the outset, just as he was later in picking them out from the dreamer's free associations. The principal "counter-wish" dream to be discussed critically below, which features an event actually dreaded by "the cleverest" of all of Freud's dreamers (1900, p. 151), could readily be explained by the dreamer's fear of the untoward state of affairs.

Yet Freud tries unsuccessfully to explain it by the dreamer's *wish* to prove him wrong, as we shall see.

In short, in virtue of Freud's crucial reliance on free association to ferret out alleged dream motives, neither his analysis of the Irma dream as a purported "Specimen Dream," nor the rest of his dream analyses in his 1900 *magnum opus* can support his attribution of dream formation to repressed infantile wishes. These criticisms so far pertain to the ill-foundedness of the dream theory, as distinct from its falsity. But here, I aim to develop two important grounds for presuming the theory to be false. These grounds are independent of those adduced by Hobson (1988). Bear in mind, however, that grounds for presuming the falsity of a theory need *not* necessarily furnish deductive refutations of it.

The first of these grounds for the presumption of falsity has gone unnoticed in the prior critical literature of which I am aware, and I overlooked it in my own earlier scrutiny of the dream theory (Grünbaum, 1984, pp. 232-234). It pertains to the two *generic* wish motives to which Freud attributes so-called "counterwish dreams." Such dreams feature "the frustration of a wish or the occurrence of something clearly unwished-for" (p. 157). For example, a one-time fellow student of Freud's had become a trial attorney and then dreamed that he had lost all of his court cases (p. 152).

As Freud points out, the distressing manifest contents of these dreams pose a *prima facie* challenge to his wish fulfillment theory of dreaming. To neutralize this challenge, he contends that, in these dreams, "the non-fulfilment of one wish meant the fulfilment of another" (p. 151). That is, these dreams do fulfill *some* wish after all, though at the cost of the nonfulfillment of another, perhaps more salient one. And we learn that "If these dreams are considered as a whole," two wish motives are at hand to explain them: "One of the two motive forces leading to such dreams is the wish that I [Freud] may be wrong," a wish cunningly fulfilled by the alleged *logical acumen* of the unconscious dream work (p. 157). The second such wish motive, which Freud considers obvious, is the masochistic wish for humiliation and mental torture, as distinct from the desire of people for "having *physical* pain inflicted on them" (p. 159).

Having called these two generic wish motives to the rescue in order to accommodate counterwish dreams "as a whole" in his fulfillment theory, Freud also appealed to miscellaneous other sorts of wishes to explain certain cases of wish-contravening dreams. One such dream depicted the thwarting of a wish consciously felt by the dreamer in the dream itself. Glymour (1983) criticized Freud's attempt to deal with this dream, and I previously discussed only that same example within the class of counterwish dreams (Grünbaum, 1984, pp. 232-234). But here I shall contend that Freud's resort to two generic wish motives is multiply flawed. Indeed, it will turn out that counterwish dreams as a whole—far from being properly explained by his wish fulfillment theory—furnish disconfirmatory evidence against *each* of the two independent theses in which Freud encapsulated that theory.

A second ground for presuming its falsity is supplied, I claim, by the failure of extensively psychoanalyzed patients to experience a significant reduction in the *frequency* of their dreams, as distinct from a systematic alteration of the thematic manifest dream content. Heretofore I merely gave an inadequate sketch of my rationale for this criticism, which is subject to the proviso that long-term psychoanalytic treatment succeeds in lifting the analysand's repressions (pp. 234-235). Therefore, I shall develop it here anew.

Finally, I here offer a critical appraisal of Freud's 1920 and 1933 revisions of his dream theory.

Returning to the 1900 theory, let us state it concisely as follows: For every dream D, there is at least one wish W such that (i) W is the motivational cause of D, and (ii) the manifest content of D graphically displays, more or less disguisedly, the state of affairs desired by W. Thus, the fulfillment of W is two-fold.

COUNTERWISH DREAMS

As Freud recognized, imputations either of a dreamer's wish to prove his dream theory wrong or of a masochistic disposition to the dreamer require evidence other than the mere occurrence of wish-contravening dreams. In the absence of independent evidence, such motivational attributions in the service of explaining these dreams would, of course, simply beg the question. Yet, as we shall see in due course, Freud ran afoul of this evidential requirement by claiming fallaciously that a patient's desire to prove him wrong was a deductive "logical consequence" of a counterwish dream reported by one of his patients.

According to Freud (1900), counterwish dreams are "very frequent" (1900, p. 157). But within the human population at large, he singles out as counterwish dreamers people who belong to at least one of the following three classes: (a) patients who become aware of his dream theory while "in a state of resistance" to him during psychoanalytic treatment (p. 157); (b) others who are exposed to his writings or lectures on his dream theory, but are unfavorably disposed toward it (p. 158); or (c) who are self-punitive masochists (p. 159).

Let us consider in some detail Freud's analysis of a counterwish dream experienced by one of his patients, whom he described as "the cleverest of all my dreamers" (p. 151). Presumably this tribute was intended to incline us to agree that the logical acumen of her unconscious was especially cunning in designing a dream allegedly fulfilling her wish to prove Freud wrong. But it will turn out that, however clever she was in waking life, her dream simply gave no evidence at all of the logical perspicacity of her unconscious.

We learn that, after Freud explained his dream theory to her, she dreamed that "she was traveling down with her mother-in-law to the place in the country where they were to spend their holidays together." Yet he "knew that she had violently rebelled against the idea of spending the summer near her mother-in-law and that a few days earlier she had successfully avoided the propinquity she dreaded by engaging rooms in a far distant resort. And now her dream had undone the solution she had wished for." Finally, Freud asks: "was not this the sharpest possible contradiction of my theory that in dreams wishes are fulfilled" (p. 151)? It is vital to be especially alert to all of the key words in the answer he then gave. Alas, I would be hard put to find any other few sentences in the writings of a comparably influential thinker that contain so high a density of fallacies as his ensuing passage.

Recall Freud's characterization of the manifest dream content as having "undone the solution she had wished for." This much is clearly correct, since that content featured a dreaded state of affairs. Then he had asked whether this vacation dream did not pose "the sharpest possible contradiction" to his wish-fulfillment theory. Yet, despite his ultimate aim of explaining counterwish dreams as wish fulfilling after all, he replied most bewilderingly:

> No doubt; it was only necessary to follow the dream's logical consequence in order to arrive at its interpretation. The dream showed that I was wrong. *Thus it was her wish that I might be wrong, and her dream showed that wish fulfilled* [p. 151].

My own English rendition of this passage differs somewhat from that of the *Standard Edition*:

> Certainly; one need only draw the logical consequence of this dream to be in possession of its interpretation. According to this dream, I was wrong; *thus, it was her wish that I should be wrong, and her dream showed her the fulfillment of that wish.*[1]

Recall Freud's own report of the manifest content of the dream experienced by "the cleverest" of all his dreamers the night after he had explained his wish-fulfillment theory to her: "Next day she brought me a dream in which she was travelling down with her mother-in-law to the place in the country where they were to spend their holidays together" (p. 151).

Astonishingly, he tells us that this description of the manifest content warrants the following series of assertions:

1. It entails logically that his wish fulfillment theory is wrong by furnishing "the sharpest possible contradiction" to it.

2. It allows him to deduce: *"Thus it was her wish that I be wrong."*

3. The dream graphically displayed to the patient the actual fulfillment of her presumed wish that Freud be wrong. And indeed that wish motive had engendered her vacation dream.

---

[1]The corresponding German original reads: "Gewiss, man brauchte nur die Konsequenz aus diesem Traum zu ziehen, um seine Deutung zu haben. Nach diesem Traum hatte ich unrecht; *es war also ihr Wunsch, dass ich unrecht haben sollte, und diesen zeigte ihr der Traum erfüllt*" (Freud, 1972, p. 167).

The *Standard Edition* translates Freud's account of what the manifest content displays graphically as *"her dream showed that wish fulfilled."* But I note that the German original uses the phrase *"zeigte ihr,"* which means "showed *to* her" or "exhibited *to* her." Therefore, I myself rendered his third assertion by speaking of what the dream displayed *to* the patient.

Evidently, Freud fancied himself to have established three results: (1) The patient harbored the wish to prove him wrong; (2) this wish, in turn, was the motive that had engendered the counterwish dream; and furthermore (3) the dream's manifest content graphically displayed the fulfillment of that wish. In this way, he believed he had demonstrated after all the conformity of the counterwish dream to both theses of his theory. First, its manifest content displayed a wish-fulfillment; secondly, its generating motive was a wish.

In fairness to Freud, observe that there is surely no requirement in his wish-fulfillment doctrine that any given dream fulfill *all* of the dreamer's wishes, conscious or unconscious. Besides being too numerous, a person's wishes often conflict with one another by not being jointly realizable. At least typically, even in a dream "You can't have your cake and eat it." Thus, Freud's dream theory *allows* the *non*fulfillment of even so salient a wish as a trial attorney's desire to win all his court cases. But, as we shall see before long, this much is quite unavailing to his generic explanation of counterwish dreams as being engendered by hostility to his dream theory or by the masochistic craving for mental torture.

Let me now appraise, one by one, the three deeply flawed inferences above, which Freud drew from his patient's vacation dream:

Inference 1. The bizarre conclusion of his first inference was that the vacation dream contradicted his theory most sharply. It is bizarre, because Freud also wants to *explain* this dream as a wishfulling positive instance of his theory after all. We are given that, in waking life, the dreamer had avowed a strong aversion to vacationing with her mother-in-law, an aversion she had implemented by means of the distant location of the rooms she had rented. Furthermore, in contravention to that stated wish, her manifest dream content visually showed her enroute to a joint vacation with the mother-in-law. I claim that this content *itself* does not contradict Freud's wish-fulfillment theory at all.

Observe that the manifest content datum logically *permits* the following state of affairs: Despite the conscious aversion to being in the company of her mother-in-law, the dreamer also ambivalently has the *unconscious* wish to be with her after all. Plainly, by featuring the two women traveling together, the manifest dream content logically *allows* the unconscious existence of the wish for the mother-in-law's company as well as *its* fulfillment in the dream. However, in asserting this compatibility, I do *not* maintain that there is any empirical evidence for this putative wish, let alone for its being the motive for the formation of the dream. What I am claiming instead is this: There is nothing at all in the manifest content that would deductively *rule out* its fulfilling the putative unconscious wish for the mother-in-law's company, both motivationally and graphically as required by Freudian theory; therefore, the truthful report of this manifest dream content cannot itself also deductively contradict this wish-fulfillment theory. Yet Freud told us that just these data stand in "the sharpest possible contradiction" to his theory (p. 151).

But suppose that, merely for argument's sake, we take Freud at his word and were to grant him that the reported vacation dream content does contradict his theory. If so, then the occurrence of this counterwish dream would be a *bona fide*—rather than only a *prima facie* or sham—refuting instance of his dream theory. By the same token, it is then patently inconsistent and futile on Freud's part to contend, as he did soon thereafter, that, after all, counterwish dreams only "appear to stand in contradiction to my theory" (p. 157), and that, moreover, two wish motives generically explain them fully in accord with his theory.

Even as a piece of pedagogy, Freud's account here is painfully bewildering. And if there is "wild analysis," as he tells us, then he has surely treated us here to a piece of theoretical wilding, as will now emerge.

We have seen that Freud sought to buttress his case by speaking of what the dream purportedly "shows." But this term harbors a serious ambiguity as used in the locution "dream *D* shows that X," and in its German cognates, such as the German counterpart of "according to this dream" (i.e., "Nach diesem Traum"). The sentence "the dream content shows that X" or "dream D shows that X" can be used to assert that the manifest content deductively or inductively warrants the conclusion that X is the case. Let me speak of this sense of "shows" as the "inferential" sense. On the other hand, the phrase "dream D shows that X" can be employed to say that "the manifest dream content graphically or otherwise *portrays* X," where X is a wish-fulfilling scenario with respect to a given wish *W*. Let me speak of the latter sense as the "graphic" sense of the term "shows."

Unfortunately, the term "shows" is used in each of these two senses in rapid succession in Freud's passage. Mindful also of the German original, note that, on the heels of speaking of drawing "the dream's logical consequence," he concludes: "The dream showed that I was wrong." Here, he is employing the *inferential* sense of "shows." But, as I have already demonstrated, Freud's inference here is flatly fallacious: Far from contradicting his wish-fulfillment theory, the manifest content—in and of itself—is entirely compatible with it. Therefore, this dream content cannot itself have shown inferentially that his theory was wrong.

Inference 2. Immediately after asserting "The dream showed that I was wrong," Freud draws an arrantly fallacious second inference, saying: "*Thus it was her wish that I might be wrong*" (p. 151). Even if he had proven the manifest dream content to be incompatible with his dream theory, so that he was in fact wrong, how could this putative fact possibly entail that the patient actually had the *wish* that he be wrong? Deductively, this motivational imputation is a patent *non-sequitur*. But, in any case, the premise of the imputation is unsound. Hence even a validly drawn conclusion from it would be ill-founded.

Apparently, Freud was uneasy about the deductive soundness of his inference "Thus it was her wish that I might be wrong" (italics omitted). And so he proceeds to offer supposedly direct *empirical* evidence for the presence of this wish: "But her wish that I might be wrong, which was fulfilled in connection with her summer holidays, related in fact to another and more serious matter" (p. 151). At the time of the dream, we are told, the patient had been rejecting his inference as to the occurrence of certain events in her life that had presumably been pathogenic, but that she could not recall. This resistance had been prompted by her "well-justified wish that the events of which she was then becoming aware for the first time might never have occurred" (p. 152). By the same token, this wish presumably also engendered her broader intellectual desire that Freud's other theorizing be quite generally wrong. Thereupon, he draws the major causal inference that the latter desire "was transformed into her dream of spending her holidays with her mother-in-law" (p. 152). Note that when Freud tells us that there was such a transformation, he means that *this* desire was the motive of the dream.

I contend that, to the serious detriment of Freud's entire case, precisely this claim of motivational causation of the dream is a house of cards. Therefore, consider his third inference.

Inference 3. The conclusion of this inference was that the vacation dream fulfilled the patient's wish that Freud be wrong, and it did so both graphically and motivationally, as required by the dream theory. I claim that the dream did neither. First, observe that, contrary to Freud, the manifest content did *not* display graphically to the patient the actual fulfillment of her presumed wish that he be wrong. What it did display instead was simply that, as Freud himself had put it, "she was travelling down with her mother-in-law to the place in the country where they were to spend their holidays together" (p. 151). But a manifest content scenario that could be said to display graphically the fulfillment of the wish that Freud be wrong can easily be imagined. For example, a public debate on the merits of Freud's own brand of psychoanalysis in which he is roundly defeated in argument by some obscure Swiss scholar, who is a thin disguise for Carl Gustav Jung.

In the second place, consider the presumed dream motive. What does Freud offer toward establishing that the putative hostile wish *produced* the vacation dream?

As he tells us, counterwish dreams are "very frequent" (p. 157). Therefore, one can only marvel at the methodological abandon with which he overlooks the following key point: Unless he provides a baseline as to the incidence of counterwish dreams in the general population, there is plainly no reason to infer that either hostile motives toward his dream theory or masochistic wishes affect the frequency of such dreams on the part of those who do harbor one or both of these motives. After all, to show that such wish motives are causally relevant to having counterwish dreams, one must provide evidence that these wishes make a difference to the incidence of these dreams in each one of the following two pairs of subclasses: (1) the subclass of dreams dreamed by any given defensively resistant patient undergoing psychoanalysis, as compared to the dreams in the patient's life prior to being analyzed; and (2) the subclass of dreamers harboring at least one of the two special wishes *vis-à-vis* the subclass of all other dreamers. If Freud were right, then in both (1) and (2), the first of the two subclasses should exhibit a significantly higher incidence of counterwish dreams than the second.

It does not even seem to have occurred to Freud to ask himself how often his cleverest female patient had experienced counterwish dreams before having heard of his wish-fulfillment theory. I can report, as an unanalyzed person, that most of my own recalled dreams are counterwish dreams, such as examination dreams in which I come unprepared to the finals. And, as we saw, the wish-contravening manifest content of these distressing dreams does not graphically portray Freud to be wrong, although I do believe him to be. But even if I had ulterior motives for *wishing* him to be wrong, there is no evidence at all that this putative wish actually engendered my counterwish dreams. In fact, I had lots of them even before I had read Freud and took up a critical attitude toward him. Nor is there any evidence, as far as I know, that I have a masochistic need for mental torture or humiliation. Indeed, the dream researcher Alan Hobson reports (private communication) that most of our dreams are unpleasant, if not counterwish dreams.

Astonishingly, Freud felt no need to offer evidence that adults, children, or animals (e.g., monkeys) who give no *independent* evidence of a significant masochistic disposition and who are in no position to harbor a wish to disprove his dream theory have at least incomparably fewer counterwish dreams than do patients who are in a resistance phase of their analysis or are otherwise hostile to Freudian ideas. Moreover, even if a desire to prove Freud wrong were to motivate some counterwish dreams, that wish fails to satisfy his requirement of being a *repressed infantile* wish! Besides, what of the counterwish dreams of those who are *ardent* believers in psychoanalysis yet are clearly not masochists? What wish motives do *they* have to dream such dreams? Is there even a shred of evidence that the renowned psychoanalysts Charles Brenner or Robert Wallerstein, not to speak of Freud himself, have *fewer* wish-contravening dreams than do the anti-Freudians Hans Eysenck or B. F. Skinner? And, finally, why does Freud feel entitled to assert that any significant number of the readers of his *The Interpretation of Dreams* "will be quite ready to have one of their wishes frustrated in a dream if only their wish that I may be wrong can be fulfilled" (p. 158)? On what grounds did he expect that *unanalyzed* educated people exposed to his wish-fulfillment theory would often have a motive for resisting it? After all, the notion that *some* dreams are wish fulfilling is a commonplace in folk (commonsense) psychology. Yet he claims that people who heard him lecture on his theory have had wish-contravening dreams "as a reaction" to its thesis of wish fulfillment (p. 158, n. 1).

It now appears that Freud's proposed explanation of the vacation dream as motivated by the patient's purported wish to prove him wrong is fundamentally and multiply flawed. He fares no better in regard to a masochistic wish. For he did not even attribute a masochistic disposition to the patient, let alone give independent evidence for it. *A fortiori*, it would be groundless to designate such a wish as the motive of this distressing dream. Thus, this counterwish dream clearly *fails to confirm* the wish-fulfillment theory with respect to either wish. Indeed, for all we know, this dream content could have been produced by none other than the patient's conscious *fear* that just this state of affairs would come to pass.

So far, my criticism asserts the ill-foundedness of Freud's dream theory as an explanation of counter-wish dreams. I shall now expand my objection to claim the following: Counterwish dreams seem to warrant the presumption that Freud's wish-fulfillment theory is false; yet, as will soon emerge, it would seem that such dreams do not deductively refute the theory outright.

Consider any manifest dream content that is wish-contravening, as Freud told us, in the sense of featuring "the frustration of a wish or the occurrence of something clearly unwished-for" (p. 157). As I have already emphasized, any such dream content does leave open whether it fulfills some other less salient *and, indeed unconscious* with W, at the expense of the nonfulfillment of the more salient wish. And we recall that, according to Freud, the fulfillment of W must be twofold: (1) W must be the motivational cause of the dream; and (2) the manifest content must graphically display—albeit in more or less disguised form—the state of affairs desired by W. Hence, for any given counterwish dream, the crucial question is: Is there such a W at all?

We have already seen that, for the vacation dream, the putative unconscious wish that Freud be wrong does not qualify as the sought-after W. This wish fails to qualify in two respects: (1) The manifest content simply does not display the desired state of affairs; and (2) Freud gave no shred of evidence that the putative wish engendered the dream. Nor, as I pointed out, would a masochistic wish do. Therefore, I ask: What *other* unconscious (repressed) wish—as distinct, of course, from a fear!—does the vacation dream realize? It is clearly the burden of Freud's wish-fulfillment theory to come up with a W of the required sort, which he himself failed to do. Be mindful again of the two constraints on W imposed by his *two*fold sense of wish fulfillment. Also note that the mere *logical possibility* of the required W, though genuine, does not constitute *empirical* evidence for its existence. Then it would seem likely that there just is no such W, and hence that the vacation dream disconfirms his theory. Yet, since the number of actual human wishes is clearly finite, though large, it might perhaps be possible to show that the required W is elusive, because it does not exist. And if that were actually shown, then Freud's dream theory would stand deductively refuted by this dream, rather than only disconfirmed. Yet what is disconfirming about the vacation dream is not its manifest content, but rather the likely nonexistence of any wish that was demonstrably the motive for this dream. Moreover, the rival explanation that the patient's *fear* of being stuck with her mother-in-law was the dream motive may well be sustainable by the evidence. As a corollary, note that these results militate still further against Popper's (1983, chap. II) charge that Freud's dream theory is unfalsifiable, a charge that I have thoroughly discredited in other respects in chapter 2.[2]

This then is my unfavorable verdict on Freud's claim that "even dreams with a distressing content are to be construed as wish-fulfilments" (p. 159), though he grants that they "appear to stand in contradiction" to his theory (p. 157).

I now turn to the second of my two grounds for presuming the falsity of Freud's dream theory.

THE FAILURE OF DREAM REDUCTION IN LONG-TERM ANALYSES

My argument will rely, in an essential way, on the import of Freud's theoretical assimilation of manifest dream contents to neurotic symptoms. Therefore, it is important that I be quite clear, at the outset, on the etiologic, explanatory, and investigative dimensions of that assimilation.

In the first instance, Freud postulated that manifest dream contents and neurotic symptoms are *etiologically homologous* by being constructed in the same manner. They are both alike compromise formations, inasmuch as the dream work, no less than neurosogenesis, features the defensive operations of repression and censorious distortion in the service of disguise, etc.:

> It will now be seen that dreams are constructed like a neurotic symptom: they are compromises between the demands of a repressed impulse and the resistance of a censoring force in the ego. Since they have a similar origin they are equally unintelligible and stand in equal need of interpretation [1925b, p. 45].

---

[2]Thirty years ago, Salmon (1959, pp. 264-265) pointed out that Freud's account of counterwish dreams does not immunize his wish-fulfillment theory against disconfirmation. But Salmon overstates the strength of the potentially disconfirming conditions countenanced by Freud, because he neglects to mention the role that Freud accorded to masochistic wishes.

Having assimilated the construction of dreams to the constitution of neurotic symptoms, Freud spells out that, in regard to the role of "causal overdetermination," dreams are "like all other psychopathological structures" (1900, p. 149).

Freudians, no less than the rest of us, are aware of the obvious differences between the hallucinatory nature of the (visual) manifest dream scenarios and the actual displays of neurotic symptoms in the real actions of waking life. But, in the context of psychoanalytic theory, the analyst Charles Rycroft (1973, p. 37) rightly stressed their deep-seated etiologic homology: "Freud's interest in dreams derived from the fact that they are normal processes with which everyone is familiar, *but which nonetheless exemplify the processes at work in the formation of neurotic symptoms*" (my italics).

In Freud's view, repressions are alike causally necessary for dream disguises no less than for neurosogenesis. In the case of a dream, a repressed wishful impulse "is the actual constructor of the dream: it provides the energy for its production and makes use of the day's residues as material" (1925b, p. 44); moreover, "*A wish which is represented in a dream must be an infantile one*" (1900, p. 553). As for neurosogenesis, the crucial pathogen is a sexual repression of some sort. Freud draws a rather unclear distinction between "*primal repression*," a first phase of denying the psychical representative of an instinct entry into consciousness, and "*repression proper*," a second stage or "after-repression" which banishes "mental derivatives of the repressed representative" (1915e, p. 148 and n. 2). But there is no textual evidence for supposing that he took the respective roles of the two phases of repression to *differ* at all as between dream formation and symptom formation. Furthermore, as shown by the function attributed to *primal fantasy* in the etiology of the Wolf-Man's obsessions (1918, pp. 89-103), such fantasies cannot be claimed to be more relevant to dream production than to neurosogenesis.

Indeed, Freud does stress the etiologic homology between dreams and neurotic symptoms once again, when he develops its momentous *investigative corollary* for the causal interpretation of dreams:

My patients were pledged to communicate to me every idea or thought that occurred to them in connection with some particular subject; amongst other things they told me their dreams and so taught me that a dream can be inserted into the psychical chain that has to be traced backwards in the memory from a pathological idea. It was then only a short step to treating the dream itself as a symptom and to applying to dreams the method of interpretation that had been worked out for symptoms [1900, pp. 100-101].

In short, having assimilated manifest dream contents to neurotic symptoms, Freud felt entitled to enlarge the epistemic role of free association from being only a method of etiologic inquiry aimed at therapy, to serving likewise as an avenue for fathoming the purported unconscious causes of dreams.

But to the detriment of his wish-fulfillment theory of dreaming, Freud completely overlooked a *therapeutic corollary* that is derivable from his assimilation of dreams to the compromise model of neurotic symptoms, in conjunction with the investigative corollary that he did draw: The effect of free association on lifting etiologic repressions should be similar for dreams and neurotic symptoms, not only *investigatively* but also, I claim, *therapeutically*. And I shall enlist just that therapeutic corollary in my impending argument against Freud's wish-fulfillment theory of dreaming.

First, let me just outline the argument. It will soon turn out that, in the context of the remainder of Freud's theory of repression and psychoanalytic therapy, his dream theory predicts a reduction in the *frequency* of dreaming among extensively psychoanalyzed patients. More precisely, Freud's assimilation of manifest dream content to minineurotic symptoms will turn out to have the following consequence: *Either* extensively analyzed patients should be "cured" of dreaming, *or* free association just fails as a means of lifting presumably repressed infantile wishes. But, as will emerge, contrary to the prediction that is derivable from the theory, there is no systematic evidence that long-term analysands experience dream reduction. Now let me supply the details and elaborate their significance.

Throughout his career, Freud explicitly linked the therapeutic and investigative functions of free association to one another in the context of full-fledged *psychopathology*. Thus, at the very start of his psychoanalytic career, Freud (1893, p. 35) said: "Breuer learnt from his first patient that the attempt at discovering the determining cause of a symptom was at the same time a therapeutic manoeuvre." And, at age 70, Freud declared: "In psychoanalysis there has existed from the very first an inseparable bond between cure and research [into etiology]. . . . Our analytic procedure [of free association] is the only one in which this precious conjunction is assured" (1927a, p. 256). I maintain that just as this linkage between the investigative and therapeutic functions of free association is appropriate to Freud's compromise model of full-fledged neurotic symptoms, so also—by full parity of reasoning—that same linkage is indeed appropriate to his extended compromise model of manifest dream content. Therefore, I claim, the etiologic homology of neurotic symptoms and manifest dream contents that is asserted by their shared compromise model spells a therapeutic corollary no less than the investigative one developed by Freud. Thus, the therapeutic effect of lifting etiologic repressions on neurotic symptoms should be paralleled by a like effect on dream formation: Lifting the infantile repressions to which Freud attributed dream generation should undermine or dissipate the very formation of dreams.

Recall that psychoanalytic theory postulates sexual repressions, in particular, to be causally necessary for neurosogenesis. Similarly, it also hypothesizes sundry sorts of repressed infantile wishes to be the causal *sine qua non* of the generation of all those dreams whose manifest content is a mendacious disguise for a latent content. Presumably, the vast majority of dreams have such latent content. Yet Freud (1900, pp. 123-126) points out that among short and simple dreams, there are many that bear their wish-fulfilling character "upon their faces without disguise" (p. 126). But Breuer and Freud (1893-95) had told us that if particular repressions are, in fact, causally necessary for psychopathology, then it follows deductively that the lifting (undoing) of these pathogenic repressions or conflicts by means of free association will issue in the conquest of the patient's afflictions. By complete parity of reasoning, I claim, if *repressed* infantile wishes are indeed the *sine qua non* of the formation of dreams that feature disguises, the patient's achievement of conscious awareness of these wishes will undercut and negate their previous causal role as dream generators. It appears, therefore, that to the extent that the patient's free associations do succeed in bringing his or her buried infantile wishes to light, the analysand should experience—and presumably exhibit neurophysiologically—a noticeable reduction in dream formation. Evidently this reduction should be a diminution in the *frequency* of dream generation, as distinct from mere thematic change in dream content.

It is a commonplace among analysts and their patients that changes in dream content occur routinely as a function of the thematic content of analytic sessions. Yet even protractedly analyzed patients do not report any remarkable subjective diminution of their recalled dream experiences. Nor, to my knowledge, have analysts been aware that the theoretical expectation of a reduction in the frequency of dreaming among such patients is indeed a logical consequence of Freud's dream theory, though an *unexpected* consequence. It is an investigative assumption of his "fundamental rule" that free associations of sufficient duration normally retrieve at least some buried infantile wishes among extensively analyzed patients.

We now see that if neurophysiological indicators (perhaps REM sleep) bear out that, among such long-term psychoanalytic patients, the expected decline in dream activity *fails* to materialize, then an important indictment would seem to follow: Either their free associations are chronically unsuccessful in retrieving their buried infantile wishes, or, if there is such retrieval, then Freud's account of dream generation is false. But if free association were to fail chronically even in just lifting repressions, that would be the therapeutic death knell of the clinical psychoanalytic enterprise, a debacle far more devastating than the mere demise of Freud's dream theory.

In response to my development of this argument, the psychoanalyst Philip Holzman invited my comment on the retort that no reduction of dream frequency is to be expected after all, because the impulse behind the emerging wishes remains undiminished in the unconscious. Mindful of the stated therapeutic import of Freud's compromise model of manifest dream content, I reply that this retort cannot obviate the discreditation of his account of dream formation, precisely because of the warranted parity of the reasoning in my argument with the basic rationale of psychoanalytic *therapy*. Why, I ask, should the *therapeutic* import of Freud's compromise model not apply alike to dream production and to the formation of ordinary neurotic symptoms? What is sauce for the goose is sauce for the gander. If lifting (and working through) the sexual repressions that are deemed pathogenic more or less cures the neuroses, then lifting (and working through) the repressions of infantile wishes should "cure" dreaming to the same extent, as it were. On the other hand, suppose, for argument's sake, that the impulse behind the previously repressed infantile wishes chronically generates new unconscious adult wishes which, in turn, engender dreams even as the patient becomes conscious of the earlier infantile ones. Why then does the pathogenic action of sexual repressions not only remain equally undiminished after *those* repressions are lifted? If psychoanalytic theory is taken to assert that we have an inexhaustible store of the wish impulses that beget dreams, how can it avoid the claim that we have a like store of pathogenic sexual impulses that are routinely renewed in adult life, if only by going to parties? By the same token, if psychoanalytic therapy is not doomed to fail at the very outset as a treatment of neuroses because of a surfeit of pathogenic impulses in neuroses, then it is impermissibly *ad hoc* for psychoanalysis to escape refutation by invoking undiminished dream generation, even as repressed infantile wishes are made conscious. In short, I deny that my "therapeutic" conclusion of dream reduction from my parity argument can be evaded without resorting to *ad hoc* devices not countenanced by Freudian theory.

In a lengthy critique of my views, David Sachs (1989, p. 371) deems the consequence I deduced from Freud's theory "startling," which I do not deny. But then he tried to parry it on the unavailing ground that the deduced diminution of dreams is a "folly" against which Freud allegedly issued an "implicit warning" (p. 371). Alas, Sachs offers nothing cogent against the *deducibility* of the so-called "folly" from Freud's major postulates. Instead, despite much textual evidence to the contrary in my writings (Grünbaum, 1984, chaps. 5, 8, 10, esp. p. 261; 1986, p. 273), he manufactures the gross red herring that "Grünbaum throughout insists that the only data on which Freud was both able and willing to draw were data of therapeutic upshot" (p. 372). How then is the embarrassing result that is deductively implicit in the Freudian corpus a "folly" of *mine*, merely because Freud would presumably reject dream diminution on straightforwardly empirical grounds? Apparently, Sachs treats us to the specious argument that an observationally false claim cannot be a logical consequence of a theory *T* just because *T*'s originator had not *intended* it. By this gambit, any theory at all could be immunized against discreditation by unexpected contrary facts.

FREUD'S 1933 "REVISION OF THE THEORY OF DREAMS"

In later writings (1920a, pp. 13-14, 32-33; 1922, p. 208), Freud acknowledged that one particular sort of wish-contravening dream calls for revision of his wish-fulfillment theory of dreaming by furnishing an exception to its validity: Victims of traumatic neuroses, such as soldiers traumatized by combat, keep reliving their shocking experiences in their dreams. Thus, Freud was willing

> . . . to admit for the first time an exception to the proposition that dreams are fulfilments of wishes. Anxiety dreams, as I have shown repeatedly and in detail, offer no such exception. Nor do 'punishment dreams', for they merely replace the forbidden wish-fulfilment by the appropriate punishment for it; that is to say, they fulfil the wish of the sense of guilt which is the reaction to the repudiated impulse. But it is impossible to classify as wish-fulfilments the dreams we have been discussing which occur in traumatic neuroses, or the dreams during psychoanalyses which bring to memory the psychical traumas of childhood [1920a, p. 32].

But if the reproductions of traumatic scenes in dreams thus prompted Freud "to revise the theory of dreams" (1922, p.

208), just what form was that revision to take? As we recall, the 1900 theory had asserted that, for every dream D, there is at least one wish W such that (1) W must be the motivational cause of D; and (2) the manifest content of D graphically displays (disguisedly) the state of affairs desired by W.

Do trauma-repeating dreams mandate the revision of (1), or of (2), or of both? In his initial 1920 modification, he retracted both (1) and (2). But, as we shall see further on, by the time he published his 1933 "Revision of the Theory of Dreams," he repudiated, in effect, his retraction of (1) and explicitly retracted only (2). His twofold disavowal in 1920 is intertwined with a phylogenetic speculation. Trauma-reproducing dreams, we learn,

> . . . arise, rather, in obedience to the compulsion to repeat, though it is true that in analysis that compulsion is supported by the wish (which is encouraged by 'suggestion') to conjure up what has been forgotten and repressed. Thus it would seem that the function of dreams, which consists in setting aside any motives that might interrupt sleep, by fulfilling the wishes of the disturbing impulses, is not their *original* function. It would not be possible for them to perform that function until the whole of mental life had accepted the dominance of the pleasure principle. If there is a 'beyond the pleasure principle', it is only consistent to grant that there was also a time before the purpose of dreams was the fulfilment of wishes. This would imply no denial of their later function [1920a, pp. 32-33].

Freud's 1920 attribution here of trauma-reenacting dreams to the compulsion to repeat repudiates not only the wish-fulfilling role of such dreams, but even the applicability of his compromise model of symptoms to their distressing manifest contents. As Laplanche and Pontalis (1973) have rightly pointed out:

> In elaborating the theory of the compulsion to repeat, Freud treats it [this compulsion] as an autonomous factor which cannot ultimately be reduced to a conflictual dynamic entirely circumscribed by the interplay between the pleasure principle and the reality principle [p. 78; italics omitted].

Equally appropriately, these authors have appraised the notion of this compulsion unfavorably:

The concept reflects all the hesitations, the deadends and even the contradictions of Freud's speculative hypotheses. This is one of the reasons why the discussion of the repetition compulsion is so confused—and so often resumed—in psychoanalytic literature. The debate inevitably involves fundamental options regarding the most vital notions of Freud's work, such as the pleasure principle, instinct, the death instincts and binding [p.78].

The incoherence of his notion of the repetition compulsion is well illustrated by the role Freud envisioned for that compulsion in the phylogeny he postulated for the function of dreams (1920a, pp. 32-33). As he told us à propos of trauma-rehearsing dreams in the last passage I quoted, the wish-fulfilling function of dreams was "not their *original* function." Instead, "there was also a time before the purpose of dreams was the fulfilment of wishes. This would imply no denial of their later function." But if the hypothesized archaic function of dreaming was "obedience to the compulsion to repeat," how are we to understand the totality of the dream productions of the traumatic neurotics who lived in the twentieth century?

Are *all* their dreams in fact just reenacted traumas? Do these people not also have *some* ordinary anxiety dreams, punishment dreams, or even innocuous ones, all of which, according to Freud, must be wish fulfilling? And is their dreaming apparatus just a historical relic that has been replaced, *in the rest of us*, by the wish-fulfilling agency of the pleasure principle? But don't some of the rest of us occasionally have nightmares that feature reenactments of traumatic episodes, such as a major automobile accident in which a loved one was killed while we were at the steering wheel? Of course, traumatic neurotics are most likely to complain about their nocturnal hallucinatory reenactments of traumas. Yet presumably, unless Freud produced evidence to the contrary, such neurotics sometimes have garden variety dreams, no less than the rest of us occasionally have a traumatically recapitulatory nightmare. If so, does the totality of dreams of each group then have the dual function of part-time obedience to the pleasure principle yet also part-time adherence to the compulsion to repeat that is "beyond" it? Astonishingly, Freud seems not to have addressed these tantalizing questions, though answers to them become imperative in his 1920 *Beyond the Pleasure Principle*.

Instead of answering those questions by the time of his 1933 "Revision" he transformed the doctrine that had generated the queries. But that 1933 modification, in turn, raised other, related difficulties that are no less troublesome.

By 1933, six years before Freud's death, we are told that "only two serious difficulties have arisen against the wish-fulfilment theory of dreams" (p. 28). But of these, only one seems insurmountable to him:

> . . . people who have experienced a shock, a severe psychical trauma—such as happened so often during the war and such as affords the basis for traumatic hysteria—are regularly taken back in their dreams into the traumatic situation. According to our hypotheses about the function of dreams this should not occur. What wishful impulse could be satisfied by harking back in this way to this exceedingly distressing traumatic experience? It is hard to guess [p. 28].

How, then, did Freud propose to deal with this difficulty? After issuing the caveat that discussion of it "has not yet, indeed, brought us to any wholly satisfying conclusion" (p. 28), he replied on the next page:

> We should not, I think, be afraid to admit that here the function of the dream has failed. . . . We say that a dream is the fulfilment of a wish; but if you want to take these latter objections into account, you can say nevertheless that a dream is an *attempt* at the fulfilment of a wish. . . . In certain circumstances a dream is only about to put its intention into effect very incompletely, or must abandon it entirely. Unconscious fixation to a trauma seems to be foremost among these obstacles to the function of dreaming. While the sleeper is obliged to dream, because the relaxation of repression at night allows the upward pressure of the traumatic fixation to become active, there is a failure in the functioning of his dream-work, which would like to transform the memory-traces of the traumatic event into the fulfilment of a wish. In these circumstances it will happen that one cannot sleep, that one gives up sleep from dread of the failure of the function of dreaming [p. 29].

Thus, according to Freud's somewhat metaphorical notion of *attempted* wish fulfillment, even in a traumatic dream, a wish is still the driving motive that *initiates* the process of dream generation. But an "unconscious fixation to a trauma" aborts the process of transformation by which the dream work normally issues in a manifest content so that the fulfillment of the given wish is portrayed more or less disguisedly.

Thus, the chronically traumatic dreams of war neurotics prompted Freud to revise his dream theory as follows: He retracted the universality of wish fulfillment in the dream *content*, but he did reiterate that a wish is universally the driving *motive* of the process of dream generation. In short, Freud gave up one conjunct of his encapsulation of his wish-fulfilling theory, while retaining the other. Such a modification of his 1900 theory is feasible, since neither of these two conjuncts is redundant with the other. This summary recasts more lucidly the compressed account of Freud's 1933 revision that I gave in my book (1984, pp. 238-239).

There I offered his revision to illustrate that, contrary to Popper (1962, p. 38, n. 3; 1938, chap. II), Freud had indeed responded to adverse evidence and had modified his theory (Grünbaum, 1984, pp. 112, 220). In defense of Popper, Mark Notturno and Paul McHugh (1986) conflated the two conjuncts of Freud's theory and, in effect, argued fallaciously against me that since Freud had reaffirmed the second of these conjuncts in 1933, he could not have retracted the first. Chapter 2 reprints my most comprehensive critique of Popper's treatment of psychoanalysis (Grünbaum, 1989), where I deal with his 1983 discussion of the issues, which is more detailed than any of his earlier ones. In response to my 1989 paper, Paul McHugh, chairman of the Department of Psychiatry at Johns Hopkins University, wrote me (private communication, January 20, 1989): "You certainly mount a tremendously powerful reply to any defender of Karl Popper. I can only wave the white flag."

But what are the merits of Freud's 1933 "Revision"?

What wish, we must ask, was the purported driving motive of the dream in which the dream work was thwarted by the "upward pressure of the traumatic fixation"? Freud does not tell us. But Eli Zaretski (private communication) has suggested that though the dream-generating process recapitulates a trauma in its manifest content, the motivational cause of the dream is the wish to *avoid* just that recapitulation. Let me assume that Zaretski's suggested reading does capture Freud's own view as to the identity of the hypothesized wish motive for the trauma dreams.

Then the question is: What evidence can Freud or Zaretski offer—without begging the question—that the motive of the traumatic dream is a wish at all, let alone that it is the wish to *avoid* experiencing a painful manifest content? Just for argument's sake, let us grant that the method of free association does have the epistemic capability of ferreting out the purportedly dream-producing wishes for all those dreams in which the dream work is not aborted. Even if we make this dubious assumption, which I reject (Grünbaum, 1984, chaps. 4 and 5), Freud's aforecited own account of the failure of the dream work in the case of the traumatic dreams at least allows that their manifest contents will not contain the causal traces of the putative wish motive. But, if so, then even by Freud's own tribute to the epistemic capacity of free associations as a means of uncovering the causes of dreams, it is unavailing to let a traumatic neurotic associate to the elements of his painful manifest dream contents: Presumably, the traces of the purported wish motives will not be carried into these contents. Moreover, Freud gave us no report on whether he or other analysts had asked traumatic neurotics systematically to associate to their distressing dreams after all, and whether an *unconscious* wish to *avoid* just these traumatic manifest contents emerged. Thus, free association has not authenticated the supposed wish to avoid traumatic dreams as the motive for just those dreams that fail to fulfill the putative wish.

Furthermore, as is clear from my discussion of the requirements for validating the attribution of counterwish dreams to wish motives, no cogent evidence has been offered at all for attributing traumatic dreams causally to the wish to avoid them. In any case, that wish does not seem to qualify as a *repressed* infantile one. Nor had Freud offered a believable warrant for his earlier 1920 ascription of such dreams to the compulsion to repeat.

It emerges that Freud validated neither his 1920 nor his 1933 revision of his 1900 dream theory.

It behooves Freudians to tell us just what they think they might still salvage from Freud's emphatic dictum: *"The interpretation of dreams is the royal road to a knowledge of the unconscious activities of the mind"* (1900, p. 608).

CONCLUSION

In an earlier monograph in this *Psychological Issues* series, the psychoanalyst and philosopher Carlo Strenger (1991, p. 10) notes that such hermeneuticist writers as R. Schafer, G. S. Klein, P. Ricoeur, and J. Habermas have offered three sorts of defense of psychoanalysis against epistemological criticisms that have been leveled against it: (1) Objections predicated on Freud's own "scientistic" conception of psychoanalysis are beside the mark, because precisely that conception suffers from his misunderstanding of his own psychoanalytic enterprise. (2) The hermeneuticist reconstruction of psychoanalysis as a theory of "meanings," and reasons for action, constructively obviates just such "scientistic" objections; and (3) "the epistemic weaknesses [of psychoanalysis] apply only to [its] metapsychology and not to what has been labeled the clinical theory of psychoanalysis." In chapters 1 and 4, I have argued that these defenses fail.

Strenger (1991, p. 5) generously characterized my (1984) book as having "presented a critique of the evidential foundations of psychoanalysis, unprecedented in its clarity and incisiveness." Furthermore, he declares (p. 10): "It is therefore a further advantage of Grünbaum's [1984] book that it is concerned exclusively with the clinical theory, thus precluding the defense that he is attacking a straw man [metapsychology], an anachronism."

For just this reason, this monograph, no less than my book (1984), is largely devoted to the clinical theory, as emphasized in its title and in chapter 1. But Freud's extension of his clinical theory to the elaboration of a psychoanalytic psychology of religion warranted chapter 7. And the fundamental challenge to the therapeutic bases of the clinical theory posed by placebogenic phenomena, which I set forth in chapter 1, prompted the generalized inquiry, in chapter 3, into the very concept of placebo throughout medicine and psychiatry.

Despite Edelson's criticisms of my pessimism concerning the validational capabilities of the psychoanalytic treatment setting (see chapters 4 and 6 above), he is of one mind with me in rejecting the stated three defenses of the clinical theory offered by the hermeneuticist writers mentioned by Strenger.

Another distinguished and philosophically informed psychoanalyst, the late Benjamin B. Rubinstein (1983), writing in his valuable contribution to a 1983 *Festschrift* for me (Cohen and Laudan, 1983), offered a major conclusion (p. 187) that I have endeavored to vindicate extensively in this monograph:

> The theory of hysteria is not all of psychoanalysis. But it epitomizes a number of the problems that beset this discipline. . . . Critical psychoanalysts are in the habit of blaming Freud's metapsychology for all the difficulties inherent in the theory [footnote omitted]. Metapsychology, however, presents a comparatively minor problem. . . .
> *It is the clinical part of psychoanalysis that is really disturbing. It is top-heavy with theory but has only a slim evidential base.* I have used the theory of hysteria to illustrate the arbitrariness, because of lack of adequate confirmation, of a great many clinical interpretations. This statement holds also beyond hysteria. That, of course, does not mean that all clinical interpretations fail in this way. But it is those that do that interest us here [italics added].

REFERENCES

ABRAHAM, K. (1922). The spider as a dream symbol. In *Selected Papers on Psychoanalysis*. New York: Basic Books, 1953, pp. 326-332.

ABRAHAMSEN, D. (1977). *Nixon vs. Nixon: An Emotional Tragedy*. New York: Farrar, Straus & Giroux.

ALBERT, H. (1979). *Das Elend der Theologie*. Hamburg: Hoffmann & Campe.

ALEXANDER, F. (1935). Concerning the genesis of the castration complex. *Psychoanal. Rev.*, 23:51-52.

—— (1963). *Fundamentals of Psychoanalysis*. New York: Norton.

—— (1966). Sandor Rado. In *Psychoanalytic Pioneers*, ed. F. Alexander, S. Eisenstein, & M. Grotjahn. New York: Basic Books, pp. 240-248.

—— & FRENCH, T. M. (1946). *Psychoanalytic Therapy*. New York: Ronald Press.

ASHER, H. (1976). *Causal Modeling*. Beverly Hills, Calif.: Sage.

BACHRACH, H. M., GALATZER-LEVY, R., SKOLNIKOFF, A., & WALDRON, S., Jr. (1991). On the efficacy of psychoanalysis. *J. Amer. Psychoanal. Assn.*, 39:871–916.

BASCH, M. (1980). *Doing Psychotherapy*. New York: Basic Books.

BEECHER, H. K. (1961). Surgery as placebo. *J. Amer. Med. Assn.*, 176:1102-1107.

—— (1972). The placebo effect as a non-specific force surrounding disease and the treatment of disease. In *Pain: Basic Principles, Pharmacology, Therapy*, ed. J. Janzen et al. Stuttgart: Thieme.

BENSON, H. & McCALLIE, D. P. (1979). Angina pectoris and the placebo effect. *New Engl. J. Med.*, 300:1424-1429.

BERGIN, A. E. & LAMBERT, M. J. (1978). The evaluation of therapeutic outcomes. In *Handbook of Psychotherapy and Behavior Change* (2nd ed.), ed. S. L. Garfield & A. E. Bergin. New York: Wiley, pp. 139-189.

BETTELHEIM, B. (1982). *Freud and Man's Soul*. New York: Random House.

BLAKISTON'S (1972). *Gould Medical Dictionary* (3rd ed.). New York: McGraw-Hill.

BLALOCK, H. (1961). *Causal Inferences in Nonexperimental Research*. New York: Norton.

—— (1969). *Theory Construction*. Englewood Cliffs, N.J.: Prentice-Hall.

BOK, S. (1974). The ethics of giving placebos. *Sci. Amer.*, 231 (November):17-23.

BOURNE, H. R. (1971). The placebo: A poorly understood and neglected therapeutic agent. *Rational Drug Therapy*, 5:1-6.

BRANDT, L. W. (1966). Process or structure? *Psychoanal. Rev.*, 53:50.

BRENNER, C. (1976). *Psychoanalytic Technique and Psychic Conflict*. New York: Int. Univ. Press.

385

────── (1982). *The Mind in Conflict*. New York: Int. Univ. Press.
BREUER, J. & FREUD, S. (1893). The psychical mechanism of hysterical phenomena: Preliminary communication. *S. E.*,* 2:3-17.
────── ────── (1893-95). Studies on Hysteria. *S. E.*, 2.
BRODY, H. (1977). *Placebos and the Philosophy of Medicine*. Chicago: Univ. Chicago Press.
────── (1985). Placebo effect: An examination of Grünbaum's definition. In *Placebo Theory, Research and Mechanisms*, ed. L. White et al. New York: Guilford Press, pp. 37-58.
BRODY, J. (1979). Placebos work, but survey shows widespread misuse. *N.Y. Times*, April 3, C. 1.
BROWN, D. (1980). Tchaikovsky. In *The New Grove's Dictionary of Music and Musicians*, ed. S. Sadie. London: Macmillan, vol. 18, pp. 626-628.
CAMPBELL, D. & STANLEY, J. (1963). *Experimental and Quasi-Experimental Designs for Research*. Chicago: Rand McNally.
CAMPBELL, R. J., Ed. (1981). *Psychiatric Dictionary* (5th ed.). New York: Oxford Univ. Press. A sixth edition appeared in 1989.
────── (1989). *Psychiatric Dictionary* (6th ed.). New York: Oxford Univ. Press.
CARNAP, R. (1936). Testability and meaning. *Phil. Sci.*, 3:419-471.
────── (1937). Testability and meaning. *Phil. Sci.*, 4:2-40.
CHRISTIANSEN, B. (1964). The scientific status of psychoanalytic clinical evidence. *Inquiry*, 7:47-49.
CIOFFI, F. (1985). Psychoanalysis, pseudo-science and testability. In *Popper and the Human Sciences*, ed. G. Currie & A. Musgrave. Dordrecht: Nijhoff, pp. 13-44.
────── (1988). "Exegetical myth-making" in Grünbaum's indictment of Popper and exoneration of Freud. In *Mind, Psychoanalysis and Science*, ed. P. Clark & C. Wright. Oxford: Blackwell, pp. 61-87.
COHEN, M. R. & NAGEL, E. (1934). *Introduction to Logic and Scientific Method*. New York: Harcourt, Brace.
COHEN, R. S. & LAUDAN, L.., eds. (1983). *Physics, Philosophy, and Psychoanalysis, Essays in Honor of Adolf Grünbaum*. Dordrect, Holland: Kluwer Academic Publishers.
CONSIDINE, D. M. (1976). *Van Nostrand's Scientific Encyclopedia* (5th ed.). New York: Van Nostrand, p. 1335.
COOK, T. & CAMPBELL, D. (1979). The design and conduct of quasi-experiments and true experiments in field settings. In *Handbook of Industrial and Organizational Psychology*, ed. M. Dunnette. Chicago: Rand McNally, pp. 223-326.
COOPER, A. M. & MICHELS, R. (1978). An era of growth. In *Controversy in Psychiatry*, ed. J. P. Brady & H. K. H. Brodie. Philadelphia: Saunders, pp. 369-385.
CREWS, F. (1986). *Skeptical Engagements*. New York: Oxford Univ. Press.
CRITELLI, J. W. & NEUMANN, K. F. (1984). The placebo. *Amer. Psychologist*, 39:32-39.
DAVIS, J. M. & COLE, J. O. (1975a). Antipsychotic drugs. In *Comprehensive Textbook of Psychiatry* (2nd ed.), ed. A. M. Freedman, H. T. Kaplan, & B. J. Sadock. Baltimore: Williams & Wilkins, Vol. 1, pp. 1922-1930.

The Standard Edition of the Complete Psychological Works of Sigmund Freud, 24 vols. London: Hogarth Press, 1955-1974.

———— & ———— (1975b). Antipsychotic drugs. In *American Handbook of Psychiatry* (2nd ed.), ed. S. Arieti. New York: Basic Books, Vol. 5, pp. 444-447.

DETRE, K. M., PEDUZZI, P., TAKARO, T., HULTGREN, N., MURPHY, M. L., & KRONCKE, G. (1984). Eleven-year survival in the Veterans Administration randomized trial of coronary bypass surgery for stable angina. *N. Engl. J. Med.*, 311:1333-1339.

DORIAN, F. (1981). Tchaikovsky's death a suicide! A biographical correction. In *Pittsburgh Symphony Orchestra Program Magazine* (October 23), pp. 224-227.

DYWAN, J. & BOWERS, K. (1983). The use of hypnosis to enhance recall. *Science*, 222:184-185.

EAGLE, M. (1983). The epistemological status of recent developments in psychoanalytic theory. In *Physics, Philosophy and Psychoanalysis: Essays in Honor of Adolf Grünbaum*, ed. R. S. Cohen & L. Laudan. Boston: Reidel, pp. 31-55.

———— (1984a). Psychoanalysis and modern psychodynamic theories. In *Personality and the Behavior Disorders* (rev. ed.), ed. N. S. Endler & J. McV. Hunt. New York: Wiley.

———— (1984b). *Recent Developments in Psychoanalysis: A Critical Evaluation.* New York: McGraw-Hill.

———— (1986). A. Grünbaum's *The Foundations of Psychoanalysis: A Philosophical Critique. Philosophy of Science*, 53:65-88.

EDELSON, M. (1984). *Hypothesis and Evidence in Psychoanalysis.* Chicago: Univ. Chicago Press.

———— (1986). Causal explanation in science and in psychoanalysis. *Psychoanal. Study Child*, 41:89-127.

———— (1988). *Psychoanalysis: A Theory in Crisis.* Chicago: Univ. Chicago Press.

EDWARDS, P. (1992). The dependence of consciousness on the brain. In *Immortality*, ed. P. Edwards. New York: Macmillan Publishing Co., pp. 292–307.

EFRON, A. (1967). Magnetic hysteresis. In *The Harper Encyclopedia of Science* (rev. ed.), ed. J. R. Newman. New York: Harper & Row, p. 694.

EISSLER, K. R. (1969). Irreverent remarks about the present and the future of psychoanalysis. *Int. J. Psycho-Anal.*, 50:461-471.

ELLENBERGER, H. F. (1970). *The Discovery of the Unconscious.* New York: Basic Books.

———— (1972). The story of "Anna O.": A critical review with new data. *J. Hist. Behav. Sci.*, 8:267-279.

ERDELYI, M. H. (1985). *Psychoanalysis.* New York: Freeman.

———— (1986). Psychoanalysis has a wider scope than the retrospective discovery of etiologies. *Behav. & Brain Sci.*, 9:234–235.

ERIKSON, E. H. (1954). The dream specimen of psychoanalysis. *J. Amer. Psychoanal. Assn.*, 2:5–56.

ERWIN, E. (1978). *Behavior Therapy.* New York: Cambridge Univ. Press.

———— (1992). Philosophers on Freudianism: Replies to Grünbaum's *Foundations*. In *Philosophical Problems of the Internal and External Worlds: Essays on the Philosophy of Adolf Grünbaum*, ed. J. Earman et al. Pittsburgh, PA: Univ. of Pittsburgh Press.

EYSENCK, H. J. (1963). *Uses and Abuses of Psychology.* Baltimore: Penguin Books.

———— (1980). A unified theory of psychotherapy, behaviour therapy and spontaneous remission. *Zschr. Psychol.*, 188:44-56.
———— & WILSON, G. D. (1973). *The Experimental Study of Freudian Theories.* London: Methuen.
FANCHER, R. E. (1973). *Psychoanalytic Psychology.* New York: Norton.
FENICHEL, O. (1945). *The Psychoanalytic Theory of Neurosis.* New York: Norton.
FERGUSON, M. (1981). Progress and theory change: The two analyses of Mr. Z. *Annu. Psychoanal.*, 9:133–160.
FEUER, L. S., Ed. (1959). *Basic Writings on Politics and Philosophy, Karl Marx and Friedrich Engels.* Garden City, N.Y.: Doubleday.
FISH, J. M. (1973). *Placebo Therapy.* San Francisco: Jossey-Bass.
FISHER, S. & GREENBERG, R. P. (1977). *The Scientific Credibility of Freud's Theory and Therapy.* New York: Basic Books.
FLAX, J. (1981). Psychoanalysis and the philosophy of science: Critique or resistance? *J. Phil.*, 78:561-569.
FLIESS, R., Ed. (1948). *The Psychoanalytic Reader.* New York: Int. Univ. Press.
FRANK, G. H. (1965). The role of the family in the development of psychopathology. *Psychol. Bull.*, 64:191-205.
FRANK, J. D. (1973). *Persuasion and Healing* (rev. ed.). Baltimore: Johns Hopkins Univ. Press.
———— (1974). Therapeutic components of psychotherapy. *J. Nerv. Ment. Dis.*, 159:325-342.
FREUD, A. (1969). Difficulties in the path of psychoanalysis. In *The Writings of Anna Freud*, Vol. 7, pp. 124-156. New York: Int. Univ. Press, 1971.
FREUD, S. (1883-1938). *Collected Papers.* New York: Basic Books, 1959.
———— (1893). On the psychical mechanism of hysterical phenomena. *S. E.*, 3:25-39.
———— (1895a). Project for a scientific psychology. *S. E.*, 1:283-397.
———— (1895b). A reply to criticisms of my paper on anxiety neurosis. *S. E.*, 3:123-139.
———— (1896). The aetiology of hysteria. *S. E.*, 3:191-221.
———— (1898). Sexuality in the aetiology of the neuroses. *S. E.*, 3:263-285.
———— (1900). The interpretation of dreams. *S. E.*, 4 & 5.
———— (1901). The psychopathology of everyday life. *S. E.*, 6:1-279.
———— (1905a). Fragment of an analysis of a case of hysteria. *S. E.*, 7:7-122.
———— (1905b). Three essays on the theory of sexuality. *S. E.*, 7:126-243.
———— (1907). Obsessive actions and religious practices. *S. E.*, 9:115-127.
———— (1908). Character and anal erotism. *S. E.*, 9:167-175.
———— (1909a). Analysis of a phobia in a five-year-old boy. *S. E.*, 10:5-147.
———— (1909b). Notes upon a case of obsessional neurosis. *S. E.*, 10:155-318.
———— (1910a). Leonardo da Vinci and a memory of his childhood. *S. E.*, 11:63-137.
———— (1910b). A special type of choice of object made by men. *S. E.*, 11:165–175.
———— (1911). Psycho-analytic notes on an autobiographical account of a case of paranoia (dementia paranoides). *S. E.*, 12:9-79.
———— (1912a). The dynamics of transference. *S. E.*, 12:99-108.
———— (1912b). A note on the unconscious in psycho-analysis. *S. E.*, 12:260-266.
———— (1912c). Recommendations to physicians practising psycho-analysis. *S. E.*, 12:111-120.

—— (1913a). On beginning the treatment. *S. E.*, 12:123-144.

—— (1913b). The disposition to obsessional neurosis. *S. E.*, 12:311–326.

—— (1913c). Animism, magic and the omnipotence of thought. *S. E.*, 13:75-99.

—— (1913d). The claims of psycho-analysis to scientific interest. *S. E.*, 13:163-190.

—— (1913e). Totem and taboo. *S. E.*, 13:1-162.

—— (1914a). Remembering, repeating and working-through. *S. E.*, 12:147-156.

—— (1914b). On the history of the psycho-analytic movement. *S. E.*, 14:7-66.

—— (1914c). On narcissism: An introduction. *S. E.*, 14:73-102.

—— (1915a). A case of paranoia running counter to the psycho-analytic theory of the disease. *S. E.*, 14:263-272.

—— (1915b). Instincts and their vicissitudes. *S. E.*, 14:117-140.

—— (1915c). The unconscious. *S. E.*, 14:166-215.

—— (1915d). Thoughts for the times on war and death. *S. E.*, 14:271-302.

—— (1915e). Repression. *S. E.*, 14:141-158.

—— (1916-17). Introductory lectures on psycho-analysis. *S. E.*, 15-16:15-463.

—— (1917). A difficulty in the path of psycho-analysis. *S. E.*, 17:137-144.

—— (1918). From the history of an infantile neurosis. *S. E.*, 17:7-122.

—— (1919). The "uncanny." *S. E.*, 17:219-256.

—— (1920a). Beyond the pleasure principle. *S. E.*, 18:7-64.

—— (1920b). The psychogenesis of a case of homosexuality in a woman. *S. E.*, 18:147-172.

—— (1921). Group psychology and the analysis of the ego. *S. E.*, 18:65-143.

—— (1922). Some neurotic mechanisms in jealousy, paranoia and homosexuality. *S. E.*, 18:223-232.

—— (1923a). The ego and the id. *S. E.*, 19:12-59.

—— (1923b). Remarks on the theory and practice of dream-interpretation. *S. E.*, 19:109-121.

—— (1923c). Two encyclopaedia articles. *S. E.*, 18:235-259.

—— (1924). A short account of psycho-analysis. *S. E.*, 19:191-209.

—— (1925a). Some psychical consequences of the anatomical distinction between the sexes. *S. E.*, 19:248-258.

—— (1925b). An autobiographical study. *S. E.*, 20:7-70.

—— (1926a). Inhibitions, symptoms and anxiety. *S. E.*, 20:87-174.

—— (1926b). The question of lay analysis. *S. E.*, 20:183-250.

—— (1926c). Psychoanalysis [Freudian school]. *S. E.*, 20:263-270 [1930].

—— (1927a). Postscript [to a discussion on lay analysis]. *S. E.*, 20:251-258.

—— (1927b). The future of an illusion. *S. E.*, 21:1-56.

—— (1930). Civilization and its discontents. *S. E.*, 21:59-145.

—— (1933). New introductory lectures on psycho-analysis. *S. E.*, 22:5-182.

—— (1934). Letter to Saul Rosenzweig. In Luborsky & Spence (1978), pp. 356-357.

—— (1937a). Analysis terminable and interminable. *S. E.*, 23:216-253.

—— (1937b). Constructions in analysis. *S. E.*, 23:257-269.

—— (1939). Moses and monotheism: Three essays. *S. E.*, 23:1-137.

390   VALIDATION: CLINICAL THEORY OF PSYCHOANALYSIS

———— (1940a). An outline of psycho-analysis. *S. E.*, 23:144-207.
———— (1940b). Some elementary lessons in psycho-analysis. *S. E.*, 23:281-286.
———— (1940-52). *Gesammelte Werke*. London: Imago.
———— (1954). *The Origins of Psychoanalysis*. New York: Basic Books.
———— (1972). *Die Traumdeutung. Freud Studienausgabe*, vol. II. Frankfurt/Main: Fischer Verlag.
———— & BULLITT, W. (1967). *Thomas Woodrow Wilson*. Boston: Houghton Mifflin.
FRIEDMAN, R. (1986). The sayings of Rabbi Kahane. *N.Y. Rev. Books* 3(February 13):19.
GADAMER, H. G. (1975). *Truth and Method*. New York: Seabury Press.
GALLIMORE, R. G. & TURNER, J. L. (1977). Contemporary studies of placebo phenomena. In *Psychopharmacology in the Practice of Medicine*, ed. M. E. Jarvik. New York: Appleton-Century-Crofts, pp. 47-57.
GALTON, F. (1872). Statistical inquiries into the efficacy of prayer. *Fortnightly Rev.*, 12:125-135.
GARDINER, M., Ed. (1971). *The Wolf Man*. New York: Basic Books.
GARDNER, M. (1986). Niebuhr and supernaturalism. *N.Y. Rev. Books* (March 27):52-53.
GARFIELD, S. L. & BERGIN, A. E., Eds. (1978). *Handbook of Psychotherapy and Behavior Change* (2nd ed.). New York: Wiley.
GAY, P. (1985). *Freud for Historians*. New York: Oxford Univ. Press.
———— (1988). *Freud*. New York: Norton.
GEDO, J. E. (1979). *Beyond Interpretation: Toward a Revised Theory of Psychoanalysis*. New York: Int. Univ. Press.
———— (1980). Reflections on some current controversies in psychoanalysis. *J. Amer. Psychoanal. Assn.*, 28:363-383.
GIBBON, E. (1899). *Decline and Fall of the Roman Empire*. New York: Peter Fenelon Collier, p. 523.
GIERE, R. (1979). *Understanding Scientific Reasoning*. New York: Holt, Rinehart & Winston.
GLIEDMAN, L. H., NASH, E. H., IMBER, S. D., STONE, A. R., & FRANK, J. D. (1958). Reduction of symptoms by pharmacologically inert substances and by short-term psychotherapy. *Arch. Neurol. & Psychiat.*, 79:345-351.
GLOVER, E. (1931). The therapeutic effect of inexact interpretation: A contribution to the theory of suggestion. *Int. J. Psychoanal.*, 12:397-411.
———— (1952). Research methods in psychoanalysis. *Int. J. Psychoanal.*, 8:403-409.
GLYMOUR, C. (1974). Freud, Kepler and the clinical evidence. In *Freud*, ed. R. Wollheim. New York: Anchor Books, pp. 285-304.
———— (1980). *Theory and Evidence*. Princeton: Princeton Univ. Press.
———— (1982). Afterword by Glymour (1974). In *Philosophical Essays on Freud*, ed. R. Wollheim & J. Hopkins. New York: Cambridge Univ. Press, pp. 29-31.
———— (1983). The theory of your dreams. In *Physics, Philosophy and Psychoanalysis: Essays in Honor of Adolf Grünbaum*, ed. R. S. Cohen & L. Laudan. Boston: Reidel, pp. 57-71.
GOODMAN, L. S. & GILMAN, A., Eds. (1975). *The Pharmacological Basis of Therapeutics* (5th ed.). London: Macmillan.

REFERENCES 391

GRÜNBAUM, A. (1972). Free will and laws of human behavior. In *New Readings in Philosophical Analysis*, ed. H. Feigl, W. Sellars, & K. Lehrer. New York: Appleton-Century-Crofts, pp. 605-627.

―――― (1973). *Philosophical Problems of Space and Time*, 2nd ed. Boston: Reidel.

―――― (1976). Is falsifiability the touchstone of scientific rationality? Karl Popper versus inductivism. In *Essays in Memory of Imre Lakatos*, ed. R. S. Cohen, P. K. Feyerabend, & M. W. Wartofsky. Boston: Reidel, pp. 213-252.

―――― (1977). How scientific is psychoanalysis? In *Science and Psychotherapy*, ed. R. Stern, L. Horowitz, & J. Lynes. New York: Haven Press, pp. 219-254.

―――― (1979a). Is Freudian psychoanalytic theory pseudo-scientific by Karl Popper's criterion of demarcation? *Amer. Phil. Q.*, 16:131-141.

―――― (1979b). Epistemological liabilities of the clinical appraisal of psychoanalytic theory. *Psychoanal. & Contemp. Thought*, 2:451-526.

―――― (1980). The role of psychological explanations of the rejection or acceptance of scientific theories. *A Festschrift for Robert Merton*. In *Trans. N.Y. Acad. Sci.*, Series II, Vol. 39, pp. 75-90.

―――― (1981). The placebo concept. *Behav. Res. & Ther.*, 19:157-167.

―――― (1982). Can psychoanalytic theory be cogently tested "on the couch"? Part II. *Psychoanal. & Contemp. Thought*, 5:311-436.

―――― (1983). Is object-relations theory better founded than orthodox psychoanalysis? A reply to Jane Flax. *J. Phil.*, 80:46-51.

―――― (1984). *The Foundations of Psychoanalysis: A Philosophical Critique*. Berkeley & Los Angeles: Univ. California Press.

―――― (1986). Précis of *The Foundations of Psychoanalysis: A Philosophical Critique*, and author's response to 39 reviewers: Is Freud's theory well-founded? *Behav. & Brain Sci.*, 9:217-284.

―――― (1988). Are hidden motives in psychoanalysis reasons but not causes of human conduct? In *Hermeneutics and Psychological Theory: Interpretative Perspectives on Personality, Psychotherapy and Psychopathology*, ed. S. B. Messer, L. A. Sass, & R. L. Woolfolk. New Brunswick, N.J.: Rutgers Univ. Press, pp. 149-167.

―――― (1989). Why thematic kinships between events DO NOT attest their causal linkage. *A Festschrift for Robert E. Butts*. In *An Intimate Relation: Studies in the History and Philosophy of Science*, ed. J. R. Brown & J Mittelstrass. Boston: Reidel.

―――― (1990a). Meaning connections and causal connections in the human sciences: The poverty of hermeneutic philosophy. *J. Amer. Psychoanal. Assn.*, 38:559-577.

―――― (1990b). Pseudo-creation of the big bang. *Nature*, 344:821-822.

―――― (1991). Creation as a pseudo-explanation in current physical cosmology. *Erkenntnis*, 35:233-254.

―――― (1992). In defense of secular humanism. *Free Inquiry*, 12:30-39.

―――― (in press). Theological pseudointerpretations of recent physical cosmology. In press for publication in the *Boston Studies in the Philosophy of Science*. Boston: Kluwer Publ. Co.

HABERMAS, J. (1970). *Zur Logik der Sozialwissenschaften*. Frankfurt: Surkamp Verlag.

——— (1971). *Knowledge and Human Interests*. Boston: Beacon Press.

——— (1984). Questions and counterquestions. *Praxis Int.*, 4:229-249.

HACKING, I. (1975). *The Emergence of Probability*. New York: Cambridge Univ. Press.

HANKOFF, L. D., ENGELHARDT, D. M., & FREEDMAN, N. (1960). Placebo responses in schizophrenic outpatients. *Arch. Gen. Psychiat.*, 2:43-52.

HARTMANN, H. (1959). Psychoanalysis as a scientific theory. In *Psychoanalysis, Scientific Method and Philosophy*, ed. S. Hook. New York: New York Univ. Press. pp. 3-37.

HEINE, R. W. (1953). A comparison of patients' reports on psychotherapeutic experience with psychoanalytic, non-directive, and Adlerian therapists. *Amer. J. Psychother.*, 7:16-23.

HEMPEL, C. G. (1965). *Aspects of Scientific Explanation*. New York: Free Press.

HERSON, M. & BARLOW, D. H. (1976). *Single Case Experimental Designs*. New York: Pergamon Press.

HINSIE, L. E. & CAMPBELL, R. J., Eds. (1970). *Psychiatric Dictionary* (4th ed.). New York: Oxford Univ. Press. (See also Campbell, R. J., 1981 and 1989.)

HIRSCHMÜLLER, A. (1989). *The Life and Work of Josef Breuer*. New York: New York University Press.

HOBSON, A. J. (1988). *The Dreaming Brain*. New York: Basic Books.

HOLT, R. R. (1978). *Methods in Clinical Psychology*, Vol. 2. New York: Plenum Press.

——— (1985). The current status of psychoanalytic theory. *Psychoanal. Psychol.*, 2:289-315.

HOLZMAN, P. S. (1976). The future of psychoanalysis and its institutes. *Psychoanal. Q.*, 45:250–273.

——— (1985). Psychoanalysis: Is the therapy destroying the science? *J. Amer. Psychoanal. Assn.*, 33:725-770.

HOOK, S., ed. (1959). *Psychoanalysis, Scientific Method, and Philosophy*. New York: New York University Press.

——— (1985). An interview with Sidney Hook. *Free Inquiry*, 5:24-33.

HOPKINS, J. (1991). The interpretation of dreams. In *The Cambridge Companion to Freud*, ed. J. Neu. New York: Cambridge University Press.

JASPERS, K. (1973). *Allgemeine Psychopathologie* (9th ed.). New York: Springer.

——— (1974). Causal and "meaningful" connexions between life history and psychosis. In *Themes and Variations in European Psychiatry*, ed. S. R. Hirsch & M. Shephers. Charlottesville: Univ. Virginia Press, pp. 80-93.

JONES, E. (1948). *Papers on Psychoanalysis*. London: Baillière, Tindall & Cox.

——— (1959). Editorial preface. In *Freud* (1883-1938), Vol. 1.

KAGAN, J. (1984). *The Nature of the Child*. New York: Basic Books.

KAPLAN, A. H. (1981). From discovery to validation: A basic challenge to psychoanalysis. *J. Amer. Psychoanal. Assn.*, 29:3-26.

KAZDIN, A. E. (1980). *Research Design in Clinical Psychology*. New York: Harper & Row.

——— (1981). Drawing valid inferences from case studies. *J. Consult. & Clin. Psychol.*, 49:183-192.

——— (1982). Single-case experimental designs. In *Handbook of Research Methods in Clinical Psychology*, ed. P. C. Kendall & J. N. Butcher. New York: Wiley, pp. 461-490.

————— & WILSON, G. T. (1978). *Evaluation of Behavior Therapy*. Cambridge, Mass.: Ballinger.

KIEV, A. (1978). The role of expectancy in behavioral change. In *Controversy in Psychiatry*, ed. J. P. Brady & H. K. H. Brodie. Philadelphia: Saunders.

KITCHER, P. W. (in press). *Freud's Dream: A Complete Interdisciplinary Cognitive Science*. Cambridge, MA: Bradford Books, MIT Press.

KLEIN, D. F. (1980). *Diagnosis and Drug Treatment of Psychiatric Disorders* (2nd ed.). Baltimore: Williams & Wilkins.

KLEIN, G. S. (1976). *Psychoanalytic Theory: An Exploration of Essentials*. New York: Int. Univ. Press.

KLINE, P. (1981). *Fact and Fantasy in Freudian Theory* (2nd ed.). London: Methuen.

KOHUT, H. (1959). Introspection, empathy, and psychoanalysis. *J. Amer. Psychoanal. Assn.*, 7:459-483.

————— (1978). *The Search for the Self*, ed. P. H. Ornstein. New York: Int. Univ. Press.

KOLATA, G. B. (1979). New drugs and the brain. *Science*, 205:774-776.

KRIS, E. (1947). The nature of psychoanalytic propositions and their validation. In *Kris* (1975), pp. 3-23.

————— (1975). *Selected Papers of Ernst Kris*. New Haven: Yale Univ. Press.

KUBIE, L. S. (1950). *Practical and Theoretical Aspects of Psychoanalysis* (2nd rev. ed.). New York: Int. Univ. Press, 1975.

————— (1952). Problems and techniques of psychoanalytic validation and progress. In *Psychoanalysis as Science*, ed. E. Pumpian-Mindlin. Stanford: Stanford Univ. Press, pp. 46-124.

KÜNG, H. (1979). *Freud and the Problem of God*. New Haven: Yale Univ. Press.

————— (1984). *Eternal Life?* Garden City, N.Y.: Doubleday.

LAPLANCHE, J. & PONTALIS, J. B. (1973). *The Language of Psychoanalysis*. New York: Norton.

LASCH, C. (1978). *The Culture of Narcissism*. New York: Norton.

LEVINE, F. J. (1979). On the clinical application of Heinz Kohut's psychology of the self: Comments on some recently published case studies. *J. Philadelphia Assn. Psychoanal.*, 6:1-19.

LEVINE, J. D., GORDON, N. C., BORNSTEIN, J. C., & FIELDS, H. L. (1979). Role of pain in placebo analgesia. *Proc. Nat. Acad. Sci.*, 76:3528-3531.

————— ————— & FIELDS, H. L. (1978). The mechanism of placebo analgesia. *Lancet*, 2:654-657.

LIBERMAN, R. (1964). An experimental study of the placebo response under three different situations of pain. *J. Psychiat. Res.*, 2:233-246.

LIFTON, R. J. (1980). Psychohistory. In *Comprehensive Textbook of Psychiatry*, 3rd ed., Vol. 3, ed. A. M. Freedman, H. T. Kaplan, & B. J. Sadock, pp. 3104-3112.

LOFTUS, E. (1980). *Memory*. Reading, Mass.: Addison-Wesley.

LUBORSKY, L. (1967). Momentary forgetting during psychotherapy and psychoanalysis. In *Motives and Thought*, ed. R. R. Holt. *Psychological Issues*, 18/19:177-217. New York: Int. Univ. Press.

————— (1973). Forgetting and remembering (momentary forgetting) during psychotherapy. In *Psychoanalytic Research*, ed. M. Mayman. *Psychological Issues*, 30:29-55. New York: Int. Univ. Press.

————— MELLON, J., ALEXANDER, K., VAN RAVENSWAAY, P., CHILDRESS, A., LEVINE, F. J., FRITS-CRISTOPH, D., COHEN, K. D., HOLD, A. V., &

MING, S. (1985). A verification of Freud's grandest clinical hypothesis: The transference. *Clin. Psychol. Rev.*, 5:231-246.

—— & MINTZ, J. (1974). What sets off momentary forgetting during a psychoanalysis? *Psychoanal. & Contemp. Sci.*, 3:233-268.

—— & SPENCE, D. P. (1978). Quantitative research on psychoanalytic therapy. In *Handbook of Psychotherapy and Behavior Change* (2nd ed.), ed. S. L. Garfield & A. E. Bergin. New York: Wiley.

MACKINNON, D. W. & DUKES, W. F. (1964). Repression. In *Psychology in the Making*, ed. L. Postman. New York: Knopf.

MAGRI, E. (1979). New Pope shows managerial skill. *Pittsburgh Post-Gazette* (January 1), p. 10.

MAHONEY, P. J. (1986). *Freud and the Rat Man.* New Haven: Yale Univ. Press.

MALAN, D. H. (1976). *Toward the Validation of Dynamic Psychotherapy.* New York: Plenum.

MALCOLM, J. (1981). *Psychoanalysis: The Impossible Profession.* New York: Knopf.

MALITZ, S. & KANZLER, M. (1971). Are antidepressants better than placebo? *Amer. J. Psychiat.*, 127:1605-1611.

MANUEL, F. (1968). *A Portrait of Isaac Newton.* Cambridge: Harvard Univ. Press.

MARCUS, S. (1984). *Freud and the Culture of Psychoanalysis.* London: Allen & Unwin.

MARGOLIN, S. (1964). The scientific status of psychoanalytic clinical evidence. *Inquiry*, 7:37-46.

MARMOR, J. (1962). Psychoanalytic therapy as an educational process. In *Psychoanalytic Education*, ed. J. Masserman. New York: Grune & Stratton, pp. 286-299.

—— (1968). New directions in psychoanalytic theory and therapy. In *Modern Psychoanalysis*, ed. J. Marmor. New York: Basic Books.

—— (1970). Limitations of free associations. *Arch. Gen. Psychiat.*, 22:160-165.

MARTIN, M. (1978). *Social Science and Philosophical Analysis.* Washington: Univ. Press of America.

MASER, J. D. & SELIGMAN, M. E. P. (1977). *Psychopathology: Experimental Models.* San Francisco: Freeman.

MASSON, J. M. (1984). *The Assault on Truth.* New York: Farrar, Straus & Giroux.

MCGRATH, W. J. (1986). *Freud's Discovery of Psychoanalysis.* Ithaca, N.Y.: Cornell Univ. Press.

MEEHL, P. E. (1973). Some methodological reflections on the difficulties of psychoanalytic research. In *Psychoanalytic Research*, ed. M. Mayr. *Psychological Issues*, 30:104-128. New York: Int. Univ. Press.

—— (1978). Theoretical risks and tabular asterisks: Sir Karl, Sir Ronald and the slow progress of soft psychology. *J. Consult. & Clin. Psychol.*, 46:806-834.

—— (1983). Subjectivity in psychoanalytic inference: The nagging persistence of Wilhelm Fliess's Achensee question. In *Testing Scientific Theories*, ed. J. Earman. Minnesota Studies in the Philosophy of Science, Vol. X. Minneapolis: Univ. Minnesota Press.

MEISSNER, W. W. (1978). *The Paranoid Process.* New York: Aronson.

———— (1984). *Psychoanalysis and Religious Experience*. New Haven: Yale Univ. Press.

———— (1990). Foundations of psychoanalysis reconsidered. *J. Amer. Psychoanal. Assn.*, 38:523–557.

———— (1992). The pathology of belief systems. *Psychoanal. & Contemp. Thought*, 15:99–128.

MENAKER, E. (1982). *Otto Rank: A Rediscovered Legacy*. New York: Columbia Univ. Press.

MEYERS, S. J. (1981). The bipolar self. *J. Amer. Psychoanal. Assn.*, 29:143-159.

MILL, J. S. (1887). *A System of Logic* (8th ed.). New York: Harper & Row, Book III, Chap. VIII.

MILLER, N. E. (1980). Applications of learning and biofeedback to psychiatry and medicine. In *Comprehensive Textbook of Psychiatry* (3rd ed.), Vol. 1, ed. A. M. Freedman, H. T. Kaplan, & B. J. Sadock. Baltimore: Williams & Wilkins.

MÖLLER, H. J. (1976). *Methodische Grundprobleme der Psychiatrie*. Stuttgart: W. Kohlhammer.

———— (1978). *Psychoanalyse*. Munich: Wilhelm Fink.

MOORE, M. (1983). The nature of psychoanalytic explanation. In *Mind and Medicine: Explanation and Evaluation in Psychiatry and the Biomedical Sciences*, ed. L. Laudan. Berkeley & Los Angeles: Univ. California Press, pp. 5-78.

MOTLEY, M. T. (1980). Verification of "Freudian slips" and semantic prearticulatory editing via laboratory induced spoonerisms. In *Errors in Linguistic Performance: Slips of the Tongue, Ear, Pen, and Hand*, ed. V. A. Fromkin. New York: Academic Press, pp. 133–147.

MOWRER, O. H. (1939). A stimulus-response analysis of anxiety and its role as a reinforcing agent. *Psychol. Rev.*, 46:553-565.

NEMIAH, J. C. (1975). Classical psychoanalysis. In *American Handbook of Psychiatry* (2nd ed.), Vol. 5, ed. S. Arieti. New York: Basic Books, pp. 163-182.

NISBETT, R. E. & ROSS, L. (1980). *Human Inference: Strategies and Shortcomings of Social Judgment*. Englewood Cliffs, N.J.: Prentice Hall.

———— & WILSON, T. D. (1977). Telling more than we can know: Verbal reports on mental processes. *Psychol. Rev.*, 84:231-259.

NOTTURNO, M. A., & McHUGH, P. R. (1986). Is Freudian psychoanalytic theory really falsifiable? *Behav. & Brain Sci.*, 9:250-252.

OBHOLZER, K. (1982). *The Wolf Man: Conversations with Freud's Patient—Sixty Years Later*. New York: Continuum.

OGDEN, C. K., & RICHARDS, I. A. (1956). *The Meaning of Meaning*. New York: Harcourt Brace.

O'LEARY, K. D. & BORKOVEC, T. D. (1978). Conceptual, methodological and ethical problems of placebo groups in psychotherapy research. *Amer. Psychologist*, 33:821-830.

PAGE, L. & ADAMS, N. I. (1940). *Electrodynamics*. New York: Van Nostrand.

PARK, L. C. & COVI, L. (1965). Nonblind placebo trial. *Arch. Gen. Psychiat.*, 12:336-345.

PERREZ, M. (1979). *Ist die Psychoanalyse eine Wissenschaft?* (2nd rev. ed.). Bern: Hans Huber.

PIECHOWIAK, H. (1982). Die namenlose Pille: Über Wirkungen und Neben-
wirkungen im therapeutischen Umgang mit Plazebopräparaten. *Inter-
nistische Praxis*, 22:759-772.
────── (1983). Die Schein-Heilung: Welche Rolle spielt das Placebo in der
ärztlichen Praxis? *Deutsches Ärzteblatt*, 80:39-50.
POPPER, K. R. (1950). *The Open Society and Its Enemies*. Princeton: Princeton
Univ. Press.
────── (1962). *Conjectures and Refutations*. New York: Basic Books.
────── (1974). Replies to my critics. In *The Philosophy of Karl Popper*, ed. P. A.
Schilpp. LaSalle, Ill.: Open Court, Vol. 2, pp. 961-1197.
────── (1983). *Realism and the Aim of Science*, ed. W. W. Bartley, III. Totowa,
N.J.: Rowman & Littlefield.
PRIOLEAU, L., MURDOCK, M., & BRODY, N. (1983). An analysis of psychother-
apy versus placebo. *Behav. Brain. Sci.*, 6:275-285.
RACHMAN, S. J. (1978). *Fear and Courage*. San Francisco: Freeman.
────── & WILSON, G. T. (1980). *The Effects of Psychological Therapy* (2nd ed.).
New York: Pergamon Press.
RAPAPORT, D. (1959). The structure of psychoanalytic theory: A systematizing
attempt. In *Psychology: A Study of a Science*, Vol. 3, ed. S. Koch. New
York: McGraw-Hill.
RAUHALA, L. (1969). *Intentionality and the Problem of the Unconscious*. Turku,
Finland: Turun Yliopisto.
REDLICH, F. C. & FREEDMAN, D. X. (1966). *The Theory and Practice of Psychiatry*.
New York: Basic Books.
REICHENBACH, H. (1956). *The Direction of Time*. Berkeley: Univ. California
Press.
REPPEN, J., Ed. (1985). *Beyond Freud: A Study of Modern Psychoanalytic Theorists*.
New York: Erlbaum.
RICE, B. (1986). Dealing with difficult bosses. *US Air Magazine*, December:32-
39.
RICOEUR, P. (1966). Der Atheismus der Psychoanalyse Freuds. *Concilium*,
2:430-435.
────── (1970). *Freud and Philosophy*. New Haven: Yale Univ. Press.
────── (1981). *Hermeneutics and the Human Sciences*. New York: Cambridge
Univ. Press.
RIEFF, P. (1959). *Freud: The Mind of the Moralist*. Chicago: Univ. Chicago Press.
ROBBINS, M. (1980). Current controversy in object relations theory as out-
growth of a schism between Klein and Fairbairn. *Int. J. Psychoanal.*,
61:477-492.
ROSENZWEIG, S. (1934). An experimental study of "repression" with special
reference to need-persistive and ego-defensive reactions to frustration.
J. Exp. Psychol., 32:64-74.
────── (1986). *Freud and Experimental Psychology: The Emergence of Idiodynamics*.
New York: McGraw-Hill.
ROTH, M. (1987). *Psycho-Analysis as History*. Ithaca, NY: Cornell University
Press.
RUBINSTEIN, B. B. (1983). Freud's early theories of hysteria. In *Physics, Philoso-
phy, and Psychoanalysis: Essays in Honor of Adolf Grünbaum*, ed. R. S.
Cohen & L. Laudan. Boston: Reidel, pp. 169-190.

RUDNITSKY, P. L. (1990). A psychoanalytic Weltanschauung. In *Philosophie und Psychoanalyse*, ed. L. Nagl et al. Frankfurt: Nexus Verlag, pp. 137-153.

RUSSELL, B. (1954). *A History of Western Philosophy.* New York: Simon & Schuster.

RYCROFT, C. (1968). *A Critical Dictionary of Psychoanalysis.* Nashville: Nelson.

——— (1973). *A Critical Dictionary of Psychoanalysis.* Totowa, N.J.: Littlefield, Adams.

SACHS, D. (1989). In fairness to Freud: A critical notice of *The Foundations of Psychoanalysis* by Adolf Grünbaum. *Philos. Rev.*, 98:349-378.

SACKEIM, H. A. & GUR, R. C. (1978). Self-deception, self-confrontation, and consciousness. In *Consciousness and Self-regulation*, ed. G. E. Schwartz & D. Shapiro. New York: Plenum Press, Vol. 2, pp. 139-197.

SAFIRE, W. (1986). Secs appeal. *New York Times Magazine* (January 26):688.

SALMON, W. C. (1959). Psychoanalytic theory and evidence. In *Psychoanalysis, Scientific Method and Philosophy*, ed. S. Hook. New York: New York Univ. Press, pp. 252-267.

——— (1984). *Scientific Explanation and the Causal Structure of the World.* Princeton: Princeton Univ. Press.

SCHACHTER, S. & SINGER, J. E. (1962). Cognitive, social and physiological determinants of emotional state. *Psychol. Rev.*, 69:379-399.

SCHWARTZ, G. E. (1978). Psychobiological foundations of psychotherapy and behavior changes. In *Handbook of Psychotherapy and Behavior Change* (2nd ed.), ed. S. L. Garfield & A. E. Bergin. New York: Wiley, pp. 63-99.

SEARLES, H. (1963). Transference psychosis in the psychotherapy of chronic schizophrenia. *Int. J. Psychoanal.*, 44:249-281.

SHAMES, M. L. (1979). On the metamethodological dimension of the "expectancy paradox." *Phil. Sci.*, 46:382-388.

SHANDS, H. C. (1978). Psychoanalysis: Caviar for the general. In *Controversy in Psychiatry*, ed. J. P. Brady & H. K. H. Brodie. Philadelphia: Saunders, pp. 386-401.

SHAPIRO, A. K. (1960). A contribution to a history of the placebo effect. *Behav. Sci.*, 5:109-135.

——— (1968). Semantics of the placebo. *Psychiat. Q.*, 4:1-43.

——— & MORRIS, L. A. (1978). The placebo effect in medical and psychological therapies. In *Handbook of Psychotherapy and Behavior Change* (2nd ed.), ed. S. L. Garfield & A. E. Bergin. New York: Wiley, pp. 369-410.

SHAPIRO, A. P., SCHWARTZ, G. E., & FERGUSON, D. C. (1977). Behavioral methods in the treatment of hypertension. *Annu. Intern. Med.*, 86:626-636.

SHEPHERD, M. (1961). Specific and non-specific factors in psychopharmacology. In *Neuropsychopharmacology*, ed. E. Rothlin. Amsterdam: Elsevier, Vol. 2, pp. 117-129.

SHINN, R. L. (1986). Tillich as interpreter and disturber of contemporary civilization. *Bull. Amer. Acad. Arts & Sci.*, 39:7-27.

SLOANE, R. B., STAPLES, F. R., CRISTOL, A. H., YORKSTON, N. J., & WHIPPLE, K. (1975). *Psychotherapy vs. Behavior Therapy.* Cambridge: Harvard Univ. Press.

SMITH, E. R., & MILLER, F. D. (1978). Limits on perception of cognitive processes: A reply to Nisbett and Wilson. *Psychol. Rev.*, 85:355-362.

SMITH, M. L., GLASS, G. V., & MILLER, T. I. (1980). *The Benefits of Psychotherapy*. Baltimore: Johns Hopkins Univ. Press.
SOBER, E. (1987). Parsimony, likelihood, and the principle of the common cause. *Phil. Sci.*, 54:465-469.
——— (1988). The principle of the common cause. In *Probability and Causality*, ed. J. Fetzer. Dordrecht, Boston: Reidel, pp. 211-228.
SPENCE, D. P. (1982). *Narrative Truth and Historical Truth*. New York: Norton.
STEELE, R. S. (1979). Psychoanalysis and hermeneutics. *Int. Rev. Psychoanal.*, 6:389-411.
STEPANSKY, P. E. (1986). Feuerbach and Jung as religious critics: With a note on Freud's psychology of religion. In *Freud, Appraisals and Reappraisals*, ed. P. E. Stepansky. Hillsdale, N.J.: Analytic Press.
STEWART, R. L. (1978). The restoration of insight: The specific results of psychoanalysis. In *Controversy in Psychiatry*, ed. J. P. Brady & H. K. H. Brodie. Philadelphia: Saunders, pp. 561-578.
STORR, A. (1986). Human understanding and scientific Validation. *Behav. & Brain Sci.* 9:259–260.
STRACHEY, J. (1955). Editor's introduction to "Studies on Hysteria." *S. E.*, 2: xvi.
STRENGER, C. (1991). *Between Hermeneutics and Science. Psychological Issues*, Monogr. 59. Madison, CT: Int. Univ. Press.
STRUPP, H. H., HADLEY, S. W., & GOMES-SCHWARTZ, B. (1977). *Psychotherapy for Better or Worse: The Problem of Negative Effects*. New York: Aronson.
SUEDFELD, P. (1984). The subtractive expectancy placebo procedure: A measure of non-specific factors in behavioural interventions. *Behav. Res. & Ther.*, 22:159-164.
SULLOWAY, F. J. (1977). *Freud, Biologist of the Mind*. New York: Basic Books.
——— (1991). Reassessing Freud's case histories. *Isis*, 82:245–275.
UHLENHUTH, E. H., CANTER, A., NEUSTADT, J. O., & PAYSON, H. E. (1959). The symptomatic relief of anxiety with meprobamate, phenobarbital and placebo. *Amer. J. Psychiat.*, 115:905-910.
VON ECKARDT, B. (1985). Adolf Grünbaum and psychoanalytic epistemology. In *Beyond Freud: A Study of Modern Psychoanalytic Theorists*, ed. J. Reppen. Hillsdale, N.J.: Analytic Press, pp. 353-403.
WAELDER, R. (1960). *Basic Theory of Psychoanalysis*. New York: Int. Univ. Press.
——— (1962). Review of *Psychoanalysis, Scientific Method and Philosophy*, ed. S. Hook. *J. Amer. Psychoanal. Assn.*, 10:617-637.
WALLACE, E. R. (1983). *Freud and Anthropology. Psychological Issues*, Monogr. 55. New York: Int. Univ. Press.
——— (1985). Freud and religion: A history and reappraisal. In *The Psychoanalytic Study of Society*, ed. L. B. Boyer, W. Muensterberger, & S. Grolnick. Hillsdale, N.J.: Analytic Press.
——— (1986). The scientific status of psychoanalysis: A review of Grünbaum's *The Foundations of Psychoanalysis*. *J. Nerv. & Ment. Dis.*, 174:379-386.
WALLERSTEIN, R. (1982). Foreword. In Spence (1982), pp. 9-14.
——— (1986). Psychoanalysis as a science: A response to the new challenges. *Psychoanal. Q.*, 55:414-451.
——— (1988). Psychoanalysis, psychoanalytic science, and psychoanalytic research—1986. *J. Amer. Psychoanal. Assn.*, 36:3-30.
WATSON, G. & McGAW, D. (1980). *Statistical Inquiry*. New York: Wiley.

WHEATLEY, D. (1967). Influence of doctors' and patients' attitudes in the treatment of neurotic illness. *Lancet*, 2:1133-1135.

WHYTE, L. L. (1960). *The Unconscious Before Freud*. New York: Basic Books.

WILKINS, W. (1985). Therapy credibility is not a non-specific event. *Cognit. Ther. & Res.*, 9:119-125.

WILSON, W. R. (1979). Feeling more than we can know: Exposure effects without learning. *J. Pers. & Soc. Psychol.*, 37:811-821.

WOLBERG, L. (1977). *The Technique of Psychotherapy* (3rd ed.). New York: Grune & Stratton.

WOLITSKY, D. L., KLEIN, G. S., & DWORKIN, S. F. (1975). An experimental approach to the study of repression: Effects of a hypnotically induced fantasy. *Psychoanal. & Contemp. Sci.*, 4:211-233.

World Book Encyclopedia 11 (1966).

WRIGHT, R. (1988). Why men are still beasts. *New Republic*, Issue #3834 (July 11):27-32.

YUDOFSKY, S. C. & HALES, R. E., eds. (1992). *Textbook of Neuropsychiatry*. Washington, D.C.: American Psychiatric Press.

ZAMANSKY, D. (1958). An investigation of the psychoanalytic theory of paranoid delusions. *J. Pers.*, 26:410-425.

ZILBOORG, G. (1962). *Psychoanalysis and Religion*. New York: Farrar, Straus & Cudahy.

ZIMMER, D. (1982). *Die Zeit*, No. 45 (November 5):18-19.

NAME INDEX

Abraham, K., 223
Abrahamsen, D., 167
Adams, J., 134–135
Adams, N. I., 14
Adler, A., 268–269
Albert, H., 263n
Alexander, F., 180–181
Alexander, K., 173, 330
Anderson, A. R., 228
Aristotle, 289–290
Arlow, J. A., 162
Asher, H., 233
Augustine, St., 308–309

Bachrach, H. M., 222
Bacon, F., 63, 67, 163, 291, 330–331
Barlow, D. H., 230, 234–237, 239–241
Bartley, W., 57
Basch, M., 325
Beecher, H. K., 96, 99
Benson, H., 96, 99–100
Bergin, A. E., 103, 171, 188, 193–194
Bettelheim, B., 4
Black, H. L., 281
Blakiston, 76
Blalock, H., 233
Bok, S., 96–98
Borkovec, T. D., 93
Bornstein, J. C., 87
Bourne, H. R., 191n
Bowers, K., 350
Brandt, L. W., 179n
Brenner, C., 157–158, 176, 180, 342, 368
Brentano, F., 258n, 263

Breuer, J., 10, 20–22, 23, 25, 27, 36, 39, 136–137, 165, 234, 237–239, 240, 311, 343–351, 373
Brody, H., 95, 103–107
Brody, J., 87
Brody, N., 31n, 188, 190
Brown, D., 19
Bryant, A., 19
Buber, M., 290–291
Bullitt, W., 167
Bush, G., 286

Campbell, D., 233, 234, 235, 244
Campbell, R. J., 305, 341
Canter, A., 191n
Carnap, R., 60
Carter, J., 287, 304
Childress, A., 173, 330
Christiansen, B., 180, 201
Cioffi, F., 25, 50, 186
Cohen, K. D., 173, 330
Cohen, M. R., 242
Cohen, R. S., 384
Cole, J. O., 75
Columbus, C., 260
Considine, D. M., 15
Cook, T., 233, 235, 244
Cooper, A. M., 178, 225, 315
Covi, L., 71, 81–82, 88
Crews, F., 168
Cristol, A. H., 192
Critelli, J. W., 83, 85–86

Darwin, C., 276, 282
Davis, J. M., 75

401

SUBJECT INDEX

epistemic role of, 216–217
failure of, 213
trustworthiness of, 208–209

Jonestown group, 286–287

Lesbianism, etiology of, 320–321
Little Hans case, 185–186
critique of, 314

Marxism
psychoanalysis and, 66–67
religion and, 264–265
Master Proposition, 28–32, 184. *See also*
Necessary Condition Thesis
(NCT)
discrediting of, 31–32
tenability of, 69
Masturbation, repressed castigation for,
141–143, 147–148, 328
Meaning
causally explanatory, 116–117
of covert wish, 206
of dreams, 117–118
psychology of, 114
semantic, 115–117, 119
unconscious, 114
Meaning connections, x, 50, 113–114
versus causal connections, 120–121
Memory
Freudian account of lapse of, 41–43
unreliability of, 35–37
Memory-jogging device, 36
Meno dialogue, 1
Mental disorders, sexual repressions in,
3–4
Mental processes
causal dynamics of, 205–206
subjective reports about, 215–217
Metaphysics, versus science, 48–49,
66–67
Metapsychology, 7, 384
Mind, bipartite structural model, 6–7
Mind-brain system hypotheses, 247
Moral majority, 286
Morality

and divine omnibenevolence, 303
and theology, 303–305
theory of, and religion, 268
Mosaic monotheism, psychoanalytic
phylogeny of, 274–279
Moses and Monotheism, 272
Motherhood, dissociation of sexuality
from, 297–298
Motivation
hypothesizing of, 164–166
in "making sense" of actions, 118–119
Motivational explanations, Mill's methods of validating, 163–166
Multiple baseline design, 239–240
Mystery, belief in, 295–305

Narcissism, culture of, 167–168
Narcissistic transferences, 184
Necessary Condition Thesis (NCT),
184–185, 187
challenge of, 191–193
disavowal of, 199–200
spuriousness of, 189
Neurological model, 6–7
Neurosis. *See also* Psychoneurosis
dynamic hypotheses of, 175–176
factors in etiology of, 33
preconditions of, 23
repression in etiology of, 46–47,
110–111, 121–128, 311
Neurotic defense, 127–129
Newtonian physics
falsifiability of, 58
errors in, 283
Nightmares, 378–379
Nonplacebo effect, 78
Nonplacebo therapy, 83
Nonspecific placebo response, 94

Object, essential versus accidental properties of, 289–290
Object relations theory, 354
epistemic critique of, 37
etiologic theory of, 38, 355
Obsessional neuroses
clinical testability of repression in etiology of, 326–330

PSYCHOLOGICAL ISSUES